THE WORLD'S CLASSICS

THE IMPORTANCE OF BEING EARNEST
AND OTHER PLAYS

OSCAR WILDE was born in Dublin in 1854. He was educated at Trinity College, Dublin and Magdalen College, Oxford where, as a disciple of Pater, he founded an aesthetic cult. His first book, a volume of poems, was published in 1881, and the following year he carried out a much publicized lecture tour in North America. He married Constance Lloyd in 1884, and his two sons Cyril and Vyvyan were born in 1885 and 1886.

He wrote short stories and critical essays, and his novel, *The Picture of Dorian Gray*, was published in 1891. This, and the social comedies *Lady Windermere's Fan* (1892), *A Woman of No Importance* (1893), *An Ideal Husband* (1895) and *The Importance of Being Earnest* (1895), swiftly built up his reputation and notoriety. His symbolist play *Salome* was refused a licence by the Lord Chamberlain in 1892, and published first in French and then English in succeeding years. In 1895, following his own libel action against the Marquess of Queensberry, Wilde was sentenced to two years' imprisonment for homosexual conduct, and from this experience emerged *The Ballad of Reading Gaol* (1898) and the confessional letter *De Profundis* (1905). After his release from prison in 1897 he lived abroad in Europe, and died in Paris in 1900.

PETER RABY is Senior Lecturer and Head of Drama at Homerton College, Cambridge, and author of *Oscar Wilde* (Cambridge University Press). His essay on *The Importance of Being Earnest* appeared in the special Wilde number of *Modern Drama* (Spring 1994), and he is currently working on a Wilde Companion to be published by Cambridge University Press.

MICHAEL CORDNER is Reader in the Department of English and Related Literature at the University of York. He has edited editions of George Farquhar's *The Beaux' Stratagem*, the *Complete Plays* of Sir George Etherege, *Four Comedies* of Sir John Vanbrugh and, for the World's Classics series, *Four Restoration Marriage Comedies*. He has also co-edited *English Comedy* (Cambridge, 1994) and is completing a book on *The Comedy of Marriage 1660–1737*.

PETER HOLLAND is Judith E. Wilson University Lecturer in Drama in the Faculty of English at the University of Cambridge.

MARTIN WIGGINS is a Fellow of the Shakespeare Institute and Lecturer in English at the University of Birmingham.

DRAMA IN WORLD'S CLASSICS

J. M. Barrie
Peter Pan and Other Plays

Aphra Behn
The Rover and Other Plays

George Farquhar
The Recruiting Officer and Other Plays

John Ford
'Tis Pity She's a Whore and Other Plays

Ben Jonson
The Alchemist and Other Plays

Christopher Marlowe
Doctor Faustus and Other Plays

Thomas Middleton
A Mad World, My Masters and Other Plays

Arthur Wing Pinero
Trelawny of the 'Wells' and Other Plays

J. M. Synge
The Playboy of the Western World and Other Plays

John Webster
The Duchess of Malfi and Other Plays

Oscar Wilde
The Importance of Being Earnest and Other Plays

William Wycherley
The Country Wife and Other Plays

Campion, Carew, Chapman, Daniel, Davenant, Jonson, Townshend
Court Masques

Chapman, Kyd, Middleton, Tourneur
Four Revenge Tragedies

Coyne, Fitzball, Jones, Lewes, Sims
The Lights o' London and Other Plays

Dryden, Lee, Otway, Southerne
Four Restoration Marriage Comedies

THE WORLD'S CLASSICS

OSCAR WILDE

Lady Windermere's Fan
Salome
A Woman of No Importance
An Ideal Husband
The Importance of Being Earnest

Edited with an Introduction by
PETER RABY

General Editor
MICHAEL CORDNER
Associate General Editors
PETER HOLLAND MARTIN WIGGINS

Oxford New York
OXFORD UNIVERSITY PRESS

Oxford University Press, Walton Street, Oxford OX2 6DP

Oxford New York
Athens Auckland Bangkok Bombay
Calcutta Cape Town Dar es Salaam Delhi
Florence Hong Kong Istanbul Karachi
Kuala Lumpur Madras Madrid Melbourne
Mexico City Nairobi Paris Singapore
Taipei Tokyo Toronto
and associated companies in
Berlin Ibadan

Oxford is a trade mark of Oxford University Press

First published as a World's Classics paperback 1995

British Library Cataloguing in Publication Data
Data available

Library of Congress Cataloging in Publication Data
Data available
ISBN 0-19-282246-2

5 7 9 10 8 6 4

Printed in Great Britain by Biddles Ltd,
Guildford & King's Lynn

CONTENTS

ACKNOWLEDGEMENTS

I WOULD like to express my thanks to Michael Cordner and Peter Holland for their meticulous comments and invariably helpful suggestions in the preparation for this edition.

This edition is for Jessica.

INTRODUCTION

IT is entirely natural that Wilde, a supreme exponent of conversation and experimenter with masks, should explore the medium of the theatre. For someone who promoted the concept of the Artist as a sacred figure, he spent a surprisingly large part of his life courting publicity, and holding public court. He marketed himself as a lecturer, and took a job as editor of a popular journal. The theatre presented him with unusual opportunities to exploit his gifts, and for an especially immediate and symbiotic interaction with his audience. It also offered a lucrative source of income. Commentary has tended to focus on the fashionable West End audiences for Wilde's comedies. In 1894 there were two companies, North and South, touring *A Woman of No Importance* in the English provinces: Wilde received a quarter of the profits.

All the plays in this volume were written and put into production between the summer of 1891 and February 1895. Wilde had written two previous plays: *Vera, or the Nihilists*, published in 1880 and produced in New York in August 1883; and *The Duchess of Padua*, written in 1883 and first presented (under the title of *Guido Ferranti*), again in New York, for a brief season in 1891. *Vera*, a melodramatic treatment of Nihilism set in contemporary Russia, was actually put into rehearsal in London in November 1881, but withdrawn, ostensibly because of political considerations. It is a play, transparently, of modern life, with a non-conforming woman in the central role and a flippant mouthpiece for Wilde's epigrams, Prince Paul, who anticipates the dandy of the later comedies. *The Duchess of Padua* reads as pastiche, a revenge verse-drama with echoes of Shakespeare, Webster, and Shelley's *The Cenci*. In a long letter to the actress Mary Anderson, Wilde gives a detailed analysis of scenery and costume which reveals his instinctive perception of the importance of the visual dimension in this and all his plays. Wilde was a regular and discriminating playgoer; he had a close knowledge of the contemporary theatre, and was on intimate terms with a number of actresses and actors. His startling emergence as a writer of polished comedies was built on more experience than was apparent.

Wilde contrived to appear a little insouciant towards his comedies, so that even his close friend Ada Leverson, the Sphinx, could comment that 'in truth he cared little for any of his plays excepting only *Salome*'.[1] Charles Ricketts recalled Wilde saying of *An Ideal Husband*, 'It was written for ridiculous puppets to play, and the critics will say, "Ah, here is Oscar unlike himself!"—though in reality I became engrossed in writing it, and it contains a great deal of the real Oscar.' Ricketts adds, 'This is a final and a severe estimate of it. Oscar was always better than he thought he was, and no one in his lifetime was able to see it.'[2] Wilde's own interest and involvement in the rehearsal process, and the numerous versions of each text, indicate his underlying commitment to dramatic form. André Gide, who once wrote disparagingly of the plays, later revised his judgement: 'they appear to me, today when I have learned to know them better, as among the most curious, the most significant and, whatever may have been said about them, the newest things in the contemporary theatre.'[3] Apart from *The Importance of Being Earnest*, these plays have consistently been subjected to adverse criticism as successful works of art, even where their value as entertainment, as vehicles for Wilde's wit, has been recognized. They are more than they appear to be, and they continue to appeal to late twentieth-century audiences in spite of the largely obtuse commentaries of generations of theatre critics.

Wilde's début as a writer of comedy was prompted by George Alexander. Alexander assumed the management of the St James's Theatre in 1890, and asked Wilde for a play. He rejected *The Duchess of Padua*, suggesting that Wilde should write on a modern subject, and made him a £50 advance. Eventually, Wilde took himself off to the Lake District: 'I wonder can I do it in a week, or will it take three?', he asked Frank Harris. 'It ought not to take long to beat the Pineros and the Joneses.'[4] When he read his script to Alexander in October, Alexander thought it wonderful and offered him £1,000. Shrewdly, Wilde insisted on a percentage and earned £7,000 from it in the first year.

Lady Windermere's Fan

Lady Windermere's Fan, in which Wilde first found his authentic voice as a playwright, is a remarkable beginning. Wilde seems to have absorbed, and to reflect, a number of theatrical traditions, and yet succeeds in formulating a distinctive style and method. There are

---

[1] Ada Leverson, 'The Last First Night', *New Criterion*, Jan. 1926.
[2] *Self-Portrait, Letters and Journals of Charles Ricketts*, ed. Cecil Lewis (1939), 124–5.
[3] André Gide, *Oscar Wilde* (1939), 9–10.
[4] Frank Harris, *Oscar Wilde, His Life and Confessions* (1930), 97.

echoes of the situations, devices, and style of English comedy, especially Congreve and Sheridan; there are clear affinities with the social dramas of Dumas *fils* and Sardou, representatives of the French plot-bank on which the English theatre drew unashamedly. Wilde was familiar with melodrama. He was also fully aware of the kinds of drama the Pineros and the Joneses were writing: Haddon Chambers's *The Idler* (1891), Sydney Grundy's *The New Woman* (1894), Jones's *The Dancing Girl* (1891), Pinero's *The Cabinet Minister* (1890) and *The Second Mrs Tanqueray* (1893), even Shaw's *Widowers' Houses* (1892), in different degrees share common ground with Wilde's social comedies. But the resemblances are far less striking than the crucial differences in style and rhythm, and, above all, in a kind of artistic distance which Wilde maintained from his material. Wilde was knowledgeable about the avant-garde theatre of Europe. He admired Ibsen, and Ibsen's London interpreters such as Elizabeth Robins. He attended the performance of Zola's *Thérèse Raquin* at the Independent Theatre, and absorbed the aesthetic experiment of Godwin's outdoor production of *As You Like It*. When he turned to the theatre, it was not just to imitate, but to create something original, translating images and patterns of modern life into his own artistic medium. His voice (and this became a subject of extensive criticism) was like no one else's.

Alexander assisted materially in nudging Wilde towards a distinctly modern tone. Wilde clung to his original wish to withhold from his audience knowledge of the mother–daughter relationship between Mrs Erlynne and Lady Windermere, and it was not until the fourth or fifth night that the earlier, gradual revelation was agreed. At Alexander's insistence, Wilde wrote a new curtain-line for Act 2, to replace a more traditional 'strong' speech from Mrs Erlynne. The play works as a subtle set of variations on the expected norms and conventions, whether of drama or of society. It moves towards a conclusion where what is concealed, and unspoken, is more significant than what is revealed. The melodrama format leads inexorably towards public recognition of relationships and misdemeanours, towards punishment, forgiveness, and reconciliation, and so a reinforcement of traditional moral values. The same holds true, formally at least, for the comic structure of *The School for Scandal*. *Lady Windermere's Fan* begins to sketch a far more complex world, in which the accepted codes are repeatedly adjusted or reversed by a new morality, just as the language system of received rectitude is exposed by the verbal brilliance of the wits.

One of the play's major principles of construction is the hierarchy of wit. In such a scheme, Mrs Erlynne and Lord Darlington dominate, their tone echoed by the choric voice of Cecil Graham. Below them rank the essentially serious Windermeres, and at the bottom the apparently witless Lord Augustus. However, Wilde achieves some surprising and ironic effects, by showing Lady Windermere on the point of eloping with Lord Darlington, and by matching Mrs Erlynne with Lord Augustus. This last marriage is achieved via a number of deceptions, and Lady Windermere's return to her husband is, significantly, not followed by the normally obligatory confession of her flight to Lord Darlington's rooms. The play's principal action privately subverts conventional morality, while superficially preserving propriety, thus exposing the fundamental hypocrisy of social conventions and values. The play functions as a concealed critique of contemporary mores: Wilde achieves this partly by his insistence on recognizable external details of modern life—telegrams, photographs, whisky and soda, the Club Train—and partly by his exposure of society as a sexual market-place. The comic force generated by the Duchess of Berwick's single-minded pursuit of a rich Australian young man for her tongue-tied daughter is balanced by Mrs Erlynne's cynical exploitation of Lord Windermere's chequebook.

The play is finely balanced between the light and the dark, between innocence and experience. The context is Lady Windermere's twenty-first birthday, and her coming-of-age is marked not only by a ball, but by a succession of gifts: the fan, a declaration of love, and finally wisdom. (Knowledge, in the form of Mrs Erlynne's true identity, is withheld.) The fan, like the mask a traditional emblem of sexual invitation, is used adroitly by Wilde in each act to point up particular encounters, and appropriately leaves the stage in Mrs Erlynne's possession. The play's action begins with the relatively private exchanges and confidences of Act 1; it opens out in the large-scale public scenes of the Act 2 dance, dominated by the women, and the oppressive masculinity of Darlington's rooms in Act 3; then contracts to the privately achieved compromises of the mother's marriage and the daughter's reconciliation. Significantly, each couple retreats from London and the social season: the Windermeres to the pastoral retreat of Selby, Mrs Erlynne and Lord Augustus to the Continent, where Lord Darlington has already gone.

Wilde did not fully resolve two major and related difficulties. The dandy is his trade mark as a dramatist, cool, hard-edged, detached, self-absorbed, the arbiter and exemplar of good taste and behaviour, at the apex in the hierarchy of wit. The transformation of Lord Darlington from a dandy to a lover, and his subsequent disappearance from the play, disturb the balance between wit and seriousness. Wilde contrives to indicate that Lady Windermere is her mother's daughter, a passionate woman capable of development. Lord Windermere, by contrast, sounds pompous and ponderous, and seems to be regressing towards the rigid morality which his wife has learnt to reject. The balance between the witty and the earnest, and their two respective languages and codes, emerges as Wilde's most taxing dramatic problem. This challenge is located within both the theatre conventions of the 1890s and in the sensibility of Wilde's immediate and predominantly upper-class audience. He answered it partly by the development of two contrasting styles and forms: the 'symbolist' theatre of *Salome* and the farcical comedy of *Earnest*.

Salome

Salome had the longest gestation period of all Wilde's plays. He had thought about the subject since he was first introduced to 'Hérodias', one of Flaubert's *Trois Contes*, by Pater at Oxford in 1877. His interest in Salome's image was stimulated by the vivid descriptions of Gustave Moreau's paintings in J.-K. Huysmans's *A Rebours*. Other literary influences include Heine's nightmarish vision in *Atta Troll*, Laforgue's Salomé in *Moralités Légendaires*, and Mallarmé's *Hérodiade*. In terms of dramatic influences, the work of Maeterlinck (and specifically *La Princesse Maleine*), with its use of colour, sound, dance, visual description, and visual effect, offered Wilde a potent theatrical vocabulary. Paris was the centre of theatrical experiment, being home both to Antoine's Théâtre Libre, grounded on naturalist theory, and to Paul Fort's symbolist Théâtre d'Art and its successor, Lugné-Poe's Théâtre de l'Œuvre. Both Fort and Lugné-Poe used painters for scene and poster design, and poets to supply the text. The genesis of *Salome* is contemporary with Artaud and Alfred Jarry. The text belongs to the Theatre of Cruelty and might be performed by marionettes, or by actors simulating marionettes.

As Richard Ellmann has persuasively argued, when Wilde went to Paris in 1891, soon after the completion of his play about a 'Good Woman', he became obsessed with the idea of writing a dark symbolist counterpart, rivalling Mallarmé on one of his own subjects and in his own language. He was drunk with words and attention.

The dream of Salome formed and reformed. Women whom he saw in the streets, a Romanian acrobat dancing on her hands in the Moulin Rouge, wild and terrible gypsy music in the Grand Café, all fed his imagination; and at various stages of the play's evolution he circulated the script amongst his friends in Paris, seeking, but mostly ignoring, their advice.

In London, in the summer of 1892, Sarah Bernhardt met Wilde at Henry Irving's house and suggested he write a play for her. Wilde offered her *Salomé*. Wilde later denied that he had written the play with Bernhardt in mind, though it seems improbable that such an appealing idea did not surface at an early stage. Charles Ricketts reported that when he read the play to her, 'She exclaimed "Mais, c'est héraldique, on dirait une fresque" [But it's heraldic, you would think it was a fresco], and for days both author and actress discussed the pitch of voice required. "Le mot doit tomber comme une perle sur une disque de cristal, pas de mouvements rapides, des gestes stylisés." [Each word must fall like a pearl on a crystal disc, no rapid movements, but stylised gestures.]'[5] The play was in rehearsal for inclusion in Bernhardt's London season, when it was refused a licence by the Lord Chamberlain's office because it depicted a biblical subject—the same grounds which prevented Saint-Saëns's *Samson et Dalila* from being produced. The notoriety which shadows the play was established. William Archer, the dramatic critic of the *World*, wrote to the *Pall Mall Gazette* to protest, Shaw was predictably supportive, while Wilde announced that he would take out letters of naturalization and settle in France: 'I will not consent to call myself a citizen of a country that shows such narrowness in artistic judgement. I am not English. I am Irish which is quite another thing.'[6] No one else had much sympathy. Although the censor, Pigott, frequently turned a blind eye to texts in French, the combination of subject-matter and treatment was too much to overlook. In a private letter he described *Salomé* as 'a miracle of impudence', and Wilde's French text as 'half Biblical, half pornographic'.[7] Pigott's comments exemplify the cast of mind which orchestrated Wilde's unsuccessful libel action in 1895, and his subsequent trials and imprisonment.

---

[5] Charles Ricketts, *Oscar Wilde: Recollections by Jean-Paul Raymond and Charles Ricketts* (1932), 53.

[6] *Pall Mall Budget*, 40 (30 June 1892).

[7] J. R. Stephens, *The Censorship of English Drama 1824–1901* (1980), 112.

Wilde went to Bad Homburg to recover. The excitement of discussing design ideas with Graham Robertson and Charles Ricketts, the mystery of how Bernhardt would execute the dance of the seven veils, came to nothing, and Wilde had to be content with publication, in February 1893. Wilde distributed complimentary copies liberally and was highly gratified by the response from France, from Loti, Maeterlinck, and, above all, from Mallarmé. Wilde decided to prepare an English version, but made the mistake of entrusting the translation to Lord Alfred Douglas. When Douglas produced his version at the end of August 1893, Wilde found it inadequate and, in places, inaccurate. Bitter recriminations followed. Beardsley, commissioned to provide the illustrations, offered to provide another translation. Wilde eventually took responsibility himself, but the text was so altered that a compromise was reached whereby Douglas's name did not appear on the title-page, but only in the dedication. The English version was finally published on 9 February 1894.

The first production of *Salomé* took place, appropriately enough, in Paris. Lugné-Poe directed it at the Théâtre de l'Œuvre on 11 February 1896, while Wilde was in prison, and himself played the role of Herod. Dowson, who accompanied Beardsley, called it 'triumphant'. Richard Strauss saw it in Berlin in November 1902, at Max Reinhardt's 'Little Theatre', with Gertrud Eysoldt as Salomé, and began to compose his opera based on the play the following summer. The first English staging was a private production by the New Stage Club at the Bijou Theatre in Archer Street, London, in May 1905. The following year, it was presented in a double bill with Wilde's *A Florentine Tragedy* by the Literary Theatre Society at the King's Hall, with designs by Ricketts. Shaw and Duse were in the audience: the press boycotted the production. Roger Fry thought it 'superbly mounted and acted and it really came out something altogether greater than one had any idea of'. Herod became a 'quite Shakespearean conception', while Ricketts's idea of colour 'surpassed belief. I've never seen anything so beautiful on the stage.'[8] In spite of—perhaps because of—the popularity of Strauss's opera, which follows though inevitably compresses Wilde's text, and in spite of isolated attempts to reveal the true nature of the work, *Salome* has been largely neglected within the English theatre. Terence Gray's 1931 production at the Festival Theatre, Cambridge, with Beatrix Lehmann as Salome, was one landmark. Gray saw the play's virtue in its verbal treatment,

---

[8] *Letters of Roger Fry*, ed. Denys Sutton (2 vols.; 1972), i. 267.

which 'corresponds to a musical composition': accordingly, he produced it for sound and movement, and not at all for character. The
1977 version at the Roundhouse was another notable exploration: 'a
colossal homo-erotic spectacle', according to Bernard Levin, 'lifted
from the absurd to the impressive by the manifest artistic integrity'
of Lindsay Kemp. But when Steven Berkoff's production, first seen
at the Gate Theatre, Dublin, filled the Lyttelton auditorium in the
National Theatre in November 1989, it had taken almost a century
for Wilde's play to be accepted into the national, as opposed to the
international, repertory.

A review of Lugné-Poe's Paris production sums up the essence of
the play: 'Salomé a presque toutes les qualités d'un poème, la prose
en est musicale et fluide comme des vers, elle est chargée d'images et
de metaphores' [Salome has almost all the qualities of a poem, the
prose is as musical and fluid as verse, it is charged with images and
metaphors].[9] Wilde often referred to *Salome* in musical terms: he
wrote that its recurring phrases 'bind it together like a piece of music
with recurring *motifs*'.[10] One of the revelations of Berkoff's production
was that, by stressing rather than concealing the elaborations and
repetitions of the text, the strange musical quality was released.
Speech, like movement, was slowed down, and the unity of style drew
attention to the choric function of the people who inhabit Herod's
palace: 'Drawling the lines as though in a Mogadon-induced trance,
they strike exaggerated attitudes of false conviviality and behave like
a single, multi-membered organism.'[11] This measured pace provides
a contrasting framework for the intensity of the central action. The
play has a precisely demarcated structure, with a prelude followed by
three episodes: the encounter between Salome and Iokanaan, marked
by the suicide of the young Syrian, the phase of the white moon; the
major and public central episode, which culminates in the dance and
the beheading, the phase of the red moon; and the swift conclusion,
when the black cloud conceals the moon, and Salome is crushed to
death.

Criticism of *Salome* has tended to treat it either as a literary text or
as a theatrical aberration. Ellmann argued in 'Overtures to Wilde's
Salome' that it was a kind of critical dialectic, with an ascetic Iokanaan
representing Ruskin and a sense-dominated Salome Pater: Wilde's

---

[9] *La Plume*, 1 Mar. 1896.
[10] *The Letters of Oscar Wilde*, ed. Rupert Hart-Davis (1962), 590.
[11] Paul Taylor, *Independent*, 9 Nov. 1989.

two opposing influences destroy each other, while Herod, associated with Wilde himself, as in Beardsley's illustrations, survives.[12] This reading can be imposed on the literary text, but lacks credibility on stage. Herod has, in fact, tended to obtrude, partly from the difficulty of casting and potraying Salome: even Berkoff's remarkable production suffered because his own performance as Herod overinflated the role. To interpret Salome's dance as a mimed striptease placed the focus on Herod as spectator and left a vacuum at the play's centre. The dance must be the key to Salome, the role and the work. It is an act of self-realization and self-expression, amoral rather than immoral because it is not social. It does not need spectators, or approval; it is instinctive, not motivated. It is art in direct opposition to the social and political order, and as such has to be destroyed.

A Woman of No Importance

Ellmann described *A Woman of No Importance* as the weakest of the plays Wilde wrote in the 1890s.[13] It is the most uneven of his comedies, and the most erratic in tone, and consequently less often revived, yet it also contains some of Wilde's most innovative dramatic writing. The distinguished actor manager Herbert Beerbohm Tree, impressed by *Lady Windermere's Fan*, had asked Wilde for a play. Wilde was initially reluctant: 'As Herod in my Salome you would be admirable. As a peer of the realm in my latest dramatic device, pray forgive me if I do not see you.'[14] But Wilde capitulated. He wrote most of the play in the late summer of 1892, in a rented farmhouse near Cromer in Norfolk—the location is reflected in the name of Lady Hunstanton—with Lord Alfred Douglas in attendance. Tree accepted the play on 14 October and began rehearsals in the following March, playing the role of Lord Illingworth himself. The rehearsal period was somewhat strained. Lord Illingworth, Wilde declared, was quite unlike anyone who had been seen on stage before: 'He is certainly not natural,' he told Tree. 'He is a figure of art. Indeed, if you can bear the truth, he is MYSELF.' He tried to restrain Tree from making Lord Illingworth too theatrical, complaining that 'every day Herbert becomes *de plus en plus oscarisé*. It is a wonderful case of nature

[12] Richard Ellmann, 'Overtures to *Salome*', in *Golden Codgers: Biographical Speculations* (1973).

[13] *Oscar Wilde* (1987), 357.

[14] Hesketh Pearson, *Beerbohm Tree: His Life and Laughter* (1956), 65.

imitating art.' Tree commented later that he had produced the play 'with the interference of Wilde'.[15]

The theme, like *Lady Windermere's Fan*, concerns a woman with a secret past: in the context of an English country house party, Mrs Arbuthnot and her former lover, Lord Illingworth, her son Gerald's natural father, meet unexpectedly. Mrs Arbuthnot lives in a cottage in a neighbouring town, doing good works, while Gerald has a job in a bank; Gerald has been invited to join the house party, and Lord Illingworth, not knowing who he is but attracted to him, offers him a post as his private secretary. In contrast to *Lady Windermere's Fan*, the truth of the relationships is revealed, when Lord Illingworth forces a kiss on the young American 'Puritan', Hester Worsley, and Gerald prepares to strike him in outraged retaliation. Lord Illingworth's offers, of a job and property to Gerald, of marriage to Rachel Arbuthnot, are rejected. The son resolves to stay with the mother, and Hester, an orphan like Gerald, declares her love for him and accepts Mrs Arbuthnot as her mother. Lord Illingworth is dismissed, slapped in the face with his own glove. Wilde's declaration that he took the situation from *The Family Herald*, a weekly downmarket domestic magazine full of remarkable events and anecdotes, does not improve the plot's banality;[16] he might have taken it from any number of French melodramas and *drames*. William Archer criticized Wilde's occasionally blatant reliance on stale convention, remarking tartly of the close of Act 3: 'It would be a just retribution if Mr Wilde were presently to be confronted with this tableau in all the horrors of chromolithography, on every hoarding in London, with the legend, "Stay, Gerald! He is your father!" in crinkly letters in the corner.'[17] Wilde is usually more convincing when expressing himself through the comic and the witty than through the serious. Mrs Arbuthnot seldom speaks with the incisiveness of, for example, Mrs Erlynne, and so lacks the dramatic authority which Wilde imparts by his gift of language. To have a dandy as villain imposes undue strain on the play's structure.

The play begins authoritatively. Wilde thought Act 1 perfect, since it contained absolutely no action at all. The English country house weekend is brilliantly evoked, as the characters come and go under the large yew tree on the lawn. Wilde assembles a cross-section of English upper-class society under the benevolent eye of Lady

[15] Pearson, *Beerbohm Tree*, 65–9.
[16] Ibid. 67.
[17] *World*, 26 Apr. 1893.

Hunstanton, who anticipates Lady Bracknell in her imperfect grasp of fact and the disconcerting conjunction of the naïve and the worldly in her analysis of social behaviour. There are two dandies, Mrs Allonby matching Lord Illingworth in both language and amorality. The beautiful young American Hester Worsley combines the function of serious lover with that of moral commentator and exposer of English hypocrisy; Gerald, the other orphan, is her counterpart with his attributes of youth and good looks. The other guests, a sparkling collection of fools and grotesques, move in and out of view, endlessly though vainly pursuing each other: the lovely but brainless Lady Stutfield; Sir John Pontefract, straining at the leash held taut by his plain, acidic wife, Lady Caroline; the earnest Kelvil; the Archdeacon, forerunner of Canon Chasuble, defined largely in terms of his absent wife's ailments. These strange characters and their obsessions create an almost Chekhovian pattern, a comparison accentuated by the sense of autumn which Wilde evokes, with references to cloaks and shawls and overshoes. Hester and Gerald are conspicuous by their youth: the other characters are middle-aged or elderly. As in L. P. Hartley's *The Go-Between* or Isobel Colegate's *The Shooting-Party*, the country house and its inhabitants evoke the end of an era. 'The future belongs to the dandy. It is the exquisites who are going to rule,' declares Lord Illingworth in Act 3. At the close of Act 4, however, he asks Mrs Arbuthnot what '*fin-de-siècle* person' persuaded Gerald that she should not accept his offer of marriage, and receives his answer: the Puritan. A new age and a new morality are beginning.

Structurally, the play moves between two gardens, the formal lawns and spacious terraces of Hunstanton, and the garden seen through the French window of Mrs Arbuthnot's cottage. The connotation is clarified by Lord Illingworth: 'The Book of Life begins with a man and a woman in a garden.' In the background lies the garden setting of the initial sexual encounter between moral, intellectual, even social opposites, so that Illingworth's kissing of Hester Worsley repeats the pattern, as he reminds Mrs Arbuthnot, 'when the whole thing began in your father's garden'. Sexual love and marriage, as in one of the more savage Restoration comedies, do not seem to agree. Only one married couple appears in this play, the Pontefracts, and Sir John is Lady Caroline's fourth husband. The others are widowed, single, or separated, at least temporarily. Sterility is rife, and the hints of decadence reflect the play's many echoes of Wilde's novel of 1890, *The Picture of Dorian Gray*. Mrs Allonby, in her complaint about her husband Ernest, seems to hint at his sexual, or at least his emotional, inexperience. She commends Lord Illingworth for never having made love to her, and challenges him to kiss someone else. Even Lady Caroline, whose brother Lord Henry Weston, a man with a hideous smile and a hideous past, has ruined other women, pronounces: 'Englishwomen conceal their feelings till after they are married. They show them then.' The beauty of English home-life, so unctuously commended by Mr Kelvil, is mercilessly exposed.

One further unusual feature of the play is the dominance of women. Mrs Arbuthnot, the woman of the title, rejects, insults, and dismisses Lord Illingworth, and her final curtain-line, 'A man of no importance', overturns his 'A woman of no importance' in Act 1. Hester Worsley undergoes a moral education, not unlike that of Lady Windermere, while also highlighting the decadence of English aristocratic values. This critique is especially effective in Act 2. Hester, a Puritan in white, sits silent while the other women talk, and Mrs Allonby defines the Ideal Man. In fact, Hester's silent presence is dramatically far more powerful than the moral lecture she delivers: 'Oh, your English society seems to me shallow, selfish, foolish. . . . It lies like a leper in purple. It sits like a dead thing smeared with gold.' The biblical rhythms sit uneasily within this play, a sudden incursion from the world of *Salome*. Mrs Arbuthnot and her apprentice, Hester, were essays on Wilde's part to create contemporary women as morally independent as Ibsen's characters. He had not, however, found a verbal language to complement their physical gestures and express their inner life in anything other than conventional terms.

The 'leper' phrases, later removed from the acting text, may not have endeared Wilde to some sections of the first-night audience. A few boos were heard when Wilde appeared. But the hints of subversion were too far beneath the surface to ruffle the fashionable public. The Prince of Wales reportedly told Wilde, 'Do not alter a single line.' The critics, too, approved, and Archer called the Act Two exchange between Lord Illingworth and Mrs Arbuthnot 'the most virile and intelligent piece of English play-writing of our day'.[18] Wilde would return to some of the elements of *A Woman of No Importance*—the orphan, the search for self-realization—in *The Importance of Being Earnest*, which can be viewed, among other perspectives, as its parody.

[18] *World*, 26 Apr. 1893.

An Ideal Husband

An Ideal Husband was begun at Goring in the summer of 1893 with constant distractions from Douglas, who encouraged Wilde to paddle about on the Thames in a Canadian canoe: it was completed early in 1894 when Douglas was abroad, and marks a clear advance in Wilde's career as a dramatist. The ironic title is somewhat misleading, for Wilde chose to set his 'new and original play of modern life' in the public arena: a world of grand receptions, the Foreign Office, speeches in the House of Commons, and visits to Downing Street. The youthful indiscretion which is the plot's spring is not a relationship in which the woman is victimized: it is a breach of trust, the selling of confidential state information, committed by a young man who is now, as Sir Robert Chiltern, a wealthy Government minister with an adoring, upright wife and a dazzling career before him. Mrs Cheveley, a reincarnation of Dumas's Milady de Winter in *The Three Muske-teers*, arrives from Vienna with a compromising letter to blackmail Chiltern into giving public support for a canal scheme which will secure her fortune. Lord Goring extricates Sir Robert from Mrs Cheveley's clutches and persuades the puritanical Lady Chiltern to forgive her husband and allow him to continue in public life. The play concludes with a seat in the cabinet for Sir Robert, a declaration of love from Lady Chiltern, and her confident affirmation: 'For both of us a new life is beginning.'

The play was advertised as 'A New and Original Play of Modern Life', which may seem initially surprising in view of the well-tried ingredients which Wilde tossed in. However, a glance at some periodical such as *Vanity Fair* will confirm that the conversation of the chattering classes Wilde depicts is a brilliant pastiche of contemporary gossip: the readers learnt that Lord Curzon dined without his wife, and Lady Helmsley dined without her husband; Lady Howe had her jewel-case stolen while staying with Lord and Lady Dorchester for Cowes week.[19] If the plot is demonstrably contrived, it is not necessarily untrue to public life. Wilde had Disraeli's handling of the Suez Canal transactions in mind, and public scandals frequently resemble the lurid inventions of melodrama, certainly in the way they are reported. Wilde had an unerring eye for trivial or mundane details which he contrives to make resonant of so much more.

Wilde repeatedly altered the mechanics of the plot in successive drafts, as though they were of little consequence, and even so it

[19] *Vanity Fair*, 27 July 1893 and 8 Aug. 1893.

functions smoothly enough. The main characters are somewhat wooden; 'horrid objective creations of serious folk', as Wilde described them to Adela Schuster.[20] His major achievement is the creation of Lord Goring, whom he places on the pinnacle of the hierarchy of wit. Goring represents the dandiacal point of view. He functions as commentator and observer, philosopher and judge. Morally, intellectually, and aesthetically superior, he stands, as Wilde describes him, 'in immediate relation to modern life, makes it indeed, and so masters it. He is the first well-dressed philosopher in the history of thought.' He is matched in wit and style by Chiltern's sister, Mabel, and characteristically distances himself by choosing, with her approval, an entirely domestic and private life. The witty lovers leave just before the close of Act 4, and the closing stage image of the serious married couple is ironically placed and diminished by their absence.

Shaw praised the 'subtle and pervading levity' of the play,[21] and this prevailing mood, established by Wilde through Lord Goring, gives the work a greater unity than he achieved in the previous comedies. Goring initiates three of the four acts, beginning the last with a soliloquy, in which Wilde draws attention to the fact that he is playing with plot, characters, dramatic form, and, indeed, the audience: 'It is a great nuisance. I can't find anyone in this house to talk to. And I am full of interesting information.' Act 3, set in Lord Goring's Library and presided over by the impassive Phipps, the Ideal Butler and as incommunicative as the Sphinx, reveals Wilde at his most masterful. Although the pattern of action veers towards melodrama, with overheard conversations, burning letters, and bracelets with secret clasps, the pace and tone are closer to those of elegant farce. This is particularly noticeable in the series of unexpected callers who arrive in rapid succession, to be neatly disposed in adjoining rooms without meeting each other. Wilde maintains a delicate balance between melodramatic action and heightened private emotion, on the one hand, and the appearance of rigid public decorum and polite conversation on the other. One illustration of this is Lord Goring's last speech to Mrs Cheveley, when for once he seems in danger of losing control: 'Give me back that letter. I'll take it from you by force. You shall not leave my room till I have got it.' Mrs Cheveley's answer is to ring the bell for Phipps, in whose presence Lord Goring feels

---

[20] Unpublished letter, William Andrews Clark Library, Los Angeles.
[21] *Saturday Review*, 12 January 1895.

compelled to remain silent. The servant, or appearance, rules, and Goring recovers his poise sufficiently to light a cigarette.

As Wilde eventually organized the final act, the supposedly incriminating letter is a false clue, easily disposed of. Mrs Cheveley is seen no more, and after some ritual obstacles have been overcome the solutions proposed by Lord Goring win acceptance. Mabel Chiltern, anticipating Gwendolen Fairfax and Cecily Cardew, arranges her own engagement. The moral scheme of the outcome has some unusual dimensions, reflecting the mature tolerance of *Lady Windermere's Fan* rather than the absolutes of *A Woman of No Importance*. The man who sold confidential information may look forward to the prospect of becoming Prime Minister, while Lady Chiltern learns to adopt a less puritanical code. Wilde, however, gives her declaration, 'A man's life is of more value than a woman's', a distinctly ironical gloss by having her repeat the lesson she has learnt from Lord Goring like a parrot in his presence. The apparently conventional ending carries a critique of public life which is all the more disconcerting for being unstated.

The Importance of Being Earnest

The year 1894 was a productive, if frenetic, one for Wilde: he completed *An Ideal Husband*, wrote most of *A Florentine Tragedy* and *La Sainte Courtisane*, and embarked on an entirely new genre in *The Importance of Being Earnest*. He was involved in detailed negotiation with producers and managers over existing plays and unwritten projects, and as his finances became increasingly inadequate to support his mother's household as well as his own in addition to the sums he spent on Lord Alfred Douglas, the need to create a lucrative new property sharpened. Just before he left with his family for Worthing, at the end of July 1894, he sent Alexander the scenario of his new comedy, asking £150 for the first refusal. (This has been reprinted in the Appendix.) The detailed outline of the plot, though unmistakably the origin of *Earnest*, is intriguingly different. The upright guardian is Mr Bertram Ashton JP, his fictitious younger brother is George, and his great friend Lord Alfred Rufford. The only name which survived into the final version is Miss Prism, dragon of propriety with designs on her employer. There is no misplaced baby, three-volume novel, nor handbag, and, in the absence of the Ernest joke, the principal concern on the part of the girls is to marry men who are bad and hence in need of reform.

Once established at Worthing, Wilde began to develop the play, which now had the working title of 'The Guardian'. Bertram became Geoffrey, and Ernest and the christening motif appear. (The Ernest joke was an elaboration from *A Woman of No Importance*, in which Mrs Allonby had been horribly deceived into believing that her husband had never loved anyone before.)

In a manuscript workbook in the Clark Library,[22] Wilde sketched out this exchange:

[LADY GWENDOLEN] Beautiful name—Ernest. I couldn't love anybody who wasn't called Ernest—

[GEOFFREY ASHTON] Oh! don't say that Gwendolen. It sounds perfectly heartless of you—why shd. love be dependent on the action of an irresponsible godfather. Is a man's whole fortune to depend on the font. I am told that there was a moment when my father contemplated calling me John—

[LADY GWENDOLEN] How very cruel of him!

The precise timing of the emergence of *Earnest*, from three-act scenario to four-act version to the three acts of Alexander's production, is difficult to determine. Few of Wilde's letters from Worthing are dated. Wilde's personal circumstances seem to inhabit the text: the railway journey from Victoria station to Worthing on the Brighton line, the names of nearby seaside resorts such as Lancing and Shoreham, the 'horrid ugly Swiss governess' who was looking after his children; while Douglas, installed at one point in the Grand Hotel at Brighton and succumbing to flu, seems a demonic echo of the invalid Bunbury. Wilde, holed up for the summer at 5, The Esplanade, Worthing, practically penniless and with a clandestine lover in tow, was already living in a world of farce. Kerry Powell, in *Oscar Wilde and the Theatre of the 1890s*, traces many parallels between *Earnest* and the popular theatre of the time, and suggests that Wilde may have attended a performance of Lestocq's and Robson's farce *The Foundling*, which opened at Terry's Theatre in London on 30 August. Certainly a few of the details are uncannily similar, and it is conceivable that Wilde may have found there the idea of the suitor who needs to find a parent. But Wilde claimed not to have the price of a rail-ticket to London and had probably completed a draft by the time he met Alexander at the Garrick in early September. He was, in any event, an avid reader of reviews, and the notice in *The Morning Post* of 31 August provided full details of the plot, though the broad

---

[22] MS Notebook, William Andrews Clark Library, Los Angeles.

situation of this orphan child is as old as comedy, and he might just as usefully have recalled *The Pirates of Penzance*. Certainly, too, Wilde was conscious that he was writing a very different kind of play, a 'farcical comedy'—'admirable for style, but fatal to handwriting', he informed Douglas.[23] Having involved Alexander at the very beginning, Wilde later suggested that the play was not entirely suited to him, though he sent him the four-act version at the end of October. Instead, he promised it to Charles Wyndham. When Alexander urgently needed a new work because of the failure of Henry James's *Guy Domville*, Wyndham agreed to concede his rights in *Earnest*, and Alexander persuaded Wilde to return to a three-act form.

Whatever the play's derivation, Wilde created something which transcended the genre of farce, delighting his contemporary audience though disconcerting some of his admirers, most notably Shaw, who found it 'heartless'.[24] (Mary McCarthy would go further: she thought the play, though extremely funny, a 'ferocious idyll': 'depravity is the hero and the only character'.[25])

The play is neither superficial, nor trivial, but purely surface, purely play. Appearance, style, fiction are treated as essence, not just by the wits and dandies, but by the butler, the 'serious' guardian, the matriarch, the *ingénue*, and, finally, by the governess and the clergyman. Miss Prism's magnificent slip, in which she substituted the baby for the manuscript of her three-volume novel, is definitive. The imaginary, fictitious love which Cecily conceives for Jack's wicked younger brother has more validity than the 'reality' of Algernon. Algernon, as Lady Bracknell remarks, 'has nothing' but 'looks everything'. Lady Bracknell will change either the fashion or Jack's residence in Belgrave Square to satisfy convention, which is exposed, or celebrated, as wholly artificial. From the lie of the disappearing cucumbers to the flurry of proposed christenings, the ceremonies of social life are stylishly exploded, just like Bunbury: death, birth, engagement, marriage, celibacy, fidelity, receive the same treatment. Everything must be arranged into an aesthetic pattern which satisfies the egotists who inhabit the story and who are endowed with the disarming innocence and ruthless tunnel-vision of children. To confuse the issue, the events do not take place in some fanciful construction such as Lewis Carroll's *Alice in Wonderland* or Samuel Butler's *Erewhon*, or in the dubious hotel or seaside boarding-house

[23] *The Letters of Oscar Wilde*, 370.
[24] *Saturday Review*, 12 Jan. 1895.
[25] Mary McCarthy, *Sights and Spectacles* (1959), 105.

of popular farce, but in the instantly recognizable world of the audience, the apartments of fashionable Mayfair and the spacious country house of the respectable home counties.

For this hard-edged dream, Wilde has fashioned a comic verbal style which embraces every character. Max Beerbohm, reviewing the 1902 revival, observed that the characters 'speak a kind of beautiful nonsense—the language of high comedy, twisted into fantasy. Throughout the dialogue is the horse-play of a distinguished intellect and a distinguished imagination—a horse-play among words and ideas, conducted with poetic dignity.'[26] Wilde always began to create his plays from dialogue. Here he succeeds in subjugating plot to dialogue so conclusively that one feels literally anything could happen without affecting his characters' aplomb. He achieves the total suspension of belief, creating a polished mirror into which his contemporary audience could gaze and see, if they chose, a disconcerting reflection, or inversion, or themselves. The contrast between style and subject is integral. To achieve the full effect, it is crucial that the cast act with complete seriousness: every statement, however preposterous or absurd, must be delivered with conviction. Lady Bracknell articulates the underlying value system, more wittily and memorably than Sir Robert Chiltern's solemn statement 'The god of this country is wealth': 'A hundred and thirty thousand pounds! And in the Funds! Miss Cardew seems to me a most attractive young lady, now that I look at her.' If the serious business of society was the achievement of satisfactory marriages, and generous marriage settlements, the closing tableau of *The Importance of Being Earnest* provides it with a superbly trivialized image.

The play achieves its power to disconcert by deploying traditional patterns, such as the dénouement, yet implying that they have no relevance for the participants. Even such gestures as a kiss or an embrace are purely conventional, undertaken for effect, not spontaneous, but a response to the search for form and symmetry. Joseph Bristow has argued that *Earnest* is a privately coded play, with a sub-text of allusions to homosexuality which would have been recognized only by the initiated, centred on the name of Ernest and the life of deception: 'there is a lot more provocative sexual innuendo than most critics have been willing to observe in *Earnest*.'[27] However, the play remains consistently detached from social reality of any kind,

[26] *Saturday Review*, 18 Jan. 1902.
[27] Joseph Bristow (ed.), *The Importance of Being Earnest and Related Writings* (1992), 208.

a critique of the absurdity of all forms and conventions. None of the characters act as if they have any but the most superficial knowledge of each other; even the speeches, once rehearsed, seem to float free of their utterers. In this world of artifice, each individual is autonomous, and separate, though it is the women who move with the greatest confidence through Wilde's absurdist dream, in which 'Life is a play scrutinized by a ring of eyes.'[28] The play's celebration of high artifice makes an appropriate, if imposed, climax to Wilde's career as a dramatist.

[28] Camille Paglia, *Sexual Personae* (1991), 537.

NOTE ON THE TEXTS

The texts printed here are, with a few minor emendations, those of the first published edition of each play (or, in the case of *Salome*, of the first English version). Wilde supervised the publication of each play, making numerous changes, and (again with the exception of *Salome*) he had the experience of the first production to draw upon. These texts, therefore, form the version which he chose to commit to print.

Writing to his agent Elisabeth Marbury in February 1893, about a proposed American production of *A Woman of No Importance*, Wilde asked that it should not open until the Haymarket production was in full swing 'as the ultimate version must be the version produced under the direct supervision of the author. I need not tell you, with your experience and artistic instinct, how a play grows at rehearsal, and what new points one can produce.'[1] However, the first published texts were substantially different from the first acting texts. Although Wilde incorporated many 'new points' developed at rehearsal, he also reworked lines and speeches, often returning to words and speeches which had appeared in earlier drafts, and had subsequently been cut or changed. The published texts of *Lady Windermere's Fan* and *A Woman of No Importance* appeared within eighteen months or so of their first productions, but *The Importance of Being Earnest* and *An Ideal Husband* were not published until 1899 because of Wilde's trials, imprisonment, and voluntary exile.

The various manuscripts, typescripts, and copies marked up as prompt-books offer a rich, verging on indigestible, source for investigating the complex process of development and revision. The New Mermaid editions provide detailed and lucid accounts of the textual history of each comedy: *Lady Windermere's Fan*, edited by Ian Small (1980); *The Importance of Being Earnest*, edited by Russell Jackson (1980); and *Two Society Comedies: A Woman of No Importance, An Ideal Husband*, edited by Ian Small and Russell Jackson (1983). I am especially indebted to these two editors. Reference is made in the notes to a number of alternative readings, where these are judged to clarify textual or performance aspects. The major sources for these details are: a manuscript of *Lady Windermere's Fan* at the Clark

---

[1] Rupert Hart-Davis (ed.), *More Letters of Oscar Wilde* (1985), 120.

Library, UCLA, marked for performance, together with a variant typescript; a typescript of *A Woman of No Importance*, also at the Clark; a typescript of *An Ideal Husband*, prepared for the New York production under the management of Frohman (New York Public Library); and Alexander's copy of *The Importance of Being Earnest*, also marked for performance (Harvard Theatre Collection). Other texts cited include the typescripts and Licensing Copies at the British Library, and French's acting editions, which, while they lack authority, undoubtedly reflect early stage practice.

The text of *Salome* presents a different problem, since Wilde never had the benefit of seeing a production, though the French text was in rehearsal when the Censor's office refused it a licence. Wilde invited Lord Alfred Douglas to make the translation, but was horrified at the result, and took the responsibility for the final version into his own hands, smoothing Douglas's feelings with the dedication: 'To my friend Lord Alfred Bruce Douglas the translator of my play'. Since Wilde saw neither French nor English text performed, it seems consistent to work from the English. The form 'Salomé' is used where the French text is specifically referred to.

A number of small emendations to the texts, mostly to correct obvious punctuation errors, have been made. The more substantial changes are explained in the notes. Some words, hyphenated in the first editions, now conform to modern practice. The lay-out of the stage directions has been emended in accordance with the series conventions.

Wilde is not consistent in his use of stage directions (s.d.), though a general shift away from recording theatre practice towards providing a text for the non-theatre-going reader may be detected: *Lady Windermere's Fan* is much closer to an acting edition, for instance, than *An Ideal Husband*. Some technical annotations remain, and are found both in the texts and notes: R. = Right, L. = Left, R.C. = Right of Centre, R.U.E. = Right Upper (i.e. Upstage) Entrance, etc. These positions are from the perspective of an actress or actor standing on-stage and facing the audience, so 'down' means 'towards the audience'.

SELECT BIBLIOGRAPHY

Wilde's Works

Until the publication of the new Oxford University Press Collected Wilde, the reader has a choice of either the *Complete Works*, with an introduction by Vyvyan Holland (London, 1966, new edn. 1994), or a variety of individual works and selections. Those edited by Isobel Murray for OUP offer crisp annotation: *The Picture of Dorian Gray* (1974); *The Complete Shorter Fiction of Oscar Wilde* (1979); and *The Writings of Oscar Wilde* (1989). Richard Ellmann edited Wilde's criticism: *The Artist as Critic: Critical Writings of Oscar Wilde* (New York, 1969; London, 1970). The fullest and best editions of the individual plays are those in the New Mermaid series: *Lady Windermere's Fan* (ed. Ian Small, 1980); *Two Society Comedies (A Woman of No Importance and An Ideal Husband)* (ed. Ian Small and Russell Jackson, 1983); and *The Importance of Being Earnest* (ed. Russell Jackson, 1980).

Bibliography

Stuart Mason's *A Bibliography of Oscar Wilde* (1916, reissued 1967) is the first significant bibliography, annotated and extended by Ian Fletcher and John Stokes in 'Oscar Wilde', in *Recent Research on Anglo-Irish Writers: A Supplement to Anglo-Irish Literature: A Review of Research*, edited by Richard J. Finneran (New York, 1983); and by E. H. Mikhail, *Oscar Wilde: An Annotated Bibliography of Criticism* (1978). Most recently, Ian Small has produced *Oscar Wilde Revalued: An Essay on New Materials & Methods of Research* (Greenboro, NC, 1993). In addition to surveying the current state of Wilde studies, and providing a commentary on recent criticism, Small publishes a selection of the extensive material, such as letters, as yet uncollected, and provides a detailed survey of the existing Wilde manuscripts and typescripts, especially useful in the case of the plays.

Biography and Letters

Richard Ellmann's *Oscar Wilde* (1987) is the best biography, incorporating much critical material. However, it includes some dubious conjectures, for instance that Wilde's last illness was 'almost certainly syphilitic in origin', an assertion that has been challenged by, among others, Wilde's grandson Merlin Holland ('What Killed Oscar Wilde?', *Spectator*, Dec. 1988). Horst Schroeder has printed privately *Additions and Corrections to Richard Ellmann's 'Oscar Wilde'* (Brunswick, 1989). Of earlier biographies, that by Hesketh Pearson (revised edition, 1954) is readable and offers insight into the theatrical context. Vyvyan Holland's *Son of Oscar Wilde* (Oxford, 1988) is moving and provides a different perspective on some aspects of Wilde's later life. E. H. Mikhail edited a rich and varied two-volume collection, *Oscar Wilde: Interviews and Recollections* (1979). Rupert Hart-Davis edited three volumes of letters: the first great collection, *The Letters of Oscar Wilde*, appeared in 1962, followed by *More Letters of Oscar Wilde* in 1985; there is also a *Selected Letters of Oscar Wilde* (Oxford, 1979). Hart-Davis's footnotes and explanations function almost as a biography. There remain a surprising number of unpublished letters, some of them of more than peripheral interest, a selection of which appears in Small (*Oscar Wilde Revalued*).

Criticism

There are four volumes of collected criticism which provide good coverage, especially of the plays: *Oscar Wilde: The Critical Heritage* (1970), edited by Karl Beckson; *Oscar Wilde: A Collection of Critical Essays*, edited by Richard Ellmann (Englewood Cliffs, NJ, 1969); *Wilde, Comedies: A Selection of Critical Essays*, edited by William Tydeman (1982); and *Critical Essays on Oscar Wilde* (New York, 1991), edited by Regenia Gagnier. The latter two bring together much recent material.

Rodney Shewan's *Oscar Wilde: Art and Egotism* (1977) is a wide-ranging monograph on Wilde's work, and especially challenging on *Salome*. An introductory study which emphasizes the centrality of the plays, and the dramatic, is that by Peter Raby (Cambridge, 1988). Katherine Worth's study in the Macmillan Modern Dramatists series (1983) was the first to concentrate on the way Wilde's plays function in performance, and to locate Wilde firmly in the context of the late Victorian theatre. Kerry Powell's important study, *Oscar Wilde and the Theatre of the 1890s* (Cambridge, 1990), explores the relationship between Wilde and the late Victorian theatre and drama, including Ibsen, and provides many new perspectives on Wilde as a playwright. Regenia Gagnier, in a vigorous and radical study *Idylls of the Marketplace: Oscar Wilde and the Victorian Public* (Standford, Calif., 1986), places Wilde in the context of his audiences and of contemporary social institutions. Studies which set Wilde within wider intellectual and cultural contexts include J. E. Chamberlin's *Ripe was the Drowsy Hour* (1977), and Jonathan Dollimore's *Sexual Dissidence: Augustine to Wilde, Freud to Foucault* (1991). Wilde is a central and recurrent figure in John Stokes's collection of essays *In the Nineties* (Hemel Hempstead, 1989). Camille Paglia has two provocative chapters on Wilde, including one centred on *The Importance of Being Earnest*, in *Sexual Personae* (New Haven, Conn., 1990).

Of more specialized individual essays, the following (some of them available in the collections) are important: Joseph Donohue's ground-breaking 'The First Production of *The Importance of Being Earnest*: A Proposal for Recon-structive Study', in Kenneth Richards and Peter Thomson (eds.), *Nineteenth Century British Theatre* (1971), 125–43; Richard Ellmann's 'Overtures to

Salome', most easily located in *Golden Codgers: Biographical Speculations* (1973); Arthur H. Ganz, 'The Divided Self in the Society Comedies of Oscar Wilde', *Modern Drama*, 3 (1960), 16–23; Ian Gregor, 'Comedy and Oscar Wilde', *Sewanee Review*, 74 (1966), 501–21, illuminating on the role of the dandy; and Jerusha McCormack, 'Masks Without Faces: The Personalities of Oscar Wilde', *English Literature in Transition*, 22 (1979), 253–69. The introductions to Ian Small's and Russell Jackson's editions of the comedies are full and detailed. Joseph Bristow's commentary to *The Importance of Being Earnest and Related Writings* (1992) is sharp and balanced on Wilde and sexual politics. The special Wilde number of *Modern Drama*, XXVII, 1 (1994), edited by Joel Kaplan, brings together the most recent researches of Wilde scholars in the field of theatre. Joel H. Kaplan and Sheila Stowell's *Theatre and Fashion: Oscar Wilde to the Suffragettes* (Cambridge, 1994) explores the relationship between theatre, fashion, and society, with detailed analysis of Wilde's social comedies.

A CHRONOLOGY OF OSCAR WILDE

1854   (16 Oct.) Born in Dublin.

1864–71 Portora Royal School, Enniskillen.

1871–4 Trinity College, Dublin.

1874–8 (Oct.) Magdalen College, Oxford.

1875   (June) Travel in Italy.

1877   (Mar.–Apr.) Travel in Greece and Italy.

1878   Wins Newdigate Prize with poem 'Ravenna', completes degree with First in Greats.

1881   *Poems* published.

1882   Lecture tour of USA and Canada.

1883   (Jan.–May) In Paris.

        (Aug.–Sept.) In New York for production of *Vera*.

        (Sept.) Lectures in UK.

        (26 Nov.) Engaged to Constance Lloyd.

1884   (29 May) Married in London.

1885   (1 Jan.) Moves into 16 Tite Street, Chelsea.

        (5 June) Elder son Cyril born.

1886   (3 Nov.) Younger son Vyvyan born.

1887–9 Editor, *Woman's World*.

1888   (May) *The Happy Prince and Other Tales* published.

1889   (July) *The Portrait of Mr W.H.* published (Blackwood's).

1890   (June) *The Picture of Dorian Gray* published (Lippincott's).

1891   Meets Lord Alfred Douglas.

        (Jan.) *The Duchess of Padua*—'*Guido Ferranti*'—produced in New York.

        (Feb.) *The Soul of Man under Socialism* published (*Fortnightly Review*).

        (Apr.) Extended version of *The Picture of Dorian Gray* published.

        (May) *Intentions* published.

        (July) *Lord Arthur Savile's Crime and Other Stories* published.

        (Nov.) *A House of Pomegranates* published.

        (Nov.–Dec.) Writes *Salomé* in Paris.

1892   (22 Feb.) *Lady Windermere's Fan* opens at St James's Theatre.

        (June) *Salomé* banned by Lord Chamberlain.

1893   (Feb.) *Salomé* published in French.

        (19 Apr.) *A Woman of No Importance* opens at Theatre Royal, Haymarket.

        (Nov.) *Lady Windermere's Fan* published.

1894   (Feb.) *Salome* published in English.

        (June) *The Sphinx* published.

	(Oct.) *A Woman of No Importance* published.
1895	(3 Jan.) *An Ideal Husband* opens at Theatre Royal, Haymarket.
	(14 Feb.) *The Importance of Being Earnest* opens at St James's Theatre.
	(28 Feb.) Finds Queensberry's card, 'To Oscar Wilde, posing (as a) Somdomite' [*sic*] at Albemarle Club. Wilde applies for warrant for Queensberry's arrest, for publishing a libel.
	(5 Apr.) Acquittal of Queensberry, arrest of Wilde.
	(25 May) Convicted and sentenced to two years' hard labour, imprisoned at Pentonville.
	(4 July) Transferred to Wandsworth.
	(20 Nov.) Transferred to Reading.
1896	(3 Feb.) Death of mother, Lady Wilde.
	(11 Feb.) *Salomé* produced by Lugné-Poe at Théâtre de l'Œuvre, Paris.
1897	(Jan.–Mar.) Writes *De Profundis*.
	(19 May) Released from prison; crosses to Dieppe. Lives abroad until his death.
1898	(Feb.) *The Ballad of Reading Gaol* published.
	(7 Apr.) Death of Constance Wilde.
1899	(Feb.) *The Importance of Being Earnest* published.
	(July) *An Ideal Husband* published.
1900	(30 Nov.) After being received into the Roman Catholic Church, dies in Hôtel d'Alsace, Paris.

LADY WINDERMERE'S FAN

A Play about a Good Woman

To the dear memory of

ROBERT EARL OF LYTTON

in affection and admiration

THE PERSONS OF THE PLAY

The play was first staged at the St James's Theatre, London, 20 February 1892.

Lord Windermere	*Mr George Alexander*
Lord Darlington	*Mr Nutcombe Gould*
Lord Augustus Lorton	*Mr H. H. Vincent*
Mr Cecil Graham	*Mr Ben Webster*
Mr Dumby	*Mr Vane-Tempest*
Mr Hopper	*Mr Alfred Holles*
Parker (Butler)	*Mr V. Sansbury*
Lady Windermere	*Miss Lily Hanbury*
The Duchess of Berwick	*Miss Fanny Coleman*
Lady Agatha Carlisle	*Miss Laura Graves*
Lady Plymdale	*Miss Granville*
Lady Jedburgh	*Miss B. Page*
Lady Stutfield	*Miss Madge Girdlestone*
Mrs Cowper-Cowper	*Miss A. de Winton*
Mrs Erlynne	*Miss Marion Terry*
Rosalie (Maid)	*Miss Winifred Dolan*

Non-Speaking Characters:

Sir James Royston, Mr Guy Berkeley, Mr Rufford, Miss Graham, Mr and Mrs Arthur Bowden, Lord and Lady Paisley.

THE SCENES OF THE PLAY

Act 1
Morning-room in Lord Windermere's house

Act 2
Drawing-room in Lord Windermere's house

Act 3
Lord Darlington's rooms

Act 4
Same as Act 1

Time *The Present*

Place *London*

The action of the play takes place within twenty-four hours, beginning on a Tuesday afternoon at five o'clock, and ending the next day at 1.30 p.m.

First Act

Scene: Morning-room of Lord Windermere's house in Carlton House Terrace. Doors C. and R. Bureau with books and papers R. Sofa with small tea-table L. Window opening on to terrace L. Table R. [with fan on it]. Lady Windermere is at table R., arranging roses in a blue bowl. Enter Parker

PARKER Is your ladyship at home° this afternoon?

LADY WINDERMERE Yes—who has called?

PARKER Lord Darlington, my lady.

LADY WINDERMERE (*hesitates for a moment*) Show him up—and I'm at home to anyone° who calls.   5

PARKER Yes, my lady.
    Exit C.

LADY WINDERMERE It's best for me to see him before tonight. I'm glad he's come.
    Enter Parker C.

PARKER Lord Darlington.
    Enter Lord Darlington C. Exit Parker

LORD DARLINGTON How do you do, Lady Windermere? [*offering to*   10
shake hands]

LADY WINDERMERE How do you do, Lord Darlington? No, I can't shake hands° with you. My hands are all wet with these roses. Aren't they lovely? They came up from Selby° this morning.

LORD DARLINGTON They are quite perfect. (*Sees a fan lying on the table.*) And what a wonderful fan! May I look at it?   15

LADY WINDERMERE Do. Pretty, isn't it! It's got my name on it, and everything. I have only just seen it myself. It's my husband's birthday present to me. You know today is my birthday?

LORD DARLINGTON No? Is it really?

LADY WINDERMERE Yes, I'm of age° today. Quite an important day   20
in my life, isn't it? That is why I am giving this party tonight. Do sit down.° (*Still arranging flowers.*)

LORD DARLINGTON (*sitting down*) I wish I had known it was your birthday, Lady Windermere. I would have covered the whole street in front of your house with flowers for you to walk on.°   25
They are made for you.
    A short pause

LADY WINDERMERE Lord Darlington, you annoyed me last night at the Foreign Office.° I am afraid you are going to annoy me again.

LORD DARLINGTON I, Lady Windermere?

Enter Parker and Footman C., with tray and tea things.

LADY WINDERMERE Put it there, Parker. That will do.° (*Wipes her hands with her pocket-handkerchief, goes to tea-table L., and sits down.*)

Won't you come over,° Lord Darlington?

Exit Parker C. [and Footman]

LORD DARLINGTON (*takes chair and goes across L.C.*) I am quite miserable, Lady Windermere. You must tell me what I did. (*Sits down at table L.*)

LADY WINDERMERE Well, you kept paying me elaborate compliments the whole evening.

LORD DARLINGTON (*smiling*) Ah, nowadays we are all of us so hard up, that the only pleasant things to pay *are* compliments. They're the only things we *can* pay.

LADY WINDERMERE (*shaking her head*) No, I am talking very seriously. You mustn't laugh, I am quite serious. I don't like compliments, and I don't see why a man should think he is pleasing a woman enormously when he says to her a whole heap of things that he doesn't mean.

LORD DARLINGTON Ah, but I did mean them. (*Takes tea which she offers him.*)

LADY WINDERMERE (*gravely*) I hope not. I should be sorry to have to quarrel with you, Lord Darlington. I like you very much, you know that. But I shouldn't like you at all if I thought you were what most other men are.° Believe me, you are better than most other men, and I sometimes think you pretend to be worse.

LORD DARLINGTON We all have our little vanities, Lady Windermere.

LADY WINDERMERE (*Still seated at table L.*) Why do you make that your special one?

LORD DARLINGTON (*still seated L.C.*) Oh, nowadays so many conceited people go about Society pretending to be good, that I think it shows rather a sweet and modest disposition to pretend to be bad. Besides, there is this to be said. If you pretend to be good, the world takes you very seriously. If you pretend to be bad, it doesn't. Such is the astounding stupidity of optimism.

LADY WINDERMERE Don't you *want* the world to take you seriously, then, Lord Darlington?

LORD DARLINGTON No, not the world. Who are the people the
world takes seriously? All the dull people one can think of, from
the Bishops down to the bores. I should like *you* to take me very
seriously, Lady Windermere, *you* more than anyone else in life. 65

LADY WINDERMERE Why—why me?

LORD DARLINGTON (*after a slight hesitation*) Because I think we
might be great friends.° Let us be great friends. You may want a
friend some day.

LADY WINDERMERE Why do you say that? 70

LORD DARLINGTON Oh!—we all want friends at times.

LADY WINDERMERE I think we're very good friends already, Lord
Darlington. We can always remain so as long as you don't——

LORD DARLINGTON Don't what?

LADY WINDERMERE Don't spoil it by saying extravagant silly things 75
to me. You think I am a Puritan,° I suppose? Well, I have
something of the Puritan in me. I was brought up like that. I am
glad of it. My mother died° when I was a mere child. I lived always
with Lady Julia, my father's elder sister you know. She was stern
to me, but she taught me, what the world is forgetting, the 80
difference that there is between what is right and what is wrong.
She allowed of no compromise. *I* allow of none.

LORD DARLINGTON My dear Lady Windermere!

LADY WINDERMERE (*leaning back on the sofa*) You look on me as
behind the age.—Well, I am! I should be sorry to be on the same 85
level as an age like this.

LORD DARLINGTON You think the age very bad?

LADY WINDERMERE Yes. Nowadays people seem to look on life as
a speculation. It is not a speculation. It is a sacrament. Its ideal is
Love. Its purification is sacrifice. 90

LORD DARLINGTON (*smiling*) Oh, anything is better than being
sacrificed!

LADY WINDERMERE (*leaning forward*) Don't say that.

LORD DARLINGTON I do say it. I feel it—I know it.
        Enter Parker° *C.*

PARKER The men want to know if they are to put the carpets on the 95
terrace for tonight, my lady?

LADY WINDERMERE You don't think it will rain, Lord Darlington,
do you?

LORD DARLINGTON I won't hear of its raining on your birthday!

LADY WINDERMERE Tell them to do it at once, Parker. 100
        Exit Parker C.

LORD DARLINGTON (*still seated*) Do you think then—of course I am only putting an imaginary instance—do you think that in the case of a young married couple, say about two years married, if the husband suddenly becomes the intimate friend of a woman° of—well, more than doubtful character, is always calling upon her, lunching with her, and probably paying her bills—do you think that the wife should not console° herself?   105

LADY WINDERMERE (*frowning*) Console herself?

LORD DARLINGTON Yes, I think she should—I think she has the right.   110

LADY WINDERMERE Because the husband is vile—should the wife be vile also?

LORD DARLINGTON Vileness is a terrible word, Lady Windermere.

LADY WINDERMERE It is a terrible thing, Lord Darlington.

LORD DARLINGTON Do you know I am afraid that good people do a great deal of harm in this world. Certainly the greatest harm they do is that they make badness of such extraordinary importance. It is absurd to divide people into good and bad. People are either charming or tedious.° I take the side of the charming, and you, Lady Windermere, can't help belonging to them.   115   120

LADY WINDERMERE Now, Lord Darlington. (*Rising and crossing R.,* [*in*] *front of him*) Don't stir,° I am merely going to finish my flowers. (*Goes to table R.C.*)

LORD DARLINGTON (*rising and moving chair*) And I must say I think you are very hard on modern life, Lady Windermere. Of course there is much against it, I admit. Most women, for instance, nowadays, are rather mercenary.   125

LADY WINDERMERE Don't talk about such people.

LORD DARLINGTON Well then, setting mercenary people aside, who, of course, are dreadful, do you think seriously that women who have committed what the world calls a fault should never be forgiven?   130

LADY WINDERMERE (*standing at table*) I think they should never be forgiven.

LORD DARLINGTON And men? Do you think that there should be the same laws for men as there are for women?   135

LADY WINDERMERE Certainly!

LORD DARLINGTON I think life too complex a thing to be settled by these hard and fast rules.

LADY WINDERMERE If we had 'these hard and fast rules', we should find life much more simple.   140

LORD DARLINGTON You allow of no exception?

LADY WINDERMERE None!

LORD DARLINGTON Ah, what a fascinating Puritan you are, Lady
Windermere!   145

LADY WINDERMERE The adjective was unnecessary, Lord Darlington.

LORD DARLINGTON I couldn't help it. I can resist everything except
temptation.

LADY WINDERMERE You have the modern affectation of weakness.   150

LORD DARLINGTON (*looking at her*)° It's only an affectation, Lady
Windermere.
  Enter Parker C.

PARKER The Duchess of Berwick and Lady Agatha Carlisle.
  Enter the Duchess of Berwick and Lady Agatha Carlisle C. Exit
  Parker C.

DUCHESS OF BERWICK (*coming down C., and shaking hands*) Dear
Margaret,° I am so pleased to see you. You remember Agatha,   155
don't you? (*Crossing L.C.*) How do you do, Lord Darlington? I
won't let you know my daughter, you are far too wicked.

LORD DARLINGTON Don't say that, Duchess. As a wicked man I am
a complete failure. Why, there are lots of people who say I have
never really done anything wrong in the whole course of my life.   160
Of course they only say it behind my back.

DUCHESS OF BERWICK Isn't he dreadful? Agatha, this is Lord
Darlington.° Mind you don't believe a word he says. (*Lord
Darlington crosses R.C.*) No, no tea, thank you, dear. (*Crosses and
sits on sofa*)° We have just had tea at Lady Markby's. Such bad tea,   165
too. It was quite undrinkable. I wasn't at all surprised. Her own
son-in-law supplies it.° Agatha is looking forward so much to your
ball tonight, dear Margaret.

LADY WINDERMERE (*seated L.C.*) Oh, you mustn't think it is going
to be a ball, Duchess. It is only a dance in honour of my birthday.   170
A small and early.°

LORD DARLINGTON (*standing L.C.*) Very small, very early, and very
select,° Duchess.

DUCHESS OF BERWICK (*on sofa L.*) Of course it's going to be select.
But we know *that*, dear Margaret, about *your* house. It is really one   175
of the few houses in London where I can take Agatha, and where
I feel perfectly secure about dear Berwick. I don't know what
society is coming to. The most dreadful people seem to go
everywhere. They certainly come to my parties—the men get quite

furious if one doesn't ask them. Really, someone should make a   180
stand against it.

LADY WINDERMERE *I* will, Duchess. I will have no one in my house
about whom there is any scandal.

LORD DARLINGTON (*R.C.*) Oh, don't say that, Lady Windermere. I
should never be admitted! (*Sitting*)   185

DUCHESS OF BERWICK Oh, men don't matter. With women it is
different. We're good. Some of us are, at least. But we are
positively getting elbowed into the corner. Our husbands would
really forget our existence if we didn't nag at them from time
to time, just to remind them that we have a perfect legal right to 190
do so.

LORD DARLINGTON It's a curious thing, Duchess, about the
game of marriage—a game, by the way, that is going out of
fashion—the wives hold all the honours,° and invariably lose the
odd trick.   195

DUCHESS OF BERWICK The odd trick? Is that the husband, Lord
Darlington?

LORD DARLINGTON It would be rather a good name for the modern
husband.

DUCHESS OF BERWICK Dear Lord Darlington, how thoroughly   200
depraved you are!

LADY WINDERMERE Lord Darlington is trivial.

LORD DARLINGTON Ah, don't say that, Lady Windermere.

LADY WINDERMERE Why do you *talk* so trivially about life, then?

LORD DARLINGTON Because I think that life is far too important a   205
thing ever to talk seriously about it. (*Moves up C.*)

DUCHESS OF BERWICK What does he mean? Do, as a concession to
my poor wits, Lord Darlington, just explain to me what you really
mean.

LORD DARLINGTON (*coming down back of table*) I think I had better   210
not, Duchess. Nowadays to be intelligible is to be found out.
Good-bye! (*Shakes hands with Duchess*) And now—(*goes up
stage*)—Lady Windermere, good-bye. I may come tonight, mayn't
I? Do let me come.

LADY WINDERMERE (*standing up stage° with Lord Darlington*)   215
Yes, certainly. But you are not to say foolish, insincere things to
people.

LORD DARLINGTON (*smiling*) Ah! you are beginning to reform me.
It is a dangerous thing to reform anyone, Lady Windermere.
    Bows, and exit C.

DUCHESS OF BERWICK (*who has risen, goes C.*) What a charming,   220
wicked creature! I like him so much. I'm quite delighted he's gone!
How sweet you're looking! Where *do* you get your gowns? And
now I must tell you how sorry I am for you, dear Margaret.
(*Crosses to sofa° and sits with Lady Windermere*)   Agatha darling!

LADY AGATHA Yes, mamma. (*Rises.*)   225

DUCHESS OF BERWICK Will you go and look over the photograph
album that I see there?

LADY AGATHA Yes, mamma. (*Goes to table up L.*)

DUCHESS OF BERWICK Dear girl! She is so fond of photographs of
Switzerland. Such a pure taste, I think. But I really am so sorry   230
for you, Margaret.

LADY WINDERMERE (*smiling*) Why, Duchess?

DUCHESS OF BERWICK Oh, on account of that horrid woman. She
dresses so well, too, which makes it much worse, sets such a
dreadful example. Augustus—you know my disreputable   235
brother—such a trial to us all—well, Augustus is completely
infatuated about her. It is quite scandalous, for she is absolutely
inadmissible into society. Many a woman has a past, but I am told
that she has at least a dozen, and that they all fit.

lady windermere Whom are you talking about, Duchess?   240

DUCHESS OF BERWICK About Mrs Erlynne.

LADY WINDERMERE Mrs Erlynne? I never heard of her, Duchess.
And what *has* she to do with me?

DUCHESS OF BERWICK My poor child! Agatha, darling!

LADY AGATHA Yes, mamma.   245

DUCHESS OF BERWICK Will you go out on the terrace and look at
the sunset?

LADY AGATHA Yes, mamma.
        Exit through window L.

DUCHESS OF BERWICK Sweet girl! So devoted to sunsets! Shows
such refinement of feeling, does it not? After all, there is nothing   250
like Nature, is there?

LADY WINDERMERE But what is it, Duchess? Why do you talk to
me about this person?

DUCHESS OF BERWICK Don't you really know? I assure you we're
all so distressed about it. Only last night at dear Lady Jansen's   255
everyone was saying how extraordinary it was that, of all men in
London, Windermere° should behave in such a way.

LADY WINDERMERE My husband—what has *he* got to do with any
woman of that kind?

DUCHESS OF BERWICK Ah, what indeed, dear? That is the point. He 260
goes to see her continually, and stops for hours at a time, and while
he is there she is not at home to anyone.° Not that many ladies
call on her, dear, but she has a great many disreputable men
friends—my own brother particularly, as I told you—and that is
what makes it so dreadful about Windermere. We looked upon *him* 265
as being such a model husband, but I am afraid there is no doubt
about it. My dear nieces—you know the Saville girls, don't
you?—such nice domestic creatures—plain, dreadfully plain, but
so good—well, they're always at the window doing fancy work, and
making ugly things for the poor, which I think so useful of them 270
in these dreadful socialistic days, and this terrible woman has taken
a house in Curzon Street,° right opposite them—such a respectable
street, too! I don't know what we're coming to! And they tell me
that Windermere goes there four and five times a week—they *see*
him. They can't help it—and although they never talk scandal, 275
they—well, of course—they remark on it to every one. And the
worst of it all is that I have been told that this woman has got a
great deal of money out of somebody, for it seems that she came
to London six months ago without anything at all to speak of, and
now she has this charming house in Mayfair, drives her ponies in 280
the Park° every afternoon and all—well, all—since she has known
poor dear Windermere.

LADY WINDERMERE Oh, I can't believe it!

DUCHESS OF BERWICK But it's quite true, my dear. The whole of
London knows it. That is why I felt it was better to come and talk 285
to you, and advise you to take Windermere away at once to
Homburg or to Aix,° where he'll have something to amuse him,
and where you can watch him all day long. I assure you, my dear,
that on several occasions after I was first married, I had to pretend
to be very ill, and was obliged to drink the most unpleasant mineral 290
waters, merely to get Berwick out of town. He was so extremely
susceptible. Though I am bound to say he never gave away any
large sums of money to anybody. He is far too high-principled for
that!

LADY WINDERMERE (*interrupting*) Duchess, Duchess, it's im- 295
possible! (*Rising and crossing stage to C.*) We are only married two
years. Our child is but six months old. (*Sits in chair R. of L. table*)

DUCHESS OF BERWICK Ah, the dear pretty baby! How is the little
darling? Is it a boy or a girl? I hope a girl—Ah, no, I remember
it's a boy! I'm so sorry. Boys are so wicked. My boy is excessively 300

immoral. You wouldn't believe at what hours he comes home. And
he's only left Oxford° a few months—I really don't know what
they teach them there.

LADY WINDERMERE Are *all* men bad?

DUCHESS OF BERWICK Oh, all of them, my dear, all of them,   305
without any exception. And they never grow any better. Men
become old, but they never become good.

LADY WINDERMERE Windermere and I married for love.

DUCHESS OF BERWICK Yes, we begin like that. It was only Berwick's brutal and incessant threats of suicide that made me accept   310
him at all, and before the year was out, he was running after all
kinds of petticoats, every colour, every shape, every material. In
fact, before the honeymoon was over, I caught him winking at my
maid, a most pretty, respectable girl. I dismissed her at once
without a character.°—No, I remember I passed her on to my   315
sister; poor dear Sir George is so short-sighted, I thought it
wouldn't matter. But it did, though—it was most unfortunate.
(*Rises*) And now, my dear child, I must go, as we are dining
out.° And mind you don't take this little aberration of Windermere's too much to heart. Just take him abroad, and he'll come   320
back to you all right.

LADY WINDERMERE Come back to me? (*C.*)

DUCHESS OF BERWICK (*L.C.*) Yes, dear, these wicked women get
our husbands away from us, but they always come back, slightly
damaged, of course. And don't make scenes, men hate them!   325

LADY WINDERMERE It is very kind of you, Duchess, to come
and tell me all this. But I can't believe that my husband is untrue
to me.

DUCHESS OF BERWICK Pretty child! I was like that once. Now I
know that all men are monsters. (*Lady Windermere rings bell*) The   330
only thing to do is to feed the wretches well. A good cook does
wonders, and that I know you have. My dear Margaret, you are
not going to cry?

LADY WINDERMERE You needn't be afraid, Duchess, I never cry.

DUCHESS OF BERWICK That's quite right, dear. Crying is the refuge   335
of plain women but the ruin of pretty ones. Agatha, darling!

    [*Enter Lady Agatha from terrace*]

LADY AGATHA Yes, mamma. (*Stands back of table L.C.*)

DUCHESS OF BERWICK Come and bid good-bye to Lady Windermere, and thank her for your charming visit. (*Coming down again*)
And by the way, I must thank you for sending a card° to Mr   340

Hopper—he's that rich young Australian people are taking such
notice of just at present. His father made a great fortune by selling
some kind of food in circular tins—most palatable, I believe—I
fancy it is the thing the servants always refuse to eat. But the son
is quite interesting. I think he's attracted by dear Agatha's clever   345
talk. Of course, we should be very sorry to lose her, but I think
that a mother who doesn't part with a daughter every season° has
no real affection. We're coming tonight, dear. (*Parker opens C.
doors*) And remember my advice, take the poor fellow out of town at
once, it is the only thing to do. Good-bye, once more; come, Agatha.   350
    Exeunt Duchess and Lady Agatha C. [*Parker closes doors*]

LADY WINDERMERE How horrible! I understand now what Lord
Darlington meant by the imaginary instance of the couple not two
years married. Oh! it can't be true—she spoke of enormous sums
of money paid to this woman. I know where Arthur keeps his bank
book—in one of the drawers of that desk. I might find out by that.   355
I *will* find out.° (*Opens drawers.*) No, it is some hideous mistake.
(*Rises and goes C.*) Some silly scandal! He loves *me*! He loves *me*!
But why should I not look? I am his wife, I have a right to look!
(*Returns to bureau, takes out book and examines it, page by page,
smiles and gives a sigh of relief*) I knew it! there is not a word of
truth in this stupid story. (*Puts book back in drawer. As she does so,*   360
starts and takes out another book) A second book—private—locked!
(*Tries to open it, but fails. Sees paper knife on bureau, and with it cuts
cover from book. Begins to start at the first page*) 'Mrs Erlynne—
£600—Mrs Erlynne—£700—Mrs Erlynne—£400.' Oh! it is true!
it is true! How horrible! (*Throws book on floor*)°
    Enter Lord Windermere C.

LORD WINDERMERE Well, dear, has the fan been sent home yet?   365
(*Going R.C. Sees book*) Margaret, you have cut open my bank
book. You have no right to do such a thing!

LADY WINDERMERE You think it wrong that you are found out,
don't you?

LORD WINDERMERE I think it wrong that a wife should spy on her   370
husband.

LADY WINDERMERE I did not spy on you. I never knew of this
woman's existence till half an hour ago. Someone who pitied me
was kind enough to tell me what everyone in London knows
already—your daily visits to Curzon Street, your mad infatuation,   375
the monstrous sums of money you squander on this infamous
woman! (*Crossing L.*)

LORD WINDERMERE Margaret! don't talk like that of Mrs Erlynne, you don't know how unjust it is!

LADY WINDERMERE (*turning to him*) You are very jealous of Mrs   380
Erlynne's honour. I wish you had been as jealous of mine.

LORD WINDERMERE Your honour is untouched, Margaret. You don't think for a moment that—(*Puts book back into desk*)

LADY WINDERMERE I think that you spend your money strangely. That is all. Oh, don't imagine I mind about the money. As far as   385
I am concerned, you may squander everything we have. But what I *do* mind is that you who have loved me, you who have taught me to love you, should pass from the love that is given to the love that is bought. Oh, it's horrible! (*Sits on sofa*)° And it is I who feel degraded! *you* don't feel anything. I feel stained, utterly   390
stained. You can't realize how hideous the last six months seems to me now—every kiss you have given me is tainted in my memory.

LORD WINDERMERE (*crossing to her*) Don't say that, Margaret. I never loved anyone in the whole world but you.   395

LADY WINDERMERE (*rises*) Who is this woman, then? Why do you take a house for her?

LORD WINDERMERE I did not take a house for her.

LADY WINDERMERE You gave her the money to do it, which is the same thing.   400

LORD WINDERMERE Margaret, as far as I have known Mrs Erlynne—

LADY WINDERMERE Is there a Mr Erlynne—or is he a myth?

LORD WINDERMERE Her husband died many years ago. She is alone in the world.   405

LADY WINDERMERE No relations?
A pause

LORD WINDERMERE None.

LADY WINDERMERE Rather curious, isn't it? (*L.*)

LORD WINDERMERE (*L.C.*) Margaret, I was saying to you—and I beg you to listen to me—that as far as I have known Mrs Erlynne,   410
she has conducted herself well. If years ago—

LADY WINDERMERE Oh! (*Crossing R.C.*) I don't want details about her life!

LORD WINDERMERE (*C.*) I am not going to give you any details about her life. I tell you simply this—Mrs Erlynne was once   415
honoured, loved, respected. She was well born, she had position— she lost everything—threw it away, if you like. That makes it all

the more bitter. Misfortunes one can endure—they come from
outside, they are accidents. But to suffer for one's own faults—
ah!—there is the sting of life. It was twenty years ago, too. She was   420
little more than a girl then. She had been a wife for even less time
than you have.

LADY WINDERMERE I am not interested in her—and—you should
not mention this woman and me in the same breath. It is an error
of taste. (*Sitting R. at desk*)   425

LORD WINDERMERE Margaret, you could save this woman. She
wants to get back into society, and she wants you to help her.
(*Crossing to her*)

LADY WINDERMERE Me!

LORD WINDERMERE Yes, you.

LADY WINDERMERE How impertinent of her!   430
     A pause

LORD WINDERMERE Margaret, I came to ask you a great favour, and
I still ask it of you, though you have discovered what I had
intended you should never have known, that I have given Mrs
Erlynne a large sum of money. I want you to send her an
invitation° for our party tonight. (*Standing L. of her*)   435

LADY WINDERMERE You are mad! (*Rises*)

LORD WINDERMERE I entreat you. People may chatter about her, do
chatter about her, of course, but they don't know anything definite
against her. She has been to several houses—not to houses where
you would go, I admit, but still to houses where women who are   440
in what is called Society nowadays do go. That does not content
her. She wants you to receive her once.°

LADY WINDERMERE As a triumph for her, I suppose?

LORD WINDERMERE No; but because she knows that you are a good
woman—and that if she comes here once she will have a chance of   445
a happier, a surer life than she has had. She will make no further
effort to know you. Won't you help a woman who is trying to get
back?

LADY WINDERMERE No! If a woman really repents, she never wishes
to return to the society that has made or seen her ruin.   450

LORD WINDERMERE I beg of you.°

LADY WINDERMERE (*crossing to door R.*) I am going to dress for
dinner, and don't mention the subject again this evening. Art-
hur° (*going to him C.*), you fancy because I have no father or
mother that I am alone in the world, and that you can treat me as   455
you choose. You are wrong, I have friends,° many friends.

LORD WINDERMERE (*L.C.*) Margaret, you are talking foolishly, recklessly. I won't argue with you, but I insist upon your asking Mrs Erlynne tonight.

LADY WINDERMERE (*R.C.*) I shall do nothing of the kind. (*Crossing L.C.*) 460

LORD WINDERMERE You refuse? (*C.*)

LADY WINDERMERE Absolutely!

LORD WINDERMERE Ah, Margaret, do this for my sake; it is her last chance.

LADY WINDERMERE What has that to do with me? 465

LORD WINDERMERE How hard good women are!

LADY WINDERMERE How weak bad men are!

LORD WINDERMERE Margaret, none of us men may be good enough for the women we marry—that is quite true—but you don't imagine I would ever—oh, the suggestion is monstrous! 470

LADY WINDERMERE Why should *you* be different from other men? I am told that there is hardly a husband in London who does not waste his life over *some* shameful passion.

LORD WINDERMERE I am not one of them.

LADY WINDERMERE I am not sure of that! 475

LORD WINDERMERE You are sure in your heart. But don't make chasm after chasm between us. God knows the last few minutes have thrust us wide enough apart. Sit down and write the card.

LADY WINDERMERE Nothing in the whole world would induce me. 480

LORD WINDERMERE (*crossing to bureau*) Then I will! (*Rings electric bell, sits and writes card*)°

LADY WINDERMERE You are going to invite this woman? (*Crossing to him*)

LORD WINDERMERE Yes.

Pause. Enter Parker

Parker!

PARKER Yes, my lord. (*Comes down L.C.*) 485

LORD WINDERMERE Have this note sent to Mrs Erlynne at No. 84A° Curzon Street. (*Crossing to L.C. and giving note to Parker*) There is no answer!

Exit Parker C.

LADY WINDERMERE Arthur, if that woman comes here, I shall insult her. 490

LORD WINDERMERE Margaret, don't say that.

LADY WINDERMERE I mean it.

LORD WINDERMERE Child,° if you did such a thing, there's not a woman in London who wouldn't pity you.

LADY WINDERMERE There is not a *good* woman in London who 495 would not applaud me. We have been too lax. We must make an example, I propose to begin tonight. (*Picking up fan*) Yes, you gave me this fan today; it was your birthday present. If that woman crosses my threshold, I shall strike her across the face with it. [*Rings bell*]°

LORD WINDERMERE Margaret, you couldn't do such a thing. 500

LADY WINDERMERE You don't know me! (*Moves R.*)
          Enter Parker
Parker!

PARKER Yes, my lady.

LADY WINDERMERE I shall dine in my own room.° I don't want dinner, in fact. See that everything is ready by half past ten. And, 505 Parker, be sure you pronounce the names° of the guests very distinctly tonight. Sometimes you speak so fast that I miss them. I am particularly anxious to hear the names quite clearly, so as to make no mistake. You understand, Parker?

PARKER Yes, my lady. 510

LADY WINDERMERE That will do!
          Exit Parker C.
(*Speaking to Lord Windermere*) Arthur, if that woman comes here—I warn you—

LORD WINDERMERE Margaret, you'll ruin us!

LADY WINDERMERE Us! From this moment my life is separate from 515 yours. But if you wish to avoid a public scandal, write at once to this woman, and tell her that I forbid her to come here!

LORD WINDERMERE I will not—I cannot—she must come!

LADY WINDERMERE Then I shall do exactly as I have said. (*Goes R.*) You leave me no choice. 520
          Exit R.

LORD WINDERMERE (*calling after her*) Margaret! Margaret!
          A pause
My God! What shall I do? I dare not tell her who this woman really is.° *The shame would kill her.* (*Sinks down into a chair and buries his face in his hands*)

ACT-DROP

Second Act

Scene: Drawing-room in Lord Windermere's house. Door R.U. opening into ball-room, where band is playing. Door L. through which guests are entering. Door L.U. opens on to illuminated terrace. Palms, flowers, and brilliant lights. Room crowded with guests. Lady Windermere is receiving them. [Parker stands by door L. Duchess of Berwick and Lady Agatha are on stage. A sofa, L., and bureau, R.]

DUCHESS OF BERWICK (*up C.*) So strange Lord Windermere isn't here. Mr Hopper is very late, too. You have kept those five dances for him, Agatha? (*Comes down*)

LADY AGATHA Yes, mamma.

DUCHESS OF BERWICK (*sitting on sofa*) Just let me see your card.° 5 I'm so glad Lady Windermere has revived cards.—They're a mother's only safeguard. You dear simple little thing! (*Scratches out two names.*) No nice girl should ever waltz with such particularly younger sons!° It looks so fast! The last two dances you might pass on the terrace with Mr Hopper. 10

Enter Mr Dumby and Lady Plymdale° from the ball-room

LADY AGATHA Yes, mamma.

DUCHESS OF BERWICK (*fanning herself*) The air is so pleasant there.

PARKER Mrs Cowper-Cowper. Lady Stutfield. Sir James Royston. Mr Guy Berkeley.

These people enter as announced

DUMBY Good evening, Lady Stutfield. I suppose this will be the last 15 ball of the season?

LADY STUTFIELD I suppose so, Mr Dumby. It's been a delightful season, hasn't it?

DUMBY Quite delightful! Good evening, Duchess. I suppose this will be the last ball of the season? 20

DUCHESS OF BERWICK I suppose so, Mr Dumby. It has been a very dull season, hasn't it?

DUMBY Dreadfully dull! Dreadfully dull!

MRS COWPER-COWPER Good evening, Mr Dumby. I suppose this will be the last ball of the season? 25

DUMBY Oh, I think not. There'll probably be two more. (*Wanders back to Lady Plymdale*)

PARKER Mr Rufford. Lady Jedburgh and Miss Graham. Mr Hopper.

These people enter as announced

HOPPER How do you do, Lady Windermere? How do you do,
Duchess? (*Bows to Lady Agatha*)

DUCHESS OF BERWICK Dear Mr Hopper, how nice of you to come   30
so early. We all know how you are run after in London.

HOPPER Capital place, London! They are not nearly so exclusive in
London as they are in Sydney.

DUCHESS OF BERWICK Ah! we know your value, Mr Hopper. We
wish there were more like you. It would make life so much easier.   35
Do you know, Mr Hopper, dear Agatha and I are so much
interested in Australia. It must be so pretty with all the dear little
kangaroos flying about. Agatha has found it on the map.° What a
curious shape it is! Just like a large packing case. However, it is a
very young country, isn't it?   40

HOPPER Wasn't it made at the same time as the others, Duchess?

DUCHESS OF BERWICK How clever you are, Mr Hopper. You have
a cleverness quite of your own. Now I mustn't keep you.

HOPPER But I should like to dance with Lady Agatha, Duchess.

DUCHESS OF BERWICK Well, I *hope* she has a dance left. Have you   45
a dance left, Agatha?

LADY AGATHA Yes, mamma.

DUCHESS OF BERWICK The next one?

LADY AGATHA Yes, mamma.

HOPPER May I have the pleasure? (*Lady Agatha bows*)   50

DUCHESS OF BERWICK Mind you take great care of my little
chatterbox, Mr Hopper.

*Lady Agatha and Mr Hopper pass into ball-room. Enter Lord
Windermere L.*

LORD WINDERMERE Margaret, I want to speak to you.

LADY WINDERMERE In a moment. (*The music stops*)

PARKER Lord Augustus Lorton.   55

Enter Lord Augustus

LORD AUGUSTUS Good evening, Lady Windermere.

DUCHESS OF BERWICK Sir James, will you take me into the ball-
room? Augustus has been dining with us tonight. I really have had
quite enough of dear Augustus for the moment.

*Sir James Royston gives the Duchess his arm and escorts her into
the ball-room*

PARKER Mr and Mrs Arthur Bowden. Lord and Lady Paisley. Lord   60
Darlington.

These people enter as announced

LORD AUGUSTUS (*coming up to Lord Windermere*) Want to speak to you particularly, dear boy. I'm worn to a shadow. Know I don't look it. None of us men do look what we really are. Demmed° good thing, too. What I want to know is this. Who is she? Where 65 does she come from? Why hasn't she got any demmed relations? Demmed nuisance, relations! But they make one so demmed respectable.

LORD WINDERMERE You are talking of Mrs Erlynne, I suppose? I only met her six months ago. Till then, I never knew of her 70 existence.

LORD AUGUSTUS You have seen a good deal of her since then.

LORD WINDERMERE (*coldly*) Yes, I have seen a good deal of her since then. I have just seen her.

LORD AUGUSTUS Egad! the women are very down on her. I have 75 been dining with Arabella this evening! By Jove! you should have heard what she said about Mrs Erlynne. She didn't leave a rag on her. . . . (*Aside*) Berwick and I told her that didn't matter much, as the lady in question must have an extremely fine figure. You should have seen Arabella's expression! . . . But, look here, dear 80 boy. I don't know what to do about Mrs Erlynne. Egad! I might be married to her; she treats me with such demmed indifference. She's deuced clever, too! She explains everything. Egad! She explains you. She has got any amount of explanations for you—and all of them different. 85

LORD WINDERMERE No explanations are necessary about my friendship with Mrs Erlynne.

LORD AUGUSTUS Hem! Well, look here, dear old fellow. Do you think she will ever get into this demmed thing called Society? Would you introduce her to your wife?° No use beating about the 90 confounded bush. Would you do that?

LORD WINDERMERE Mrs Erlynne is coming here tonight.

LORD AUGUSTUS Your wife has sent her a card?

LORD WINDERMERE Mrs Erlynne has received a card.°

LORD AUGUSTUS Then she's all right, dear boy. But why didn't you 95 tell me that before? It would have saved me a heap of worry and demmed misunderstandings!

Lady Agatha and Mr Hopper cross° and exit on terrace L.U.E.

PARKER Mr Cecil Graham!

Enter Mr Cecil Graham

CECIL GRAHAM (*bows to Lady Windermere, passes over and shakes hands with Lord Windermere*). Good evening, Arthur. Why don't 100

23

you ask me how I am?° I like people to ask me how I am. It shows
a widespread interest in my health. Now, tonight I am not at all
well. Been dining with my people. Wonder why it is one's people
are always so tedious? My father would talk morality after dinner.
I told him he was old enough to know better. But my experience   105
is that as soon as people are old enough to know better, they don't
know anything at all. Hullo, Tuppy! Hear you're going to be
married again; thought you were tired of that game.

LORD AUGUSTUS You're excessively trivial, my dear boy, excessively
trivial!   110

CECIL GRAHAM By the way, Tuppy, which is it? Have you been
twice married and once divorced, or twice divorced and once
married? I say you've been twice divorced and once married. It
sounds so much more probable.

LORD AUGUSTUS I have a very bad memory. I really don't remember   115
which. (*Moves away R.*)°

LADY PLYMDALE Lord Windermere, I've something most particular
to ask you.

LORD WINDERMERE I am afraid—if you will excuse me—I must join
my wife.   120

LADY PLYMDALE Oh, you mustn't dream of such a thing. It's
most dangerous nowadays for a husband to pay any attention to
his wife in public. It always makes people think that he beats her
when they're alone. The world has grown so suspicious of
anything that looks like a happy married life. But I'll tell you   125
what it is at supper.

    Moves towards door of ball-room

LORD WINDERMERE (*C.*) Margaret! I *must* speak to you.

LADY WINDERMERE Will you hold my fan for me, Lord Darlington?° Thanks. (*Comes down to him*)

LORD WINDERMERE (*crossing to her*) Margaret, what you said before 130
dinner was, of course, impossible?

LADY WINDERMERE That woman is not coming here tonight.

LORD WINDERMERE (*R.C.*) Mrs Erlynne is coming here, and if you
in any way annoy her or wound her, you will bring shame and
sorrow on us both. Remember that! Ah, Margaret! only trust me!   135
A wife should trust her husband!

LADY WINDERMERE (*C.*) London is full of women who trust their
husbands. One can always recognize them. They look so thoroughly unhappy. I am not going to be one of them. (*Moves up*) Lord
Darlington, will you give me back my fan, please? Thanks. . . . A   140

useful thing a fan, isn't it? . . . I want a friend tonight, Lord Darlington: I didn't know I would want one so soon.

LORD DARLINGTON Lady Windermere! I knew the time would come some day; but why tonight?

LORD WINDERMERE I *will* tell her. I must. It would be terrible if   145
there were any scene. Margaret . . .

PARKER Mrs Erlynne!

> *Lord Windermere starts. Mrs Erlynne enters,° very beauti-fully dressed and very dignified. Lady Windermere clutches at her fan, then lets it drop on the floor. She bows coldly to Mrs Erlynne, who bows to her sweetly in turn, and sails into the room*

LORD DARLINGTON You have dropped your fan, Lady Windermere. (*Picks it up and hands it to her*)

MRS ERLYNNE (*C.*) How do you do, again, Lord Windermere? How charming your sweet wife looks! Quite a picture!   150

LORD WINDERMERE (*in a low voice*) It was terribly rash of you to come!

MRS ERLYNNE (*smiling*) The wisest thing I ever did in my life. And, by the way, you must pay me a good deal of attention this evening. I am afraid of the women. You must introduce me to   155 some of them. The men I can always manage. How do you do, Lord Augustus? You have quite neglected me lately. I have not seen you since yesterday. I am afraid you're faithless. Everyone told me so.

LORD AUGUSTUS (*R.*) Now really, Mrs Erlynne, allow me to explain.   160

MRS ERLYNNE (*R.C.*) No, dear Lord Augustus, you can't explain anything. It is your chief charm.

LORD AUGUSTUS Ah! if you find charms in me, Mrs Erlynne—

> *They converse together. Lord Windermere moves uneasily about the room watching Mrs Erlynne*

LORD DARLINGTON (*to Lady Windermere*) How pale you are!

LADY WINDERMERE Cowards are always pale!   165

LORD DARLINGTON You look faint. Come out on the terrace.°

LADY WINDERMERE Yes. (*To Parker*) Parker, send my cloak out.

MRS ERLYNNE (*crossing to her*) Lady Windermere, how beautifully your terrace is illuminated. Reminds me of Prince Doria's° at Rome.   170

> *Lady Windermere bows coldly, and goes off with Lord Darlington*

Oh, how do you do, Mr Graham? Isn't that your aunt, Lady Jedburgh? I should so much like to know her.°

25

CECIL GRAHAM (*after a moment's hesitation and embarrassment*) Oh, certainly, if you wish it. Aunt Caroline, allow me to introduce Mrs Erlynne.

MRS ERLYNNE So pleased to meet you, Lady Jedburgh. (*Sits beside her on the sofa*) Your nephew and I are great friends. I am so much interested in his political career. I think he's sure to be a wonderful success. He thinks like a Tory and talks like a Radical, and that's so important nowadays. He's such a brilliant talker, too. But we all know from whom he inherits that. Lord Allendale was saying to me only yesterday, in the Park, that Mr Graham talks almost as well as his aunt.

LADY JEDBURGH (*R.*) Most kind of you to say these charming things to me!

    Mrs Erlynne smiles, and continues conversation

DUMBY (*to Cecil Graham*) Did you introduce Mrs Erlynne to Lady Jedburgh?

CECIL GRAHAM Had to, my dear fellow. Couldn't help it! That woman can make one do anything she wants. How, I don't know.

DUMBY Hope to goodness she won't speak to me! (*Saunters towards Lady Plymdale*)

MRS ERLYNNE (*C. To Lady Jedburgh*) On Thursday? With great pleasure. (*Rises, and speaks to Lord Windermere, laughing*) What a bore it is to have to be civil to these old dowagers! But they always insist on it!

LADY PLYMDALE (*to Mr Dumby*) Who is that well-dressed woman talking to Windermere?

DUMBY Haven't got the slightest idea! Looks like an *édition de luxe* of a wicked French novel,° meant specially for the English market.

MRS ERLYNNE So that is poor Dumby with Lady Plymdale? I hear she is frightfully jealous of him. He doesn't seem anxious to speak to me tonight. I suppose he is afraid of her. Those straw-coloured women have dreadful tempers. Do you know, I think I'll dance with you first,° Windermere. (*Lord Windermere bites his lip and frowns*) It will make Lord Augustus so jealous! Lord Augustus! (*Lord Augustus comes down*) Lord Windermere insists on my dancing with him first, and, as it's his own house, I can't well refuse. You know I would much sooner dance with you.

LORD AUGUSTUS (*with a low bow*) I wish I could think so, Mrs Erlynne.

MRS ERLYNNE You know it far too well. I can fancy a person dancing through life with you and finding it charming.

LORD AUGUSTUS (*placing his hand on his white waistcoat*) Oh, thank you, thank you. You are the most adorable of all ladies!

MRS ERLYNNE What a nice speech! So simple and so sincere! Just the sort of speech I like. Well, you shall hold my bouquet.° (*Goes towards ball-room on Lord Windermere's arm*) Ah, Mr Dumby, how are you? I am so sorry I have been out the last three times you have called. Come and lunch on Friday.

DUMBY (*with perfect nonchalance*) Delighted!°

> *Lady Plymdale glares with indignation at Mr Dumby. Lord Augustus follows Mrs Erlynne and Lord Windermere into the ball-room holding bouquet*

LADY PLYMDALE (*to Mr Dumby*) What an absolute brute you are! I never can believe a word you say! Why did you tell me you didn't know her? What do you mean by calling on her three times running? You are not to go to lunch there; of course you understand that?

DUMBY My dear Laura, I wouldn't dream of going!

LADY PLYMDALE You haven't told me her name yet! Who is she?

DUMBY (*coughs slightly and smooths his hair*) She's a Mrs Erlynne.

LADY PLYMDALE *That* woman!°

DUMBY Yes; that is what everyone calls her.

LADY PLYMDALE How very interesting! How intensely interesting! I really must have a good stare at her. (*Goes to door of ball-room and looks in*) I have heard the most shocking things about her. They say she is ruining poor Windermere. And Lady Windermere, who goes in for being so proper, invites her! How extremely amusing! It takes a thoroughly good woman to do a thoroughly stupid thing. You are to lunch there on Friday!

DUMBY Why?

LADY PLYMDALE Because I want you to take my husband with you. He has been so attentive lately, that he has become a perfect nuisance. Now, this woman is just the thing for him.° He'll dance attendance upon her as long as she lets him, and won't bother me. I assure you, women of that kind are most useful. They form the basis of other people's marriages.

DUMBY What a mystery you are!

LADY PLYMDALE (*looking at him*) I wish *you* were!

DUMBY I am—to myself. I am the only person in the world I should like to know thoroughly; but I don't see any chance of it just at present.

> *They pass into the ball-room*° [*Stage quite clear.*] *Lady Windermere and Lord Darlington enter from the terrace*

LADY WINDERMERE Yes. Her coming here is monstrous, unbear-   250
able. I know now what you meant today at tea-time. Why didn't
you tell me right out? You should have!

LORD DARLINGTON I couldn't! A man can't tell these things about
another man! But if I had known he was going to make you ask
her here tonight, I think I would have told you. That insult, at any   255
rate, you would have been spared.

LADY WINDERMERE I did not ask her. He insisted on her coming—
against my entreaties—against my commands. Oh! the house is
tainted for me! I feel that every woman here sneers at me as she
dances by with my husband. What have I done to deserve this? I   260
gave him all my life. He took it—used it—spoiled it! I am degraded
in my own eyes; and I lack courage—I am a coward! (*Sits down on
sofa*)

LORD DARLINGTON If I know you at all, I know that you can't live
with a man who treats you like this! What sort of life would you
have with him? You would feel that he was lying to you every   265
moment of the day. You would feel that the look in his eyes was
false, his voice false, his touch false, his passion false. He would
come to you when he was weary of others; you would have to
comfort him. He would come to you when he was devoted to
others; you would have to charm him. You would have to be   270
to him the mask of his real life, the cloak to hide his secret.

LADY WINDERMERE You are right—you are terribly right. But
where am I to turn? You said you would be my friend, Lord
Darlington.—Tell me, what am I to do? Be my friend now.

LORD DARLINGTON Between men and women there is no friendship   275
possible. There is passion, enmity, worship, love, but no friendship. I love you—

LADY WINDERMERE No, no! (*Rises*)

LORD DARLINGTON Yes, I love you! You are more to me than
anything in the world. What does your husband give you?   280
Nothing. Whatever is in him he gives to this wretched woman,
whom he has thrust into your society, into your home, to shame
you before everyone. I offer you my life—

LADY WINDERMERE Lord Darlington!

LORD DARLINGTON My life—my whole life. Take it, and do with it   285
what you will. . . . I love you—love you as I have never loved any
living thing. From the moment I met you I loved you, loved you
blindly, adoringly, madly! You did not know it then—you know it
now! Leave this house tonight. I won't tell you that the world

matters nothing, or the world's voice, or the voice of society. They   290
matter a great deal. They matter far too much. But there are
moments when one has to choose between living one's own life,
fully, entirely, completely—or dragging out some false, shallow,
degrading existence that the world in its hypocrisy demands. You
have that moment now. Choose! Oh, my love, choose.   295

LADY WINDERMERE (*moving slowly away from him, and looking at him
with startled eyes*) I have not the courage.

LORD DARLINGTON (*following her*) Yes; you have the courage.
There may be six months of pain, of disgrace even, but when you
no longer bear his name, when you bear mine, all will be well.   300
Margaret, my love, my wife that shall be some day—yes, my wife!
You know it! What are you now? This woman has the place that
belongs by right to you. Oh! go—go out of this house, with head
erect, with a smile upon your lips, with courage in your eyes. All
London will know why you did it; and who will blame you? No   305
one. If they did, what matter? Wrong? What is wrong? It's wrong
for a man to abandon his wife for a shameless woman. It is wrong
for a wife to remain with a man who so dishonours her. You said
once you would make no compromise with things. Make none
now. Be brave! Be yourself!   310

LADY WINDERMERE I am afraid of being myself. Let me think. Let
me wait! My husband may return to me. (*Sits down on sofa*)

LORD DARLINGTON And you would take him back! You are not
what I thought you were. You are just the same as every other
woman. You would stand anything rather than face the censure of   315
a world, whose praise you would despise. In a week you will be
driving with this woman in the Park. She will be your constant
guest—your dearest friend. You would endure anything rather
than break with one blow this monstrous tie. You are right. You
have no courage; none!   320

LADY WINDERMERE Ah, give me time to think. I cannot answer you
now. (*Passes her hand nervously over her brow*)

LORD DARLINGTON It must be now or not at all.

LADY WINDERMERE (*rising from the sofa*) Then, not at all!
      A pause°

LORD DARLINGTON You break my heart!°   325

LADY WINDERMERE Mine is already broken.
      A pause

LORD DARLINGTON Tomorrow I leave England. This is the last
time I shall ever look on you. You will never see me again. For

one moment our lives met—our souls touched. They must never
meet or touch again. Good-bye, Margaret.   330
  Exit
LADY WINDERMERE How alone I am in life! How terribly alone!
  The music stops.° Enter the Duchess of Berwick and Lord
  Paisley laughing and talking. Other guests come in from the
  ball-room
DUCHESS OF BERWICK Dear Margaret, I've just been having such a
delightful chat with Mrs Erlynne. I am so sorry for what I said to
you this afternoon about her. Of course, she must be all right if
you invite her. A most attractive woman, and has such sensible   335
views on life. Told me she entirely disapproved of people marrying
more than once, so I feel quite safe about poor Augustus. Can't
imagine why people speak against her. It's those horrid nieces of
mine—the Saville girls—they're always talking scandal. Still, I
should go to Homburg, dear, I really should. She is just a little too 340
attractive. But where is Agatha? Oh, there she is. (*Lady Agatha and*
Mr Hopper enter from terrace L.U.E.) Mr Hopper, I am very, very
angry with you. You have taken Agatha out on the terrace, and she
is so delicate.
HOPPER (*L.C.*) Awfully sorry, Duchess. We went out for a moment   345
and then got chatting together.
DUCHESS OF BERWICK (*C.*) Ah, about dear Australia, I suppose?
HOPPER Yes!
DUCHESS OF BERWICK Agatha, darling! (*Beckons her over*)
LADY AGATHA Yes, mamma!   350
DUCHESS OF BERWICK (*aside*) Did Mr Hopper definitely—
LADY AGATHA Yes, mamma.
DUCHESS OF BERWICK And what answer did you give him, dear
child?
LADY AGATHA Yes, mamma.   355
DUCHESS OF BERWICK (*affectionately*) My dear one! You always say
the right thing. Mr Hopper! James!° Agatha has told me every-
thing. How cleverly you have both kept your secret.
HOPPER You don't mind my taking Agatha off to Australia, then,
Duchess?   360
DUCHESS OF BERWICK (*indignantly*) To Australia? Oh, don't men-
tion that dreadful vulgar place.
HOPPER But she said she'd like to come with me.
DUCHESS OF BERWICK (*severely*) Did you say that, Agatha?
LADY AGATHA Yes, mamma.   365

DUCHESS OF BERWICK Agatha, you say the most silly things possible. I think on the whole that Grosvenor Square° would be a more healthy place to reside in. There are lots of vulgar people live in Grosvenor Square, but at any rate there are no horrid kangaroos crawling about. But we'll talk about that tomorrow. James, you can   370
take Agatha down.° You'll come to lunch, of course, James. At half-past one, instead of two. The Duke will wish to say a few words to you, I am sure.

HOPPER I should like to have a chat with the Duke,° Duchess. He has not said a single word to me yet.   375

DUCHESS OF BERWICK I think you'll find he will have a great deal to say to you tomorrow.

    Exit Lady Agatha with Mr Hopper

And now good night, Margaret. I'm afraid it's the old, old story, dear. Love—well, not love at first sight, but love° at the end of the season, which is so much more satisfactory.   380

LADY WINDERMERE Good night, Duchess.

    Exit the Duchess of Berwick on Lord Paisley's arm

LADY PLYMDALE My dear Margaret, what a handsome woman your husband has been dancing with! I should be quite jealous if I were you! Is she a great friend of yours?

LADY WINDERMERE No!   385

LADY PLYMDALE Really? Good night, dear.

    Looks at Mr Dumby and exit

DUMBY Awful manners young Hopper has!

CECIL GRAHAM Ah! Hopper is one of Nature's gentlemen, the worst type of gentleman I know.

DUMBY Sensible woman, Lady Windermere. Lots of wives would   390
have objected to Mrs Erlynne coming. But Lady Windermere has that uncommon thing called common sense.

CECIL GRAHAM And Windermere knows that nothing looks so like innocence as an indiscretion.

DUMBY Yes, dear Windermere is becoming almost modern.° Never   395
thought he would.

    Bows to Lady Windermere and exit

LADY JEDBURGH Good night, Lady Windermere. What a fascinating woman Mrs Erlynne is! She is coming to lunch on Thursday; won't you come too? I expect the Bishop and dear Lady Merton.   400

LADY WINDERMERE I am afraid I am engaged, Lady Jedburgh.

LADY JEDBURGH So sorry. Come, dear.

*Exeunt Lady Jedburgh and Miss Graham. Enter Mrs Erlynne
and Lord Windermere*

MRS ERLYNNE Charming ball it has been! Quite reminds me of old
days. (*Sits on sofa*) And I see that there are just as many fools in
society as there used to be. So pleased to find that nothing has   405
altered! Except Margaret. She's grown quite pretty. The last time
I saw her°—twenty years ago, she was a fright in flannel. Positive
fright, I assure you. The dear Duchess! and that sweet Lady
Agatha! Just the type of girl I like! Well, really, Windermere, if I
am to be the Duchess's sister-in-law—   410

LORD WINDERMERE (*sitting L. of her*) But are you—?

*Exit° Mr Cecil Graham with the rest of guests. Lady Windermere
watches, with a look of scorn and pain, Mrs Erlynne and her
husband. They are unconscious of her presence.*

MRS ERLYNNE Oh, yes. He's to call tomorrow at twelve o'clock! He
wanted to propose tonight. In fact he did. He kept on proposing.
Poor Augustus, you know how he repeats himself. Such a bad
habit! But I told him I wouldn't give him an answer till tomorrow.   415
Of course I am going to take him. And I dare say I'll make him
an admirable wife, as wives go. And there is a great deal of good
in Lord Augustus. Fortunately it is all on the surface. Just where
good qualities should be. Of course you must help me in this
matter.   420

LORD WINDERMERE I am not called on to encourage Lord Augustus, I suppose?

MRS ERLYNNE Oh, no! I do the encouraging. But you will make me
a handsome settlement,° Windermere, won't you?

LORD WINDERMERE (*frowning*) Is that what you want to talk to me   425
about tonight?

MRS ERLYNNE Yes.

LORD WINDERMERE (*with a gesture of impatience*) I will not talk of it
here.

MRS ERLYNNE (*laughing*) Then we will talk of it on the terrace. Even   430
business should have a picturesque background. Should it not,
Windermere? With a proper background women can do anything.

LORD WINDERMERE Won't tomorrow do as well?

MRS ERLYNNE No; you see, tomorrow I am going to accept him.
And I think it would be a good thing if I was able to tell him that   435
I had—well, what shall I say?—£2,000 a year left me by a third
cousin—or a second husband—or some distant relative of that
kind. It would be an additional attraction, wouldn't it? You have a

delightful opportunity of paying me a compliment, Windermere. But you are not very clever at paying compliments. I am afraid 440 Margaret doesn't encourage you in that excellent habit. It's a great mistake on her part. When men give up saying what is charming, they give up thinking what is charming. But seriously, what do you say to £2,000? £2,500, I think. In modern life margin is everything. Windermere, don't you think the world an intensely 445 amusing place? I do!

> *Exit on terrace with Lord Windermere. Music strikes up° in ball-room*

LADY WINDERMERE To stay in this house any longer is impossible. Tonight a man who loves me offered me his whole life. I refused it. It was foolish of me. I will offer him mine now. I will give him mine. I will go to him! (*Puts on cloak and goes to the door, then turns* 450 *back. Sits down at table and writes a letter, puts it into an envelope, and leaves it on table*) Arthur has never understood me. When he reads this, he will. He may do as he chooses now with his life. I have done with mine as I think best, as I think right. It is he who has broken the bond of marriage—not I! I only break its bondage. 455

> *Exit° [Lady Windermere.] Parker enters L. and crosses towards the ball-room R. Enter Mrs Erlynne*

MRS ERLYNNE Is Lady Windermere in the ball-room?

PARKER Her ladyship has just gone out.

MRS ERLYNNE Gone out? She's not on the terrace?

PARKER No, madam. Her ladyship has just gone out of the house.

MRS ERLYNNE (*starts, and looks at the servant with a puzzled expression on her face*) Out of the house? 460

PARKER Yes, madam—her ladyship told me she had left a letter for his lordship on the table.

MRS ERLYNNE A letter for Lord Windermere?

PARKER Yes, madam!

MRS ERLYNNE Thank you.

> *Exit Parker. The music in the ball-room stops°*

Gone out of her house! A letter addressed to her husband! (*Goes* 465 *over to bureau and looks at letter. Takes it up and lays it down again with a shudder of fear*) No, no! It would be impossible! Life doesn't repeat its tragedies like that! Oh, why does this horrible fancy come across me? Why do I remember now the one moment of my life I most wish to forget? Does life repeat its tragedies? (*Tears letter open and reads it, then sinks down into a chair with a gesture of anguish*) Oh, how terrible! The same words that twenty years ago 470

I wrote to her father! and how bitterly I have been punished for it! No; my punishment, my real punishment is tonight, is now! (*Still seated R.*)

    Enter Lord Windermere L.U.E.

LORD WINDERMERE Have you said good-night to my wife? (*Comes C.*)

MRS ERLYNNE (*crushing letter in hand*) Yes.

LORD WINDERMERE Where is she?   475

MRS ERLYNNE She is very tired. She has gone to bed. She said she had a headache.

LORD WINDERMERE I must go to her. You'll excuse me?

MRS ERLYNNE (*rising hurriedly*) Oh, no! It's nothing serious. She's only very tired, that is all. Besides, there are people still in the   480 supper room. She wants you to make her apologies to them. She said she didn't wish to be disturbed. (*Drops letter*)° She asked me to tell you!

LORD WINDERMERE (*picks up letter*) You have dropped something.

MRS ERLYNNE Oh, yes, thank you, that is mine. (*Puts out her hand*   485 *to take it*)

LORD WINDERMERE (*still looking at letter*) But it's my wife's handwriting, isn't it?

MRS ERLYNNE (*takes the letter° quickly*) Yes, it's—an address. Will you ask them to call my carriage, please?

LORD WINDERMERE Certainly.   490

    Goes L. and exit

MRS ERLYNNE Thanks! What can I do? What can I do? I feel a passion awakening within me that I never felt before. What can it mean? The daughter must not be like the mother—that would be terrible. How can I save her? How can I save my child? A moment may ruin a life. Who knows that better than I? Windermere must   495 be got out of the house; that is absolutely necessary. (*Goes L.*) But how shall I do it? It must be done somehow. Ah!

    Enter Lord Augustus° R.U.E. carrying bouquet

LORD AUGUSTUS Dear lady, I am in such suspense! May I not have an answer to my request?

MRS ERLYNNE Lord Augustus, listen to me. You are to take Lord   500 Windermere down to your club at once, and keep him there as long as possible. You understand?

LORD AUGUSTUS But you said you wished me to keep early hours!

MRS ERLYNNE (*nervously*) Do what I tell you. Do what I tell you.

LORD AUGUSTUS And my reward?   505

MRS ERLYNNE Your reward? Your reward? Oh, ask me that tomorrow. But don't let Windermere out of your sight tonight. If you do I will never forgive you. I will never speak to you again. I'll have nothing to do with you. Remember you are to keep Windermere at your club, and don't let him come back tonight.   510
    Exit L.

LORD AUGUSTUS Well, really,° I might be her husband already. Positively I might.
Follows her in a bewildered manner

    ACT DROP

Third Act

Scene: Lord Darlington's rooms. A large sofa is in front of fireplace R. At the back of the stage a curtain is drawn across the window. Doors L. and R. Table R. with writing materials. Table C. with syphons, glasses, and Tantalus frame. Table L. with cigar and cigarette-box. Lamps lit.

LADY WINDERMERE (*standing by the fireplace*) Why doesn't he come?° This waiting is horrible. He should be here. Why is he not here, to wake by passionate words some fire within me? I am cold—cold as a loveless thing. Arthur must have read my letter by this time. If he cared for me he would have come after me, would have taken me back by force. But he doesn't care. He's entrammelled by this woman—fascinated by her—dominated by her. If a woman wants to hold a man, she has merely to appeal to what is worst in him. We make gods of men and they leave us. Others make brutes of them and they fawn and are faithful. How hideous life is! . . . Oh! it was mad of me to come here, horribly mad. And yet, which is the worst, I wonder, to be at the mercy of a man who loves one, or the wife of a man who in one's own house dishonours one? What woman knows? What woman in the whole world? But will he love me always, this man to whom I am giving my life? What do I bring him? Lips that have lost the note of joy, eyes that are blinded by tears, chill hands and icy heart. I bring him nothing. I must go back—no; I can't go back, my letter has put me in their power—Arthur would not take me back! That fatal letter! No! Lord Darlington leaves England tomorrow. I will go with him—I have no choice. (*Sits down for a few moments. Then starts up and puts on her cloak*)° No, no! I will go back, let Arthur do with me what he pleases. I can't wait here. It has been madness my coming. I must go at once. As for Lord Darlington—Oh, here he is! What shall I do? What can I say to him? Will he let me go away at all? I have heard that men are brutal, horrible . . . Oh (*Hides her face in her hands*)

    Enter Mrs Erlynne L.

MRS ERLYNNE Lady Windermere! (*Lady Windermere starts and looks up. Then recoils in contempt*) Thank Heaven I am in time. You must go back to your husband's house immediately.

LADY WINDERMERE Must?

MRS ERLYNNE (*authoritatively*) Yes, you must! There is not a second to be lost. Lord Darlington may return at any moment.

LADY WINDERMERE Don't come near me!

MRS ERLYNNE Oh! You are on the brink of ruin, you are on the brink of a hideous precipice. You must leave this place at once, my carriage is waiting at the corner of the street. You must come with me and drive straight home.   35

Lady Windermere throws off her cloak° and flings it on the sofa

MRS ERLYNNE What are you doing?

LADY WINDERMERE Mrs Erlynne—if you had not come here, I would have gone back. But now that I see you, I feel that nothing in the whole world would induce me to live under the same roof   40 as Lord Windermere. You fill me with horror. There is something about you that stirs the wildest—rage within me. And I know why you are here. My husband sent you to lure me back that I might serve as a blind to whatever relations exist between you and him.   45

MRS ERLYNNE Oh! You don't think that—you can't.

LADY WINDERMERE Go back to my husband, Mrs Erlynne. He belongs to you and not to me. I suppose he is afraid of a scandal. Men are such cowards. They outrage every law of the world, and are afraid of the world's tongue. But he had better prepare himself.   50 He shall have a scandal. He shall have the worst scandal there has been in London for years. He shall see his name in every vile paper, mine on every hideous placard.

MRS ERLYNNE No—no—

LADY WINDERMERE Yes! he shall. Had he come himself, I admit I   55 would have gone back to the life of degradation you and he had prepared for me—I was going back—but to stay himself at home, and to send you as his messenger—oh! it was infamous—infamous.

MRS ERLYNNE (*C.*) Lady Windermere, you wrong me horribly—you wrong your husband horribly. He doesn't know you are here—he   60 thinks you are safe in your own house. He thinks you are asleep in your own room. He never read the mad letter you wrote to him!

LADY WINDERMERE (*R.*) Never read it!

MRS ERLYNNE No—he knows nothing about it.

LADY WINDERMERE How simple you think me! (*Going to her*) You   65 are lying to me!

MRS ERLYNNE (*restraining herself*) I am not. I am telling you the truth.

LADY WINDERMERE If my husband didn't read my letter, how is it that you are here? Who told you I had left the house you were   70

shameless enough to enter? Who told you where I had gone
to? My husband told you, and sent you to decoy me back.
(*Crosses L.*)

MRS ERLYNNE (*R.C.*) Your husband has never seen the letter.
I—saw it, I opened it. I—read it.

LADY WINDERMERE (*turning to her*) You opened a letter of mine to   75
my husband? You wouldn't dare!

MRS ERLYNNE Dare! Oh! to save you from the abyss into which you
are falling, there is nothing in the world I would not dare, nothing
in the whole world. Here is the letter. Your husband has never
read it. He never shall read it. (*Going to fireplace*) It should never   80
have been written.
        Tears it and throws it into the fire°

LADY WINDERMERE (*with infinite contempt in her voice and look*) How
do I know that that was my letter after all? You seem to think the
commonest device can take me in!

MRS ERLYNNE Oh! why do you disbelieve everything I tell you?   85
What object do you think I have in coming here, except to save
you from utter ruin, to save you from the consequence of a hideous
mistake? That letter that is burnt now *was* your letter. I swear it
to you!

LADY WINDERMERE (*slowly*) You took good care to burn it before I   90
had examined it. I cannot trust you. You, whose whole life is a lie,
how could you speak the truth about anything? (*Sits down*)

MRS ERLYNNE (*hurriedly*) Think as you like about me—say what you
choose against me, but go back, go back to the husband you love.

LADY WINDERMERE (*sullenly*) I do *not* love him!   95

MRS ERLYNNE You do, and you know that he loves you.

LADY WINDERMERE He does not understand what love is. He
understands it as little as you do—but I see what you want. It
would be a great advantage for you to get me back. Dear Heaven!
what a life I would have then! Living at the mercy of a woman   100
who has neither mercy nor pity in her, a woman whom it is an
infamy to meet, a degradation to know, a vile woman, a woman
who comes between husband and wife!

MRS ERLYNNE (*with a gesture of despair*) Lady Windermere, Lady
Windermere, don't say such terrible things. You don't know how   105
terrible they are, how terrible and how unjust. Listen, you must
listen! Only go back to your husband, and I promise you never to
communicate with him again on any pretext—never to see him—
never to have anything to do with his life or yours. The money

that he gave me, he gave me not through love, but through hatred,   110
not in worship, but in contempt. The hold I have over him—

LADY WINDERMERE (*rising*) Ah! you admit you have a hold!

MRS ERLYNNE Yes, and I will tell you what it is. It is his love for
you, Lady Windermere.

LADY WINDERMERE You expect me to believe that?   115

MRS ERLYNNE You must believe it! It is true. It is his love for you
that has made him submit to—oh! call it what you like, tyranny,
threats, anything you choose. But it is his love for you. His desire
to spare you—shame, yes, shame and disgrace.

LADY WINDERMERE What do you mean? You are insolent! What   120
have I to do with you?

MRS ERLYNNE (*humbly*) Nothing. I know it—but I tell you that your
husband loves you—that you may never meet with such love again
in your whole life—that such love you will never meet—and that
if you throw it away, the day may come when you will starve for   125
love and it will not be given to you, beg for love and it will be
denied you—Oh! Arthur° loves you!

LADY WINDERMERE Arthur? And you tell me there is nothing
between you?

MRS ERLYNNE Lady Windermere, before Heaven your husband is   130
guiltless of all offence towards you! And I—I tell you that had it
ever occurred to me that such a monstrous suspicion would have
entered your mind I would have died rather than have crossed
your life or his—oh! died, gladly died! (*Moves away to sofa R.*)

LADY WINDERMERE You talk as if you had a heart. Women like you   135
have no hearts. Heart is not in you. You are bought and sold. (*Sits
L.C.*)

MRS ERLYNNE (*Starts, with a gesture of pain. Then restrains herself,
and comes over to where Lady Windermere is sitting. As she speaks,
she stretches out her hands towards her, but does not dare to touch her*)°
Believe what you choose about me. I am not worth a moment's
sorrow. But don't spoil your beautiful young life on my account!
You don't know what may be in store for you, unless you leave   140
this house at once. You don't know what it is to fall into the pit,
to be despised, mocked, abandoned, sneered at—to be an outcast!
to find the door shut against one, to have to creep in by hideous
byways, afraid every moment lest the mask should be stripped
from one's face, and all the while to hear the laughter, the horrible   145
laughter of the world, a thing more tragic than all the tears the
world has ever shed. You don't know what it is. One pays for one's

sin, and then one pays again, and all one's life one pays. You must never know that.—As for me, if suffering be an expiation, then at this moment I have expiated all my faults, whatever they have been; for tonight you have made a heart in one who had it not, made it and broken it.—But let that pass. I may have wrecked my own life, but I will not let you wreck yours. You—why, you are a mere girl, you would be lost. You haven't got the kind of brains that enables a woman to get back. You have neither the wit nor the courage. You couldn't stand dishonour. No! Go back, Lady Windermere, to the husband who loves you, whom you love. You have a child,° Lady Windermere. Go back to that child who even now, in pain or in joy, may be calling to you. (*Lady Windermere rises*)   God gave you that child. He will require from you that you make his life fine, that you watch over him. What answer will you make to God if his life is ruined through you? Back to your house, Lady Windermere—your husband loves you! He has never swerved for a moment from the love he bears you. But even if he had a thousand loves, you must stay with your child. If he was harsh to you, you must stay with your child. If he ill-treated you, you must stay with your child. If he abandoned you, your place is with your child.

> *Lady Windermere bursts into tears and buries her face in her hands*
> *(Rushing to her)* Lady Windermere!

LADY WINDERMERE (*holding out her hands to her, helplessly, as a child might do*) Take me home. Take me home.

MRS ERLYNNE (*is about to embrace her. Then restrains herself. There is a look of wonderful joy° in her face*) Come! Where is your cloak? (*Getting it from sofa*) Here. Put it on. Come at once!

> *They go to the door*

LADY WINDERMERE Stop! Don't you hear voices?

MRS ERLYNNE No, no! There is no one!

LADY WINDERMERE Yes, there is! Listen! Oh! that is my husband's voice! He is coming in! Save me!° Oh, it's some plot! You have sent for him.

> *Voices outside*°

MRS ERLYNNE Silence! I'm here to save you, if I can. But I fear it is too late! There! (*Points to the curtain across the window*) The first chance you have, slip out, if you ever get a chance!

LADY WINDERMERE But you?

MRS ERLYNNE Oh! never mind me. I'll face them.

Lady Windermere hides herself behind the curtain

LORD AUGUSTUS (*outside*) Nonsense, dear Windermere,° you must   185
not leave me!

MRS ERLYNNE Lord Augustus! Then it is I who am lost!
  *Hesitates for a moment, then looks round and sees door R.,° and
  exit through it
  Enter Lord Darlington, Mr Dumby, Lord Windermere, Lord
  Augustus Lorton, and Mr Cecil Graham*

DUMBY What a nuisance their turning us out of the club° at this
hour! It's only two o'clock. (*Sinks into a chair*) The lively part of
the evening is only just beginning. (*Yawns and closes his eyes*)   190

LORD WINDERMERE It is very good of you, Lord Darlington,
allowing Augustus to force our company on you, but I'm afraid I
can't stay long.

LORD DARLINGTON Really! I am so sorry! You'll take a cigar, won't
you?   195

LORD WINDERMERE Thanks! (*Sits down*)

LORD AUGUSTUS (*to Lord Windermere*) My dear boy, you must not
dream of going. I have a great deal to talk to you about, of demmed
importance, too. (*Sits down with him at L. table.*)

CECIL GRAHAM Oh! We all know what that is! Tuppy can't talk   200
about anything but Mrs Erlynne.

LORD WINDERMERE Well, that is no business of yours,° is it, Cecil?

CECIL GRAHAM None! That is why it interests me. My own business
always bores me to death. I prefer other people's.

LORD DARLINGTON Have something to drink, you fellows. Cecil,   205
you'll have a whisky and soda?

CECIL GRAHAM Thanks. (*Goes to table with Lord Darlington*) Mrs
Erlynne looked very handsome tonight, didn't she?

LORD DARLINGTON I am not one of her admirers.

CECIL GRAHAM I usen't to be, but I am now. Why! she actually   210
made me introduce her to poor dear Aunt Caroline. I believe she
is going to lunch there.

LORD DARLINGTON (*in surprise*) No?

CECIL GRAHAM She is, really.

LORD DARLINGTON Excuse me, you fellows. I'm going away tomor-   215
row. And I have to write a few letters.
  Goes to writing table and sits down

DUMBY Clever woman, Mrs Erlynne.

CECIL GRAHAM Hallo, Dumby! I thought you were asleep.

DUMBY I am, I usually am!

LORD AUGUSTUS A very clever woman. Knows perfectly well what   220
a demmed fool I am—knows it as well as I do myself.
    Cecil Graham comes towards him laughing
Ah, you may laugh, my boy, but it is a great thing to come across
a woman who thoroughly understands one.

DUMBY It is an awfully dangerous thing. They always end by
marrying one.   225

CECIL GRAHAM But I thought, Tuppy, you were never going to see
her again! Yes! you told me so yesterday evening at the club. You
said you'd heard—(*Whispering to him*)

LORD AUGUSTUS Oh, she's explained that.

CECIL GRAHAM And the Wiesbaden° affair?   230

LORD AUGUSTUS She's explained that too.

DUMBY And her income, Tuppy? Has she explained that?

LORD AUGUSTUS (*in a very serious voice*) She's going to explain that
tomorrow.
    Cecil Graham goes back to C. table

DUMBY Awfully commercial, women nowadays. Our grandmothers   235
threw their caps over the mills, of course, but, by Jove, their
granddaughters only throw their caps over mills that can raise the
wind for them.°

LORD AUGUSTUS You want to make her out a wicked woman. She
is not!   240

CECIL GRAHAM Oh! Wicked women bother one. Good women bore
one. That is the only difference between them.

LORD AUGUSTUS (*puffing a cigar*) Mrs Erlynne has a future before
her.

DUMBY Mrs Erlynne has a past before her.   245

LORD AUGUSTUS I prefer women with a past. They're always so
demmed amusing to talk to.

CECIL GRAHAM Well, you'll have lots of topics of conversation with
her, Tuppy. (*Rising and going to him*)

LORD AUGUSTUS You're getting annoying, dear boy; you're getting   250
demmed annoying.

CECIL GRAHAM (*puts his hands on his shoulders*)° Now, Tuppy, you've
lost your figure and you've lost your character. Don't lose your
temper; you have only got one.

LORD AUGUSTUS My dear boy, if I wasn't the most good-natured   255
man in London—

CECIL GRAHAM We'd treat you with more respect, wouldn't we,
Tuppy? (*Strolls away*)

DUMBY The youth of the present day are quite monstrous. They have absolutely no respect for dyed hair. *(Lord Augustus looks round angrily)* 260

CECIL GRAHAM Mrs Erlynne has a very great respect for dear Tuppy.

DUMBY Then Mrs Erlynne sets an admirable example to the rest of her sex. It is perfectly brutal the way most women nowadays behave to men who are not their husbands.° 265

LORD WINDERMERE Dumby, you are ridiculous, and Cecil, you let your tongue run away with you. You must leave Mrs Erlynne alone. You don't really know anything about her, and you're always talking scandal against her.

CECIL GRAHAM *(coming towards him L.C.)* My dear Arthur, I never 270 talk scandal. *I* only talk gossip.

LORD WINDERMERE What is the difference between scandal and gossip?

CECIL GRAHAM Oh! gossip is charming! History is merely gossip. But scandal is gossip made tedious by morality. Now, I never 275 moralize. A man who moralizes is usually a hypocrite, and a woman who moralizes is invariably plain. There is nothing in the whole world so unbecoming to a woman as a Nonconformist° conscience. And most women know it, I'm glad to say.

LORD AUGUSTUS Just my sentiments, dear boy, just my senti- 280 ments.

CECIL GRAHAM Sorry to hear it, Tuppy; whenever people agree with me, I always feel I must be wrong.

LORD AUGUSTUS My dear boy, when I was your age—

CECIL GRAHAM But you never were, Tuppy, and you never will be. 285 *(Goes up C.)* I say, Darlington, let us have some cards. You'll play, Arthur, won't you?

LORD WINDERMERE No, thanks, Cecil.

DUMBY *(with a sigh)* Good heavens! how marriage ruins a man! It's as demoralizing as cigarettes, and far more expensive. 290

CECIL GRAHAM You'll play, of course, Tuppy?

LORD AUGUSTUS *(pouring himself out a brandy and soda at table)* Can't, dear boy. Promised Mrs Erlynne never to play or drink again.°

CECIL GRAHAM Now, my dear Tuppy, don't be led astray into the 295 paths of virtue. Reformed, you would be perfectly tedious. That is the worst of women. They always want one to be good. And if we are good, when they meet us, they don't love us at all. They like

to find us quite irretrievably bad, and to leave us quite unattract-   300
ively good.

LORD DARLINGTON (*rising from R. table, where he has been writing
letters*) They always do find us bad!

DUMBY I don't think we are bad. I think we are all good, except
Tuppy.

LORD DARLINGTON No, we are all in the gutter, but some of us are   305
looking at the stars. (*Sits down at C. table*)

DUMBY We are all in the gutter,° but some of us are looking at
the stars? Upon my word, you are very romantic tonight, Darlington.

CECIL GRAHAM Too romantic! You must be in love. Who is the girl?   310

LORD DARLINGTON The woman I love is not free, or thinks she
isn't. (*Glances instinctively at Lord Windermere while he speaks*)

CECIL GRAHAM A married woman, then! Well, there's nothing in the
world like the devotion of a married woman. It's a thing no
married man knows anything about.   315

LORD DARLINGTON Oh! she doesn't love me. She is a good woman.°
She is the only good woman I have ever met in my life.

CECIL GRAHAM The only good woman you have ever met in your
life?

LORD DARLINGTON Yes!   320

CECIL GRAHAM (*lighting a cigarette*) Well, you are a lucky fellow!
Why, I have met hundreds of good women. I never seem to meet
any but good women. The world is perfectly packed with good
women. To know them is a middle-class education.°

LORD DARLINGTON This woman has purity and innocence. She has   325
everything we men have lost.

CECIL GRAHAM My dear fellow, what on earth should we men do
going about with purity and innocence? A carefully thought-out
buttonhole is much more effective.

DUMBY She doesn't really love you then?   330

LORD DARLINGTON No, she does not!

DUMBY I congratulate you, my dear fellow. In this world there are
only two tragedies. One is not getting what one wants, and the
other is getting it. The last is much the worst, the last is a real
tragedy! But I am interested to hear she does not love you. How   335
long could you love a woman who didn't love you, Cecil?

CECIL GRAHAM A woman who didn't love me? Oh, all my life!

DUMBY So could I. But it's so difficult to meet one.

LORD DARLINGTON How can you be so conceited, Dumby?

44

DUMBY I didn't say it as a matter of conceit. I said it as a matter of   340
regret. I have been wildly, madly adored. I am sorry I have. It has
been an immense nuisance. I should like to be allowed a little time
to myself now and then.

LORD AUGUSTUS (*looking round*) Time to educate yourself, I suppose.   345

DUMBY No, time to forget all I have learned. That is much
more important, dear Tuppy. (*Lord Augustus moves uneasily in his
chair*)

LORD DARLINGTON What cynics you fellows are!

CECIL GRAHAM What is a cynic? (*Sitting on the back of the sofa*)

LORD DARLINGTON A man who knows the price of everything and   350
the value of nothing.

CECIL GRAHAM And a sentimentalist, my dear Darlington, is a man
who sees an absurd value in everything, and doesn't know the
market price of any single thing.

LORD DARLINGTON You always amuse me, Cecil. You talk as if you   355
were a man of experience.

CECIL GRAHAM I am. (*Moves up to front of fireplace*)

LORD DARLINGTON You are far too young!

CECIL GRAHAM That is a great error. Experience is a question of
instinct about life. I have got it. Tuppy hasn't. Experience is the   360
name Tuppy gives to his mistakes. That is all. (*Lord Augustus looks
round indignantly*)

DUMBY Experience is the name everyone gives to their mistakes.

CECIL GRAHAM (*standing with his back to the fireplace*) One shouldn't
commit any. (*Sees Lady Windermere's fan° on sofa*)

DUMBY Life would be very dull without them.   365

CECIL GRAHAM Of course you are quite faithful to this woman you
are in love with, Darlington, to this good woman?

LORD DARLINGTON Cecil, if one really loves a woman, all other
women in the world become absolutely meaningless to one. Love
changes one—*I* am changed.   370

CECIL GRAHAM Dear me! How very interesting! Tuppy, I want to
talk to you. (*Lord Augustus takes no notice*)

DUMBY It's no use talking to Tuppy. You might just as well talk to
a brick wall.

CECIL GRAHAM But I like talking to a brick wall—it's the only thing   375
in the world that never contradicts me! Tuppy!

LORD AUGUSTUS Well, what is it? What is it?
    Rising and going over to Cecil Graham

CECIL GRAHAM Come over here. I want you particularly. [*Aside*] Darlington has been moralizing and talking about the purity of love, and that sort of thing, and he has got some woman° in his rooms all the time. 380

LORD AUGUSTUS No, really! really!

CECIL GRAHAM (*in a low voice*) Yes, here is her fan. (*Points to the fan*)

LORD AUGUSTUS (*chuckling*) By Jove! By Jove!

LORD WINDERMERE (*up by the door*) I am really off now, Lord Darlington. I am sorry you are leaving England so soon. Pray call on us when you come back! My wife and I will be charmed to see you! 385

LORD DARLINGTON (*up stage with Lord Windermere*) I am afraid I shall be away for many years. Good-night! 390

CECIL GRAHAM Arthur!

LORD WINDERMERE What?

CECIL GRAHAM I want to speak to you for a moment. No, do come!

LORD WINDERMERE (*putting on his coat*) I can't—I'm off!

CECIL GRAHAM It is something very particular. It will interest you enormously. 395

LORD WINDERMERE (*smiling*) It is some of your nonsense, Cecil.

CECIL GRAHAM It isn't! It isn't really.

LORD AUGUSTUS (*going to him*) My dear fellow, you mustn't go yet. I have a lot to talk to you about. And Cecil has something to show you. 400

LORD WINDERMERE (*walking over*) Well, what is it?

CECIL GRAHAM Darlington has got a woman here in his rooms. Here is her fan. Amusing, isn't it?

  A pause

LORD WINDERMERE Good God! (*Seizes the fan—Dumby rises*) 405

CECIL GRAHAM What is the matter?

LORD WINDERMERE Lord Darlington!

LORD DARLINGTON (*turning round*) Yes!

LORD WINDERMERE What is my wife's fan doing here in your rooms? Hands off, Cecil.° Don't touch me. 410

LORD DARLINGTON Your wife's fan?

LORD WINDERMERE Yes, here it is!

LORD DARLINGTON (*walking towards him*) I don't know!

LORD WINDERMERE You must know. I demand an explanation. (*To* CECIL GRAHAM) Don't hold me, you fool. 415

LORD DARLINGTON (*aside*) She is here after all!

LORD WINDERMERE Speak, sir! Why is my wife's fan here? Answer me! By God! I'll search your rooms, and if my wife's here, I'll—° (*Moves*)

LORD DARLINGTON You shall not search my rooms. You have no   420
right to do so. I forbid you!

LORD WINDERMERE You scoundrel! I'll not leave your room till I have searched every corner of it! What moves behind that curtain?
  Rushes towards the curtain C.

MRS ERLYNNE (*enters behind R.*)° Lord Windermere!

LORD WINDERMERE Mrs Erlynne!   425
  Everyone starts and turns round. Lady Windermere slips out from behind the curtain and glides from the room L.

MRS ERLYNNE I am afraid I took your wife's fan in mistake for my own, when I was leaving your house tonight. I am so sorry.
  Takes fan from him. Lord Windermere looks at her in contempt. Lord Darlington in mingled astonishment and anger. Lord Augustus turns away. The other men smile at each other

ACT DROP

Fourth Act

Scene: Same as in Act I

LADY WINDERMERE (*lying on sofa*) How can I tell him? I can't tell him. It would kill me. I wonder what happened after I escaped from that horrible room. Perhaps she told them the true reason of her being there, and the real meaning of that—fatal fan of mine. Oh, if he knows—how can I look him in the face again? He would never forgive me. (*Touches bell*) How securely one thinks one lives—out of reach of temptation, sin, folly. And then suddenly— Oh! Life is terrible. It rules us, we do not rule it.

Enter Rosalie R.

ROSALIE Did your ladyship ring for me?

LADY WINDERMERE Yes. Have you found out at what time Lord Windermere came in last night?

ROSALIE His lordship did not come in till five o'clock.

LADY WINDERMERE Five o'clock? He knocked at my door this morning, didn't he?

ROSALIE Yes, my lady—at half-past nine. I told him° your ladyship was not awake yet.

LADY WINDERMERE Did he say anything?

ROSALIE Something about your ladyship's fan. I didn't quite catch what his lordship said. Has the fan been lost, my lady? I can't find it, and Parker says it was not left in any of the rooms. He has looked in all of them and on the terrace as well.

LADY WINDERMERE It doesn't matter. Tell Parker not to trouble. That will do.

Exit Rosalie

LADY WINDERMERE (*rising*) She is sure to tell him. I can fancy a person doing a wonderful act of self-sacrifice, doing it spontaneously, recklessly, nobly—and afterwards finding out that it costs too much. Why should she hesitate between her ruin and mine? . . . How strange! I would have publicly disgraced her° in my own house. She accepts public disgrace in the house of another to save me. . . . There is a bitter irony in things, a bitter irony in the way we talk of good and bad women. . . . Oh, what a lesson! and what a pity that in life we only get our lessons when they are of no use to us! For even if she doesn't tell, I must. Oh, the shame of it, the shame of it. To tell it is to live through it all again.

Actions are the first tragedy in life, words are the second. Words   35
are perhaps the worst. Words are merciless. . . . Oh! (*starts as Lord
Windermere enters*)

LORD WINDERMERE (*kisses her*) Margaret—how pale you look!

LADY WINDERMERE I slept very badly.

LORD WINDERMERE (*sitting on sofa with her*) I am so sorry. I came
in dreadfully late, and didn't like to wake you. You are crying,   40
dear.

LADY WINDERMERE Yes, I am crying, for I have something to tell
you, Arthur.

LORD WINDERMERE My dear child, you are not well. You've been
doing too much. Let us go away° to the country. You'll be all right   45
at Selby. The season is almost over. There is no use staying on.
Poor darling! We'll go away today, if you like. (*Rises*) We can
easily catch the 3.40. I'll send a wire to Fannen. (*Crosses and sits
down at table to write a telegram*)

LADY WINDERMERE Yes; let us go away today. No; I can't go today,
Arthur. There is someone I must see before I leave town—some-   50
one who has been kind to me.

LORD WINDERMERE (*rising and leaning over sofa*) Kind to you?

LADY WINDERMERE Far more than that. (*Rises and goes to him*) I will
tell you, Arthur, but only love me, love me as you used to love me.

LORD WINDERMERE Used to? You are not thinking of that wretched   55
woman who came here last night? (*Coming round and sitting R. of
her*) You don't still imagine—no, you couldn't.

LADY WINDERMERE I don't. I know now I was wrong and foolish.

LORD WINDERMERE It was very good of you to receive her last
night—but you are never to see her again.   60

LADY WINDERMERE Why do you say that?

   A pause

LORD WINDERMERE (*holding her hand*) Margaret, I thought Mrs
Erlynne was a woman more sinned against than sinning, as the
phrase goes. I thought she wanted to be good, to get back into a
place that she had lost by a moment's folly, to lead again a decent   65
life. I believed what she told me—I was mistaken in her. She is
bad—as bad as a woman can be.

LADY WINDERMERE Arthur, Arthur, don't talk so bitterly about any
woman. I don't think now that people can be divided into the good
and the bad,° as though they were two separate races or creations.   70
What are called good women may have terrible things in them,
mad moods of recklessness, assertion, jealousy, sin. Bad women, as

49

they are termed, may have in them sorrow, repentance, pity, sacrifice. And I don't think Mrs Erlynne a bad woman—I know she's not.   75

LORD WINDERMERE My dear child, the woman's impossible. No matter what harm she tries to do us, you must never see her again. She is inadmissible anywhere.

LADY WINDERMERE But I want to see her. I want her to come here.

LORD WINDERMERE Never!   80

LADY WINDERMERE She came here once as *your* guest. She must come now as *mine*. That is but fair.

LORD WINDERMERE She should never have come here.

LADY WINDERMERE (*rising*) It is too late, Arthur, to say that now.
        Moves away

LORD WINDERMERE (*rising*) Margaret, if you knew where Mrs   85
Erlynne went last night, after she left this house, you would not sit in the same room with her. It was absolutely shameless, the whole thing.

LADY WINDERMERE Arthur, I can't bear it any longer. I must tell you. Last night—   90
        *Enter Parker with a tray on which lie Lady Windermere's
        fan° and a card*

PARKER Mrs Erlynne has called to return your ladyship's fan which she took away by mistake last night. Mrs Erlynne has written a message on the card.

LADY WINDERMERE Oh, ask Mrs Erlynne to be kind enough to come up. (*Reads card*) Say I shall be very glad to see her.   95
        Exit Parker
She wants to see me, Arthur.

LORD WINDERMERE (*takes card and looks at it*) Margaret, I *beg* you not to. Let me see her first, at any rate. She's a very dangerous woman. She is the most dangerous woman I know. You don't realize what you're doing.   100

LADY WINDERMERE. It is right that I should see her.

LORD WINDERMERE My child, you may be on the brink of a great sorrow. Don't go to meet it. It is absolutely necessary that I should see her before you do.

LADY WINDERMERE Why should it be necessary?   105
        Enter Parker

PARKER Mrs Erlynne.
        Enter Mrs Erlynne.° Exit Parker

MRS ERLYNNE How do you do, Lady Windermere? (*To Lord Windermere*) How do you do? Do you know, Lady Windermere, I am so sorry about your fan. I can't imagine how I made such a silly mistake. Most stupid of me. And as I was driving in your direction, I thought I would take the opportunity of returning your property in person with many apologies for my carelessness, and of bidding you good-bye.

LADY WINDERMERE Good-bye? (*Moves towards sofa with Mrs Erlynne and sits down beside her*)° Are you going away, then, Mrs Erlynne?

MRS ERLYNNE Yes; I am going to live abroad again. The English climate doesn't suit me. My—heart is affected here, and that I don't like. I prefer living in the south. London is too full of fogs and—serious people,° Lord Windermere. Whether the fogs produce the serious people or whether the serious people produce the fogs, I don't know, but the whole thing rather gets on my nerves, and so I'm leaving this afternoon by the Club Train.°

LADY WINDERMERE This afternoon? But I wanted so much to come and see you.

MRS ERLYNNE How kind of you! But I am afraid I have to go.

LADY WINDERMERE Shall I never see you again, Mrs Erlynne?

MRS ERLYNNE I am afraid not. Our lives lie too far apart. But there is a little thing I would like you to do for me. I want a photograph of you, Lady Windermere—would you give me one? You don't know how gratified I should be.

LADY WINDERMERE Oh, with pleasure. There is one on that table. I'll show it to you. (*Goes across to the table*)

LORD WINDERMERE (*coming up to Mrs Erlynne and speaking in a low voice*) It is monstrous your intruding yourself here after your conduct last night.

MRS ERLYNNE (*with an amused smile*) My dear Windermere, manners before morals!

LADY WINDERMERE (*returning*) I'm afraid it is very flattering—I am not so pretty as that. (*Showing photograph*)

MRS ERLYNNE You are much prettier. But haven't you got one of yourself with your little boy?

LADY WINDERMERE I have. Would you prefer one of those?

MRS ERLYNNE Yes.

LADY WINDERMERE I'll go and get it for you, if you'll excuse me for a moment. I have one upstairs.

MRS ERLYNNE So sorry, Lady Windermere, to give you so much trouble.

LADY WINDERMERE (*moves to door R.*) No trouble at all, Mrs Erlynne.°

MRS ERLYNNE Thanks so much.
    Exit Lady Windermere R.
  You seem rather out of temper this morning, Windermere. Why
should you be? Margaret and I get on charmingly together.

LORD WINDERMERE I can't bear to see you with her. Besides, you
have not told me the truth, Mrs Erlynne.   155

MRS ERLYNNE I have not told *her* the truth, you mean.

LORD WINDERMERE (*standing C.*) I sometimes wish you had. I
should have been spared then the misery, the anxiety, the annoyance of the last six months. But rather than my wife should
know—that the mother whom she was taught to consider as dead, 160
the mother whom she has mourned as dead, is living—a divorced
woman, going about under an assumed name, a bad woman
preying upon life, as I know you now to be—rather than that, I
was ready to supply you with money to pay bill after bill,
extravagance after extravagance, to risk what occurred yesterday, 165
the first quarrel I have ever had with my wife. You don't
understand what that means to me. How could you? But I tell you
that the only bitter words that ever came from those sweet lips of
hers were on your account, and I hate to see you next her. You
sully the innocence that is in her. (*Moves L.C.*) And then I used 170
to think that with all your faults you were frank and honest. You
are not.

MRS ERLYNNE Why do you say that?

LORD WINDERMERE You made me get you an invitation to my
wife's ball.   175

MRS ERLYNNE For my daughter's ball—yes.

LORD WINDERMERE You came, and within an hour of your leaving
the house you are found in a man's rooms—you are disgraced
before everyone. (*Goes up stage C.*)

MRS ERLYNNE Yes.   180

LORD WINDERMERE (*turning round on her*) Therefore I have a right
to look upon you as what you are—a worthless, vicious woman. I
have the right to tell you never to enter this house again, never to
attempt to come near my wife—

MRS ERLYNNE (*coldly*) My daughter, you mean.   185

LORD WINDERMERE You have no right to claim her as your
daughter. You left her, abandoned her when she was but a child in
the cradle, abandoned her for your lover, who abandoned you in
turn.

MRS ERLYNNE (*rising*)° Do you count that to his credit, Lord 190
Windermere—or to mine?

LORD WINDERMERE To his, now that I know you.

MRS ERLYNNE Take care—you had better be careful.

LORD WINDERMERE Oh, I am not going to mince words for you. I know you thoroughly. 195

MRS ERLYNNE (*looking steadily at him*) I question that.

LORD WINDERMERE I *do* know you. For twenty years of your life you lived without your child, without a thought of your child. One day you read in the papers that she had married a rich man. You saw your hideous chance. You knew that to spare her the ignominy 200 of learning that a woman like you was her mother, I would endure anything. You began your blackmailing.°

MRS ERLYNNE (*shrugging her shoulders*) Don't use ugly words, Windermere. They are vulgar. I saw my chance, it is true, and took it.

LORD WINDERMERE Yes, you took it—and spoiled it all last night 205 by being found out.

MRS ERLYNNE (*with a strange smile*) You are quite right, I spoiled it all last night.

LORD WINDERMERE And as for your blunder in taking my wife's fan from here and then leaving it about in Darlington's rooms, it is 210 unpardonable. I can't bear the sight of it now. I shall never let my wife use it again. The thing is soiled for me. You should have kept it and not brought it back.

MRS ERLYNNE I think I *shall* keep it. (*Goes up*) It's extremely pretty. (*Takes up fan*) I shall ask Margaret to give it to me. 215

LORD WINDERMERE I hope my wife will give it to you.

MRS ERLYNNE Oh, I'm sure she will have no objection.

LORD WINDERMERE I wish that at the same time she would give you a miniature she kisses every night before she prays—It's the miniature of a young innocent-looking girl° with beautiful dark 220 hair.

MRS ERLYNNE Ah, yes, I remember. How long ago that seems. (*Goes to a sofa and sits down*) It was done before I was married. Dark hair and an innocent expression were the fashion then, Windermere!
A pause

LORD WINDERMERE What do you mean by coming here this 225 morning? What is your object? (*Crossing L.C. and sitting*)

MRS ERLYNNE (*with a note of irony in her voice*) To bid good-bye to my dear daughter, of course. (*Lord Windermere bites his underlip in anger. Mrs Erlynne looks at him, and her voice and manner become serious. In her accents as she talks there is a note of deep tragedy. For a moment she reveals herself*) Oh, don't imagine I am going to have a pathetic scene with her, weep on her neck and tell her who I am, 230 and all that kind of thing. I have no ambition to play the part of a mother. Only once in my life have I known a mother's feelings. That was last night. They were terrible—they made me suffer—they made me suffer too much. For twenty years, as you say, I have lived childless—I want to live childless still. (*Hiding her* 235 *feelings with a trivial laugh*) Besides, my dear Windermere, how on earth could I pose as a mother with a grown-up daughter? Margaret is twenty-one, and I have never admitted that I am more than twenty-nine, or thirty at the most. Twenty-nine when there are pink shades,° thirty when there are not. So you see what 240 difficulties it would involve. No, as far as I am concerned, let your wife cherish the memory of this dead, stainless mother. Why should I interfere with her illusions? I find it hard enough to keep my own. I lost one illusion last night. I thought I had no heart. I find I have, and a heart doesn't suit me,° Windermere. Somehow 245 it doesn't go with modern dress. It makes one look old. (*Takes up hand-mirror from table and looks into it*) And it spoils one's career at critical moments.

LORD WINDERMERE You fill me with horror—with absolute horror.

MRS ERLYNNE (*rising*) I suppose, Windermere, you would like me to 250 retire into a convent, or become a hospital nurse, or something of that kind, as people do in silly modern novels. That is stupid of you, Arthur; in real life we don't do such things°—not so long as we have any good looks left, at any rate. No—what consoles one nowadays is not repentance, but pleasure. Repentance is quite out 255 of date. And besides, if a woman really repents, she has to go to a bad dressmaker, otherwise no one believes in her. And nothing in the world would induce me to do that.° No; I am going to pass entirely out of your two lives. My coming into them has been a mistake—I discovered that last night. 260

LORD WINDERMERE A fatal mistake.°

MRS ERLYNNE (*smiling*) Almost fatal.

LORD WINDERMERE I am sorry now I did not tell my wife the whole thing at once.

MRS ERLYNNE I regret my bad actions. You regret your good 265 ones—that is the difference between us.

LORD WINDERMERE I don't trust you. I *will* tell my wife. It's better for her to know, and from me. It will cause her infinite pain—it will humiliate her terribly, but it's right that she should know.

MRS ERLYNNE You propose to tell her? 270

LORD WINDERMERE I am going to tell her.

MRS ERLYNNE (*going up to him*) If you do, I will make my name so infamous that it will mar every moment of her life. It will ruin her, and make her wretched. If you dare to tell her, there is no depth of degradation I will not sink to, no pit of shame I will not enter. You shall not tell her—I forbid you.   275

LORD WINDERMERE Why?

MRS ERLYNNE (*after a pause*) If I said to you that I cared for her, perhaps loved her even—you would sneer at me, wouldn't you?

LORD WINDERMERE I should feel it was not true. A mother's love   280 means devotion, unselfishness, sacrifice. What could you know of such things?

MRS ERLYNNE You are right. What could I know of such things? Don't let us talk any more about it—as for telling my daughter who I am, that I do not allow. It is my secret,° it is not yours. If   285 I make up my mind to tell her, and I think I will, I shall tell her before I leave the house—if not, I shall never tell her.

LORD WINDERMERE (*angrily*) Then let me beg of you to leave our house at once. I will make your excuses to Margaret.

> *Enter Lady Windermere R. She goes over to Mrs Erlynne with the photograph in her hand. Lord Windermere moves to back of sofa, and anxiously watches Mrs Erlynne as the scene progresses*

LADY WINDERMERE I am so sorry, Mrs Erlynne, to have kept you   290 waiting. I couldn't find the photograph anywhere. At last I discovered it in my husband's dressing-room—he had stolen it.

MRS ERLYNNE (*takes the photograph from her and looks at it*) I am not surprised—it is charming. (*Goes over to sofa with Lady Windermere, and sits down beside her. Looks again at the photograph*) And so that   295 is your little boy! What is he called?

LADY WINDERMERE Gerard, after my dear father.

MRS ERLYNNE (*laying the photograph down*) Really?

LADY WINDERMERE Yes. If it had been a girl, I would have called it after my mother. My mother had the same name as myself,   300 Margaret.

MRS ERLYNNE My name is Margaret too.

LADY WINDERMERE Indeed!

MRS ERLYNNE Yes. (*Pause*) You are devoted to your mother's memory, Lady Windermere, your husband tells me.   305

LADY WINDERMERE We all have ideals in life. At least we all should have. Mine is my mother.

MRS ERLYNNE Ideals are dangerous things. Realities are better. They wound, but they're better.

LADY WINDERMERE (*shaking her head*) If I lost my ideals, I should 310
lose everything.

MRS ERLYNNE Everything?

LADY WINDERMERE Yes.

    Pause

MRS ERLYNNE Did your father often speak to you of your mother?

LADY WINDERMERE No, it gave him too much pain. He told me 315
how my mother had died a few months after I was born. His eyes
filled with tears as he spoke. Then he begged me never to mention
her name to him again. It made him suffer even to hear it. My
father—my father really died of a broken heart. His was the most
ruined life I know. 320

MRS ERLYNNE (*rising*) I am afraid I must go now, Lady Windermere.

LADY WINDERMERE (*rising*) Oh no, don't.

MRS ERLYNNE I think I had better. My carriage must have come
back by this time. I sent it to Lady Jedburgh's with a note. 325

LADY WINDERMERE Arthur, would you mind seeing if Mrs
Erlynne's carriage has come back?

MRS ERLYNNE Pray don't trouble, Lord Windermere.

LADY WINDERMERE Yes, Arthur, do go, please.

    Lord Windermere hesitates for a moment and looks at Mrs
    Erlynne. She remains quite impassive. He leaves the room

(*To Mrs Erlynne*) Oh! What am I to say to you? You saved me last 330
night. (*Goes towards her*)

MRS ERLYNNE Hush—don't speak of it.

LADY WINDERMERE I must speak of it. I can't let you think that I
am going to accept this sacrifice. I am not. It is too great. I am
going to tell my husband everything. It is my duty. 335

MRS ERLYNNE It is not your duty—at least you have duties to others
besides him. You say you owe me something?

LADY WINDERMERE I owe you everything.

MRS ERLYNNE Then pay your debt by silence.° That is the only way
in which it can be paid. Don't spoil the one good thing I have done 340
in my life by telling it to anyone. Promise me that what passed last
night will remain a secret between us. You must not bring misery
into your husband's life. Why spoil his love? You must not spoil
it. Love is easily killed. Oh! how easily love is killed. Pledge me
your word, Lady Windermere, that you will *never* tell him. I insist 345
upon it.

LADY WINDERMERE (*with bowed head*) It is your will, not mine.

MRS ERLYNNE Yes, it is my will. And never forget your child—I like
to think of you as a mother. I like you to think of yourself as one.

LADY WINDERMERE (*looking up*) I always will now. Only once in my   350
life I have forgotten my own mother—that was last night. Oh, if I
had remembered her I should not have been so foolish, so wicked.

MRS ERLYNNE (*with a slight shudder*) Hush, last night is quite over.
    Enter Lord Windermere

LORD WINDERMERE Your carriage has not come back yet, Mrs
Erlynne.   355

MRS ERLYNNE It makes no matter. I'll take a hansom. There is
nothing in the world so respectable as a good Shrewsbury and
Talbot.° And now, dear Lady Windermere, I am afraid it is really
good-bye. (*Moves up C.*) Oh, I remember. You'll think me absurd,
but do you know I've taken a great fancy to this fan that I was silly   360
enough to run away with last night from your ball. Now, I wonder
would you give it to me? Lord Windermere says you may. I know
it is his present.

LADY WINDERMERE Oh, certainly, if it will give you any pleasure.
But it has my name on it. It has 'Margaret' on it.   365

MRS ERLYNNE But we have the same Christian name.

LADY WINDERMERE Oh, I forgot. Of course, do have it. What a
wonderful chance our names being the same!

MRS ERLYNNE Quite wonderful. Thanks—it will always remind me
of you. (*Shakes hands° with her*)   370
    Enter Parker

PARKER Lord Augustus Lorton. Mrs Erlynne's carriage has come.
    Enter Lord Augustus

LORD AUGUSTUS Good morning, dear boy. Good morning, Lady
Windermere. (*Sees Mrs Erlynne*) Mrs Erlynne!

MRS ERLYNNE How do you do, Lord Augustus? Are you quite well
this morning?   375

LORD AUGUSTUS (*coldly*). Quite well, thank you, Mrs Erlynne.

MRS ERLYNNE You don't look at all well, Lord Augustus. You stop
up too late—it is so bad for you. You really should take more care
of yourself. Good-bye, Lord Windermere. (*Goes towards door with
a bow to Lord Augustus. Suddenly smiles and looks back at him*) Lord   380
Augustus! Won't you see me to my carriage? You might carry the
fan.°

LORD WINDERMERE Allow me!

MRS ERLYNNE No; I want Lord Augustus. I have a special message
for the dear Duchess. Won't you carry the fan, Lord Augustus?   385

57

LORD AUGUSTUS If you really desire it, Mrs Erlynne.

MRS ERLYNNE (*laughing*) Of course I do. You'll carry it so gracefully. You would carry off anything gracefully, dear Lord Augustus.

> *When she reaches the door she looks back for a moment at Lady*
> *Windermere. Their eyes meet. Then she turns, and exit C.*
> *followed by Lord Augustus* [*Exit Parker*]

LADY WINDERMERE You will never speak against Mrs Erlynne   390
again, Arthur, will you?

LORD WINDERMERE (*gravely*) She is better than one thought her.

LADY WINDERMERE She is better than I am.

LORD WINDERMERE (*smiling as he strokes her hair*) Child, you and
she belong to different worlds. Into your world evil has never   395
entered.

LADY WINDERMERE Don't say that, Arthur. There is the same
world for all of us, and good and evil, sin and innocence, go
through it hand in hand. To shut one's eyes to half of life that one
may live securely is as though one blinded oneself that one might   400
walk with more safety in a land of pit and precipice.

LORD WINDERMERE (*moves down with her*) Darling, why do you say
that?

LADY WINDERMERE (*sits on sofa*)° Because I, who had shut my eyes
to life, came to the brink. And one who had separated us—   405

LORD WINDERMERE We were never separated.

LADY WINDERMERE We never must be again. Oh Arthur, don't love
me less, and I will trust you more. I will trust you absolutely. Let
us go to Selby. In the Rose Garden at Selby the roses are white
and red.°   410

> *Enter Lord Augustus C.*

LORD AUGUSTUS Arthur, she has explained everything. (*Lady Win-*
dermere looks horribly frightened at this. Lord Windermere starts. Lord
Augustus takes Windermere by the arm and brings him to front of stage.
He talks rapidly and in a low voice. Lady Windermere stands watching
them in terror) My dear fellow, she has explained every demmed
thing. We all wronged her immensely. It was entirely for my sake
she went to Darlington's rooms. Called first at the Club—fact is,
wanted to put me out of suspense—and being told I had gone   415
on—followed—naturally frightened when she heard a lot of us
coming in—retired to another room—I assure you, most gratifying
to me, the whole thing. We all behaved brutally to her. She is just
the woman for me. Suits me down to the ground. All the

conditions she makes are that we live entirely out of England. A   420
very good thing too. Demmed clubs, demmed climate, demmed
cooks, demmed everything. Sick of it all!

LADY WINDERMERE (*frightened*) Has Mrs Erlynne—?

LORD AUGUSTUS (*advancing towards her with a low bow*). Yes, Lady
Windermere—Mrs Erlynne has done me the honour of accepting   425
my hand.

LORD WINDERMERE Well, you are certainly marrying a very clever
woman!

LADY WINDERMERE (*taking her husband's hand*) Ah, you're marrying
a very good woman!°   430

CURTAIN

SALOME

To my friend
LORD ALFRED BRUCE DOUGLAS
the translator of my play

THE PERSONS OF THE PLAY

The play was first staged in French at the Théâtre de l'Œuvre, Paris, 11 February 1896. It was first staged in English at the Bijou Theatre, London (New Stage Club), 10 May 1905.

Herod Antipas, Tetrarch of Judaea
Iokanaan, the Prophet
The Young Syrian, Captain of the Guard
Tigellinus, a young Roman
A Cappadocian
A Nubian
First Soldier
Second Soldier
The Page of Herodias
Jews, Nazarenes, etc.
A Slave
Naaman, the Executioner
Herodias, wife of the Tetrarch
Salome, daughter of Herodias
The Slaves of Salome

Scene: *A great terrace in the Palace of Herod, set above the banqueting-hall. Some soldiers are leaning over the balcony. To the right there is a gigantic staircase, to the left, at the back, an old cistern surrounded by a wall of green bronze. The moon is shining very brightly.* [*Present on stage are Narraboth (the Young Syrian) and the Page of Herodias, with four soldiers (first, second, the Nubian and the Cappadocian) and, at one side, Naaman, the executioner*]

THE YOUNG SYRIAN How beautiful is the Princess Salome tonight!

THE PAGE OF HERODIAS Look at the moon. How strange the moon seems! She is like a woman rising from a tomb. She is like a dead woman. One might fancy she was looking for dead things.

THE YOUNG SYRIAN She has a strange look. She is like a little   5
princess who wears a yellow veil, and whose feet are of silver. She is like a princess who has little white doves for feet. One might fancy she was dancing.

THE PAGE OF HERODIAS She is like a woman who is dead. She moves very slowly.   10

    Noise in the banqueting-hall

FIRST SOLDIER What an uproar! Who are those wild beasts howling?

SECOND SOLDIER The Jews. They are always like that. They are disputing about their religion.

FIRST SOLDIER Why do they dispute about their religion?

SECOND SOLDIER I cannot tell. They are always doing it. The   15
Pharisees,° for instance, say that there are angels, and the Sadducees° declare that angels do not exist.

FIRST SOLDIER I think it is ridiculous to dispute about such things.

THE YOUNG SYRIAN How beautiful is the Princess Salome tonight!

THE PAGE OF HERODIAS You are always looking at her. You look   20
at her too much. It is dangerous to look at people in such fashion. Something terrible may happen.

THE YOUNG SYRIAN She is very beautiful tonight.

FIRST SOLDIER The tetrarch has a sombre aspect.

SECOND SOLDIER Yes; he has a sombre aspect.   25

FIRST SOLDIER He is looking at something.

SECOND SOLDIER He is looking at someone.

FIRST SOLDIER At whom is he looking?

SECOND SOLDIER I cannot tell.

THE YOUNG SYRIAN How pale the Princess is! Never have I seen   30
her so pale. She is like the shadow of a white rose in a mirror of
silver.

THE PAGE OF HERODIAS You must not look at her. You look too
much at her.

FIRST SOLDIER Herodias has filled the cup of the Tetrarch.   35

THE CAPPADOCIAN Is that the Queen Herodias, she who wears a
black mitre sewed with pearls, and whose hair is powdered with
blue dust?

FIRST SOLDIER Yes; that is Herodias, the Tetrarch's wife.

SECOND SOLDIER The Tetrarch is very fond of wine. He has wine   40
of three sorts. One which is brought from the Island of Samothrace,° and is purple like the cloak of Caesar.°

THE CAPPADOCIAN I have never seen Caesar.

SECOND SOLDIER Another that comes from a town called Cyprus,°
and is as yellow as gold.   45

THE CAPPADOCIAN I love gold.

SECOND SOLDIER And the third is a wine of Sicily. That wine is as
red as blood.

THE NUBIAN The gods of my country are very fond of blood. Twice
in the year we sacrifice to them young men and maidens: fifty   50
young men and a hundred maidens. But I am afraid that we never
give them quite enough, for they are very harsh to us.

THE CAPPADOCIAN In my country there are no gods left. The
Romans have driven them out.° There are some who say that they
have hidden themselves in the mountains, but I do not believe it.   55
Three nights I have been on the mountains seeking them everywhere. I did not find them, and at last I called them by their
names, and they did not come. I think they are dead.

FIRST SOLDIER The Jews worship a God that one cannot see.

THE CAPPADOCIAN I cannot understand that.   60

FIRST SOLDIER In fact, they only believe in things that one cannot
see.

THE CAPPADOCIAN That seems to me altogether ridiculous.

THE VOICE OF IOKANAAN [*From within the cistern*] After me shall
come another° mightier than I. I am not worthy so much as to   65
unloose the latchet of his shoes. When he cometh the solitary
places shall be glad. They shall blossom like the rose. The eyes of
the blind shall see the day, and the ears of the deaf shall be opened.
The sucking child shall put his hand upon the dragon's lair, he
shall lead the lions by their manes.   70

SECOND SOLDIER Make him be silent. He is always saying ridiculous things.

FIRST SOLDIER No, no. He is a holy man. He is very gentle, too. Every day when I give him to eat he thanks me.

THE CAPPADOCIAN Who is he?

FIRST SOLDIER A prophet.

THE CAPPADOCIAN What is his name?

FIRST SOLDIER Iokanaan.

THE CAPPADOCIAN Whence comes he?

FIRST SOLDIER From the desert, where he fed on locusts and wild honey.° He was clothed in camel's hair, and round his loins he had a leathern belt. He was very terrible to look upon. A great multitude used to follow him. He even had disciples.

THE CAPPADOCIAN What is he talking of?

FIRST SOLDIER We can never tell. Sometimes he says things that affright one, but it is impossible to understand what he says.

THE CAPPADOCIAN May one see him?

FIRST SOLDIER No. The Tetrarch has forbidden it.

THE YOUNG SYRIAN The Princess has hidden her face behind her fan! Her little white hands are fluttering like doves that fly to their dove-cots. They are like white butterflies. They are just like white butterflies.

THE PAGE OF HERODIAS What is that to you? Why do you look at her? You must not look at her.... Something terrible may happen.

THE CAPPADOCIAN (*pointing to the cistern*) What a strange prison!

SECOND SOLDIER It is an old cistern.

THE CAPPADOCIAN An old cistern! That must be a poisonous place in which to dwell!

SECOND SOLDIER Oh no! For instance, the Tetrarch's brother,° his elder brother, the first husband of Herodias the Queen, was imprisoned there for twelve years. It did not kill him. At the end of the twelve years he had to be strangled.

THE CAPPADOCIAN Strangled? Who dared to do that?

SECOND SOLDIER (*Pointing to the Executioner, a huge negro*) That man yonder, Naaman.

THE CAPPADOCIAN He was not afraid?

SECOND SOLDIER Oh no! The Tetrarch sent him the ring.

THE CAPPADOCIAN What ring?

SECOND SOLDIER The death ring. So he was not afraid.

THE CAPPADOCIAN Yet it is a terrible thing to strangle a king.

FIRST SOLDIER Why? Kings have but one neck, like other folk.

THE CAPPADOCIAN I think it terrible.

THE YOUNG SYRIAN The Princess is getting up! She is leaving the table! She looks very troubled. Ah, she is coming this way. Yes, she is coming towards us. How pale she is! Never have I seen her so pale. 115

THE PAGE OF HERODIAS Do not look at her. I pray you not to look at her.

THE YOUNG SYRIAN She is like a dove that has strayed. . . . She is like a narcissus trembling in the wind. . . . She is like a silver flower. 120

Enter Salome

SALOME I will not stay. I cannot stay. Why does the Tetrarch look at me all the while with his mole's eyes under his shaking eyelids? It is strange that the husband of my mother looks at me like that. I know not what it means. Of a truth I know it too well. 125

THE YOUNG SYRIAN You have left the feast, Princess?

SALOME How sweet is the air here! I can breathe here! Within there are Jews from Jerusalem who are tearing each other in pieces over their foolish ceremonies, and barbarians who drink and drink and spill their wine on the pavement, and Greeks from Smyrna° with painted eyes and painted cheeks, and frizzed hair curled in columns, and Egyptians silent and subtle, with long nails of jade and russet cloaks, and Romans brutal and coarse, with their uncouth jargon. Ah! how I loathe the Romans! They are rough and common, and they give themselves the airs of noble lords. 130 135

THE YOUNG SYRIAN Will you be seated, Princess.

THE PAGE OF HERODIAS Why do you speak to her? Oh! something terrible will happen. Why do you look at her? 140

SALOME How good to see the moon! She is like a little piece of money, a little silver flower. She is cold and chaste. I am sure she is a virgin. She has the beauty of a virgin. Yes, she is a virgin. She has never defiled herself. She has never abandoned herself to men, like the other goddesses. 145

THE VOICE OF IOKANAAN Behold! the Lord hath come. The Son of Man is at hand. The centaurs have hidden themselves in the rivers, and the nymphs have left the rivers, and are lying beneath the leaves in the forests.

SALOME Who was that who cried out? 150

SECOND SOLDIER The prophet, Princess.

SALOME Ah, the prophet! He of whom the Tetrarch is afraid?

SECOND SOLDIER We know nothing of that, Princess. It was the
prophet Iokanaan who cried out.

THE YOUNG SYRIAN Is it your pleasure that I bid them bring your   155
litter, Princess? The night is fair in the garden.

SALOME He says terrible things about my mother, does he not?

SECOND SOLDIER We never understand what he says, Princess.

SALOME Yes; he says terrible things about her.

Enter a Slave

THE SLAVE Princess, the Tetrarch prays you to return to the feast.   160

SALOME I will not return.

THE YOUNG SYRIAN Pardon me, Princess, but if you return not
some misfortune may happen.

SALOME Is he an old man, this prophet?

THE YOUNG SYRIAN Princess, it were better to return. Suffer me to   165
lead you in.

SALOME This prophet . . . is he an old man?

FIRST SOLDIER No, Princess, he is quite young.

SECOND SOLDIER One cannot be sure. There are those who say that
he is Elias.°   170

SALOME Who is Elias?

SECOND SOLDIER A prophet of this country in bygone days, Princess.

THE SLAVE What answer may I give the Tetrarch from the Princess?   175

THE VOICE OF IOKANAAN Rejoice not, O land of Palestine, because
the rod of him who smote thee is broken. For from the seed of the
serpent shall come a basilisk, and that which is born of it shall
devour the birds.

SALOME What a strange voice! I would speak with him.   180

FIRST SOLDIER I fear it may not be, Princess. The Tetrarch does not
suffer anyone to speak with him. He has even forbidden the high
priest to speak with him.

SALOME I desire to speak with him.

FIRST SOLDIER It is impossible, Princess.   185

SALOME I will speak with him.

THE YOUNG SYRIAN Would it not be better to return to the
banquet?

SALOME Bring forth this prophet.

Exit the Slave

FIRST SOLDIER We dare not, Princess.   190

SALOME (*approaching the cistern and looking down into it*) How black it is, down there! It must be terrible to be in so black a hole! It is like a tomb. . . . (*To the soldiers*) Did you not hear me? Bring out the prophet. I would look on him.

SECOND SOLDIER Princess, I beg you, do not require this of us. 195

SALOME You are making me wait upon your pleasure.

FIRST SOLDIER Princess, our lives belong to you, but we cannot do what you have asked of us. And indeed, it is not of us that you should ask this thing.

SALOME (*looking at the young Syrian*) Ah! 200

THE PAGE OF HERODIAS Oh! what is going to happen? I am sure that something terrible will happen.

SALOME (*going up to the young Syrian*) Thou wilt do this thing for me, wilt thou not, Narraboth? Thou wilt do this thing for me. I have ever been kind towards thee. Thou wilt do it for me. I would 205 but look at him, this strange prophet. Men have talked so much of him. Often I have heard the Tetrarch talk of him. I think he is afraid of him, the Tetrarch. Art thou, even thou, also afraid of him, Narraboth?

THE YOUNG SYRIAN I fear him not, Princess; there is no man I fear. 210 But the Tetrarch has formally forbidden that any man should raise the cover of this well.°

SALOME Thou wilt do this thing for me, Narraboth, and tomorrow when I pass in my litter beneath the gateway of the idol sellers I will let fall for thee a little flower, a little green flower.° 215

THE YOUNG SYRIAN Princess, I cannot, I cannot.

SALOME (*smiling*) Thou wilt do this thing for me, Narraboth. Thou knowest that thou wilt do this thing for me. And on the morrow when I shall pass in my litter by the bridge of the idol-buyers, I will look at thee through the muslin veils, I will look at thee, 220 Narraboth, it may be I will smile at thee. Look at me, Narraboth, look at me. Ah! thou knowest that thou wilt do what I ask of thee. Thou knowest it. . . . I know that thou wilt do this thing.

THE YOUNG SYRIAN (*signing to the third Soldier*) Let the prophet come forth. . . . The Princess Salome desires to see him. 225

SALOME Ah!

THE PAGE OF HERODIAS Oh! How strange the moon looks! Like the hand of a dead woman who is seeking to cover herself with a shroud.

THE YOUNG SYRIAN She has a strange aspect! She is like a little princess, whose eyes are eyes of amber. Through the clouds of 230 muslin she is smiling like a little princess.

The prophet comes out of the cistern. Salome looks at him and steps slowly back

IOKANAAN Where is he whose cup of abominations is now full? Where is he, who in a robe of silver shall one day die in the face of all the people? Bid him come forth, that he may hear the voice of him who hath cried in the waste places and in the houses of kings. 235

SALOME Of whom is he speaking?

THE YOUNG SYRIAN No one can tell, Princess.

IOKANAAN Where is she who saw the images of men painted on the walls, even the images of the Chaldaeans painted with colours, and gave herself up unto the lust of her eyes, and sent ambassadors into 240 the land of Chaldaea?°

SALOME It is of my mother that he is speaking.

THE YOUNG SYRIAN Oh no, Princess.

SALOME Yes: it is of my mother that he is speaking.

IOKANAAN Where is she who gave herself unto the Captains of 245 Assyria, who have baldricks° on their loins, and crowns of many colours on their heads? Where is she who hath given herself to the young men of the Egyptians, who are clothed in fine linen and hyacinth, whose shields are of gold, whose helmets are of silver, whose bodies are mighty? Go, bid her rise up from the bed of her 250 abominations, from the bed of her incestuousness, that she may hear the words of him who prepareth the way of the Lord, that she may repent her of her iniquities. Though she will not repent, but will stick fast in her abominations, go bid her come, for the fan of the Lord° is in His hand. 255

SALOME Ah, but he is terrible, he is terrible!

THE YOUNG SYRIAN Do not stay here, Princess, I beseech you.

SALOME It is his eyes above all that are terrible. They are like black holes burned by torches in a tapestry of Tyre. They are like the black caverns where the dragons live, the black caverns of Egypt in 260 which the dragons make their lairs. They are like black lakes troubled by fantastic moons. . . . Do you think he will speak again?

THE YOUNG SYRIAN Do not stay here, Princess. I pray you do not stay here.

SALOME How wasted he is! He is like a thin ivory statue. He is like 265 an image of silver. I am sure he is chaste, as the moon is. He is like a moonbeam, like a shaft of silver. His flesh must be very cold, cold as ivory. . . . I would look closer at him.

THE YOUNG SYRIAN No, no, Princess!

SALOME I must look at him closer. 270

THE YOUNG SYRIAN Princess! Princess!

IOKANAAN Who is this woman who is looking at me? I will not have her look at me. Wherefore doth she look at me, with her golden eyes, under her gilded eyelids? I know not who she is. I do not desire to know who she is. Bid her begone. It is not to her that I would speak. 280

SALOME I am Salome, daughter of Herodias, Princess of Judaea.

IOKANAAN Back! daughter of Babylon! Come not near the chosen of the Lord. Thy mother hath filled the earth with the wine of her iniquities, and the cry of her sinning hath come up even to the ears of God. 285

SALOME Speak again, Iokanaan. Thy voice is as music to mine ear.

THE YOUNG SYRIAN Princess! Princess! Princess!

SALOME Speak again! Speak again, Iokanaan, and tell me what I must do. 290

IOKANAAN Daughter of Sodom,° come not near me! But cover thy face with a veil, and scatter ashes upon thine head, and get thee to the desert, and seek out the Son of Man.°

SALOME Who is he, the Son of Man? Is he as beautiful as thou art, Iokanaan? 295

IOKANAAN Get thee behind me! I hear in the palace the beating of the wings of the angel of death.°

THE YOUNG SYRIAN Princess, I beseech thee to go within.

IOKANAAN Angel of the Lord God, what dost thou here with thy sword? Whom seekest thou in this palace? The day of him who shall die in a robe of silver has not yet come. 300

SALOME Iokanaan!

IOKANAAN Who speaketh?

SALOME I am amorous of thy body, Iokanaan! Thy body is white,° like the lilies of a field that the mower hath never mowed. Thy body is white like the snows that lie on the mountains of Judaea, and come down into the valleys. The roses in the garden of the Queen of Arabia are not so white as thy body. Neither the roses of the garden of the Queen of Arabia, the garden of spices of the Queen of Arabia, nor the feet of the dawn when they light on the leaves, nor the breast of the moon when she lies on the breast of the sea. . . . There is nothing in the world so white as thy body. Suffer me to touch thy body. 305 310

IOKANAAN Back! daughter of Babylon! By woman came evil into the world. Speak not to me. I will not listen to thee. I listen but to the voice of the Lord God. 315

SALOME Thy body is hideous. It is like the body of a leper. It is like
a plastered wall, where vipers have crawled; like a plastered wall
where the scorpions have made their nest. It is like a whited
sepulchre, full of loathsome things. It is horrible, thy body is   320
horrible. It is of thy hair that I am enamoured, Iokanaan. Thy hair
is like clusters of grapes, like the clusters of black grapes that hang
from the vine-trees of Edom° in the land of the Edomites. Thy
hair is like the cedars of Lebanon, like the great cedars of Lebanon
that give their shade to the lions and to the robbers who would   325
hide them by day. The long black nights, when the moon hides
her face, when the stars are afraid, are not so black as thy hair. The
silence that dwells in the forest is not so black. There is nothing
in the world that is so black as thy hair. . . . Suffer me to touch thy
hair.   330
IOKANAAN Back, daughter of Sodom! Touch me not. Profane not
the temple of the Lord God.
SALOME Thy hair is horrible. It is covered with mire and dust. It is
like a crown of thorns placed on thy head. It is like a knot of
serpents coiled round thy neck. I love not thy hair. . . . It is thy   335
mouth that I desire, Iokanaan. Thy mouth is like a band of scarlet
on a tower of ivory. It is like a pomegranate cut in twain with a
knife of ivory. The pomegranate flowers that blossom in the
gardens of Tyre, and are redder than roses, are not so red. The
red blasts of trumpets that herald the approach of kings, and make   340
afraid the enemy, are not so red. Thy mouth is redder than the
feet of those who tread the wine in the wine-press. It is redder than
the feet of the doves who inhabit the temples and are fed by the
priests. It is redder than the feet of him who cometh from a forest
where he hath slain a lion, and seen gilded tigers. Thy mouth is   345
like a branch of coral that fishers have found in the twilight of the
sea, the coral that they keep for the kings! . . . It is like the
vermilion that the Moabites find in the mines of Moab,° the
vermilion that the kings take from them. It is like the bow of the
King of the Persians, that is painted with vermilion, and is tipped   350
with coral. There is nothing in the world so red as thy mouth. . . .
Suffer me to kiss thy mouth.
IOKANAAN Never! daughter of Babylon! Daughter of Sodom!
never!
SALOME I will kiss thy mouth, Iokanaan. I will kiss thy mouth.   355
THE YOUNG SYRIAN Princess, Princess, thou who art like a garden
of myrrh, thou who art the dove of all doves, look not at this man,

look not at him! Do not speak such words to him. I cannot endure it. . . . Princess, do not speak these things.

SALOME I will kiss thy mouth, Iokanaan.   360

THE YOUNG SYRIAN Ah!

He kills himself,° and falls between Salome and Iokanaan

THE PAGE OF HERODIAS The young Syrian has slain himself! The young captain has slain himself! He has slain himself who was my friend! I gave him a little box of perfumes and ear-rings wrought in silver, and now he has killed himself! Ah, did he not say that   365 some misfortune would happen? I, too, said it, and it has come to pass. Well I knew that the moon was seeking a dead thing, but I knew not that it was he whom she sought. Ah! why did I not hide him from the moon? If I had hidden him in a cavern she would not have seen him.   370

FIRST SOLDIER Princess, the young captain has just slain himself.

SALOME Suffer me to kiss thy mouth, Iokanaan.

IOKANAAN Art thou not afraid, daughter of Herodias? Did I not tell thee that I had heard in the palace the beating of the wings of the angel of death, and hath he not come, the angel of death?   375

SALOME Suffer me to kiss thy mouth.

IOKANAAN Daughter of adultery, there is but one who can save thee. It is He of whom I spake. Go seek Him. He is in a boat on the sea of Galilee, and He talketh with His disciples. Kneel down on the shore of the sea, and call unto Him by His name. When He cometh   380 to thee, and to all who call on Him He cometh, bow thyself at His feet and ask of Him the remission of thy sins.°

SALOME Suffer me to kiss thy mouth.

IOKANAAN Cursed be thou! daughter of an incestuous mother, be thou accursed!   385

SALOME I will kiss thy mouth, Iokanaan.

IOKANAAN I will not look at thee. Thou art accursed, Salome, thou art accursed.

He goes down into the cistern.

SALOME I will kiss thy mouth, Iokanaan; I will kiss thy mouth.

FIRST SOLDIER We must bear away the body to another place. The   390 Tetrarch does not care to see dead bodies, save the bodies of those whom he himself has slain.

THE PAGE OF HERODIAS He was my brother, and nearer to me than a brother. I gave him a little box full of perfumes, and a ring of agate that he wore always on his hand. In the evening we were   395 wont to walk by the river, and among the almond-trees, and he

used to tell me of the things of his country. He spake ever very
low.° The sound of his voice was like the sound of the flute, of
one who playeth upon the flute. Also he had much joy to gaze at
himself in the river. I used to reproach him for that.   400

SECOND SOLDIER You are right; we must hide the body. The
Tetrarch must not see it.

FIRST SOLDIER The Tetrarch will not come to this place. He never
comes on the terrace. He is too much afraid of the prophet.

    Enter Herod, Herodias, and all the Court° [*: Tigellinus
    (Caesar's ambassador) and one other Roman, five Jews, two
    Nazarenes, three Slaves (Manasseh, Issachar, Ozias), and
    Salome's Slaves*]

HEROD Where is Salome? Where is the Princess? Why did she not   405
return to the banquet as I commanded her? Ah! there she is!

HERODIAS You must not look at her! You are always looking at her!

HEROD The moon has a strange look tonight. Has she not a strange
look? She is like a mad woman, a mad woman who is seeking
everywhere for lovers. She is naked too. She is quite naked. The   410
clouds are seeking to clothe her nakedness, but she will not let
them. She shows herself naked in the sky. She reels through the
clouds like a drunken woman. . . . I am sure she is looking for
lovers. Does she not reel like a drunken woman? She is like a mad
woman, is she not?   415

HERODIAS No; the moon is like the moon, that is all. Let us go
within. . . . We have nothing to do here.

HEROD I will stay here! Manasseh, lay carpets there.° Light torches.
Bring forth the ivory tables, and the tables of jasper. The air here
is sweet. I will drink more wine with my guests. We must show   420
all honours to the ambassadors of Caesar.

HERODIAS It is not because of them that you remain.

HEROD Yes; the air is very sweet. Come, Herodias, our guests await
us. Ah! I have slipped! I have slipped in blood! It is an ill omen.
It is a very ill omen. Wherefore is there blood here? . . . and this   425
body, what does this body here? Think you I am like the King of
Egypt, who gives no feast to his guests but that he shows them a
corpse? Whose is it? I will not look on it.

FIRST SOLDIER It is our captain, sire. It is the young Syrian whom
you made captain of the guard but three days gone.   430

HEROD I issued no order that he should be slain.

SECOND SOLDIER He slew himself, sire.

HEROD For what reason? I had made him captain of my guard!

SECOND SOLDIER We do not know, sire. But with his own hand he
slew himself.   435

HEROD That seems strange to me. I had thought it was but the
Roman philosophers who slew themselves. Is it not true, Tigellinus, that the philosophers at Rome slay themselves?

TIGELLINUS There be some who slay themselves, sire. They are the
Stoics.° The Stoics are people of no cultivation. They are ridicu- 440
lous people. I myself regard them as being perfectly ridiculous.

HEROD I also. It is ridiculous to kill one's self.

TIGELLINUS Everybody at Rome laughs at them. The Emperor has
written a satire against them. It is recited everywhere.

HEROD Ah! he has written a satire against them? Caesar is wonderful. 445
He can do everything. . . . It is strange that the young Syrian has
slain himself. I am sorry he has slain himself. I am very sorry. For
he was fair to look upon. He was even very fair. He had very
languorous eyes. I remember that I saw that he looked languorous-
ly at Salome. Truly, I thought he looked too much at her.   450

HERODIAS There are others who look too much at her.

HEROD His father was a king. I drave him from his kingdom. And
of his mother, who was a queen, you made a slave, Herodias. So
he was here as my guest, as it were, and for that reason I made
him my captain. I am sorry he is dead. Ho! why have you left the 455
body here? It must be taken to some other place. I will not look at
it,—away with it! (*They take away the body*)° It is cold here. There
is a wind blowing. Is there not a wind blowing?

HERODIAS No; there is no wind.

HEROD I tell you there is a wind that blows. . . . And I hear in the 460
air something that is like the beating of wings, like the beating of
vast wings. Do you not hear it?

HERODIAS I hear nothing.

HEROD I hear it no longer. But I heard it. It was the blowing of the
wind. It has passed away. But no, I hear it again. Do you not hear 465
it? It is just like a beating of wings.

HERODIAS I tell you there is nothing. You are ill. Let us go within.

HEROD I am not ill. It is your daughter who is sick to death. Never
have I seen her so pale.

HERODIAS I have told you not to look at her.   470

HEROD Pour me forth wine. (*Wine is brought*) Salome, come drink a
little wine with me. I have here a wine that is exquisite. Caesar
himself sent it me. Dip into it thy little red lips, that I may drain
the cup.

SALOME I am not thirsty, Tetrarch.   475

HEROD You hear how she answers me, this daughter of yours?

HERODIAS She does right. Why are you always gazing at her?

HEROD Bring me ripe fruits. (*Fruits are brought*). Salome, come and
    eat fruits with me. I love to see in a fruit the mark of thy little
    teeth. Bite but a little of this fruit, that I may eat what is left.   480

SALOME I am not hungry, Tetrarch.

HEROD (*to Herodias*) You see how you have brought up this daughter
    of yours.

HERODIAS My daughter and I come of a royal race. As for thee, thy
    father was a camel driver! He was a thief and a robber to boot!   485

HEROD Thou liest!

HERODIAS Thou knowest well that it is true.

HEROD Salome, come and sit next to me. I will give thee the throne
    of thy mother.

SALOME I am not tired, Tetrarch.   490

HERODIAS You see in what regard she holds you.

HEROD Bring me——What is it that I desire? I forget. Ah! ah! I
    remember.

THE VOICE OF IOKANAAN Behold the time is come! That which I
    foretold has come to pass. The day that I spake of is at hand.   495

HERODIAS Bid him be silent. I will not listen to his voice. This man
    is for ever hurling insults against me.

HEROD He has said nothing against you. Besides, he is a very great
    prophet.

HERODIAS I do not believe in prophets. Can a man tell what will   500
    come to pass? No man knows it. Also he is for ever insulting me.
    But I think you are afraid of him. . . . I know well that you are
    afraid of him.

HEROD I am not afraid of him. I am afraid of no man.

HERODIAS I tell you you are afraid of him. If you are not afraid of   505
    him why do you not deliver him to the Jews who for these six
    months past have been clamouring for him?

A JEW Truly, my lord, it were better to deliver him into our hands.

HEROD Enough on this subject. I have already given you my answer.
    I will not deliver him into your hands. He is a holy man. He is a   510
    man who has seen God.

A JEW That cannot be. There is no man who hath seen God since
    the prophet Elias. He is the last man who saw God face to face.
    In these days God doth not show Himself. God hideth Himself.
    Therefore great evils have come upon the land.   515

ANOTHER JEW Verily, no man knoweth if Elias the prophet did indeed see God. Peradventure it was but the shadow of God that he saw.

A THIRD JEW God is at no time hidden. He showeth Himself at all times and in all places. God is in what is evil even as He is in what is good. 520

A FOURTH JEW Thou shouldst not say that. It is a very dangerous doctrine. It is a doctrine that cometh from Alexandria, where men teach the philosophy of the Greeks. And the Greeks are Gentiles.° They are not even circumcised. 525

A FIFTH JEW No man can tell how God worketh. His ways are very dark. It may be that the things which we call evil are good, and that the things which we call good are evil. There is no knowledge of anything. We can but bow our heads to His will, for God is very strong. He breaketh in pieces the strong together with the weak, 530 for He regardeth not any man.

FIRST JEW Thou speakest truly. Verily, God is terrible. He breaketh in pieces the strong and the weak as men break corn in a mortar. But as for this man, he hath never seen God. No man hath seen God since the prophet Elias. 535

HERODIAS Make them be silent. They weary me.

HEROD But I have heard it said that Iokanaan is in very truth your prophet Elias.

THE JEW That cannot be. It is more than three hundred years since the days of the prophet Elias. 540

HEROD There be some who say that this man is Elias the prophet.

A NAZARENE I am sure that he is Elias the prophet.

THE JEW Nay, but he is not Elias the prophet.

THE VOICE OF IOKANAAN Behold the day is at hand, the day of the Lord, and I hear upon the mountains the feet of Him who shall 545 be the Saviour of the world.

HEROD What does that mean? The Saviour of the world?

TIGELLINUS It is a title that Caesar adopts.

HEROD But Caesar is not coming into Judaea. Only yesterday I received letters from Rome. They contained nothing concerning 550 this matter. And you, Tigellinus, who were at Rome during the winter, you heard nothing concerning this matter, did you?

TIGELLINUS Sire, I heard nothing concerning the matter. I was but explaining the title. It is one of Caesar's titles.

HEROD But Caesar cannot come. He is too gouty. They say that his 555 feet are like the feet of an elephant. Also there are reasons of state.

He who leaves Rome loses Rome. He will not come. Howbeit, Caesar is lord, he will come if such be his pleasure. Nevertheless, I think he will not come.

FIRST NAZARENE It was not concerning Caesar that the prophet   560
spake these words, sire.

HEROD How?—it was not concerning Caesar?

FIRST NAZARENE No, my lord.

HEROD Concerning whom then did he speak?

FIRST NAZARENE Concerning Messias,° who hath come.   565

A JEW Messias hath not come.

FIRST NAZARENE He hath come, and everywhere He worketh miracles!

HERODIAS Ho! ho! miracles! I do not believe in miracles. I have seen too many. (*To the Page*) My fan.   570

FIRST NAZARENE This Man worketh true miracles. Thus, at a marriage which took place in a little town of Galilee, a town of some importance, He changed water into wine.° Certain persons who were present related it to me. Also He healed two lepers that were seated before the Gate of Capernaum simply by touching   575
them.

SECOND NAZARENE Nay; it was two blind men that He healed at Capernaum.

FIRST NAZARENE Nay; they were lepers. But He hath healed blind people also, and He was seen on a mountain talking with angels.°   580

A SADDUCEE Angels do not exist.

A PHARISEE Angels exist, but I do not believe that this Man has talked with them.

FIRST NAZARENE He was seen by a great multitude of people talking with angels.   585

HERODIAS How these men weary me! They are ridiculous! They are altogether ridiculous! (*To the Page*) Well! my fan? (*The Page gives her the fan*) You have a dreamer's look. You must not dream. It is only sick people who dream. (*She strikes the Page with her fan*)

SECOND NAZARENE There is also the miracle of the daughter of   590
Jairus.°

FIRST NAZARENE Yea, that is sure. No man can gainsay it.

HERODIAS Those men are mad. They have looked too long on the moon. Command them to be silent.

HEROD What is this miracle of the daughter of Jairus?   595

FIRST NAZARENE The daughter of Jairus was dead. This Man raised her from the dead.

HEROD How! He raises people from the dead?

FIRST NAZARENE Yea, sire; He raiseth the dead.

HEROD I do not wish Him to do that. I forbid Him to do that. I 600
suffer no man to raise the dead. This Man must be found and
told that I forbid Him to raise the dead. Where is this Man at
present?

SECOND NAZARENE He is in every place, my lord, but it is hard to
find Him. 605

FIRST NAZARENE It is said that He is now in Samaria.°

A JEW It is easy to see that this is not Messias, if He is in Samaria.
It is not to the Samaritans that Messias shall come. The Samaritans are accursed. They bring no offerings to the Temple.

SECOND NAZARENE He left Samaria a few days since. I think that at 610
the present moment He is in the neighbourhood of Jerusalem.

FIRST NAZARENE No; He is not there. I have just come from
Jerusalem. For two months they have had no tidings of Him.

HEROD No matter! But let them find Him, and tell Him, thus saith
Herod the King, 'I will not suffer Thee to raise the dead.' To 615
change water into wine, to heal the lepers and the blind. . . . He
may do these things if He will. I say nothing against these things.
In truth I hold it a kindly deed to heal a leper. But no man shall
raise the dead. . . . It would be terrible if the dead came back.

THE VOICE OF IOKANAAN Ah! The wanton one! The harlot! Ah! the 620
daughter of Babylon with her golden eyes and her gilded eyelids!
Thus saith the Lord God, Let there come up against her a
multitude of men. Let the people take stones and stone her. . . .

HERODIAS Command him to be silent!

THE VOICE OF IOKANAAN Let the captains of the hosts pierce her 625
with their swords, let them crush her beneath their shields.

HERODIAS Nay, but it is infamous.

THE VOICE OF IOKANAAN It is thus that I will wipe out all
wickedness from the earth, and that all women shall learn not to
imitate her abominations. 630

HERODIAS You hear what he says against me? You suffer him to
revile her who is your wife!

HEROD He did not speak your name.

HERODIAS What does that matter? You know well that it is I whom
he seeks to revile. And I am your wife, am I not? 635

HEROD Of a truth, dear and noble Herodias, you are my wife, and
before that you were the wife of my brother.

HERODIAS It was thou didst snatch me from his arms.

HEROD Of a truth I was stronger than he was. . . . But let us not talk
of that matter. I do not desire to talk of it. It is the cause of the   640
terrible words that the prophet has spoken. Peradventure on
account of it a misfortune will come. Let us not speak of this
matter. Noble Herodias, we are not mindful of our guests. Fill
thou my cup, my well-beloved. Ho! fill with wine the great goblets
of silver, and the great goblets of glass. I will drink to Caesar.   645
There are Romans here, we must drink to Caesar.

ALL Caesar! Caesar!

HEROD Do you not see your daughter, how pale she is?

HERODIAS What is it to you if she be pale or not?

HEROD Never have I seen her so pale.   650

HERODIAS You must not look at her.

THE VOICE OF IOKANAAN In that day the sun shall become black
like sackcloth of hair, and the moon shall become like blood, and
the stars of the heaven shall fall upon the earth like unripe figs°
that fall from the fig-tree, and the kings of the earth shall be afraid.   655

HERODIAS Ah! ah! I should like to see that day of which he speaks,
when the moon shall become like blood, and when the stars shall
fall upon the earth like unripe figs. This prophet talks like a
drunken man, . . . but I cannot suffer the sound of his voice. I hate
his voice. Command him to be silent.   660

HEROD I will not. I cannot understand what it is that he saith, but it
may be an omen.

HERODIAS I do not believe in omens. He speaks like a drunken man.

HEROD It may be he is drunk with the wine of God.

HERODIAS What wine is that, the wine of God? From what vineyards   665
is it gathered? In what wine-press may one find it?

HEROD (*from this point he looks all the while at Salome*) Tigellinus,
when you were at Rome of late, did the Emperor speak with you
on the subject of . . . ?

TIGELLINUS On what subject, my lord?   670

HEROD On what subject? Ah! I asked you a question, did I not? I
have forgotten what I would have asked you.

HERODIAS You are looking again at my daughter. You must not look
at her. I have already said so.

HEROD You say nothing else.   675

HERODIAS I say it again.

HEROD And that restoration of the Temple about which they have
talked so much, will anything be done? They say that the veil of
the sanctuary° has disappeared, do they not?

HERODIAS It was thyself didst steal it. Thou speakest at random and 680
without wit. I will not stay here. Let us go within.

HEROD Dance for me, Salome.

HERODIAS I will not have her dance.

SALOME I have no desire to dance, Tetrarch.

HEROD Salome, daughter of Herodias, dance for me. 685

HERODIAS Peace. Let her alone.

HEROD I command thee to dance, Salome.

SALOME I will not dance, Tetrarch.

HERODIAS (*Laughing*) You see how she obeys you.

HEROD What is it to me whether she dance or not? It is nought to 690
me. Tonight I am happy. I am exceeding happy. Never have I been
so happy.

FIRST SOLDIER The Tetrarch has a sombre look. Has he not a
sombre look?

SECOND SOLDIER Yes, he has a sombre look. 695

HEROD Wherefore should I not be happy? Caesar, who is lord of the
world, Caesar, who is lord of all things, loves me well. He has just
sent me most precious gifts. Also he has promised me to summon
to Rome the King of Cappadocia, who is mine enemy. It may be
that at Rome he will crucify him, for he is able to do all things that 700
he has a mind to do. Verily, Caesar is lord. Therefore I do well to
be happy. I am very happy, never have I been so happy. There is
nothing in the world that can mar my happiness.

THE VOICE OF IOKANAAN He shall be seated on his throne. He shall
be clothed in scarlet and purple. In his hand he shall bear a golden 705
cup full of his blasphemies. And the angel of the Lord shall smite
him. He shall be eaten of worms.

HERODIAS You hear what he says about you. He says that you shall
be eaten of worms.°

HEROD It is not of me that he speaks. He speaks never against me. 710
It is of the King of Cappadocia that he speaks; the King of
Cappadocia who is mine enemy. It is he who shall be eaten of
worms. It is not I. Never has he spoken word against me, this
prophet, save that I sinned in taking to wife the wife of my brother.
It may be he is right. For, of a truth, you are sterile. 715

HERODIAS I am sterile, I? You say that, you that are ever looking
at my daughter, you that would have her dance for your
pleasure? You speak as a fool. I have borne a child. You have
gotten no child, no, not on one of your slaves. It is you who are
sterile, not I. 720

HEROD Peace, woman! I say that you are sterile. You have borne me
no child, and the prophet says that our marriage is not a true
marriage. He says that it is a marriage of incest, a marriage that
will bring evils. . . . I fear he is right; I am sure that he is right.
But it is not the hour to speak of these things. I would be happy   725
at this moment. Of a truth, I am happy. There is nothing I lack.

HERODIAS I am glad you are of so fair a humour tonight. It is not
your custom. But it is late. Let us go within. Do not forget that
we hunt at sunrise. All honours must be shown to Caesar's
ambassadors, must they not?   730

SECOND SOLDIER The Tetrarch has a sombre look.

FIRST SOLDIER Yes, he has a sombre look.

HEROD Salome, Salome, dance for me. I pray thee dance for me. I
am sad tonight. Yes, I am passing sad tonight. When I came hither
I slipped in blood, which is an ill omen; also I heard in the air a   735
beating of wings, a beating of giant wings. I cannot tell what that
may mean. . . . I am sad tonight. Therefore dance for me. Dance
for me, Salome, I beseech thee. If thou dancest for me thou mayest
ask of me what thou wilt, and I will give it thee. Yes, dance for
me, Salome, and whatsoever thou shalt ask of me I will give it thee,   740
even unto the half of my kingdom.

SALOME (rising) Will you indeed give me whatsoever I shall ask of
you, Tetrarch?

HERODIAS Do not dance, my daughter.

HEROD Whatsoever thou shalt ask of me, even unto the half of my   745
kingdom.

SALOME You swear it, Tetrarch?

HEROD I swear it, Salome.

HERODIAS Do not dance, my daughter.

SALOME By what will you swear this thing, Tetrarch?   750

HEROD By my life, by my crown, by my gods. Whatsoever thou shalt
desire I will give it thee, even to the half of my kingdom, if thou
wilt but dance for me. O Salome, Salome, dance for me!

SALOME You have sworn an oath, Tetrarch.

HEROD I have sworn an oath.   755

HERODIAS My daughter, do not dance.

HEROD Even to the half of my kingdom. Thou wilt be passing fair
as a queen, Salome, if it please thee to ask for the half of my
kingdom. Will she not be fair as a queen? Ah! it is cold here! There
is an icy wind, and I hear . . . wherefore do I hear in the air this   760
beating of wings? Ah! one might fancy a huge black bird that

hovers over the terrace. Why can I not see it, this bird? The beat
of its wings is terrible. The breath of the wind of its wings is
terrible. It is a chill wind. Nay, but it is not cold, it is hot. I am
choking. Pour water on my hands. Give me snow to eat. Loosen   765
my mantle. Quick! quick! loosen my mantle. Nay, but leave it. It
is my garland that hurts me, my garland of roses. The flowers are
like fire.° They have burned my forehead. (*He tears the wreath from
his head, and throws it on the table*) Ah! I can breathe now. How
red those petals are! They are like stains of blood on the cloth.   770
That does not matter. It is not wise to find symbols in everything
that one sees. It makes life too full of terrors. It were better to say
that stains of blood are as lovely as rose-petals. It were better far
to say that. . . . But we will not speak of this. Now I am happy. I
am passing happy. Have I not the right to be happy? Your   775
daughter is going to dance for me. Wilt thou not dance for me,
Salome? Thou hast promised to dance for me.

HERODIAS I will not have her dance.

SALOME I will dance for you, Tetrarch.

HEROD You hear what your daughter says. She is going to dance for   780
me. Thou doest well to dance for me, Salome. And when thou hast
danced for me, forget not to ask of me whatsoever thou hast a
mind to ask. Whatsoever thou shalt desire I will give it thee, even
to the half of my kingdom. I have sworn it, have I not?

SALOME Thou hast sworn it, Tetrarch.   785

HEROD And I have never failed of my word. I am not of those who
break their oaths. I know not how to lie. I am the slave of my word,
and my word is the word of a king. The King of Cappadocia had
ever a lying tongue, but he is no true king. He is a coward. Also
he owes me money that he will not repay. He has even insulted   790
my ambassadors. He has spoken words that were wounding. But
Caesar will crucify him when he comes to Rome. I know that
Caesar will crucify him. And if he crucify him not, yet will he die,
being eaten of worms. The prophet has prophesied it. Well!
Wherefore dost thou tarry, Salome?   795

SALOME I am waiting until my slaves bring perfumes to me and the
seven veils,° and take from off my feet my sandals.

> *Slaves bring perfumes and the seven veils, and take off the
> sandals of Salome*

HEROD Ah, thou art to dance with naked feet! 'Tis well! 'Tis well!
Thy little feet will be like white doves. They will be like little
white flowers that dance upon the trees. . . . No, no, she is going   800

to dance on blood! There is blood spilt on the ground. She must not dance on blood. It were an evil omen.

HERODIAS What is it to thee if she dance on blood? Thou hast waded deep enough in it.° . . .

HEROD What is it to me? Ah! look at the moon! She has become red. 805 She has become red as blood. Ah! the prophet prophesied truly. He prophesied that the moon would become as blood. Did he not prophesy it? All of ye heard him prophesying it. And now the moon has become as blood. Do ye not see it?

HERODIAS Oh yes, I see it well, and the stars are falling like unripe 810 figs, are they not? and the sun is becoming black like sackcloth of hair, and the kings of the earth are afraid. That at least one can see. The prophet is justified of his words in that at least, for truly the kings of the earth are afraid. . . . Let us go within. You are sick. They will say at Rome that you are mad. Let us go within, I tell 815 you.

THE VOICE OF IOKANAAN Who is this who cometh from Edom,° who is this who cometh from Bozra, whose raiment is dyed with purple, who shineth in the beauty of his garments, who walketh mighty in his greatness? Wherefore is thy raiment stained with 820 scarlet?

HERODIAS Let us go within. The voice of that man maddens me. I will not have my daughter dance while he is continually crying out. I will not have her dance while you look at her in this fashion. In a word, I will not have her dance. 825

HEROD Do not rise, my wife, my queen, it will avail thee nothing. I will not go within till she hath danced. Dance, Salome, dance for me.

HERODIAS Do not dance, my daughter.

SALOME I am ready, Tetrarch. 830
Salome dances the dance of the seven veils°

HEROD Ah! wonderful! wonderful! You see that she has danced for me, your daughter. Come near, Salome, come near, that I may give thee thy fee. Ah! I pay a royal price to those who dance for my pleasure. I will pay thee royally. I will give thee whatsoever thy soul desireth. What wouldst thou have? Speak. 835

SALOME (*kneeling*) I would that they presently bring me in a silver charger° . . .

HEROD (*laughing*) In a silver charger? Surely yes, in a silver charger. She is charming, is she not? What is it that thou wouldst have in a silver charger, O sweet and fair Salome, thou that art fairer than 840 all the daughters of Judaea? What wouldst thou have them bring thee in a silver charger? Tell me. Whatsoever it may be, thou shalt receive it. My treasures belong to thee. What is it that thou wouldst have, Salome?

SALOME (*rising*) The head of Iokanaan.   845

HERODIAS Ah! that is well said, my daughter.

HEROD No, no!

HERODIAS That is well said, my daughter.

HEROD No, no, Salome. It is not that thou desirest. Do not listen to thy mother's voice. She is ever giving thee evil counsel. Do not   850 heed her.

SALOME It is not my mother's voice that I heed. It is for mine own pleasure that I ask the head of Iokanaan in a silver charger. You have sworn an oath, Herod. Forget not that you have sworn an oath.   855

HEROD I know it. I have sworn an oath by my gods. I know it well. But I pray thee, Salome, ask of me something else. Ask of me the half of my kingdom, and I will give it thee. But ask not of me what thy lips have asked.

SALOME I ask of you the head of Iokanaan.   860

HEROD No, no, I will not give it thee.

SALOME You have sworn an oath, Herod.

HERODIAS Yes, you have sworn an oath. Everybody heard you. You swore it before everybody.

HEROD Peace, woman! It is not to you I speak.   865

HERODIAS My daughter has done well to ask the head of Iokanaan. He has covered me with insults. He has said unspeakable things against me. One can see that she loves her mother well. Do not yield, my daughter. He has sworn an oath, he has sworn an oath.   870

HEROD Peace! Speak not to me! . . . Salome, I pray thee be not stubborn. I have ever been kind toward thee. . . . It may be that I have loved thee too much. Therefore ask not this thing of me. This is a terrible thing, an awful thing to ask of me. Surely, I think thou art jesting. The head of a man that is cut from his body is ill to   875 look upon, is it not? It is not meet that the eyes of a virgin should look upon such a thing. What pleasure couldst thou have in it? There is no pleasure that thou couldst have in it. No, no, it is not that thou desirest. Hearken to me. I have an emerald, a great emerald and round, that the minion of Caesar has sent unto me.   880 When thou lookest through this emerald thou canst see that which

86

passeth afar off. Caesar himself carries such an emerald when he goes to the circus. But my emerald is the larger. I know well that it is the larger. It is the largest emerald in the whole world. Thou wilt take that, wilt thou not? Ask it of me and I will give it thee. 885

SALOME I demand the head of Iokanaan.

HEROD Thou art not listening. Thou art not listening. Suffer me to speak, Salome.

SALOME The head of Iokanaan!

HEROD No, no, thou wouldst not have that. Thou sayest that but to 890
trouble me, because that I have looked at thee and ceased not this night. It is true, I have looked at thee and ceased not this night. Thy beauty has troubled me. Thy beauty has grievously troubled me, and I have looked at thee overmuch. Nay, but I will look at thee no more. One should not look at anything. Neither at things, 895
nor at people should one look. Only in mirrors is it well to look, for mirrors do but show us masks. Oh! oh! bring wine! I thirst. . . . Salome, Salome, let us be as friends. Bethink thee. . . . Ah! what would I say? What was't? Ah! I remember it! . . . Salome,—nay but come nearer to me; I fear thou wilt not hear my 900
words,—Salome, thou knowest my white peacocks, my beautiful white peacocks, that walk in the garden between the myrtles and the tall cypress-trees. Their beaks are gilded with gold and the grains that they eat are smeared with gold, and their feet are stained with purple. When they cry out the rain comes, and the 905
moon shows herself in the heavens when they spread their tails. Two by two they walk between the cypress-trees and the black myrtles, and each has a slave to tend it. Sometimes they fly across the trees, and anon they couch in the grass, and round the pools of the water. There are not in all the world birds so wonderful. I 910
know that Caesar himself has no birds so fair as my birds. I will give thee fifty of my peacocks. They will follow thee whithersoever thou goest, and in the midst of them thou wilt be like unto the moon in the midst of a great white cloud. . . . I will give them to thee, all. I have but a hundred, and in the whole world there is no 915
king who has peacocks like unto my peacocks. But I will give them all to thee. Only thou must loose me from my oath, and must not ask of me that which thy lips have asked of me.

He empties the cup of wine

SALOME Give me the head of Iokanaan!

HERODIAS Well said, my daughter! As for you, you are ridiculous 920
with your peacocks.

HEROD Peace! you are always crying out. You cry out like a beast of
prey. You must not cry in such fashion. Your voice wearies me.
Peace, I tell you! . . . Salome, think on what thou art doing. It may
be that this man comes from God. He is a holy man. The finger   925
of God has touched him. God has put terrible words into his
mouth. In the palace, as in the desert, God is ever with him. . . .
It may be that He is, at least. One cannot tell, but it is possible
that God is with him and for him. If he die also, peradventure
some evil may befall me. Verily, he has said that evil will befall   930
someone on the day whereon he dies. On whom should it fall if it
fall not on me? Remember, I slipped in blood when I came hither.
Also did I not hear a beating of wings in the air, a beating of vast
wings? These are ill omens. And there were other things. I am sure
that there were other things, though I saw them not. Thou wouldst   935
not that some evil should befall me, Salome? Listen to me again.

SALOME Give me the head of Iokanaan!

HEROD Ah! thou art not listening to me. Be calm. As for me, am I
not calm? I am altogether calm. Listen. I have jewels hidden in this
place—jewels that thy mother even has never seen; jewels that are   940
marvellous to look at. I have a collar of pearls, set in four rows.
They are like unto moons chained with rays of silver. They are
even as half a hundred moons caught in a golden net. On the ivory
breast of a queen they have rested. Thou shalt be as fair as a queen
when thou wearest them. I have amethysts of two kinds; one that   945
is black like wine, and one that is red like wine that one has
coloured with water. I have topazes yellow as are the eyes of tigers,
and topazes that are pink as the eyes of a wood-pigeon, and green
topazes that are as the eyes of cats. I have opals that burn always,
with a flame that is cold as ice, opals that make sad men's minds,   950
and are afraid of the shadows. I have onyxes like the eyeballs of a
dead woman. I have moonstones that change when the moon
changes, and are wan when they see the sun. I have sapphires big
like eggs, and as blue as blue flowers. The sea wanders within
them, and the moon comes never to trouble the blue of their   955
waves. I have chrysolites° and beryls, and chrysoprases and rubies;
I have sardonyx and hyacinth stones, and stones of chalcedony, and
I will give them all unto thee, all, and other things will I add to
them. The King of the Indies has but even now sent me four fans
fashioned from the feathers of parrots, and the King of Numidia   960
a garment of ostrich feathers. I have a crystal, into which it is not
lawful for a woman to look, nor may young men behold it until

88

they have been beaten with rods. In a coffer of nacre I have three
wondrous turquoises. He who wears them on his forehead can
imagine things which are not, and he who carries them in his hand   965
can turn the fruitful woman into a woman that is barren. These
are great treasures. They are treasures above all price. But this is
not all. In an ebony coffer I have two cups of amber that are like
apples of pure gold. If an enemy pour poison into these cups they
become like apples of silver. In a coffer incrusted with amber I   970
have sandals incrusted with glass. I have mantles that have been
brought from the land of the Seres,° and bracelets decked about
with carbuncles and with jade that come from the city of Eu-
phrates. . . . What desirest thou more than this, Salome? Tell me
the thing that thou desirest, and I will give it thee. All that thou   975
askest I will give thee, save one thing only. I will give thee all that
is mine, save only the life of one man. I will give thee the mantle
of the high priest. I will give thee the veil of the sanctuary.°

THE JEWS Oh! oh!

SALOME Give me the head of Iokanaan!   980

HEROD (*sinking back in his seat*) Let her be given what she asks! Of
a truth she is her mother's child! (*The first Soldier approaches.
Herodias draws from the hand of the Tetrarch the ring of death, and
gives it to the Soldier, who straightway bears it to the Executioner. The
Executioner looks scared*) Who has taken my ring? There was a ring
on my right hand. Who has drunk my wine? There was wine in
my cup. It was full of wine. Someone has drunk it! Oh! surely   985
some evil will befall some one. (*The Executioner goes down into the
cistern*) Ah! wherefore did I give my oath? Hereafter let no king
swear an oath. If he keep it not, it is terrible, and if he keep it, it
is terrible also.

HERODIAS My daughter has done well.   990

HEROD I am sure that some misfortune will happen.

SALOME (*She leans over the cistern and listens*) There is no sound. I
hear nothing. Why does he not cry out, this man? Ah! if any man
sought to kill me, I would cry out, I would struggle, I would not
suffer. . . . Strike, strike, Naaman, strike, I tell you. . . . No, I hear   995
nothing. There is a silence, a terrible silence. Ah! something has
fallen upon the ground. I heard something fall. It was the sword
of the executioner. He is afraid, this slave. He has dropped his
sword. He dares not kill him. He is a coward, this slave! Let
soldiers be sent. (*She sees the Page of Herodias and addresses him*) 1000
Come hither. Thou wert the friend of him who is dead, wert thou

not? Well, I tell thee, there are not dead men enough. Go to the soldiers and bid them go down and bring me the thing I ask, the thing the Tetrarch has promised me, the thing that is mine. (*The Page recoils. She turns to the soldiers*) Hither, ye soldiers. Get ye 1005 down into this cistern and bring me the head of this man. Tetrarch, Tetrarch, command your soldiers that they bring me the head of Iokanaan.

> *A huge black arm, the arm of the Executioner, comes forth from the cistern, bearing on a silver shield the head of Iokanaan. Salome seizes it. Herod hides his face with his cloak. Herodias smiles and fans herself. The Nazarenes fall on their knees and begin to pray*

SALOME Ah! thou wouldst not suffer me to kiss thy mouth, Iokanaan. Well! I will kiss it now. I will bite it with my teeth as one bites a 1010 ripe fruit. Yes, I will kiss thy mouth, Iokanaan. I said it; did I not say it? I said it. Ah! I will kiss it now. . . . But wherefore dost thou not look at me, Iokanaan? Thine eyes that were so terrible, so full of rage and scorn, are shut now. Wherefore are they shut? Open thine eyes! Lift up thine eyelids, Iokanaan! Wherefore dost thou 1015 not look at me? Art thou afraid of me, Iokanaan, that thou wilt not look at me? . . . And thy tongue, that was like a red snake darting poison, it moves no more, it speaks no words, Iokanaan, that scarlet viper that spat its venom upon me. It is strange, is it not? How is it that the red viper stirs no longer? . . . Thou wouldst have none 1020 of me, Iokanaan. Thou rejectedst me. Thou didst speak evil words against me. Thou didst bear thyself toward me as to a harlot, as to a woman that is a wanton, to me, Salome, daughter of Herodias, Princess of Judaea! Well, I still live, but thou art dead, and thy head belongs to me. I can do with it what I will. I can throw it to 1025 the dogs and to the birds of the air. That which the dogs leave, the birds of the air shall devour. . . . Ah, Iokanaan, Iokanaan, thou wert the man that I loved alone among men! All other men were hateful to me. But thou wert beautiful! Thy body was a column of ivory set upon feet of silver. It was a garden full of doves and lilies 1030 of silver. It was a tower of silver decked with shields of ivory. There was nothing in the world so white as thy body. There was nothing in the world so black as thy hair. In the whole world there was nothing so red as thy mouth. Thy voice was a censer that scattered strange perfumes, and when I looked on thee I heard a 1035 strange music. Ah! wherefore didst thou not look at me, Iokanaan? With the cloak of thine hands, and with the cloak of thy blasphemies thou didst hide thy face. Thou didst put upon thine eyes the covering of him who would see his God. Well, thou hast seen thy God, Iokanaan, but me, me, thou didst never see. If thou hadst seen me thou hadst loved me. I saw thee, and I loved thee. Oh, how I loved thee! I love thee yet, Iokanaan. I love only thee. . . . I am athirst for thy beauty; I am hungry for thy body; and neither wine nor apples can appease my desire. What shall I do now, Iokanaan? Neither the floods nor the great waters can quench my passion. I was a princess, and thou didst scorn me. I was a virgin, and thou didst take my virginity from me. I was chaste, and thou didst fill my veins with fire. . . . Ah! ah! wherefore didst thou not look at me? If thou hadst looked at me thou hadst loved me. Well I know that thou wouldst have loved me, and the mystery of Love is greater than the mystery of Death.

HEROD She is monstrous, thy daughter; I tell thee she is monstrous. In truth, what she has done is a great crime. I am sure that it is a crime against some unknown God.

HERODIAS I am well pleased with my daughter.° She has done well. And I would stay here now.

HEROD (*rising*) Ah! There speaks my brother's wife! Come! I will not stay in this place. Come, I tell thee. Surely some terrible thing will befall. Manasseh, Issachar, Ozias, put out the torches. I will not look at things, I will not suffer things to look at me. Put out the torches! Hide the moon! Hide the stars! Let us hide ourselves in our palace, Herodias. I begin to be afraid.

The slaves put out the torches. The stars disappear. A great cloud crosses the moon and conceals it completely. The stage becomes quite dark.° The Tetrarch begins to climb the staircase

THE VOICE OF SALOME Ah! I have kissed thy mouth, Iokanaan, I have kissed thy mouth. There was a bitter taste on thy lips. Was it the taste of blood? . . . Nay; but perchance it was the taste of love. . . . They say that love hath a bitter taste. . . . But what matter? what matter? I have kissed thy mouth, Iokanaan, I have kissed thy mouth.

A ray of moonlight falls on Salome and illumines her

HEROD (*turning round and seeing Salome*) Kill that woman!°

The soldiers rush forward and crush beneath their shields Salome, daughter of Herodias, Princess of Judaea.

CURTAIN.

A WOMAN OF NO
IMPORTANCE

To

GLADYS

Countess de Grey

[Marchioness of Ripon]

THE PERSONS OF THE PLAY

The play was first staged at the Theatre Royal, Haymarket, London, 19 April 1893.

Lord Illingworth	*Mr Tree*
Sir John Pontefract	*Mr Holman Clark*
Lord Alfred Rufford	*Mr Lawford*
Mr Kelvil, MP	*Mr Allan*
The Ven. James Daubeny, DD (Rector of Wrockley)	*Mr Kemble*
Gerald Arbuthnot	*Mr Fred Terry*
Farquhar (Butler)	*Mr Hay*
Francis (Footman)	*Mr Montagu*
Lady Hunstanton	*Miss Rose Leclercq*
Lady Caroline Pontefract	*Miss Le Thière*
Lady Stutfield	*Miss Horlock*
Mrs Allonby	*Mrs Tree*
Hester Worsley	*Miss Julia Neilson*
Alice (Maid)	*Miss Kelly*
Mrs Arbuthnot	*Mrs Bernard Beere*

THE SCENES OF THE PLAY

Act 1
The terrace at Hunstanton Chase

Act 2
The drawing-room at Hunstanton Chase

Act 3
The hall at Hunstanton Chase

Act 4
Sitting-room in Mrs Arbuthnot's house at Wrockley

Time
The Present

Place
The Shires

The action of the play takes place within twenty-four hours

First Act

Scene: Lawn in front of the terrace at Hunstanton. Sir John and Lady Caroline Pontefract, Miss Worsley, on chairs under large yew tree

LADY CAROLINE I believe this is the first English country house you have stayed at, Miss Worsley?

HESTER Yes, Lady Caroline.

LADY CAROLINE You have no country houses, I am told, in America?

HESTER We have not many.

LADY CAROLINE Have you any country? What we should call country?

HESTER (*smiling*) We have the largest country in the world, Lady Caroline. They used to tell us at school that some of our states are as big as France and England put together.

LADY CAROLINE Ah! you must find it very draughty, I should fancy. (*To Sir John*) John, you should have your muffler. What is the use of my always knitting mufflers for you if you won't wear them?

SIR JOHN I am quite warm, Caroline, I assure you.

LADY CAROLINE I think not, John. Well, you couldn't come to a more charming place than this, Miss Worsley, though the house is excessively damp, quite unpardonably damp, and dear Lady Hunstanton is sometimes a little lax° about the people she asks down here. (*To Sir John*) Jane mixes too much. Lord Illingworth, of course, is a man of high distinction. It is a privilege to meet him. And that member of Parliament, Mr Kettle—

SIR JOHN Kelvil, my love, Kelvil.

LADY CAROLINE He must be quite respectable. One° has never heard his name before in the whole course of one's life, which speaks volumes for a man, nowadays. But Mrs Allonby is hardly a very suitable person.

HESTER I dislike Mrs Allonby.° I dislike her more than I can say.

LADY CAROLINE I am not sure, Miss Worsley, that foreigners like yourself should cultivate likes or dislikes about the people they are invited to meet. Mrs Allonby is very well born. She is a niece of Lord Brancaster's. It is said, of course, that she ran away twice before she was married. But you know how unfair people often are. I myself don't believe she ran away more than once.

HESTER Mr Arbuthnot is very charming.   35

LADY CAROLINE Ah, yes! the young man who has a post in a bank.
Lady Hunstanton is most kind in asking him here, and Lord
Illingworth seems to have taken quite a fancy to him. I am not
sure, however, that Jane is right in taking him out of his position.
In my young days, Miss Worsley, one never met anyone in society   40
who worked for their living.° It was not considered the thing.

HESTER In America those are the people we respect most.

LADY CAROLINE I have no doubt of it.

HESTER Mr Arbuthnot has a beautiful nature! He is so simple, so
sincere. He has one of the most beautiful natures I have ever come   45
across. It is privilege to meet *him*.

LADY CAROLINE It is not customary in England, Miss Worsley, for
a young lady to speak with such enthusiasm of any person of the
opposite sex. Englishwomen conceal their feelings till after they are
married. They show them then.   50

HESTER Do you, in England, allow no friendship to exist between a
young man and a young girl?

> *Enter Lady Hunstanton, followed by Footman° with shawls and
> a cushion*

LADY CAROLINE We think it very inadvisable. Jane, I was just saying
what a pleasant party you have asked us to meet. You have a
wonderful power of selection. It is quite a gift.   55

LADY HUNSTANTON Dear Caroline, how kind of you! I think we all
do fit in very nicely together. And I hope our charming American
visitor will carry back pleasant recollections of our English country
life. (*To Footman*) The cushion, there, Francis. And my shawl.
The Shetland. Get the Shetland.°   60

> *Exit Footman for shawl. Enter Gerald Arbuthnot*

GERALD Lady Hunstanton, I have such good news to tell you. Lord
Illingworth has just offered to make me his secretary.

LADY HUNSTANTON His secretary? That is good news indeed,
Gerald. It means a very brilliant future in store for you. Your dear
mother will be delighted. I really must try and induce her to come   65
up here tonight. Do you think she would, Gerald? I know how
difficult it is to get her to go anywhere.

GERALD Oh! I am sure she would, Lady Hunstanton, if she knew
Lord Illingworth had made me such an offer.

> *Enter Footman with shawl*

LADY HUNSTANTON I will write and tell her about it, and ask her   70
to come up and meet him. (*To Footman*) Just wait, Francis.

Writes letter

LADY CAROLINE That is a very wonderful opening for so young a man as you are, Mr Arbuthnot.

GERALD It is indeed, Lady Caroline. I trust I shall be able to show myself worthy of it. 75

LADY CAROLINE I trust so.

GERALD (*to Hester*) You have not congratulated me yet, Miss Worsley.

HESTER Are you very pleased about it?°

GERALD Of course I am. It means everything to me—things that 80 were out of the reach of hope before may be within hope's reach now.

HESTER Nothing should be out of the reach of hope. Life is a hope.

LADY HUNSTANTON I fancy, Caroline, that Diplomacy is what Lord 85 Illingworth is aiming at. I heard that he was offered Vienna.° But that may not be true.

LDY CAROLINE I don't think that England should be repre-sented abroad by an unmarried man, Jane. It might lead to complications. 90

LADY HUNSTANTON You are too nervous, Caroline. Believe me, you are too nervous. Besides, Lord Illingworth may marry any day. I was in hopes he would have married Lady Kelso. But I believe he said her family was too large. Or was it her feet? I forget which. I regret it very much. She was made to be an ambassador's 95 wife.

LADY CAROLINE She certainly has a wonderful faculty of remember-ing people's names, and forgetting their faces.

LADY HUNSTANTON Well, that is very natural, Caroline, is it not? (*To Footman*) Tell Henry to wait for an answer. I have written a 100 line to your dear mother, Gerald, to tell her your good news, and to say she really must come to dinner.

Exit Footman

GERALD That is awfully kind of you, Lady Hunstanton. (*To Hester*) Will you come for a stroll, Miss Worsley?

HESTER With pleasure. 105

Exit with Gerald

LADY HUNSTANTON I am very much gratified at Gerald Arbuth-not's good fortune. He is quite a *protégé* of mine. And I am particularly pleased that Lord Illingworth should have made the offer of his own accord without my suggesting anything. Nobody

likes to be asked favours. I remember poor Charlotte Pagden   110
making herself quite unpopular one season, because she had a
French governess she wanted to recommend to everyone.

LADY CAROLINE I saw the governess, Jane. Lady Pagden sent her to
me. It was before Eleanor came out.° She was far too good-looking
to be in any respectable household. I don't wonder Lady Pagden   115
was so anxious to get rid of her.

LADY HUNSTANTON Ah, that explains it.

LADY CAROLINE John, the grass is too damp for you. You had better
go and put on your overshoes at once.

SIR JOHN I am quite comfortable, Caroline, I assure you.   120

LADY CAROLINE You must allow me to be the best judge of that,
John. Pray do as I tell you.
    Sir John gets up and goes off

LADY HUNSTANTON You spoil him, Caroline, you do indeed!
    Enter Mrs Allonby° and Lady Stutfield
    (*To Mrs Allonby*) Well, dear, I hope you like the park. It is said
to be well timbered.   125

MRS ALLONBY The trees are wonderful, Lady Hunstanton.

LADY STUTFIELD Quite, quite wonderful.°

MRS ALLONBY But somehow, I feel sure that if I lived in the country
for six months, I should become so unsophisticated that no one
would take the slightest notice of me.   130

LADY HUNSTANTON I assure you, dear, that the country has not that
effect at all. Why, it was from Melthorpe, which is only two miles
from here, that Lady Belton eloped with Lord Fethersdale. I
remember the occurrence perfectly. Poor Lord Belton died three
days afterwards of joy, or gout. I forget which. We had a large   135
party staying here at the time, so we were all very much interested
in the whole affair.

MRS ALLONBY I think to elope is cowardly. It's running away from
danger. And danger has become so rare in modern life.

LADY CAROLINE As far as I can make out, the young women° of the   140
present day seem to make it the sole object of their lives to be
always playing with fire.

MRS ALLONBY The one advantage of playing with fire, Lady
Caroline, is that one never gets even singed. It is the people who
don't know how to play with it who get burned up.   145

LADY STUTFIELD Yes; I see that. It is very, very helpful.

LADY HUNSTANTON I don't know how the world would get on with
such a theory as that, dear Mrs Allonby.

LADY STUTFIELD Ah! The world was made for men and not for women.   150

MRS ALLONBY Oh, don't say that, Lady Stutfield. We have a much better time than they have. There are far more things forbidden to us than are forbidden to them.

LADY STUTFIELD Yes; that is quite, quite true. I had not thought of that.   155

    Enter Sir John and Mr Kelvil

LADY HUNSTANTON Well, Mr Kelvil, have you got through your work?

KELVIL I have finished my writing for the day, Lady Hunstanton. It has been an arduous task. The demands on the time of a public man are very heavy nowadays, very heavy indeed. And I don't 160 think they meet with adequate recognition.

LADY CAROLINE John, have you got your overshoes on?

SIR JOHN Yes, my love.

LADY CAROLINE I think you had better come over here, John. It is more sheltered.   165

SIR JOHN I am quite comfortable, Caroline.

LADY CAROLINE I think not, John.° You had better sit beside me.

    Sir John rises and goes across

LADY STUTFIELD And what have you been writing about this morning, Mr Kelvil?

KELVIL On the usual subject, Lady Stutfield. On Purity.   170

LADY STUTFIELD That must be such a very, very interesting thing to write about.

KELVIL It is the one subject of really national importance nowadays, Lady Stutfield. I purpose addressing my constituents on the question before Parliament meets. I find that the poorer classes 175 of this country display a marked desire for a higher ethical standard.

LADY STUTFIELD How quite, quite nice of them.

LADY CAROLINE Are you in favour of women taking part in politics, Mr Kettle?   180

SIR JOHN Kelvil, my love, Kelvil.

KELVIL The growing influence of women is the one reassuring thing in our political life, Lady Caroline. Women are always on the side of morality, public and private.

LADY STUTFIELD It is so very, very gratifying to hear you say that. 185

LADY HUNSTANTON Ah, yes!—the moral qualities in women—that is the important thing. I am afraid, Caroline, that dear Lord

Illingworth doesn't value the moral qualities in women as much as he should.

Enter Lord Illingworth°

LADY STUTFIELD The world says that Lord Illingworth is very, very   190
wicked.

LORD ILLINGWORTH But what world says that, Lady Stutfield? It must be the next world. This world and I are on excellent terms.

Sits down beside Mrs Allonby

LADY STUTFIELD Everyone *I* know says you are very, very wicked.   195

LORD ILLINGWORTH It is perfectly monstrous the way people go about, nowadays, saying things against one behind one's back that are absolutely and entirely true.

LADY HUNSTANTON Dear Lord Illingworth is quite hopeless, Lady Stutfield. I have given up trying to reform him. It would take a   200
Public Company with a Board of Directors and a paid Secretary to do that. But you have the secretary already, Lord Illingworth, haven't you? Gerald Arbuthnot has told us of his good fortune; it is really most kind of you.

LORD ILLINGWORTH Oh, don't say that, Lady Hunstanton. Kind is   205
a dreadful word. I took a great fancy to young Arbuthnot the moment I met him, and he'll be of considerable use to me in something I am foolish enough to think of doing.

LADY HUNSTANTON He is an admirable young man. And his mother is one of my dearest friends. He has just gone for a walk   210
with our pretty American. She is very pretty, is she not?

LADY CAROLINE Far too pretty. These American girls° carry off all the good matches. Why can't they stay in their own country? They are always telling us it is the Paradise of women.

LORD ILLINGWORTH It is, Lady Caroline. That is why, like Eve,   215
they are so extremely anxious to get out of it.

LADY CAROLINE Who are Miss Worsley's parents?

LORD ILLINGWORTH American women are wonderfully clever in concealing their parents.

LADY HUNSTANTON My dear Lord Illingworth, what do you mean?   220
Miss Worsley, Caroline, is an orphan.° Her father was a very wealthy millionaire or philanthropist, or both, I believe, who entertained my son quite hospitably, when he visited Boston. I don't know how he made his money, originally.

KELVIL I fancy in American dry goods.°   225

LADY HUNSTANTON What are American dry goods?

LORD ILLINGWORTH American novels.

LADY HUNSTANTON How very singular! . . . Well, from whatever source her large fortune came, I have a great esteem for Miss Worsley. She dresses exceedingly well. All Americans do dress well. They get their clothes in Paris. 230

MRS ALLONBY They say, Lady Hunstanton, that when good Americans die they go to Paris.

LADY HUNSTANTON Indeed? And when bad Americans die, where do they go to? 235

LORD ILLINGWORTH Oh, they go to America.

KELVIL I am afraid you don't appreciate America, Lord Illingworth. It is a very remarkable country, especially considering its youth.

LORD ILLINGWORTH The youth of America is their oldest tradition. It has been going on now for three hundred years. To hear them 240 talk one would imagine they were in their first childhood. As far as civilization goes they are in their second.

KELVIL There is undoubtedly a great deal of corruption in American politics. I suppose you allude to that?

LORD ILLINGWORTH I wonder. 245

LADY HUNSTANTON Politics are in a sad way everywhere, I am told. They certainly are in England. Dear Mr Cardew is ruining the country. I wonder Mrs Cardew allows him. I am sure, Lord Illingworth, you don't think that uneducated people should be allowed to have votes? 250

LORD ILLINGWORTH I think they are the only people who should.

KELVIL Do you take no side then in modern politics, Lord Illingworth?

LORD ILLINGWORTH One should never take sides in anything, Mr Kelvil. Taking sides is the beginning of sincerity, and earnestness follows shortly afterwards, and the human being becomes a bore. 255 However, the House of Commons really does very little harm. You can't make people good by Act of Parliament,—that is something.

KELVIL You cannot deny that the House of Commons has always shown great sympathy with the sufferings of the poor.

LORD ILLINGWORTH That is its special vice. That is the special vice 260 of the age. One should sympathize with the joy, the beauty, the colour of life. The less said about life's sores the better, Mr Kelvil.

KELVIL Still our East End° is a very important problem.

LORD ILLINGWORTH Quite so. It is the problem of slavery. And we are trying to solve it by amusing the slaves. 265

LADY HUNSTANTON Certainly, a great deal may be done by means of cheap entertainments, as you say, Lord Illingworth. Dear Dr

Daubeny, our rector here, provides, with the assistance of his curates, really admirable recreations for the poor during the winter. And much good may be done by means of a magic lantern, or a missionary, or some popular amusement of that kind.   270

LADY CAROLINE I am not at all in favour of amusements for the poor, Jane. Blankets and coals° are sufficient. There is too much love of pleasure amongst the upper classes as it is. Health is what we want in modern life. The tone is not healthy, not healthy at all.   275

KELVIL You are quite right, Lady Caroline.

LADY CAROLINE I believe I am usually right.

MRS ALLONBY Horrid word 'health'.

LORD ILLINGWORTH Silliest word in our language, and one knows so well the popular idea of health. The English country gentleman   280
galloping after a fox—the unspeakable in full pursuit of the uneatable.°

KELVIL May I ask, Lord Illingworth, if you regard the House of Lords as a better institution than the House of Commons?

LORD ILLINGWORTH A much better institution, of course. We in   285
the House of Lords are never in touch with public opinion. That makes us a civilized body.

KELVIL Are you serious in putting forward such a view?

LORD ILLINGWORTH Quite serious, Mr Kelvil. (*To Mrs Allonby*) Vulgar habit° that is people have nowadays of asking one, after one   290
has given them an idea, whether one is serious or not. Nothing is serious except passion. The intellect is not a serious thing, and never has been. It is an instrument on which one plays, that is all. The only serious form of intellect I know is the British intellect. And on the British intellect the illiterates play the drum.   295

LADY HUNSTANTON What are you saying, Lord Illingworth, about the drum?

LORD ILLINGWORTH I was merely talking to Mrs Allonby about the leading articles in the London newspapers.

LADY HUNSTANTON But do you believe all that is written in the   300
newspapers?

LORD ILLINGWORTH I do. Nowadays it is only the unreadable that occurs.

Rises with Mrs Allonby

LADY HUNSTANTON Are you going, Mrs Allonby?

MRS ALLONBY Just as far as the conservatory. Lord Illingworth told   305
me this morning that there was an orchid° there as beautiful as the seven deadly sins.

LADY HUNSTANTON My dear, I hope there is nothing of the kind, I will certainly speak to the gardener.

Exit Mrs Allonby and Lord Illingworth

LADY CAROLINE Remarkable type, Mrs Allonby.   310

LADY HUNSTANTON She lets her clever tongue run away with her sometimes.

LADY CAROLINE Is that the only thing, Jane, Mrs Allonby allows to run away with her?

LADY HUNSTANTON I hope so, Caroline, I am sure.   315

Enter Lord Alfred

Dear Lord Alfred, do join us.

Lord Alfred sits down beside Lady Stutfield

LADY CAROLINE You believe good of everyone, Jane. It is a great fault.

LADY STUTFIELD Do you really, really think, Lady Caroline, that one should believe evil of everyone?   320

LADY CAROLINE I think it is much safer to do so, Lady Stutfield. Until, of course, people are found out to be good. But that requires a great deal of investigation nowadays.

LADY STUTFIELD But there is so much unkind scandal in modern life.

LADY CAROLINE Lord Illingworth remarked to me last night at   325
dinner that the basis of every scandal is an absolutely immoral certainty.

KELVIL Lord Illingworth is, of course, a very brilliant man, but he seems to me to be lacking in that fine faith in the nobility and purity of life which is so important in this century.   330

LADY STUTFIELD Yes, quite, quite important, is it not?

KELVIL He gives me the impression of a man who does not appreciate the beauty of our English home-life.° I would say that he was tainted with foreign ideas on the subject.

LADY STUTFIELD There is nothing, nothing like the beauty of home   335
life, is there?

KELVIL It is the mainstay of our moral system in England, Lady Stutfield. Without it we would become like our neighbours.

LADY STUTFIELD That would be so, so sad, would it not?

KELVIL I am afraid, too, that Lord Illingworth regards woman   340
simply as a toy. Now, I have never regarded woman as a toy. Woman is the intellectual helpmeet of man in public as in private life. Without her we should forget the true ideals.

Sits down beside Lady Stutfield

LADY STUTFIELD I am so very, very glad to hear you say that.

LADY CAROLINE You a married man, Mr Kettle?°   345

SIR JOHN Kelvil, dear, Kelvil.

KELVIL I am married, Lady Caroline.

LADY CAROLINE Family?

KELVIL Yes.

LADY CAROLINE How many?   350

KELVIL Eight.

  Lady Stutfield turns her attention to Lord Alfred

LADY CAROLINE Mrs Kettle and the children are, I suppose, at the
 seaside?

  Sir John shrugs his shoulders

KELVIL My wife is at the seaside with the children, Lady Caroline.

LADY CAROLINE You will join them later on, no doubt?

KELVIL If my public engagements permit me.   355

LADY CAROLINE Your public life must be a great source of gratifi-
 cation to Mrs Kettle.

SIR JOHN Kelvil, my love, Kelvil.

LADY STUTFIELD (*to Lord Alfred*) How very, very charming those
 gold-tipped cigarettes° of yours are, Lord Alfred.   360

LORD ALFRED They are awfully expensive. I can only afford them
 when I'm in debt.

LADY STUTFIELD It must be terribly, terribly distressing to be in
 debt.

LORD ALFRED One must have some occupation nowadays. If I 365
 hadn't my debts I shouldn't have anything to think about. All the
 chaps I know are in debt.

LADY STUTFIELD But don't the people to whom you owe the money
 give you a great, great deal of annoyance?

  Enter Footman [with a letter]

LORD ALFRED Oh, no, they write; I don't.   370

LADY STUTFIELD How very, very strange.

LADY HUNSTANTON Ah, here is a letter, Caroline, from dear Mrs
 Arbuthnot. She won't dine. I am so sorry. But she will come in
 the evening. I am very pleased indeed. She is one of the sweetest
 of women. Writes a beautiful hand, too, so large, so firm. 375

  Hands letter to Lady Caroline

LADY CAROLINE (*looking at it*) A little lacking in femininity, Jane.
 Femininity is the quality I admire most in women.

LADY HUNSTANTON (*taking back letter and leaving it on table*) Oh!
 she is very feminine, Caroline, and so good too. You should hear
 what the Archdeacon says of her. He regards her as his right   380
 hand in the parish. (*Footman speaks to her*) In the Yellow

Drawing-room.° Shall we all go in? Lady Stutfield, shall we go in
to tea?

LADY STUTFIELD With pleasure, Lady Hunstanton.

*They rise and proceed to go off. Sir John offers to carry Lady
Stutfield's cloak*

LADY CAROLINE John! If you would allow your nephew° to look   385
after Lady Stutfield's cloak, you might help me with my work-
basket.

Enter Lord Illingworth and Mrs Allonby

SIR JOHN Certainly, my love.

Exeunt°

MRS ALLONBY Curious thing, plain women are always jealous of
their husbands, beautiful women never are!   390

LORD ILLINGWORTH Beautiful women never have time. They are
always so occupied in being jealous of other people's husbands.

MRS ALLONBY I should have thought Lady Caroline would have
grown tired of conjugal anxiety by this time! Sir John is her fourth!

LORD ILLINGWORTH So much marriage is certainly not becoming.   395
Twenty years of romance make a woman look like a ruin; but
twenty years of marriage make her something like a public building.

MRS ALLONBY Twenty years of romance! Is there such a thing?

LORD ILLINGWORTH Not in our day. Women have become too
brilliant. Nothing spoils a romance so much as a sense of humour   400
in the woman.

MRS ALLONBY Or the want of it in the man.

LORD ILLINGWORTH You are quite right. In a Temple everyone
should be serious, except the thing that is worshipped.

MRS ALLONBY And that should be man?   405

LORD ILLINGWORTH Women kneel so gracefully; men don't.

MRS ALLONBY You are thinking of Lady Stutfield!

LORD ILLINGWORTH I assure you I have not thought of Lady
Stutfield for the last quarter of an hour.

MRS ALLONBY Is she such a mystery?   410

LORD ILLINGWORTH She is more than a mystery—she is a mood.

MRS ALLONBY Moods don't last.

LORD ILLINGWORTH It is their chief charm.

Enter Hester and Gerald

GERALD Lord Illingworth, everyone° has been congratulating me,
Lady Hunstanton and Lady Caroline, and . . . everyone. I hope I   415
shall make a good secretary.

LORD ILLINGWORTH You will be the pattern secretary, Gerald.

(Talks to him) [apart]

MRS ALLONBY You enjoy country life, Miss Worsley?

HESTER Very much indeed.

MRS ALLONBY Don't find yourself longing for a London dinner-   420
party?

HESTER I dislike London dinner-parties.

MRS ALLONBY I adore them. The clever people never listen, and the
stupid people never talk.

HESTER I think the stupid people talk a great deal.   425

MRS ALLONBY Ah, I never listen!

LORD ILLINGWORTH My dear boy, if I didn't like you I wouldn't
have made you the offer. It is because I like you so much that I
want to have you with me.

      Exit Hester with Gerald

Charming fellow, Gerald Arbuthnot!   430

MRS ALLONBY He is very nice; very nice indeed. But I can't stand
the American young lady.

LORD ILLINGWORTH Why?

MRS ALLONBY She told me yesterday, and in quite a loud voice too,
that she was only eighteen. It was most annoying.   435

LORD ILLINGWORTH One should never trust a woman who tells one
her real age. A woman who would tell one that would tell one
anything.

MRS ALLONBY She is a Puritan besides—

LORD ILLINGWORTH Ah, that is inexcusable. I don't mind plain   440
women being Puritans. It is the only excuse they have for being
plain. But she is decidedly pretty.° I admire her immensely.

      Looks steadfastly at Mrs Allonby

MRS ALLONBY What a thoroughly bad man you must be!

LORD ILLINGWORTH What do you call a bad man?

MRS ALLONBY The sort of man who admires innocence.   445

LORD ILLINGWORTH And a bad woman?

MRS ALLONBY Oh! the sort of woman a man never gets tired of.

LORD ILLINGWORTH You are severe—on yourself.

MRS ALLONBY Define us as a sex.

LORD ILLINGWORTH Sphinxes without secrets.   450

MRS ALLONBY Does that include the Puritan women?

LORD ILLINGWORTH Do you know, I don't believe in the existence
of Puritan women? I don't think there is a woman in the world
who would not be a little flattered if one made love to her. It is
that which makes women so irresistibly adorable.   455

MRS ALLONBY You think there is no woman in the world who would object to being kissed?

LORD ILLINGWORTH Very few.

MRS ALLONBY Miss Worsley would not let you kiss her.

LORD ILLINGWORTH Are you sure?   460

MRS ALLONBY Quite.

LORD ILLINGWORTH What do you think she'd do if I kissed her?

MRS ALLONBY Either marry you, or strike you across the face with her glove. What would you do if she struck you across the face with her glove?   465

LORD ILLINGWORTH Fall in love with her, probably.

MRS ALLONBY Then it is lucky you are not going to kiss her!

LORD ILLINGWORTH Is that a challenge?

MRS ALLONBY It is an arrow shot into the air.

LORD ILLINGWORTH Don't you know that I always succeed in   470
whatever I try?

MRS ALLONBY I am sorry to hear it. We women adore failures. They lean on us.

LORD ILLINGWORTH You worship successes. You cling to them.

MRS ALLONBY We are the laurels to hide their baldness.   475

LORD ILLINGWORTH And they need you always, except at the moment of triumph.

MRS ALLONBY They are uninteresting then.

LORD ILLINGWORTH How tantalizing you are!

        A pause

MRS ALLONBY Lord Illingworth, there is one thing I shall always   480
like you for.

LORD ILLINGWORTH Only one thing? And I have so many bad qualities.

MRS ALLONBY Ah, don't be too conceited about them. You may lose them as you grow old.   485

LORD ILLINGWORTH I never intend to grow old. The soul is born old but grows young. That is the comedy of life.

MRS ALLONBY And the body is born young and grows old. That is life's tragedy.

LORD ILLINGWORTH It's comedy also, sometimes. But what is the   490
mysterious reason why you will always like me?

MRS ALLONBY It is that you have never made love to me.

LORD ILLINGWORTH I have never done anything else.

MRS ALLONBY Really? I have not noticed it.

LORD ILLINGWORTH How fortunate! It might have been a tragedy   495
for both of us.

MRS ALLONBY We should each have survived.

LORD ILLINGWORTH One can survive everything nowadays, except
death, and live down anything except a good reputation.

MRS ALLONBY Have you tried a good reputation?   500

LORD ILLINGWORTH It is one of the many annoyances to which I
have never been subjected.

MRS ALLONBY It may come.

LORD ILLINGWORTH Why do you threaten me?

MRS ALLONBY I will tell you when you have kissed the Puritan.   505
Enter Footman

FRANCIS Tea is served in the Yellow Drawing-room, my lord.

LORD ILLINGWORTH Tell her ladyship we are coming in.

FRANCIS Yes, my lord.
Exit [Footman]

LORD ILLINGWORTH Shall we go into tea?

MRS ALLONBY Do you like such simple pleasures?   510

LORD ILLINGWORTH I adore simple pleasures. They are the last
refuge of the complex. But, if you wish, let us stay here. Yes, let
us stay here. The Book of Life begins with a man and a woman in
a garden.

MRS ALLONBY It ends with Revelations.   515

LORD ILLINGWORTH You fence divinely. But the button has come
off your foil.

MRS ALLONBY I have still the mask.

LORD ILLINGWORTH It makes your eyes lovelier.

MRS ALLONBY Thank you. Come.   520

LORD ILLINGWORTH (*sees Mrs Arbuthnot's letter on table, and takes it
up and looks at envelope*) What a curious handwriting! It reminds
me of the handwriting of a woman I used to know years ago.

MRS ALLONBY Who?

LORD ILLINGWORTH Oh! no one. No one in particular. A woman   525
of no importance.°
*Throws letter down, and passes up the steps of the terrace with
Mrs Allonby. They smile at each other*

ACT DROP

Second Act

Scene: Drawing-room at Hunstanton, after dinner, lamps lit.
Door L.C. Door R.C. Ladies seated on sofas

MRS ALLONBY What a comfort it is to have got rid of the men for
a little!

LADY STUTFIELD Yes; men persecute us dreadfully, don't they?

MRS ALLONBY Persecute us? I wish they did.

LADY HUNSTANTON My dear!   5

MRS ALLONBY The annoying thing is that the wretches can be
perfectly happy without us. That is why I think it is every woman's
duty never to leave them alone for a single moment, except during
this short breathing space° after dinner; without which I believe we
poor women would be absolutely worn to shadows.   10

    Enter Servants with coffee

LADY HUNSTANTON Worn to shadows, dear?

MRS ALLONBY Yes, Lady Hunstanton. It is such a strain keeping
men up to the mark. They are always trying to escape from us.

LADY STUTFIELD It seems to me that it is we who are always trying
to escape from them. Men are so very, very heartless. They know   15
their power and use it.

LADY CAROLINE (*takes coffee from Servant*) What stuff and nonsense
all this about men is! The thing to do is to keep men in their
proper place.

MRS ALLONBY But what is their proper place, Lady Caroline?   20

LADY CAROLINE Looking after their wives, Mrs Allonby.

MRS ALLONBY (*takes coffee from Servant*) Really? And if they're not
married?

LADY CAROLINE If they are not married, they should be looking
after a wife. It's perfectly scandalous the amount of bachelors who   25
are going about society. There should be a law passed to compel
them all to marry within twelve months.

LADY STUTFIELD (*refuses coffee*) But if they're in love with someone
who, perhaps, is tied to another?

LADY CAROLINE In that case, Lady Stutfield, they should be   30
married off in a week to some plain respectable girl, in order to
teach them not to meddle with other people's property.

MRS ALLONBY I don't think that we should ever be spoken of as
other people's property. All men are married women's property.°

That is the only true definition of what married women's property   35
really is. But we don't belong to anyone.

[*Exeunt Servants*]

LADY STUTFIELD Oh, I am so very, very glad to hear you say so.

LADY HUNSTANTON But do you really think, dear Caroline, that
legislation would improve matters in any way? I am told that,
nowadays, all the married men live like bachelors, and all the   40
bachelors like married men.

MRS ALLONBY I certainly never know one from the other.

LADY STUTFIELD Oh, I think one can always know at once whether
a man has home claims upon his life or not. I have noticed a very,
very sad expression in the eyes of so many married men.   45

MRS ALLONBY Ah, all that I have noticed is that they are horribly
tedious when they are good husbands, and abominably conceited
when they are not.

LADY HUNSTANTON Well, I suppose the type of husband has
completely changed since my young days, but I'm bound to state   50
that poor dear Hunstanton° was the most delightful of creatures,
and as good as gold.

MRS ALLONBY Ah, my husband is a sort of promissory note;° I'm
tired of meeting him.

LADY CAROLINE But you renew him from time to time, don't   55
you?

MRS ALLONBY Oh no, Lady Caroline. I have only had one husband°
as yet. I suppose you look upon me as quite an amateur.

LADY CAROLINE With your views on life I wonder you married at
all.   60

MRS ALLONBY So do I.

LADY HUNSTANTON My dear child, I believe you are really very
happy in your married life, but that you like to hide your happiness
from others.

MRS ALLONBY I assure you I was horribly deceived in Ernest.   65

LADY HUNSTANTON Oh, I hope not, dear. I knew his mother quite
well. She was a Stratton, Caroline, one of Lord Crowland's
daughters.

LADY CAROLINE Victoria Stratton? I remember her perfectly. A silly
fair-haired woman with no chin.   70

MRS ALLONBY Ah, Ernest has a chin. He has a very strong chin, a
square chin. Ernest's chin is far too square.

LADY STUTFIELD But do you really think a man's chin can be too
square? I think a man should look very, very strong, and that his
chin should be quite, quite square.   75

MRS ALLONBY Then you should certainly know Ernest, Lady
Stutfield. It is only fair to tell you beforehand he has got no
conversation at all.

LADY STUTFIELD I adore silent men.

MRS ALLONBY Oh, Ernest isn't silent. He talks the whole time. But   80
he has got no conversation. What he talks about I don't know. I
haven't listened to him for years.

LADY STUTFIELD Have you never forgiven him then? How sad that
seems! But all life is very, very sad, is it not?

MRS ALLONBY Life, Lady Stutfield, is simply a *mauvais quart*   85
d'heure° made up of exquisite moments.

LADY STUTFIELD Yes, there are moments, certainly. But was it
something very, very wrong° that Mr Allonby did? Did he become
angry with you, and say anything that was unkind or true?

MRS ALLONBY Oh dear, no. Ernest is invariably calm. That is one   90
of the reasons he always gets on my nerves. Nothing is so
aggravating as calmness. There is something positively brutal
about the good temper of most modern men. I wonder we women
stand it as well as we do.

LADY STUTFIELD Yes; men's good temper shows they are not so   95
sensitive as we are, not so finely strung. It makes a great barrier
often between husband and wife, does it not? But I would so much
like to know what was the wrong thing Mr Allonby did.

MRS ALLONBY Well, I will tell you, if you solemnly promise to tell
everybody else.   100

LADY STUTFIELD Thank you, thank you. I will make a point of
repeating it.

MRS ALLONBY When Ernest and I were engaged, he swore to me
positively on his knees that he had never loved anyone before in
the whole course of his life. I was very young at the time, so I   105
didn't believe him, I needn't tell you. Unfortunately, however, I
made no inquiries of any kind till after I had been actually married
four or five months. I found out then that what he had told me
was perfectly true. And that sort of thing makes a man so
absolutely uninteresting.   110

LADY HUNSTANTON My dear!

MRS ALLONBY Men always want to be a woman's first love. That is
their clumsy vanity. We women have a more subtle instinct about
things. What we like is to be a man's last romance.

LADY STUTFIELD I see what you mean. It's very, very beautiful.   115

LADY HUNSTANTON My dear child, you don't mean to tell me that
you won't forgive your husband because he never loved anyone

else? Did you ever hear such a thing, Caroline? I am quite
surprised.

LADY CAROLINE Oh, women have become so highly educated, Jane,   120
that nothing should surprise us nowadays, except happy marriages.
They apparently are getting remarkably rare.

MRS ALLONBY Oh, they're quite out of date.

LADY STUTFIELD Except amongst the middle classes,° I have been
told.   125

MRS ALLONBY How like the middle classes!

LADY STUTFIELD Yes—is it not?—very, very like them.

LADY CAROLINE If what you tell us about the middle classes is true,
Lady Stutfield, it redounds greatly to their credit. It is much to be
regretted that in our rank of life the wife should be so persistently   130
frivolous, under the impression apparently that it is the proper
thing to be. It is to that I attribute the unhappiness of so many
marriages we all know of in society.

MRS ALLONBY Do you know, Lady Caroline, I don't think the
frivolity of the wife has ever anything to do with it. More   135
marriages are ruined nowadays by the common sense of the
husband than by anything else. How can a woman be expected to
be happy with a man who insists on treating her as if she were a
perfectly rational being?

LADY HUNSTANTON My dear!   140

MRS ALLONBY Man, poor, awkward, reliable, necessary man belongs
to a sex that has been rational for millions and millions of years. He
can't help himself. It is in his race. The History of Woman is very
different. We have always been picturesque protests against the
mere existence of common sense. We saw its dangers from the first.   145

LADY STUTFIELD Yes, the common sense of husbands is certainly
most, most trying. Do tell me your conception of the Ideal
Husband. I think it would be so very, very helpful.

MRS ALLONBY The Ideal Husband? There couldn't be such a thing.
The institution is wrong.   150

LADY STUTFIELD The Ideal Man,° then, in his relations to *us*.

LADY CAROLINE He would probably be extremely realistic.

MRS ALLONBY The Ideal Man! Oh, the Ideal Man should talk to us
as if we were goddesses, and treat us as if we were children. He
should refuse all our serious requests, and gratify every one of our   155
whims. He should encourage us to have caprices, and forbid us to
have missions. He should always say much more than he means,
and always mean much more than he says.

LADY HUNSTANTON But how could he do both, dear?

MRS ALLONBY He should never run down other pretty women. 160
That would show he had no taste, or make one suspect that he had
too much. No; he should be nice about them all, but say that
somehow they don't attract him.

LADY STUTFIELD Yes, that is always very, very pleasant to hear
about other women. 165

MRS ALLONBY If we ask him a question about anything, he should
give us an answer all about ourselves. He should invariably praise
us for whatever qualities he knows we haven't got. But he should
be pitiless, quite pitiless, in reproaching us for the virtues that we
have never dreamed of possessing. He should never believe that we 170
know the use of useful things. That would be unforgiveable. But
he should shower on us everything we don't want.

LADY CAROLINE As far as I can see, he is to do nothing but pay bills
and compliments.

MRS ALLONBY He should persistently compromise us in public, and 175
treat us with absolute respect when we are alone. And yet he
should be always ready to have a perfectly terrible scene, whenever
we want one, and to become miserable, absolutely miserable, at a
moment's notice, and to overwhelm us with just reproaches in less
than twenty minutes, and to be positively violent at the end of half 180
an hour, and to leave us for ever at a quarter to eight, when we
have to go and dress for dinner. And when, after that, one has seen
him for really the last time, and he has refused to take back the
little things he has given one, and promised never to communicate
with one again, or to write one any foolish letters, he should be 185
perfectly broken-hearted, and telegraph to one all day long, and
send one little notes every half-hour by a private hansom, and dine
quite alone at the club, so that every one should know how
unhappy he was. And after a whole dreadful week, during which
one has gone about everywhere with one's husband, just to show 190
how absolutely lonely one was, he may be given a third last
parting, in the evening, and then, if his conduct has been quite
irreproachable, and one has behaved really badly to him, he should
be allowed to admit that he has been entirely in the wrong, and
when he has admitted that, it becomes a woman's duty to forgive, 195
and one can do it all over again from the beginning, with
variations.

LADY HUNSTANTON How clever you are, my dear! You never mean
a single word you say.

LADY STUTFIELD Thank you, thank you. It has been quite, quite   200
    entrancing. I must try and remember it all. There are such a
    number of details that are so very, very important.

LADY CAROLINE But you have not told us yet what the reward of
    the Ideal Man is to be.

MRS ALLONBY His reward? Oh, infinite expectation. That is quite   205
    enough for him.

LADY STUTFIELD But men are so terribly, terribly, exacting, are they
    not?

MRS ALLONBY That makes no matter. One should never surrender.°

LADY STUTFIELD Not even to the Ideal Man?   210

MRS ALLONBY Certainly not to him. Unless, of course, one wants to
    grow tired of him.

LADY STUTFIELD Oh! . . . yes. I see that. It is very, very helpful. Do
    you think, Mrs Allonby, I shall ever meet the Ideal Man? Or are
    there more than one?   215

MRS ALLONBY There are just four in London, Lady Stutfield.

LADY HUNSTANTON Oh, my dear!

MRS ALLONBY (going over to her) What has happened? Do tell
    me.

LADY HUNSTANTON (in a low voice) I had completely forgotten that   220
    the American young lady has been in the room all the time. I am
    afraid some of this clever talk may have shocked her a little.

MRS ALLONBY Ah, that will do her so much good!

LADY HUNSTANTON Let us hope she didn't understand much. I
    think I had better go over and talk to her. (Rises and goes across to 225
    Hester Worsley) Well, dear Miss Worsley. (Sitting down beside her)
    How quiet you have been in your nice little corner all this time! I
    suppose you have been reading a book? There are so many books
    here in the library.

HESTER No, I have been listening to the conversation.   230

LADY HUNSTANTON You mustn't believe everything that was said,
    you know, dear.

HESTER I didn't believe any of it.

LADY HUNSTANTON That is quite right, dear.

HESTER (continuing)° I couldn't believe that any women could really 235
    hold such views of life as I have heard tonight from some of your
    guests.

    An awkward pause

LADY HUNSTANTON I hear you have such pleasant society in
    America. Quite like our own in places, my son wrote to me.

HESTER There are cliques in America as elsewhere, Lady Hunstan-   240
ton. But true American society consists simply of all the good
women and good men we have in our country.

LADY HUNSTANTON What a sensible system, and I dare say quite
pleasant too. I am afraid in England we have too many artificial
social barriers. We don't see as much as we should of the middle   245
and lower classes.

HESTER In America we have no lower classes.

LADY HUNSTANTON Really? What a very strange arrangement!

MRS ALLONBY What is that dreadful girl talking about?

LADY STUTFIELD She is painfully natural, is she not?   250

LADY CAROLINE There are a great many things you haven't got in
America, I am told, Miss Worsley. They say you have no ruins,
and no curiosities.

MRS ALLONBY (to Lady Stutfield) What nonsense! They have their
mothers and their manners.   255

HESTER The English aristocracy supply us with our curiosities, Lady
Caroline. They are sent over to us every summer, regularly, in the
steamers, and propose to us the day after they land. As for ruins,
we are trying to build up something that will last longer than brick
or stone.   260

> Gets up° to take her fan from table

LADY HUNSTANTON What is that, dear? Ah, yes, an iron Exhibition,° is it not, at that place that has the curious name?

HESTER (standing by table) We are trying to build up life, Lady
Hunstanton, on a better, truer, purer basis than life rests on here.
This sounds strange to you all, no doubt. How could it sound   265
other than strange? You rich people in England, you don't know
how you are living. How could you know? You shut out from your
society the gentle and the good. You laugh at the simple and the
pure. Living, as you all do, on others and by them, you sneer at
self-sacrifice, and if you throw bread to the poor, it is merely to   270
keep them quiet for a season. With all your pomp and wealth and
art you don't know how to live—you don't even know that. You
love the beauty that you can see and touch and handle, the beauty
that you can destroy, and do destroy, but of the unseen beauty of
life, of the unseen beauty of a higher life, you know nothing. You   275
have lost life's secret. Oh, your English society seems to me
shallow, selfish, foolish. It has blinded its eyes, and stopped its
ears. It lies like a leper in purple.° It sits like a dead thing smeared
with gold. It is all wrong, all wrong.

LADY STUTFIELD I don't think one should know of these things. It   280
is not very, very nice, is it?

LADY HUNSTANTON My dear Miss Worsley, I thought you liked
English society so much. You were such a success in it. And you
were so much admired by the best people. I quite forget what Lord
Henry Weston° said of you—but it was most complimentary, and   285
you know what an authority he is on beauty.

HESTER Lord Henry Weston! I remember him, Lady Hunstanton. A
man with a hideous smile and a hideous past. He is asked
everywhere. No dinner-party is complete without him. What of
those whose ruin is due to him? They are outcasts. They are   290
nameless. If you met them in the street you would turn your head
away. I don't complain of their punishment. Let all women who
have sinned° be punished.

> *Mrs Arbuthnot enters from terrace behind in a cloak with a lace
> veil over her head. She hears the last words and starts*

LADY HUNSTANTON My dear young lady!

HESTER It is right that they should be punished, but don't let them   295
be the only ones to suffer. If a man and woman have sinned, let
them both go forth into the desert to love or loathe each other
there. Let them both be branded. Set a mark, if you wish, on each,
but don't punish the one and let the other go free. Don't have one
law for men and another for women. You are unjust to women in   300
England. And till you count what is a shame in a woman to be an
infamy in a man, you will always be unjust, and Right, that pillar
of fire,° and Wrong, that pillar of cloud, will be made dim to your
eyes, or be not seen at all, or if seen, not regarded.

LADY CAROLINE Might I, dear Miss Worsley, as you are standing   305
up, ask you for my cotton° that is just behind you? Thank you.

LADY HUNSTANTON My dear Mrs Arbuthnot! I am so pleased you
have come up. But I didn't hear you announced.°

MRS ARBUTHNOT Oh, I came straight in from the terrace, Lady
Hunstanton, just as I was. You didn't tell me you had a party.°   310

LADY HUNSTANTON Not a party. Only a few guests who are staying
in the house, and whom you must know. Allow me. (*Tries to help
her* [*with cloak*] *Rings bell*) Caroline, this is Mrs Arbuthnot, one of
my sweetest friends. Lady Caroline Pontefract, Lady Stutfield,
Mrs Allonby, and my young American friend, Miss Worsley, who   315
has just been telling us all how wicked we are.

HESTER I am afraid you think I spoke too strongly, Lady Hunstanton. But there are some things in England—

LADY HUNSTANTON My dear young lady, there was a great deal of truth, I dare say, in what you said, and you looked very pretty   320
while you said it, which is much more important, Lord Illingworth would tell us. The only point where I thought you were a little hard was about Lady Caroline's brother, about poor Lord Henry. He is really such good company.

    Enter Footman

Take Mrs Arbuthnot's things.°   325

    Exit Footman with wraps

HESTER Lady Caroline, I had no idea it was your brother. I am sorry for the pain I must have caused you—I——

LADY CAROLINE My dear Miss Worsley, the only part of your little speech, if I may so term it, with which I thoroughly agreed, was the part about my brother. Nothing that you could possibly say   330
could be too bad for him. I regard Henry as infamous, absolutely infamous. But I am bound to state, as you were remarking, Jane, that he is excellent company, and he has one of the best cooks in London, and after a good dinner one can forgive anybody, even one's own relations.   335

LADY HUNSTANTON (*to Miss Worsley*) Now, do come,° dear, and make friends with Mrs Arbuthnot. She is one of the good, sweet, simple people you told us we never admitted into society. I am sorry to say Mrs Arbuthnot comes very rarely to me. But that is not my fault.   340

MRS ALLONBY What a bore it is the men staying so long after dinner! I expect they are saying the most dreadful things about us.

LADY STUTFIELD Do you really think so?

MRS ALLONBY I am sure of it.

LADY STUTFIELD How very, very horrid of them! Shall we go on to   345
the terrace?

MRS ALLONBY Oh, anything to get away from the dowagers and the dowdies. (*Rises and goes with Lady Stutfield to door L.C.*) We are only going to look at the stars, Lady Hunstanton.

LADY HUNSTANTON You will find a great many, dear, a great many.   350
But don't catch cold. (*To Mrs Arbuthnot*) We shall all miss Gerald so much, dear Mrs Arbuthnot.

MRS ARBUTHNOT But has Lord Illingworth really offered to make Gerald his secretary?

LADY HUNSTANTON Oh, yes! He has been most charming about it.   355
He has the highest possible opinion of your boy. You don't know Lord Illingworth, I believe, dear.

MRS ARBUTHNOT I have never met him.

LADY HUNSTANTON You know him by name, no doubt?

MRS ARBUTHNOT I am afraid I don't. I live so much out of the 360
world, and see so few people. I remember hearing years ago of an
old Lord Illingworth who lived in Yorkshire, I think.

LADY HUNSTANTON Ah, yes. That would be the last Earl but one.
He was a very curious man. He wanted to marry beneath him. Or
wouldn't, I believe. There was some scandal about it. The present 365
Lord Illingworth is quite different. He is very distinguished. He
does—well, he does nothing,° which I am afraid our pretty
American visitor here thinks very wrong of anybody, and I don't
know that he cares much for the subjects in which you are so
interested, dear Mrs Arbuthnot. Do you think, Caroline, that Lord 370
Illingworth is interested in the Housing of the Poor?

LADY CAROLINE I should fancy not at all, Jane.

LADY HUNSTANTON We all have our different tastes, have we not?
But Lord Illingworth has a very high position, and there is nothing
he couldn't get if he chose to ask for it. Of course, he is 375
comparatively a young man still, and he has only come to his title
within—how long exactly is it, Caroline, since Lord Illingworth
succeeded?

LADY CAROLINE About four years, I think, Jane. I know it was the
same year in which my brother had his last exposure in the evening 380
newspapers.

LADY HUNSTANTON Ah, I remember. That would be about four
years ago. Of course, there were a great many people between the
present Lord Illingworth and the title, Mrs Arbuthnot. There
was—who was there, Caroline? 385

LADY CAROLINE There was poor Margaret's baby. You remember
how anxious she was to have a boy, and it was a boy, but it died
and her husband died shortly afterwards, and she married almost
immediately one of Lord Ascot's sons, who, I am told, beats her.

LADY HUNSTANTON Ah, that is in the family, dear, that is in the 390
family. And there was also, I remember, a clergyman who wanted
to be a lunatic, or a lunatic who wanted to be a clergyman, I forget
which, but I know the Court of Chancery investigated the matter,
and decided that he was quite sane. And I saw him afterwards at
poor Lord Plumstead's with straws in his hair,° or something very 395
odd about him. I can't recall what. I often regret, Lady Caroline,
that dear Lady Cecilia never lived to see her son get the title.

MRS ARBUTHNOT Lady Cecilia?

LADY HUNSTANTON Lord Illingworth's mother, dear Mrs Arbuth- 400
not, was one of the Duchess of Jerningham's pretty daughters, and
she married Sir Thomas Harford, who wasn't considered a very
good match for her° at the time, though he was said to be the
handsomest man in London. I knew them all quite intimately, and
both the sons, Arthur and George.

MRS ARBUTHNOT It was the eldest son who succeeded, of course, 405
Lady Hunstanton?

LADY HUNSTANTON No, dear, he was killed in the hunting field. Or
was it fishing, Caroline? I forget. But George came in for
everything.° I always tell him that no younger son has ever had
such good luck as he has had. 410

MRS ARBUTHNOT Lady Hunstanton, I want to speak to Gerald at
once. Might I see him? Can he be sent for?

LADY HUNSTANTON Certainly, dear. I will send one of the servants
into the dining-room to fetch him. I don't know what keeps the
gentlemen so long. (*Rings bell*) When I knew Lord Illingworth 415
first as plain George Harford, he was simply a very brilliant young
man about town, with not a penny of money except what poor
dear Lady Cecilia gave him. She was quite devoted to him.
Chiefly, I fancy, because he was on bad terms with his father.
[*Enter Servant*] Oh, here is the dear Archdeacon. [*To Servant*] It 420
doesn't matter.

> *Enter Sir John° and Dr Daubeny [and Mr Kelvil]. Sir John*
> *goes over to Lady Stutfield, Dr Daubeny to Lady Hunstanton*

DR DAUBENY Lord Illingworth has been most entertaining. I have
never enjoyed myself more. (*Sees Mrs Arbuthnot*)   Ah, Mrs
Arbuthnot.

LADY HUNSTANTON (*to Dr Daubeny*) You see I have got Mrs 425
Arbuthnot to come to me at last.

DR DAUBENY That is a great honour, Lady Hunstanton. Mrs
Daubeny will be quite jealous of you.

LADY HUNSTANTON Ah, I am so sorry Mrs Daubeny could not
come with you tonight. Headache as usual, I suppose. 430

DR DAUBENY Yes, Lady Hunstanton; a perfect martyr. But she is
happiest alone. She is happiest alone.

LADY CAROLINE (*to her husband*) John!

> *Sir John goes over° to his wife. Dr Daubeny talks to Lady*
> *Hunstanton and Mrs Arbuthnot. [Enter Lord Illingworth.] Mrs*
> *Arbuthnot watches Lord Illingworth the whole time. He has*
> *passed across the room without noticing her, and approaches Mrs*

Allonby, who with Lady Stutfield is standing by the door looking on to the terrace

LORD ILLINGWORTH How is the most charming woman in the world? 435

MRS ALLONBY (*taking Lady Stutfield by the hand*) We are both quite well, thank you, Lord Illingworth. But what a short time you have been in the dining-room! It seems as if we had only just left.

LORD ILLINGWORTH I was bored to death. Never opened my lips 440 the whole time. Absolutely longing to come in to you.

MRS ALLONBY You should have. The American girl has been giving us a lecture.

LORD ILLINGWORTH Really? All Americans lecture, I believe. I suppose it is something in their climate. What did she lecture 445 about?

MRS ALLONBY Oh, Puritanism, of course.

LORD ILLINGWORTH I am going to convert her, am I not? How long do you give me?

MRS ALLONBY A week. 450

LORD ILLINGWORTH A week is more than enough.
          Enter Gerald and Lord Alfred
GERALD (*going to Mrs Arbuthnot*) Dear mother.

MRS ARBUTHNOT Gerald, I don't feel at all well. See me home, Gerald. I shouldn't have come.

GERALD I am so sorry, mother. Certainly. But you must know Lord 455 Illingworth first.
          Goes across room
MRS ARBUTHNOT Not tonight, Gerald.

GERALD Lord Illingworth, I want you so much to know my mother.

LORD ILLINGWORTH With the greatest pleasure. (*To Mrs Allonby*) I'll be back in a moment. People's mothers always bore me to 460 death. All women° become like their mothers. That is their tragedy.

MRS ALLONBY No man does. That is his.

LORD ILLINGWORTH What a delightful mood you are in to-night! 465
          Turns round and goes across with Gerald to Mrs Arbuthnot. When he sees her, he starts back in wonder. Then slowly his eyes turn towards Gerald
GERALD Mother, this is Lord Illingworth, who has offered to take me as his private secretary. (*Mrs Arbuthnot bows coldly*) It is a

wonderful opening for me, isn't it? I hope he won't be disappointed in me, that is all. You'll thank Lord Illingworth, mother, won't you? 470

MRS ARBUTHNOT Lord Illingworth is very good, I am sure, to interest himself in you for the moment.°

LORD ILLINGWORTH (*putting his hand on Gerald's shoulder*) Oh, Gerald and I are great friends already, Mrs . . . Arbuthnot.

MRS ARBUTHNOT There can be nothing in common between you 475
and my son, Lord Illingworth.

GERALD Dear mother, how can you say so? Of course Lord Illingworth is awfully clever and that sort of thing. There is nothing Lord Illingworth doesn't know.

LORD ILLINGWORTH My dear boy! 480

GERALD He knows more about life than anyone I have ever met. I feel an awful duffer when I am with you, Lord Illingworth. Of course, I have had so few advantages. I have not been to Eton or Oxford like other chaps. But Lord Illingworth doesn't seem to mind that. He has been awfully good to me, mother. 485

MRS ARBUTHNOT Lord Illingworth may change his mind. He may not really want you as his secretary.

GERALD Mother!

MRS ARBUTHNOT You must remember, as you said yourself, you have had so few advantages. 490

MRS ALLONBY Lord Illingworth, I want to speak to you for a moment. Do come over.

LORD ILLINGWORTH Will you excuse me, Mrs Arbuthnot? Now, don't let your charming mother make any more difficulties, Gerald. The thing is quite settled, isn't it? 495

GERALD I hope so.

Lord Illingworth goes across to Mrs Allonby

MRS ALLONBY I thought you were never going to leave the lady in black velvet.°

LORD ILLINGWORTH She is excessively handsome. (*Looks at Mrs Arbuthnot*)

LADY HUNSTANTON Caroline, shall we all make a move to the 500
music-room? Miss Worsley is going to play. You'll come too, dear Mrs Arbuthnot, won't you? You don't know what a treat is in store for you. (*To Dr Daubeny*) I must really take Miss Worsley down some afternoon to the rectory. I should so much like dear Mrs Daubeny to hear her on the violin. Ah, I forgot. Dear Mrs 505
Daubeny's hearing is a little defective, is it not?

DR DAUBENY Her deafness is a great privation to her. She can't even
hear my sermons now. She reads them at home. But she has many
resources in herself, many resources.

LADY HUNSTANTON She reads a good deal, I suppose?   510

DR DAUBENY Just the very largest print. The eyesight is rapidly
going. But she's never morbid, never morbid.

GERALD (to Lord Illingworth) Do speak to my mother, Lord Illingworth, before you go into the music-room. She seems to think,
somehow, you don't mean what you said to me.   515

MRS ALLONBY Aren't you coming?

LORD ILLINGWORTH In a few moments. Lady Hunstanton, if Mrs
Arbuthnot would allow me, I would like to say a few words to her,
and we will join you later on.

LADY HUNSTANTON Ah, of course. You will have a great deal to say   520
to her, and she will have a great deal to thank you for. It is not
every son who gets such an offer, Mrs Arbuthnot. But I know you
appreciate that, dear.

LADY CAROLINE John!°

LADY HUNSTANTON Now, don't keep Mrs Arbuthnot too long,   525
Lord Illingworth. We can't spare her.

      Exit following the other guests. Sound of violin° heard from
      music-room

LORD ILLINGWORTH So that is our son, Rachel!° Well, I am very
proud of him. He is a Harford, every inch of him. By the way,
why Arbuthnot, Rachel?

MRS ARBUTHNOT One name is as good as another, when one has no   530
right° to any name.

LORD ILLINGWORTH I suppose so—but why Gerald?

MRS ARBUTHNOT After a man whose heart I broke—after my father.

LORD ILLINGWORTH Well, Rachel, what is over is over. All I have
got to say now is that I am very, very much pleased with our boy.   535
The world will know him merely as my private secretary, but to
me he will be something very near, and very dear. It is a curious
thing, Rachel; my life seemed to be quite complete. It was not so.
It lacked something, it lacked a son. I have found my son now, I
am glad I have found him.   540

MRS ARBUTHNOT You have no right to claim him, or the smallest
part of him. The boy is entirely mine, and shall remain mine.

LORD ILLINGWORTH My dear Rachel, you have had him to yourself
for over twenty years. Why not let me have him for a little now?
He is quite as much mine as yours.   545

MRS ARBUTHNOT Are you talking of the child you abandoned? Of the child who, as far as you are concerned, might have died of hunger and of want?

LORD ILLINGWORTH You forget, Rachel, it was you who left me. It was not I who left you.   550

MRS ARBUTHNOT I left you because you refused to give the child a name. Before my son was born, I implored you to marry me.

LORD ILLINGWORTH I had no expectations then. And besides, Rachel, I wasn't much older than you were. I was only twenty-two. I was twenty-one, I believe, when the whole thing began in your 555 father's garden.

MRS ARBUTHNOT When a man is old enough to do wrong he should be old enough to do right also.

LORD ILLINGWORTH My dear Rachel, intellectual generalities are always interesting, but generalities in morals mean absolutely 560 nothing. As for saying I left our child to starve, that, of course, is untrue and silly. My mother offered you six hundred a year.° But you wouldn't take anything. You simply disappeared, and carried the child away with you.

MRS ARBUTHNOT I wouldn't have accepted a penny from her. Your 565 father was different. He told you, in my presence, when we were in Paris, that it was your duty to marry me.

LORD ILLINGWORTH Oh, duty is what one expects from others, it is not what one does oneself. Of course, I was influenced by my mother. Every man is when he is young.   570

MRS ARBUTHNOT I am glad to hear you say so. Gerald shall certainly not go away with you.

LORD ILLINGWORTH What nonsense, Rachel!

MRS ARBUTHNOT Do you think I would allow my son—

LORD ILLINGWORTH *Our* son.   575

MRS ARBUTHNOT My son (*Lord Illingworth shrugs his shoulders*)—to go away with the man who spoiled my youth, who ruined my life, who has tainted every moment of my days? You don't realize what my past has been in suffering and in shame.

LORD ILLINGWORTH My dear Rachel, I must candidly say that I 580 think Gerald's future considerably more important than your past.

MRS ARBUTHNOT Gerald cannot separate his future from my past.

LORD ILLINGWORTH That is exactly what he should do. That is exactly what you should help him to do. What a typical woman 585 you are! You talk sentimentally, and you are thoroughly selfish the whole time. But don't let us have a scene. Rachel, I want you to look at this matter from the common-sense point of view, from the point of view of what is best for our son, leaving you and me out of the question. What is our son at present? An underpaid clerk in   590 a small provincial bank in a third-rate English town. If you imagine he is quite happy in such a position, you are mistaken. He is thoroughly discontented.

MRS ARBUTHNOT He was not discontented till he met you. You have made him so.   595

LORD ILLINGWORTH Of course, I made him so. Discontent is the first step in the progress of a man or a nation. But I did not leave him with a mere longing for things he could not get. No, I made him a charming offer. He jumped at it, I need hardly say. Any young man would. And now, simply because it turns out that I am   600 the boy's own father and he my own son, you propose practically to ruin his career. That is to say, if I were a perfect stranger, you would allow Gerald to go away with me, but as he is my own flesh and blood you won't. How utterly illogical you are!

MRS ARBUTHNOT I will not allow him to go.   605

LORD ILLINGWORTH How can you prevent it? What excuse can you give to him for making him decline such an offer as mine? I won't tell him in what relation I stand to him, I need hardly say. But you daren't tell him. You know that. Look how you have brought him up.   610

MRS ARBUTHNOT I have brought him up to be a good man.

LORD ILLINGWORTH Quite so. And what is the result? You have educated him to be your judge if he ever finds you out. And a bitter, an unjust judge he will be to you. Don't be deceived, Rachel. Children begin by loving their parents.° After a time they   615 judge them. Rarely, if ever, do they forgive them.

MRS ARBUTHNOT George,° don't take my son away from me. I have had twenty years of sorrow, and I have only had one thing to love me, only one thing to love. You have had a life of joy, and pleasure, and success. You have been quite happy, you have never thought   620 of us. There was no reason, according to your views of life, why you should have remembered us at all. Your meeting us was a mere accident, a horrible accident. Forget it. Don't come now, and rob me of . . . of all I have in the whole world. You are so rich in other things. Leave me the little vineyard of my life; leave me the   625 walled-in garden and the well of water; the ewe-lamb God sent me,

in pity or in wrath, oh! leave me that. George, don't take Gerald
from me.

LORD ILLINGWORTH Rachel, at the present moment you are not
necessary to Gerald's career; I am. There is nothing more to be   630
said on the subject.

MRS ARBUTHNOT I will not let him go.

LORD ILLINGWORTH Here is Gerald. He has a right to decide for
himself.

Enter Gerald   635

GERALD Well, dear mother, I hope you have settled it all with Lord
Illingworth?

MRS ARBUTHNOT I have not, Gerald.

LORD ILLINGWORTH Your mother seems not to like your coming
with me, for some reason.

GERALD Why, mother?   640

MRS ARBUTHNOT I thought you were quite happy here with me,
Gerald. I didn't know you were so anxious to leave me.

GERALD Mother, how can you talk like that? Of course I have been
quite happy with you. But a man can't stay always with his mother.
No chap does. I want to make myself a position, to do something,   645
I thought you would have been proud to see me Lord Illingworth's
secretary.

MRS ARBUTHNOT I do not think you would be suitable as a private
secretary to Lord Illingworth. You have no qualifications.

LORD ILLINGWORTH I don't wish to seem to interfere for a   650
moment, Mrs Arbuthnot, but as far as your last objection is
concerned, I surely am the best judge. And I can only tell you that
your son has all the qualifications I had hoped for. He has more,
in fact, than I had even thought of. Far more. (*Mrs Arbuthnot
remains silent*) Have you any other reason, Mrs Arbuthnot, why   655
you don't wish your son to accept this post?

GERALD Have you, mother? Do answer.

LORD ILLINGWORTH If you have, Mrs Arbuthnot, pray, pray say it.
We are quite by ourselves here. Whatever it is, I need not say I
will not repeat it.   660

GERALD Mother?

LORD ILLINGWORTH If you would like to be alone with your son, I
will leave you. You may have some other reason you don't wish
me to hear.

MRS ARBUTHNOT I have no other reason.   665

LORD ILLINGWORTH Then, my dear boy, we may look on the thing as settled. Come, you and I will smoke a cigarette on the terrace together. And Mrs Arbuthnot, pray let me tell you, that I think you have acted very, very wisely.

> *Exit with Gerald. Mrs Arbuthnot is left alone. She stands immobile, with a look of unutterable sorrow on her face*

ACT DROP

Third Act

Scene: The picture gallery at Hunstanton. Door at back leading on to terrace. Lord Illingworth and Gerald, R.C. Lord Illingworth lolling on a sofa. Gerald in a chair

LORD ILLINGWORTH Thoroughly sensible woman, your mother, Gerald. I knew she would come round in the end.

GERALD My mother is awfully conscientious, Lord Illingworth, and I know she doesn't think I am educated enough to be your secretary. She is perfectly right, too. I was fearfully idle when I was at school, and I couldn't pass an examination now to save my life.

LORD ILLINGWORTH My dear Gerald, examinations are of no value whatsoever. If a man is a gentleman, he knows quite enough, and if he is not a gentleman, whatever he knows is bad for him.

GERALD But I am so ignorant of the world, Lord Illingworth.

LORD ILLINGWORTH Don't be afraid, Gerald. Remember that you've got on your side the most wonderful thing in the world— youth! There is nothing like youth. The middle-aged are mort- gaged to Life. The old are in Life's lumber-room. But youth is the Lord of Life. Youth has a kingdom waiting for it. Everyone is born a king, and most people die in exile, like most kings. To win back my youth, Gerald, there is nothing I wouldn't do—except take exercise, get up early, or be a useful member of the community.

GERALD But you don't call yourself old, Lord Illingworth?

LORD ILLINGWORTH I am old enough to be your father, Gerald.

GERALD I don't remember my father; he died years ago.

LORD ILLINGWORTH So Lady Hunstanton told me.

GERALD It is very curious, my mother never talks to me about my father. I sometimes think she must have married beneath her.

LORD ILLINGWORTH (*winces slightly*) Really? (*Goes over and puts his hand on Gerald's shoulder*)° You have missed not having a father, I suppose, Gerald?

GERALD Oh, no; my mother has been so good to me. No one ever had such a mother as I have had.

LORD ILLINGWORTH I am quite sure of that. Still I should imagine that most mothers don't quite understand their sons. Don't realize, I mean, that a son has ambitions, a desire to see life, to make himself a name. After all, Gerald, you couldn't be expected to pass all your life in such a hole as Wrockley, could you?

GERALD Oh, no! It would be dreadful!   35

LORD ILLINGWORTH A mother's love is very touching, of course,
but it is often curiously selfish. I mean, there is a good deal of
selfishness in it.

GERALD (*slowly*) I suppose there is.

LORD ILLINGWORTH Your mother is a thoroughly good woman.   40
But good women have such limited views of life, their horizon is
so small, their interests are so petty, aren't they?

GERALD They are awfully interested, certainly, in things we don't
care much about.

LORD ILLINGWORTH I suppose your mother is very religious, and   45
that sort of thing.

GERALD Oh, yes, she's always going to church.

LORD ILLINGWORTH Ah! she is not modern, and to be modern is
the only thing worth being nowadays. You want to be modern,
don't you, Gerald? You want to know life as it really is. Not to be   50
put off with any old-fashioned theories about life. Well, what you
have to do at present is simply to fit yourself for the best society.
A man who can dominate a London dinner-table can dominate the
world. The future belongs to the dandy. It is the exquisites who
are going to rule.   55

GERALD I should like to wear nice things awfully, but I have always
been told that a man should not think too much about his clothes.

LORD ILLINGWORTH People nowadays are so absolutely superficial
that they don't understand the philosophy of the superficial. By
the way, Gerald, you should learn how to tie your tie better.   60
Sentiment is all very well for the buttonhole. But the essential
thing for a necktie is style. A well-tied tie is the first serious step
in life.°

GERALD (*laughing*) I might be able to learn how to tie a tie, Lord
Illingworth, but I should never be able to talk as you do. I don't   65
know how to talk.

LORD ILLINGWORTH Oh! talk to every woman as if you loved her,
and to every man as if he bored you, and at the end of your first
season you will have the reputation of possessing the most perfect
social tact.   70

GERALD But it is very difficult to get into society, isn't it?

LORD ILLINGWORTH To get into the best society, nowadays, one
has either to feed people, amuse people, or shock people—that is
all.°

GERALD I suppose society is wonderfully delightful!   75

LORD ILLINGWORTH To be in it is merely a bore. But to be out of it simply a tragedy. Society is a necessary thing. No man has any real success in this world unless he has got women to back him, and women rule society. If you have not got women on your side you are quite over. You might just as well be a barrister, or a   80
stockbroker, or a journalist at once.

GERALD It is very difficult to understand women, is it not?

LORD ILLINGWORTH You should never try to understand them. Women are pictures.° Men are problems. If you want to know what a woman really means—which, by the way, is always a   85
dangerous thing to do—look at her, don't listen to her.

GERALD But women are awfully clever, aren't they?

LORD ILLINGWORTH One should always tell them so. But, to the philosopher, my dear Gerald, women represent the triumph of matter over mind—just as men represent the triumph of mind over   90
morals.

GERALD How then can women have so much power as you say they have?

LORD ILLINGWORTH The history of women is the history of the worst form of tyranny the world has ever known. The tyranny of   95
the weak over the strong. It is the only tyranny that lasts.

GERALD But haven't women got a refining influence?

LORD ILLINGWORTH Nothing refines but the intellect.

GERALD Still, there are many different kinds of women, aren't there?   100

LORD ILLINGWORTH Only two kinds in society: the plain and the coloured.°

GERALD But there are good women in society, aren't there?

LORD ILLINGWORTH Far too many.

GERALD But do you think women shouldn't be good?   105

LORD ILLINGWORTH One should never tell them so, they'd all become good at once. Women are a fascinatingly wilful sex. Every woman is a rebel, and usually in wild revolt against herself.

GERALD You have never been married, Lord Illingworth, have you?

LORD ILLINGWORTH Men marry because they are tired; women   110
because they are curious. Both are disappointed.

GERALD But don't you think one can be happy when one is married?

LORD ILLINGWORTH Perfectly happy. But the happiness of a married man, my dear Gerald, depends on the people he has not married.   115

GERALD But if one is in love?

LORD ILLINGWORTH One should always be in love. That is the
reason one should never marry.

GERALD Love is a very wonderful thing, isn't it?

LORD ILLINGWORTH When one is in love one begins by deceiving   120
oneself. And one ends by deceiving others. That is what the world
calls a romance. But a really *grande passion* is comparatively rare
nowadays. It is the privilege of people who have nothing to do.
That is the one use of the idle classes in a country, and the only
possible explanation of us Harfords.   125

GERALD Harfords, Lord Illingworth?

LORD ILLINGWORTH That is my family name. You should study
the Peerage,° Gerald. It is the one book a young man about town
should know thoroughly, and it is the best thing in fiction the
English have ever done. And now, Gerald, you are going into a   130
perfectly new life with me, and I want you to know how to live.
(*Mrs Arbuthnot appears on terrace behind*)° For the world has been
made by fools that wise men should live in it!

> *Enter L.C. Lady Hunstanton and Dr Daubeny*

LADY HUNSTANTON Ah! here you are, dear Lord Illingworth. Well,
I suppose you have been telling our young friend, Gerald, what his   135
new duties are to be, and giving him a great deal of good advice
over a pleasant cigarette.

LORD ILLINGWORTH I have been giving him the best of advice,
Lady Hunstanton, and the best of cigarettes.

LADY HUNSTANTON I am so sorry I was not here to listen to you,   140
but I suppose I am too old now to learn. Except from you, dear
Archdeacon, when you are in your nice pulpit. But then I always
know what you are going to say, so I don't feel alarmed. (*Sees Mrs
Arbuthnot*) Ah! dear Mrs Arbuthnot, do come and join us. Come,
dear.   145

> *Enter Mrs Arbuthnot*

Gerald has been having such a long talk with Lord Illingworth; I
am sure you must feel very much flattered at the pleasant way in
which everything has turned out for him. Let us sit down. (*They
sit down*) And how is your beautiful embroidery going on?

MRS ARBUTHNOT I am always at work, Lady Hunstanton.   150

LADY HUNSTANTON Mrs Daubeny embroiders a little, too, doesn't
she?

DR DAUBENY She was very deft with her needle once, quite a
Dorcas.° But the gout has crippled her fingers a good deal. She
has not touched the tambour frame° for nine or ten years. But she   155

134

has many other amusements. She is very much interested in her
own health.

LADY HUNSTANTON Ah! that is always a nice distraction, is it not?
Now, what are you talking about, Lord Illingworth? Do tell us.

LORD ILLINGWORTH I was on the point of explaining to Gerald that   160
the world has always laughed at its own tragedies, that being the
only way in which it has been able to bear them. And that,
consequently, whatever the world has treated seriously belongs to
the comedy side of things.

LADY HUNSTANTON Now I am quite out of my depth. I usually am   165
when Lord Illingworth says anything. And the Humane Society°
is most careless. They never rescue me. I am left to sink. I have a
dim idea, dear Lord Illingworth, that you are always on the side
of the sinners, and I know I always try to be on the side of the
saints, but that is as far as I get. And after all, it may be merely   170
the fancy of a drowning person.

LORD ILLINGWORTH The only difference between the saint and
the sinner is that every saint has a past,° and every sinner has a
future.

LADY HUNSTANTON Ah! that quite does for me. I haven't a word to   175
say. You and I, dear Mrs Arbuthnot, are behind the age. We can't
follow Lord Illingworth. Too much care was taken with our
education, I am afraid. To have been well brought up is a great
drawback nowadays. It shuts one out from so much.

MRS ARBUTHNOT I should be sorry to follow Lord Illingworth in   180
any of his opinions.

LADY HUNSTANTON You are quite right, dear.
          *Gerald shrugs his shoulders and looks irritably over at his
          mother. Enter Lady Caroline*

LADY CAROLINE Jane, have you seen John anywhere?°

LADY HUNSTANTON You needn't be anxious about him, dear. He is
with Lady Stutfield; I saw them some time ago, in the Yellow   185
Drawing-room. They seem quite happy together. You are not
going, Caroline? Pray sit down.

LADY CAROLINE I think I had better look after John.
          Exit Lady Caroline

LADY HUNSTANTON It doesn't do to pay men so much attention.
And Caroline has really nothing to be anxious about. Lady   190
Stutfield is very sympathetic. She is just as sympathetic about one
thing as she is about another. A beautiful nature.
          Enter Sir John and Mrs Allonby

Ah! here is Sir John! And with Mrs Allonby too! I suppose it was Mrs Allonby I saw him with. Sir John, Caroline has been looking everywhere for you.   195

MRS ALLONBY We have been waiting for her in the Music-room, dear Lady Hunstanton.

LADY HUNSTANTON Ah! the Music-room, of course. I thought it was the Yellow Drawing-room, my memory is getting so defective. (*To Dr Daubeny*) Mrs Daubeny has a wonderful memory, hasn't   200
she?

DR DAUBENY She used to be quite remarkable for her memory, but since her last attack she recalls chiefly the events of her early childhood. But she finds great pleasure in such retrospections, great pleasure.   205

Enter Lady Stutfield and Mr Kelvil

LADY HUNSTANTON Ah! dear Lady Stutfield! and what has Mr Kelvil been talking to you about?

LADY STUTFIELD About Bimetallism,° as well as I remember.

LADY HUNSTANTON Bimetallism! Is that quite a nice subject? However, I know people discuss everything very freely nowadays.   210
What did Sir John talk to you about, dear Mrs Allonby?

MRS ALLONBY About Patagonia.°

LADY HUNSTANTON Really? What a remote topic! But very improving, I have no doubt.

MRS ALLONBY He has been most interesting on the subject of   215
Patagonia. Savages seem to have quite the same views as cultured people on almost all subjects. They are excessively advanced.

LADY HUNSTANTON What do they do?

MRS ALLONBY Apparently everything.

LADY HUNSTANTON Well, it is very gratifying, dear Archdeacon, is   220
it not, to find that Human Nature is permanently one.—On the whole, the world is the same world, is it not?

LORD ILLINGWORTH The world is simply divided into two classes—those who believe the incredible, like the public—and those who do the improbable—   225

MRS ALLONBY Like yourself?

LORD ILLINGWORTH Yes; I am always astonishing myself. It is the only thing that makes life worth living.

LADY STUTFIELD And what have you been doing lately that astonishes you?   230

LORD ILLINGWORTH I have been discovering all kinds of beautiful qualities in my own nature.

MRS ALLONBY Ah! don't become quite perfect all at once. Do it
gradually!

LORD ILLINGWORTH I don't intend to grow perfect at all. At least,   235
I hope I shan't. It would be most inconvenient. Women love us
for our defects. If we have enough of them, they will forgive us
everything, even our gigantic intellects.

MRS ALLONBY It is premature to ask us to forgive analysis. We
forgive adoration; that is quite as much as should be expected from   240
us.

      Enter Lord Alfred [Rufford]. He joins Lady Stutfield

LADY HUNSTANTON Ah! we women should forgive everything,
shouldn't we, dear Mrs Arbuthnot? I am sure you agree with me
in that.

MRS ARBUTHNOT I do not, Lady Hunstanton. I think there are   245
many things women should never forgive.

LADY HUNSTANTON What sort of things?

MRS ARBUTHNOT The ruin of another woman's life.

      Moves slowly away to back of stage°

LADY HUNSTANTON Ah! those things are very sad, no doubt, but I
believe there are admirable homes where people of that kind are   250
looked after and reformed, and I think on the whole that the secret
of life is to take things very, very easily.

MRS ALLONBY The secret of life is never to have an emotion that is
unbecoming.

LADY STUTFIELD The secret of life is to appreciate the pleasure of   255
being terribly, terribly deceived.

KELVIL The secret of life is to resist temptation, Lady Stutfield.

LORD ILLINGWORTH There is no secret of life. Life's aim, if it has
one, is simply to be always looking for temptations. There are not
nearly enough. I sometimes pass a whole day without coming   260
across a single one. It is quite dreadful. It makes one so nervous
about the future.

LADY HUNSTANTON (*shakes her fan at him*) I don't know how it is,
dear Lord Illingworth, but everything you have said today seems
to me excessively immoral. It has been most interesting, listening   265
to you.

LORD ILLINGWORTH All thought is immoral. Its very essence is
destruction. If you think of anything, you kill it. Nothing survives
being thought of.

LADY HUNSTANTON I don't understand a word, Lord Illingworth.   270
But I have no doubt it is all quite true. Personally, I have very little

to reproach myself with, on the score of thinking. I don't believe
in women thinking too much. Women should think in moderation,
as they should do all things in moderation.

LORD ILLINGWORTH Moderation is a fatal thing, Lady Hunstanton. 275
Nothing succeeds like excess.

LADY HUNSTANTON I hope I shall remember that. It sounds an
admirable maxim. But I'm beginning to forget everything. It's a
great misfortune.

LORD ILLINGWORTH It is one of your most fascinating qualities, 280
Lady Hunstanton. No woman should have a memory. Memory in
a woman° is the beginning of dowdiness. One can always tell from
a woman's bonnet whether she has got a memory or not.

LADY HUNSTANTON How charming you are, dear Lord Illingworth.
You always find out that one's most glaring fault is one's most 285
important virtue. You have the most comforting views of life.

    Enter Farquhar

FARQUHAR Doctor Daubeny's carriage!°

LADY HUNSTANTON My dear Archdeacon! It is only half-past ten.

DR DAUBENY (*rising*) I am afraid I must go, Lady Hunstanton.
Tuesday is always one of Mrs Daubeny's bad nights. 290

LADY HUNSTANTON (*rising*) Well, I won't keep you from her. (*Goes
with him towards door*) I have told Farquhar to put a brace of
partridge into the carriage. Mrs Daubeny may fancy them.

DR DAUBENY It is very kind of you, but Mrs Daubeny never touches
solids now. Lives entirely on jellies. But she is wonderfully 295
cheerful, wonderfully cheerful. She has nothing to complain of.

    Exit with Lady Hunstanton [and Farquhar]

MRS ALLONBY (*goes over to Lord Illingworth*) There is a beautiful
moon tonight.°

LORD ILLINGWORTH Let us go and look at it. To look at anything
that is inconstant is charming nowadays. 300

MRS ALLONBY You have your looking-glass.

LORD ILLINGWORTH It is unkind. It merely shows me my wrinkles.

MRS ALLONBY Mine is better behaved. It never tells me the truth.

LORD ILLINGWORTH Then it is in love with you.

    Exeunt Sir John, Lady Stutfield, Mr Kelvil, and Lord Alfred

GERALD (*to Lord Illingworth*) May I come too? 305

LORD ILLINGWORTH Do, my dear boy.

    *Moves towards door with Mrs Allonby and Gerald. Lady
    Caroline enters, looks rapidly round and goes out in opposite
    direction to that taken by Sir John and Lady Stutfield*

MRS ARBUTHNOT Gerald!

GERALD What, mother!

   Exit Lord Illingworth with Mrs Allonby

MRS ARBUTHNOT It is getting late. Let us go home.

GERALD My dear mother. Do let us wait a little longer. Lord 310
Illingworth is so delightful, and, by the way, mother, I have a great
surprise for you. We are starting for India° at the end of this
month.

MRS ARBUTHNOT Let us go home.

GERALD If you really want to, of course, mother, but I must bid 315
good-bye to Lord Illingworth first. I'll be back in five minutes.

   Exit

MRS ARBUTHNOT Let him leave me if he chooses, but not with
him—not with him! I couldn't bear it.

   Walks up and down. Enter Hester

HESTER What a lovely night it is, Mrs Arbuthnot.

MRS ARBUTHNOT Is it? 320

HESTER Mrs Arbuthnot, I wish you would let us be friends. You are
so different from the other women here. When you came into the
drawing-room this evening, somehow you brought with you a
sense of what is good and pure in life. I had been foolish. There
are things that are right to say, but that may be said at the wrong 325
time and to the wrong people.

MRS ARBUTHNOT I heard what you said. I agree with it, Miss
Worsley.

HESTER I didn't know you had heard it. But I knew you would agree
with me. A woman who has sinned should be punished, shouldn't 330
she?

MRS ARBUTHNOT Yes.

HESTER She shouldn't be allowed to come into the society of good
men and women?

MRS ARBUTHNOT She should not. 335

HESTER And the man should be punished in the same way?

MRS ARBUTHNOT In the same way. And the children, if there are
children, in the same way also?

HESTER Yes, it is right that the sins of the parents° should be visited
on the children. It is a just law. It is God's law. 340

MRS ARBUTHNOT It is one of God's terrible laws.

   Moves away to fireplace°

HESTER You are distressed about your son leaving you, Mrs Arbuthnot?

MRS ARBUTHNOT Yes.

HESTER Do you like him going away with Lord Illingworth? Of 345
course there is position, no doubt, and money, but position and
money are not everything, are they?

MRS ARBUTHNOT They are nothing; they bring misery.

HESTER Then why do you let your son go with him?

MRS ARBUTHNOT He wishes it himself. 350

HESTER But if you asked him he would stay, would he not?

MRS ARBUTHNOT He has set his heart on going.

HESTER He couldn't refuse you anything. He loves you too much.
Ask him to stay. Let me send him in to you. He is on the terrace
at this moment with Lord Illingworth. I heard them laughing 355
together as I passed through the Music-room.

MRS ARBUTHNOT Don't trouble, Miss Worsley, I can wait. It is of
no consequence.

HESTER No, I'll tell him you want him. Do—do ask him to stay.
        Exit Hester

MRS ARBUTHNOT He won't come°—I know he won't come. 360
        Enter Lady Caroline. She looks round anxiously. Enter Gerald

LADY CAROLINE Mr Arbuthnot, may I ask you is Sir John anywhere
on the terrace?

GERALD No, Lady Caroline, he is not on the terrace.

LADY CAROLINE It is very curious. It is time for him to retire.
        Exit Lady Caroline

GERALD Dear mother, I am afraid I kept you waiting. I forgot all 365
about it. I am so happy tonight, mother; I have never been so
happy.

MRS ARBUTHNOT At the prospect of going away?

GERALD Don't put it like that, mother. Of course I am sorry to
leave you. Why, you are the best mother in the whole world. But 370
after all, as Lord Illingworth says, it is impossible to live in
such a place as Wrockley. You don't mind it. But I'm ambitious;
I want something more than that. I want to have a career. I want
to do something that will make you proud of me, and Lord
Illingworth is going to help me. He is going to do everything for 375
me.

MRS ARBUTHNOT Gerald, don't go away with Lord Illingworth. I
implore you not to. Gerald, I beg you!

GERALD Mother, how changeable you are! You don't seem to know
your own mind for a single moment. An hour and a half ago in 380
the drawing-room you agreed to the whole thing; now you turn

round and make objections, and try to force me to give up my one
chance in life. Yes, my one chance. You don't suppose that men
like Lord Illingworth are to be found every day, do you, mother?
It is very strange that when I have had such a wonderful piece of   385
good luck, the one person to put difficulties in my way should be
my own mother. Besides, you know, mother, I love Hester
Worsley. Who could help loving her? I love her more than I have
ever told you, far more. And if I had a position, if I had prospects,
I could—I could ask her to—Don't you understand now, mother,   390
what it means to me to be Lord Illingworth's secretary? To start
like this is to find a career ready for one—before one—waiting for
one. If I were Lord Illingworth's secretary I could ask Hester to
be my wife. As a wretched bank clerk with a hundred a year it
would be an impertinence.   395

MRS ARBUTHNOT I fear you need have no hopes of Miss Worsley. I
know her views on life. She has just told them to me.

    A pause

GERALD Then I have my ambition left, at any rate. That is something—I am glad I have that! You have always tried to crush my
ambition, mother—haven't you? You have told me that the world   400
is a wicked place, that success is not worth having, that society is
shallow, and all that sort of thing—well, I don't believe it, mother.
I think the world must be delightful. I think society must be
exquisite. I think success is a thing worth having. You have been
wrong in all that you taught me, mother, quite wrong. Lord   405
Illingworth is a successful man. He is a fashionable man. He is a
man who lives in the world and for it. Well, I would give anything
to be just like Lord Illingworth.

MRS ARBUTHNOT I would sooner see you dead.

GERALD Mother, what is your objection to Lord Illingworth? Tell   410
me—tell me right out. What is it?

MRS ARBUTHNOT He is a bad man.

GERALD In what way bad? I don't understand what you mean.

MRS ARBUTHNOT I will tell you.

GERALD I suppose you think him bad, because he doesn't believe the   415
same things as you do. Well, men are different from women,
mother. It is natural that they should have different views.

MRS ARBUTHNOT It is not what Lord Illingworth believes, or what
he does not believe, that makes him bad. It is what he is.

GERALD Mother, is it something you know of him? Something you   420
actually know?

MRS ARBUTHNOT It is something I know.

GERALD Something you are quite sure of?

MRS ARBUTHNOT Quite sure of.

GERALD How long have you known it?   425

MRS ARBUTHNOT For twenty years.

GERALD Is it fair to go back twenty years in any man's career? And
what have you or I to do with Lord Illingworth's early life? What
business is it of ours?

MRS ARBUTHNOT What this man has been, he is now, and will be   430
always.

GERALD Mother, tell me what Lord Illingworth did. If he did
anything shameful, I will not go away with him. Surely you know
me well enough for that?

MRS ARBUTHNOT Gerald, come near to me. Quite close to me, as   435
you used to do when you were a little boy, when you were
mother's own boy. (*Gerald sits down beside his mother.° She runs her
fingers through his hair, and strokes his hands*) Gerald, there was a
girl once, she was very young, she was little over eighteen at the
time. George Harford—that was Lord Illingworth's name then—   440
George Harford met her. She knew nothing about life. He—knew
everything. He made this girl love him. He made her love him so
much that she left her father's house with him one morning. She
loved him so much, and he had promised to marry her! He had
solemnly promised to marry her, and she had believed him. She   445
was very young, and—and ignorant of what life really is. But he
put the marriage off from week to week, and month to month.—
She trusted in him all the while. She loved him.—Before her child
was born—for she had a child—she implored him for the child's
sake to marry her, that the child might have a name, that her sin   450
might not be visited on the child, who was innocent. He refused.
After the child was born she left him, taking the child away, and
her life was ruined, and her soul ruined, and all that was sweet,
and good, and pure in her ruined also. She suffered terribly—she
suffers now. She will always suffer. For her there is no joy, no   455
peace, no atonement. She is a woman who drags a chain like a
guilty thing. She is a woman who wears a mask, like a thing that
is a leper. The fire cannot purify her. The waters cannot quench
her anguish. Nothing can heal her! no anodyne can give her sleep!
no poppies forgetfulness! She is lost! She is a lost soul!—That is   460
why I call Lord Illingworth a bad man. That is why I don't want
my boy to be with him.

GERALD My dear mother, it all sounds very tragic, of course. But I
dare say the girl was just as much to blame as Lord Illingworth
was.—After all, would a really nice girl, a girl with any nice   465
feelings at all, go away from her home with a man to whom she
was not married, and live with him as his wife? No nice girl would.
    [*A pause*]

MRS ARBUTHNOT Gerald, I withdraw all my objections. You are at
liberty to go away with Lord Illingworth, when and where you
choose.   470

GERALD Dear mother, I knew you wouldn't stand in my way. You
are the best woman God ever made. And, as for Lord Illingworth,
I don't believe he is capable of anything infamous or base. I can't
believe it of him—I can't.

HESTER (*outside*) Let me go! Let me go!   475
    Enter Hester in terror, and rushes over to Gerald and flings
    herself in his arms

HESTER Oh! save me—save me from him!

GERALD From whom?

HESTER He has insulted me! Horribly insulted me! Save me!

GERALD Who? Who has dared—?
    Lord Illingworth enters at back of stage. Hester breaks from
    Gerald's arms and points to him

GERALD (*he is quite beside himself with rage and indignation*) Lord   480
Illingworth, you have insulted the purest thing on God's earth,° a
thing as pure as my own mother. You have insulted the woman I
love most in the world with my own mother. As there is a God in
Heaven, I will kill you!

MRS ARBUTHNOT (*rushing across and catching hold of him*) No! no!   485

GERALD (*thrusting her back*) Don't hold me, mother. Don't hold
me—I'll kill him!

MRS ARBUTHNOT Gerald!

GERALD Let me go, I say!

MRS ARBUTHNOT Stop, Gerald, stop! He is your own father!   490
    Gerald clutches his mother's hands and looks into her face. She
    sinks slowly on the ground in shame. Hester steals towards the
    door. Lord Illingworth frowns and bites his lip. After a time
    Gerald raises his mother up, puts his arm round her, and leads
    her from the room

ACT DROP

Fourth Act

Scene: Sitting-room at Mrs Arbuthnot's. Large open French window at back, looking on to garden. Doors R.C. and L.C. Gerald Arbuthnot writing at table. Enter Alice R.C. followed by Lady Hunstanton and Mrs Allonby

ALICE Lady Hunstanton and Mrs Allonby.

Exit L.C.

LADY HUNSTANTON Good morning, Gerald.

GERALD (*rising*) Good morning, Lady Hunstanton. Good morning, Mrs Allonby.

LADY HUNSTANTON (*sitting down*) We came to inquire for your dear   5
mother, Gerald. I hope she is better?

GERALD My mother has not come down yet, Lady Hunstanton.

LADY HUNSTANTON Ah, I am afraid the heat was too much for her
last night. I think there must have been thunder in the air. Or
perhaps it was the music. Music makes one feel so romantic—at   10
least it always gets on one's nerves.

MRS ALLONBY It's the same thing, nowadays.

LADY HUNSTANTON I am so glad I don't know what you mean,
dear. I am afraid you mean something wrong. Ah, I see you're
examining Mrs Arbuthnot's pretty room. Isn't it nice and old-fa-   15
shioned?

MRS ALLONBY (*surveying the room through her lorgnette*) It looks quite
the happy English home.°

LADY HUNSTANTON That's just the word, dear; that just describes
it. One feels your mother's good influence in everything she has   20
about her, Gerald.

MRS ALLONBY Lord Illingworth says that all influence is bad, but
that a good influence is the worst in the world.

LADY HUNSTANTON When Lord Illingworth knows Mrs Arbuthnot better he will change his mind. I must certainly bring him   25
here.

MRS ALLONBY I should like to see Lord Illingworth in a happy
English home.

LADY HUNSTANTON It would do him a great deal of good, dear.
Most women in London, nowadays, seem to furnish their rooms   30
with nothing but orchids, foreigners, and French novels. But here
we have the room of a sweet saint. Fresh natural flowers,° books

that don't shock one, pictures that one can look at without
blushing.

MRS ALLONBY But I like blushing.   35

LADY HUNSTANTON Well, there *is* a good deal to be said for
blushing, if one can do it at the proper moment. Poor dear
Hunstanton used to tell me I didn't blush nearly often enough. But
then he was so very particular. He wouldn't let me know any of
his men friends, except those who were over seventy, like poor   40
Lord Ashton: who afterwards, by the way, was brought into the
Divorce Court.° A most unfortunate case.

MRS ALLONBY I delight in men over seventy. They always offer one
the devotion of a lifetime. I think seventy an ideal age for a man.

LADY HUNSTANTON She is quite incorrigible, Gerald, isn't she?   45
By-the-by, Gerald, I hope your dear mother will come and see me
more often now. You and Lord Illingworth start almost immediately, don't you?

GERALD I have given up my intention of being Lord Illingworth's
secretary.   50

LADY HUNSTANTON Surely not, Gerald! It would be most unwise
of you. What reason can you have?

GERALD I don't think I should be suitable for the post.

MRS ALLONBY I wish Lord Illingworth would ask me to be his
secretary. But he says I am not serious enough.   55

LADY HUNSTANTON My dear, you really mustn't talk like that in
this house. Mrs Arbuthnot doesn't know anything about the
wicked society in which we all live. She won't go into it. She is far
too good. I consider it was a great honour her coming to me last
night. It gave quite an atmosphere of respectability to the party.   60

MRS ALLONBY Ah, that must have been what you thought was
thunder in the air.

LADY HUNSTANTON My dear, how can you say that? There is no
resemblance between the two things at all. But really, Gerald, what
do you mean by not being suitable?   65

GERALD Lord Illingworth's views of life and mine are too different.

LADY HUNSTANTON But, my dear Gerald, at your age you shouldn't
have any views of life. They are quite out of place. You must be
guided by others in this matter. Lord Illingworth has made you
the most flattering offer, and travelling with him you would see the 70
world—as much of it, at least, as one should look at—under the
best auspices possible, and stay with all the right people, which is
so important at this solemn moment in your career.

GERALD I don't want to see the world: I've seen enough of it.

MRS ALLONBY I hope you don't think you have exhausted life, Mr   75
Arbuthnot. When a man says that° one knows that life has
exhausted him.

GERALD I don't wish to leave my mother.

LADY HUNSTANTON Now, Gerald, that is pure laziness on your
part. Not leave your mother! If I were your mother I would insist   80
on your going.

    Enter Alice L.C.

ALICE Mrs Arbuthnot's compliments, my lady, but she has a bad
headache,° and cannot see anyone this morning.

    Exit R.C.

LADY HUNSTANTON (*rising*) A bad headache! I am so sorry! Perhaps
you'll bring her up to Hunstanton this afternoon, if she is better,   85
Gerald.

GERALD I am afraid not this afternoon, Lady Hunstanton.

LADY HUNSTANTON Well, tomorrow, then. Ah, if you had a father,
Gerald, he wouldn't let you waste your life here. He would send
you off to Lord Illingworth at once. But mothers are so weak.°   90
They give up to their sons in everything. We are all heart, all heart.
Come, dear, I must call at the rectory and inquire for Mrs
Daubeny, who, I am afraid, is far from well. It is wonderful how
the Archdeacon bears up, quite wonderful. He is the most
sympathetic of husbands. Quite a model. Good-bye, Gerald, give   95
my fondest love to your mother.

MRS ALLONBY Good-bye, Mr Arbuthnot.

GERALD Good-bye.

    Exit Lady Hunstanton and Mrs Allonby, Gerald sits down and
    reads over his letter

GERALD What name can I sign?° I, who have no right to any name.
    Signs name, puts letter into envelope, addresses it, and is about
    to seal it, when door L.C. opens and Mrs Arbuthnot enters.
    Gerald lays down sealing-wax. Mother and son look at each
    other

LADY HUNSTANTON (*through French window at the back*) Good-bye   100
again, Gerald. We are taking the short cut across your pretty
garden. Now, remember my advice to you—start at once with
Lord Illingworth.

MRS ALLONBY *Au revoir*, Mr Arbuthnot. Mind you bring me back
something nice° from your travels—not an Indian shawl—on no   105
account an Indian shawl.

Exeunt

GERALD Mother, I have just written to him.

MRS ARBUTHNOT To whom?

GERALD To my father. I have written to tell him to come here at
four o'clock this afternoon.   110

MRS ARBUTHNOT He shall not come here. He shall not cross the
threshold of my house.

GERALD He must come.

MRS ARBUTHNOT Gerald, if you are going away with Lord Illingworth,
go at once. Go before it kills me: but don't ask me to meet him.   115

GERALD Mother, you don't understand. Nothing in the world would
induce me to go away with Lord Illingworth, or to leave you.
Surely you know me well enough for that. No: I have written to
him to say—

MRS ARBUTHNOT What can you have to say to him?   120

GERALD Can't you guess, mother, what I have written in this letter?

MRS ARBUTHNOT No.

GERALD Mother, surely you can. Think, think what must be done,
now, at once, within the next few days.

MRS ARBUTHNOT There is nothing to be done.   125

GERALD I have written to Lord Illingworth to tell him that he must
marry you.

MRS ARBUTHNOT Marry me?

GERALD Mother, I will force him to do it. The wrong that has been
done you must be repaired. Atonement must be made. Justice may   130
be slow, mother, but it comes in the end. In a few days you shall
be Lord Illingworth's lawful wife.

MRS ARBUTHNOT But, Gerald——

GERALD I will insist upon his doing it. I will make him do it: he will
not dare to refuse.   135

MRS ARBUTHNOT But, Gerald, it is I who refuse. I will not marry
Lord Illingworth.°

GERALD Not marry him? Mother!

MRS ARBUTHNOT I will not marry him.

GERALD But you don't understand: it is for your sake I am talking,   140
not for mine. This marriage, this necessary marriage, this marriage
which for obvious reasons must inevitably take place, will not help
me, will not give me a name that will be really, rightly mine to
bear. But surely it will be something for you, that you, my mother,
should, however late, become the wife of the man who is my   145
father. Will not that be something?

MRS ARBUTHNOT I will not marry him.

GERALD Mother, you must.

MRS ARBUTHNOT I will not. You talk of atonement for a wrong done. What atonement can be made to me? There is no atonement 150 possible. I am disgraced: he is not. That is all. It is the usual history of a man and a woman as it usually happens, as it always happens. And the ending is the ordinary ending. The woman suffers. The man goes free.

GERALD I don't know if that is the ordinary ending, mother: I hope 155 it is not. But your life, at any rate, shall not end like that. The man shall make whatever reparation is possible. It is not enough. It does not wipe out the past, I know that. But at least it makes the future better, better for you, mother.

MRS ARBUTHNOT I refuse to marry Lord Illingworth. 160

GERALD If he came to you himself and asked you to be his wife you would give him a different answer. Remember, he is my father.

MRS ARBUTHNOT If he came himself, which he will not do, my answer would be the same. Remember I am your mother. 165

GERALD Mother, you make it terribly difficult for me by talking like that, and I can't understand why you won't look at this matter from the right, from the only proper standpoint. It is to take away the bitterness out of your life, to take away the shadow that lies on your name, that this marriage must take place. There is no 170 alternative: and after the marriage you and I can go away together. But the marriage must take place first. It is a duty that you owe, not merely to yourself, but to all other women—yes: to all the other women in the world, lest he betray more.

MRS ARBUTHNOT I owe nothing to other women. There is not one 175 of them to help me. There is not one woman in the world to whom I could go for pity, if I would take it, or for sympathy, if I could win it. Women are hard on each other. That girl, last night, good though she is, fled from the room as though I were a tainted thing. She was right. I am a tainted thing. But my wrongs are my own, 180 and I will bear them alone. I must bear them alone. What have women who have not sinned to do with me, or I with them? We do not understand each other.

    Enter Hester behind °

GERALD I implore you to do what I ask you.

MRS ARBUTHNOT What son has ever asked of his mother to make 185 so hideous a sacrifice? None.

GERALD What mother has ever refused to marry the father of her
own child? None.

MRS ARBUTHNOT Let me be the first, then. I will not do it.

GERALD Mother, you believe in religion, and you brought me up to   190
believe in it also. Well, surely your religion, the religion that you
taught me when I was a boy, mother, must tell you that I am right.
You know it, you feel it.

MRS ARBUTHNOT I do not know it. I do not feel it, nor will I ever
stand before God's altar and ask God's blessing on so hideous a   195
mockery as a marriage between me and George Harford. I will not
say the words the Church bids us to say. I will not say them. I
dare not. How could I swear to love the man I loathe, to honour
him who wrought you dishonour, to obey him who, in his mastery,
made me to sin? No: marriage is a sacrament for those who love   200
each other. It is not for such as him, or such as me. Gerald, to save
you from the world's sneers and taunts I have lied to the world.
For twenty years I have lied to the world. I could not tell the world
the truth. Who can, ever? But not for my own sake will I lie to
God, and in God's presence. No, Gerald, no ceremony, Church-   205
hallowed or State-made, shall ever bind me to George Harford. It
may be that I am too bound to him already, who, robbing me, yet
left me richer, so that in the mire of my life I found the pearl of
price, or what I thought would be so.

GERALD I don't understand you now.   210

MRS ARBUTHNOT Men don't understand what mothers are. I am no
different from other women except in the wrong done me and the
wrong I did, and my very heavy punishments and great disgrace.
And yet, to bear you I had to look on death. To nurture you I had
to wrestle with it. Death fought with me for you. All women have   215
to fight with death to keep their children. Death, being childless,
wants our children from us. Gerald, when you were naked° I
clothed you, when you were hungry I gave you food. Night and
day all that long winter I tended you. No office is too mean, no
care too lowly for the thing we women love—and oh! how *I* loved   220
you. Not Hannah° Samuel more. And you needed love, for you
were weakly, and only love could have kept you alive. Only love
can keep anyone alive. And boys are careless often and without
thinking give pain, and we always fancy that when they come to
man's estate° and know us better, they will repay us. But it is not   225
so. The world draws them from our side, and they make friends
with whom they are happier than they are with us, and have

amusements from which we are barred, and interests that are not
ours: and they are unjust to us often, for when they find life bitter
they blame us for it, and when they find it sweet we do not taste   230
its sweetness with them. . . . You made many friends and went into
their houses and were glad with them, and I, knowing my secret,
did not dare to follow, but stayed at home and closed the door,
shut out the sun and sat in darkness. What should I have done in
honest households? My past was ever with me. . . . And you   235
thought I didn't care for the pleasant things of life. I tell you I
longed for them, but did not dare to touch them, feeling I had no
right. You thought I was happier working amongst the poor. That
was my mission, you imagined. It was not, but where else was I to
go? The sick do not ask if the hand that smoothes their pillow is   240
pure, nor the dying care if the lips that touch their brow have
known the kiss of sin. It was you I thought of all the time; I gave
to them the love you did not need: lavished on them a love that
was not theirs. . . . And you thought I spent too much of my time
in going to Church, and in Church duties. But where else could I   245
turn? God's house is the only house where sinners are made
welcome, and you were always in my heart, Gerald, too much in
my heart. For, though day after day, at morn or evensong, I have
knelt in God's house, I have never repented of my sin. How could
I repent of my sin when you, my love, were its fruit! Even now   250
that you are bitter to me I cannot repent. I do not. You are more
to me than innocence. I would rather be your mother—oh! much
rather!—than have been always pure. . . . Oh, don't you see? don't
you understand? It is my dishonour that has made you so dear to
me. It is my disgrace that has bound you so closely to me. It is the   255
price I paid for you—the price of soul and body—that makes me
love you as I do. Oh, don't ask me to do this horrible thing. Child
of my shame, be still the child of my shame!

GERALD Mother, I didn't know you loved me so much as that. And
I will be a better son to you than I have been. And you and I must   260
never leave each other . . . but, mother . . . I can't help it . . . you
must become my father's wife. You must marry him. It is your
duty.

HESTER (*running forward and embracing Mrs Arbuthnot*) No, no: you
shall not. That would be real dishonour, the first you have ever   265
known. That would be real disgrace: the first to touch you. Leave
him and come with me. There are other countries than England.
. . . Oh! other countries over sea, better, wiser, and less unjust
lands. The world is very wide and very big.

MRS ARBUTHNOT No, not for me. For me the world is shrivelled to   270
a palm's breadth, and where I walk there are thorns.

HESTER It shall not be so. We shall somewhere find green valleys and
fresh waters, and if we weep, well, we shall weep together. Have
we not both loved him?

GERALD Hester!   275

HESTER (*waving him back*) Don't, don't! You cannot love me at all,
unless you love her also. You cannot honour me, unless she's holier
to you. In her all womanhood is martyred. Not she alone, but all
of us are stricken in her house.

GERALD Hester, Hester, what shall I do?   280

HESTER Do you respect the man who is your father?

GERALD Respect him? I despise him! He is infamous!

HESTER I thank you for saving me from him last night.

GERALD Ah, that is nothing. I would die to save you. But you don't
tell me what to do now!   285

HESTER Have I not thanked you for saving *me*?

GERALD But what should I do?

HESTER Ask your own heart, not mine. I never had a mother to save,
or shame.

MRS ARBUTHNOT He is hard—he is hard. Let me go away.   290

GERALD (*rushes over and kneels down° beside his mother*) Mother,
forgive me: I have been to blame.

MRS ARBUTHNOT Don't kiss my hands: they are cold. My heart is
cold: something has broken it.

HESTER Ah, don't say that. Hearts live by being wounded. Pleasure   295
may turn a heart to stone, riches may make it callous, but
sorrow—oh, sorrow cannot break it. Besides, what sorrows have
you now? Why, at this moment you are more dear to him than
ever, *dear* though you have *been*, and oh! how dear you *have* been
always. Ah! be kind to him.   300

GERALD You are my mother and my father all in one. I need no
second parent. It was for you I spoke, for you alone. Oh, say
something, mother. Have I but found one love to lose another?
Don't tell me that. O mother, you are cruel.

Gets up and flings himself sobbing on a sofa°

MRS ARBUTHNOT (*to Hester*) But has he found indeed another love?   305

HESTER You know I have loved him always.

MRS ARBUTHNOT But we are very poor.

HESTER Who, being loved, is poor? Oh, no one. I hate my riches.
They are a burden. Let him share it with me.

MRS ARBUTHNOT But we are disgraced. We rank among the out- 310
casts. Gerald is nameless. The sins of the parents should be visited
on the children. It is God's law.

HESTER I was wrong. God's law is only Love.

MRS ARBUTHNOT (*rises, and taking Hester by the hand, goes slowly
over to where Gerald is lying on the sofa with his head buried in his
hands. She touches him and he looks up*) Gerald, I cannot give you 315
a father, but I have brought you a wife.

GERALD Mother, I am not worthy either of her or you.

MRS ARBUTHNOT So she comes first, you are worthy. And when you
are away, Gerald . . . with . . . her—oh, think of me sometimes.
Don't forget me. And when you pray, pray for me. We should pray 320
when we are happiest, and you will be happy, Gerald.

HESTER Oh, you don't think of leaving us?

GERALD Mother, you won't leave us?

MRS ARBUTHNOT I might bring shame upon you!

GERALD Mother! 325

MRS ARBUTHNOT For a little then: and if you let me, near you
always.

HESTER (*to Mrs Arbuthnot*) Come out with us to the garden.

MRS ARBUTHNOT Later on, later on.

> *Exeunt Hester and Gerald. Mrs Arbuthnot goes towards door
> L.C. Stops at looking-glass over mantelpiece and looks into it.
> Enter Alice R.C.*

ALICE A gentleman to see you, ma'am. 330

MRS ARBUTHNOT Say I am not at home. Show me the card. (*Takes
card from salver and looks at it*) Say I will not see him.

> *Lord Illingworth enters. Mrs Arbuthnot sees him in the glass and
> starts,° but does not turn round. Exit Alice*

What can you have to say to me today, George Harford? You can
have nothing to say to me. You must leave this house.

LORD ILLINGWORTH Rachel, Gerald knows everything about you 335
and me now, so some arrangement must be come to that will suit
us all three. I assure you, he will find in me the most charming
and generous of fathers.

MRS ARBUTHNOT My son may come in at any moment. I saved you
last night. I may not be able to save you again. My son feels my 340
dishonour strongly, terribly strongly. I beg you to go.

LORD ILLINGWORTH (*sitting down*) Last night was excessively unfortunate. That silly Puritan girl making a scene merely because I
wanted to kiss her. What harm is there in a kiss?

MRS ARBUTHNOT (*turning round*) A kiss may ruin a human life, 345
George Harford. *I* know that. *I* know that too well.

LORD ILLINGWORTH We won't discuss that at present. What is of
importance today, as yesterday, is still our son. I am extremely
fond of him, as you know, and odd though it may seem to you, I
admired his conduct last night immensely. He took up the cudgels 350
for that pretty prude with wonderful promptitude. He is just what
I should have liked a son of mine to be. Except that no son of mine
should ever take the side of the Puritans: that is always an error.
Now, what I propose is this.

MRS ARBUTHNOT Lord Illingworth, no proposition of yours inter- 355
ests me.

LORD ILLINGWORTH According to our ridiculous English laws, I
can't legitimize Gerald. But I can leave him my property. Illingworth is entailed,° of course, but it is a tedious barrack of a place.
He can have Ashby, which is much prettier, Harborough, which 360
has the best shooting in the north of England, and the house in St
James's Square. What more can a gentleman require in this world?

MRS ARBUTHNOT Nothing more, I am quite sure.

LORD ILLINGWORTH As for a title, a title is really rather a nuisance
in these democratic days. As George Harford I had everything I 365
wanted. Now I have merely everything that other people want,
which isn't nearly so pleasant. Well, my proposal is this.

MRS ARBUTHNOT I told you I was not interested, and I beg you to
go.

LORD ILLINGWORTH The boy is to be with you for six months in 370
the year, and with me for the other six. That is perfectly fair, is it
not? You can have whatever allowance you like, and live where you
choose. As for your past, no one knows anything about it except
myself and Gerald. There is the Puritan, of course, the Puritan in
white muslin, but she doesn't count. She couldn't tell the story 375
without explaining that she objected to being kissed, could she?
And all the women would think her a fool and the men think her
a bore. And you need not be afraid that Gerald won't be my heir.
I needn't tell you I have not the slightest intention of marrying.

MRS ARBUTHNOT You come too late. My son has no need of you. 380
You are not necessary.

LORD ILLINGWORTH What do you mean, Rachel?

MRS ARBUTHNOT That you are not necessary° to Gerald's career.
He does not require you.

LORD ILLINGWORTH I do not understand you. 385

MRS ARBUTHNOT Look into the garden. *(Lord Illingworth rises and goes towards window)* You had better not let them see you: you bring unpleasant memories. *(Lord Illingworth looks out and starts)* She loves him. They love each other. We are safe from you, and we are going away.   390

LORD ILLINGWORTH Where?

MRS ARBUTHNOT We will not tell you, and if you find us we will not know you. You seem surprised. What welcome would you get from the girl whose lips you tried to soil, from the boy whose life you have shamed, from the mother whose dishonour comes from   395
you?

LORD ILLINGWORTH You have grown hard, Rachel.

MRS ARBUTHNOT I was too weak once. It is well for me that I have changed.

LORD ILLINGWORTH I was very young at the time. We men know   400
life too early.

MRS ARBUTHNOT And we women know life too late. That is the difference between men and women.

    A pause°

LORD ILLINGWORTH Rachel, I want my son. My money may be of no use to him now. I may be of no use to him, but I want my son.   405
Bring us together, Rachel. You can do it if you choose. *(Sees letter on table)*

MRS ARBUTHNOT There is no room in my boy's life for *you*. He is not interested in *you*.

LORD ILLINGWORTH Then why does he write to me?

MRS ARBUTHNOT What do you mean?   410

LORD ILLINGWORTH What letter is this?
    Takes up letter

MRS ARBUTHNOT That—is nothing. Give it to me.

LORD ILLINGWORTH It is addressed to *me*.

MRS ARBUTHNOT You are not to open it. I forbid you to open it.

LORD ILLINGWORTH And in Gerald's handwriting.   415

MRS ARBUTHNOT It was not to have been sent. It is a letter he wrote to you this morning before he saw me. But he is sorry now he wrote it, very sorry. You are not to open it. Give it to me.

LORD ILLINGWORTH It belongs to me. *(Opens it, sits down, and reads it slowly.*° *Mrs Arbuthnot watches him all the time)* You have read   420
this letter, I suppose, Rachel?

MRS ARBUTHNOT No.

LORD ILLINGWORTH You know what is in it?

MRS ARBUTHNOT Yes!

LORD ILLINGWORTH I don't admit for a moment that the boy is   425
right in what he says. I don't admit that it is any duty of mine to
marry you. I deny it entirely. But to get my son back I am
ready—yes, I am ready to marry you, Rachel—and to treat you
always with the deference and respect due to my wife. I will marry
you as soon as you choose. I give you my word of honour.   430

MRS ARBUTHNOT You made that promise to me once before and
broke it.

LORD ILLINGWORTH I will keep it now. And that will show you that
I love my son, at least as much as you love him. For when I marry
you, Rachel, there are some ambitions I shall have to surrender.   435
High ambitions, too, if any ambition is high.

MRS ARBUTHNOT I decline to marry you, Lord Illingworth.

LORD ILLINGWORTH Are you serious?

MRS ARBUTHNOT Yes.

LORD ILLINGWORTH Do tell me your reasons. They would interest   440
me enormously.

MRS ARBUTHNOT I have already explained them to my son.

LORD ILLINGWORTH I suppose they were intensely sentimental,
weren't they? You women live by your emotions and for them.
You have no philosophy of life.   445

MRS ARBUTHNOT You are right. We women live by our emotions
and for them. By our passions, and for them, if you will. I have
two passions, Lord Illingworth; my love of him, my hate of you.
You cannot kill those. They feed each other.

LORD ILLINGWORTH What sort of love is that which needs to have   450
hate as its brother?

MRS ARBUTHNOT It is the sort of love I have for Gerald. Do you
think that terrible? Well, it is terrible. All love is terrible. All love
is a tragedy. I loved you once, Lord Illingworth. Oh, what a
tragedy for a woman to have loved you!   455

LORD ILLINGWORTH So you really refuse to marry me?

MRS ARBUTHNOT Yes.

LORD ILLINGWORTH Because you hate me?

MRS ARBUTHNOT Yes.

LORD ILLINGWORTH And does my son hate me as you do?   460

MRS ARBUTHNOT No.

LORD ILLINGWORTH I am glad of that, Rachel.

MRS ARBUTHNOT He merely despises you.

LORD ILLINGWORTH What a pity! What a pity for him, I mean.

MRS ARBUTHNOT Don't be deceived, George. Children begin by 465
loving their parents. After a time they judge them. Rarely if ever
do they forgive them.

LORD ILLINGWORTH (*reads letter over again, very slowly*) May I ask
by what arguments you made the boy who wrote this letter, this
beautiful, passionate letter, believe that you should not marry his 470
father, the father of your own child?

MRS ARBUTHNOT It was not I who made him see it. It was another.

LORD ILLINGWORTH What *fin-de-siècle* person?°

MRS ARBUTHNOT The Puritan, Lord Illingworth.

> *A pause. Lord Illingworth winces, then rises slowly and goes over
> to table where his hat and gloves are. Mrs Arbuthnot is standing
> close to the table. He picks up one of the gloves, and begins
> putting it on*°

LORD ILLINGWORTH There is not much then for me to do here, 475
Rachel?

MRS ARBUTHNOT Nothing.

LORD ILLINGWORTH It is good-bye, is it?

MRS ARBUTHNOT For ever, I hope, this time, Lord Illingworth.

LORD ILLINGWORTH How curious! At this moment you look exact- 480
ly as you looked the night you left me twenty years ago. You have
just the same expression in your mouth. Upon my word, Rachel,
no woman ever loved me as you did. Why, you gave yourself to
me like a flower, to do anything I liked with. You were the prettiest
of playthings, the most fascinating of small romances. . . . (*Pulls* 485
out watch) Quarter to two! Must be strolling back to Hunstanton.
Don't suppose I shall see you there again. I'm sorry, I am, really.
It's been an amusing experience to have met amongst people of
one's own rank, and treated quite seriously too, one's mistress, and
one's——° 490

MRS ARBUTHNOT *snatches up glove and strikes Lord Illingworth across
the face with it. Lord Illingworth starts. He is dazed by the insult of
his punishment. Then he controls himself, and goes to window and looks
out at his son. Sighs and leaves the room*

MRS ARBUTHNOT (*falls sobbing on the sofa*) He would have said it.
He would have said it.

> *Enter Gerald and Hester from the garden*

GERALD Well, dear mother. You never came out after all. So we have
come in to fetch you. Mother, you have not been crying?

> *Kneels down beside her*

MRS ARBUTHNOT My boy! My boy! My boy! 495

Running her fingers through his hair

HESTER (*coming over*) But you have two children now. You'll let me be your daughter?

MRS ARBUTHNOT (*looking up*) Would you choose me for a mother?

HESTER You of all women I have ever known.

They move towards the door leading into garden with their arms round each other's waists. Gerald goes to table L.C. for his hat. On turning round he sees Lord Illingworth's glove lying on the floor, and picks it up°

GERALD Hallo, mother, whose glove is this? You have had a visitor.   500
Who was it?

MRS ARBUTHNOT (*turning round*) Oh! no one. No one in particular.
A man of no importance.

CURTAIN

AN IDEAL HUSBAND

To

FRANK HARRIS

*A slight tribute to
his power and distinction as an artist
his chivalry and nobility as a friend*

THE PERSONS OF THE PLAY

The play was first staged at the Theatre Royal, Haymarket, London, 3 January 1895.

The Earl of Caversham, KG	*Mr Alfred Bishop*
Viscount Goring (his son)	*Mr Charles H. Hawtrey*
Sir Robert Chiltern, Bt. (Under-Secretary for Foreign Affairs)	*Mr Lewis Waller*
Vicomte de Nanjac (Attaché at the French Embassy in London)	*Mr Cosmo Stuart*
Mr Montford	*Mr Henry Stanford*
Mason (Butler to Sir Robert Chiltern)	*Mr H. Deane*
Phipps (Lord Goring's servant)	*Mr C. H. Brookfield*
James (Footman at Lord Goring's)	*Mr Charles Meyrick*
Harold (Footman at Sir Robert Chiltern's)	*Mr Goodhart*
Lady Chiltern	*Miss Julia Neilson*
Lady Markby	*Miss Fanny Brough*
The Countess of Basildon	*Miss Vane Featherston*
Mrs Marchmont	*Miss Helen Forsyth*
Miss Mabel Chiltern (Sir Robert's sister)	*Miss Maude Millett*
Mrs Cheveley	*Miss Florence West*

THE SCENES OF THE PLAY

Act 1
The Octagon Room in Sir Robert Chiltern's house in Grosvenor Square

Act 2
Morning-room in Sir Robert Chiltern's house

Act 3
The Library of Lord Goring's house in Curzon Street

Act 4
Same as Act 2

Time
The Present

Place
London

The action of the play is completed within twenty-four hours

First Act

Scene: The Octagon room at Sir Robert Chiltern's house in Grosvenor Square.

The room is brilliantly lighted and full of guests [including the Viconte de Nanjac, the Duchess of Maryborough, and Mabel Chiltern]. At the top of the staircase stands Lady Chiltern, a woman of grave Greek beauty, about twenty-seven years of age. She receives the guests as they come up. [Mason stands in the background]. Over the well of the staircase hangs a great chandelier with wax lights, which illumine a large eighteenth-century French tapestry—representing the Triumph of Love, from a design by Boucher—that is stretched on the staircase well. On the right is the entrance to the music-room. The sound of a string quartet is faintly heard. The entrance on the left leads to other reception-rooms. Mrs Marchmont and Lady Basildon, two very pretty women, are seated together on a Louis Seize sofa. They are types of exquisite fragility. Their affectation of manner has a delicate charm. Watteau would have loved to paint them

MRS MARCHMONT Going on° to the Hartlocks' tonight, Olivia?

LADY BASILDON I suppose so. Are you?

MRS MARCHMONT Yes. Horribly tedious parties they give, don't they?

LADY BASILDON Horribly tedious! Never know why I go. Never know why I go anywhere.   5

MRS MARCHMONT I come here to be educated.

LADY BASILDON Ah! I hate being educated!

MRS MARCHMONT So do I. It puts one almost on a level with the commercial classes, doesn't it? But dear Gertrude Chiltern is always telling me that I should have some serious purpose in life. So I come here to try to find one.   10

LADY BASILDON (*looking round through her lorgnette*) I don't see anybody here tonight whom one could possibly call a serious purpose. The man who took me in to dinner talked to me about his wife the whole time.   15

MRS MARCHMONT How very trivial° of him!

LADY BASILDON Terribly trivial! What did your man talk about?

MRS MARCHMONT About myself.

LADY BASILDON (*languidly*) And were you interested?   20

MRS MARCHMONT (*shaking her head*) Not in the smallest degree.

LADY BASILDON What martyrs we are, dear Margaret!

MRS MARCHMONT (*rising*) And how well it becomes us, Olivia!

> *They rise and go towards the music-room. The Vicomte De Nanjac, a young attaché known for his neckties° and his Anglomania, approaches with a low bow, and enters into conversation*

MASON (*announcing guests from the top of the staircase*) Mr and Lady Jane Barford. Lord Caversham.   25

> *Enter Lord Caversham, an old gentleman of seventy, wearing the riband and star of the Garter.° A fine Whig type. Rather like a portrait by Lawrence*

LORD CAVERSHAM Good evening, Lady Chiltern! Has my good-for-nothing young son been here?

LADY CHILTERN (*smiling*) I don't think Lord Goring has arrived yet.

MABEL CHILTERN (*coming up to Lord Caversham*) Why do you call Lord Goring good-for-nothing?   30

> *Mabel Chiltern is a perfect example of the English type of prettiness,° the apple-blossom type. She has all the fragrance and freedom of a flower. There is ripple after ripple of sunlight in her hair, and the little mouth, with its parted lips, is expectant, like the mouth of a child. She has the fascinating tyranny of youth, and the astonishing courage of innocence. To sane people she is not reminiscent of any work of art. But she is really like a Tanagra° statuette, and would be rather annoyed if she were told so*

LORD CAVERSHAM Because he leads such an idle life.

MABEL CHILTERN How can you say such a thing? Why, he rides in the Row° at ten o'clock in the morning, goes to the Opera three times a week, changes his clothes at least five times a day, and dines out every night of the season. You don't call that leading an   35 idle life, do you?

LORD CAVERSHAM (*looking at her with a kindly twinkle in his eyes*) You are a very charming young lady!

MABEL CHILTERN How sweet of you to say that, Lord Caversham! Do come to us more often. You know we are always at home on   40 Wednesdays,° and you look so well with your star!

LORD CAVERSHAM Never go anywhere now. Sick of London Society. Shouldn't mind being introduced to my own tailor; he always votes on the right side. But object strongly to being sent down to dinner with my wife's milliner. Never could stand Lady   45 Caversham's bonnets.

MABEL CHILTERN Oh, I love London Society! I think it has immensely improved. It is entirely composed now of beautiful idiots and brilliant lunatics. Just what Society should be.

LORD CAVERSHAM Hum! Which is Goring? Beautiful idiot, or the other thing? 50

MABEL CHILTERN (*gravely*) I have been obliged for the present to put Lord Goring into a class quite by himself. But he is developing charmingly!

LORD CAVERSHAM Into what? 55

MABEL CHILTERN (*with a little curtsey*) I hope to let you know very soon, Lord Caversham!

MASON (*announcing guests*) Lady Markby. Mrs Cheveley.

> *Enter Lady Markby and Mrs Cheveley. Lady Markby is a pleasant, kindly, popular woman, with grey hair à la mar-quise° and good lace. Mrs Cheveley, who accompanies her, is tall and rather slight. Lips very thin and highly-coloured, a line of scarlet on a pallid face. Venetian red hair, aquiline nose, and long throat. Rouge accentuates the natural paleness of her complexion. Grey-green eyes that move restlessly. She is in heliotrope, with diamonds. She looks rather like an orchid, and makes great demands on one's curiosity. In all her movements she is extremely graceful. A work of art, on the whole, but showing the influence of too many schools*

LADY MARKBY Good evening, dear Gertrude! So kind of you to let me bring my friend, Mrs Cheveley. Two such charming women should know each other! 60

LADY CHILTERN (*advances toward Mrs Cheveley with a sweet smile. Then suddenly stops, and bows rather distantly*) I think Mrs Cheveley and I have met before. I did not know she had married a second time. 65

LADY MARKBY (*genially*) Ah, nowadays people marry as often as they can, don't they? It is most fashionable. (*To Duchess of Maryborough*) Dear Duchess, and how is the Duke? Brain still weak, I suppose? Well, that is only to be expected, is it not? His good father was just the same. There is nothing like race, is there? 70

MRS CHEVELEY (*playing with her fan*) But have we really met before, Lady Chiltern? I can't remember where. I have been out of England for so long.

LADY CHILTERN We were at school together, Mrs Cheveley.

MRS CHEVELEY (*superciliously*) Indeed? I have forgotten all about my schooldays. I have a vague impression that they were detestable. 75

LADY CHILTERN (*coldly*) I am not surprised!

MRS CHEVELEY (*in her sweetest manner*) Do you know, I am quite looking forward to meeting your clever husband, Lady Chiltern. Since he has been at the Foreign Office,° he has been so much talked of in Vienna.° They actually succeed in spelling his name right in the newspapers. That in itself is fame, on the continent. 80

LADY CHILTERN: I hardly think there will be much in common between you and my husband, Mrs Cheveley!

    Moves away°

VICOMTE DE NANJAC Ah! chère Madame, quelle surprise! I have not seen you since Berlin! 85

MRS CHEVELEY Not since Berlin, Vicomte. Five years ago!

VICOMTE DE NANJAC And you are younger and more beautiful than ever. How do you manage it?

MRS CHEVELEY By making it a rule only to talk to perfectly charming people like yourself. 90

VICOMTE DE NANJAC Ah! you flatter me. You butter me,° as they say here.

MRS CHEVELEY Do they say that here? How dreadful of them!

VICOMTE DE NANJAC Yes, they have a wonderful language. It should be more widely known. 95

    Sir Robert Chiltern° *enters. A man of forty, but looking somewhat younger. Clean-shaven, with finely-cut features, dark-haired and dark-eyed. A personality of mark. Not popular—few personalities are. But intensely admired by the few, and deeply respected by the many. The note of his manner is that of perfect distinction, with a slight touch of pride. One feels that he is conscious of the success he has made in life. A nervous temperament, with a tired look. The firmly-chiselled mouth and chin contrast strikingly with the romantic expression in the deep-set eyes. The variance is suggestive of an almost complete separation of passion and intellect, as though thought and emotion were each isolated in its own sphere through some violence of will-power. There is nervousness in the nostrils, and in the pale, thin, pointed hands. It would be inaccurate to call him picturesque. Pic-turesqueness cannot survive the House of Commons. But Van-dyck would have liked to have painted his head*

SIR ROBERT CHILTERN Good evening, Lady Markby!° I hope you have brought Sir John with you?

LADY MARKBY. Oh! I have brought a much more charming person than Sir John. Sir John's temper since he has taken seriously to politics has become quite unbearable. Really, now that the House 100 of Commons is trying to become useful, it does a great deal of harm.

SIR ROBERT CHILTERN I hope not, Lady Markby. At any rate we do our best to waste the public time, don't we? But who is this charming person you have been kind enough to bring to us?

LADY MARKBY Her name is Mrs Cheveley. One of the Dorsetshire Cheveleys, I suppose. But I really don't know. Families are so mixed nowadays. Indeed, as a rule, everybody turns out to be somebody else.

SIR ROBERT CHILTERN Mrs Cheveley? I seem to know the name.

LADY MARKBY She has just arrived from Vienna.

SIR ROBERT CHILTERN: Ah! yes. I think I know whom you mean.

LADY MARKBY Oh! she goes everywhere there, and has such pleasant scandals about all her friends. I really must go to Vienna next winter. I hope there is a good chef° at the Embassy.

SIR ROBERT CHILTERN If there is not, the Ambassador will certainly have to be recalled. Pray point out Mrs Cheveley to me. I should like to see her.

LADY MARKBY Let me introduce you. (*To Mrs Cheveley*) My dear, Sir Robert Chiltern is dying to know you!

SIR ROBERT CHILTERN (*bowing*) Every one is dying to know the brilliant Mrs Cheveley. Our attachés at Vienna write to us about nothing else.

MRS CHEVELEY Thank you, Sir Robert. An acquaintance that begins with a compliment is sure to develop into a real friendship. It starts in the right manner. And I find that I know Lady Chiltern already.

SIR ROBERT CHILTERN Really?

MRS CHEVELEY Yes. She has just reminded me that we were at school together. I remember it perfectly now. She always got the good conduct prize. I have a distinct recollection of Lady Chiltern always getting the good conduct prize!

SIR ROBERT CHILTERN (*smiling*) And what prizes did you get, Mrs Cheveley?

MRS CHEVELEY My prizes came a little later on in life. I don't think any of them were for good conduct. I forget!

SIR ROBERT CHILTERN I am sure they were for something charming!

MRS CHEVELEY I don't know that women are always rewarded for being charming. I think they are usually punished for it! Certainly, more women grow old nowadays through the faithfulness of their admirers than through anything else! At least that is the only way

I can account for the terribly haggard look of most of your pretty women in London!

SIR ROBERT CHILTERN What an appalling philosophy that sounds! To attempt to classify you, Mrs Cheveley, would be an impertinence. But may I ask, at heart, are you an optimist or a pessimist? Those seem to be the only two fashionable religions left to us nowadays.

MRS CHEVELEY Oh, I'm neither. Optimism begins in a broad grin, and Pessimism ends with blue spectacles.° Besides, they are both of them merely poses.

SIR ROBERT CHILTERN You prefer to be natural?

MRS CHEVELEY Sometimes. But it is such a very difficult pose to keep up.

SIR ROBERT CHILTERN What would those modern psychological novelists, of whom we hear so much, say to such a theory as that?

MRS CHEVELEY Ah! the strength of women comes from the fact that psychology cannot explain us. Men can be analysed, women . . . merely adored.

SIR ROBERT CHILTERN You think science cannot grapple with the problem of women?

MRS CHEVELEY Science can never grapple with the irrational. That is why it has no future before it, in this world.

SIR ROBERT CHILTERN And women represent the irrational.

MRS CHEVELEY Well-dressed women do.

SIR ROBERT CHILTERN (*with a polite bow*) I fear I could hardly agree with you there. But do sit down. And now tell me, what makes you leave your brilliant Vienna for our gloomy London—or perhaps the question is indiscreet?

MRS CHEVELEY Questions are never indiscreet. Answers sometimes are.

SIR ROBERT CHILTERN Well, at any rate, may I know if it is politics or pleasure?

MRS CHEVELEY Politics are my only pleasure. You see nowadays it is not fashionable to flirt till one is forty, or to be romantic till one is forty-five, so we poor women who are under thirty, or say we are, have nothing open to us but politics or philanthropy. And philanthropy seems to me to have become simply the refuge of people who wish to annoy their fellow-creatures. I prefer politics. I think they are more . . . becoming!

SIR ROBERT CHILTERN A political life is a noble career!

MRS CHEVELEY Sometimes. And sometimes it is a clever game, Sir
Robert. And sometimes it is a great nuisance.   185

SIR ROBERT CHILTERN Which do you find it?

MRS CHEVELEY I? A combination of all three. (*Drops her fan*)°

SIR ROBERT CHILTERN (*picks up fan*) Allow me!

MRS CHEVELEY Thanks.

SIR ROBERT CHILTERN But you have not told me yet what makes   190
you honour London so suddenly. Our season is almost over.

MRS CHEVELEY Oh! I don't care about the London season! It is too
matrimonial. People are either hunting for husbands, or hiding
from them. I wanted to meet you. It is quite true. You know what
a woman's curiosity is. Almost as great as a man's! I wanted   195
immensely to meet you, and . . . to ask you to do something for
me.

SIR ROBERT CHILTERN I hope it is not a little thing, Mrs Cheveley.
I find that little things are so very difficult to do.

MRS CHEVELEY (*after a moment's reflection*) No, I don't think it is   200
quite a little thing.

SIR ROBERT CHILTERN I am so glad. Do tell me what it is.

MRS CHEVELEY: Later on. (*Rises*) And now may I walk through your
beautiful house? I hear your pictures are charming. Poor Baron
Arnheim°—you remember the Baron?—used to tell me you had   205
some wonderful Corots.

SIR ROBERT CHILTERN (*with an almost imperceptible start*) Did you
know Baron Arnheim well?

MRS CHEVELEY (*smiling*) Intimately. Did you?

SIR ROBERT CHILTERN At one time.   210

MRS CHEVELEY Wonderful man, wasn't he?
  [*A pause*]

SIR ROBERT CHILTERN He was very remarkable, in many ways.

MRS CHEVELEY I often think it such a pity he never wrote his
memoirs. They would have been most interesting.

SIR ROBERT CHILTERN Yes: he knew men and cities well, like the   215
old Greek.°

MRS CHEVELEY Without the dreadful disadvantage of having a
Penelope waiting at home for him.

MASON Lord Goring.
  Enter Lord Goring.° Thirty-four, but always says he is younger.
  A well-bred, expressionless face. He is clever, but would not like
  to be thought so. A flawless dandy, he would be annoyed if he
  were considered romantic. He plays with life, and is on perfectly

*good terms with the world. He is fond of being misunderstood. It
gives him a post of vantage.*

SIR ROBERT CHILTERN Good evening, my dear Arthur! Mrs Cheve-   220
ley, allow me to introduce to you Lord Goring, the idlest man in
London.

MRS CHEVELEY I have met Lord Goring before.

LORD GORING (*bowing*) I did not think you would remember me,
Mrs Cheveley.   225

MRS CHEVELEY My memory is under admirable control. And are
you still a bachelor?

LORD GORING I . . . believe so.

MRS CHEVELEY How very romantic!

LORD GORING Oh! I am not at all romantic. I am not old enough. I   230
leave romance to my seniors.

SIR ROBERT CHILTERN Lord Goring is the result of Boodle's Club,°
Mrs Cheveley.

MRS CHEVELEY He reflects every credit on the institution.

LORD GORING May I ask are you staying in London long?   235

MRS CHEVELEY That depends partly on the weather, partly on the
cooking, and partly on Sir Robert.

SIR ROBERT CHILTERN You are not going to plunge us into a
European war, I hope?

MRS CHEVELEY There is no danger, at present!   240
*She nods to Lord Goring, with a look of amusement in her eyes,
and goes out with Sir Robert Chiltern. Lord Goring saunters
over to Mabel Chiltern*

MABEL CHILTERN You are very late!

LORD GORING Have you missed me?

MABEL CHILTERN Awfully!

LORD GORING Then I am sorry I did not stay away longer. I like
being missed.   245

MABEL CHILTERN How very selfish of you!

LORD GORING I am very selfish.

MABEL CHILTERN You are always telling me of your bad qualities,
Lord Goring.

LORD GORING I have only told you half of them as yet, Miss Mabel!   250

MABEL CHILTERN Are the others very bad?

LORD GORING Quite dreadful! When I think of them at night I go
to sleep at once.

MABEL CHILTERN Well, I delight in your bad qualities. I wouldn't
have you part with one of them.   255

LORD GORING How very nice of you! But then you are always nice.
  By the way, I want to ask you a question, Miss Mabel. Who
  brought Mrs Cheveley here? That woman in heliotrope, who has
  just gone out of the room with your brother?

MABEL CHILTERN Oh, I think Lady Markby brought her. Why do   260
  you ask?

LORD GORING I hadn't seen her for years, that is all.

MABEL CHILTERN What an absurd reason!

LORD GORING All reasons are absurd.

MABEL CHILTERN What sort of a woman is she?°   265

LORD GORING Oh! a genius in the daytime and a beauty at night!

MABEL CHILTERN I dislike her already.

LORD GORING That shows your admirable good taste.

VICOMTE DE NANJAC (*approaching*) Ah, the English young lady is the
  dragon of good taste,° is she not? Quite the dragon of good taste.   270

LORD GORING So the newspapers are always telling us.

VICOMTE DE NANJAC I read all your English newspapers, I find
  them so amusing.

LORD GORING Then, my dear Nanjac, you must certainly read
  between the lines.   275

VICOMTE DE NANJAC I should like to, but my professor objects. (*To
  Mabel Chiltern*) May I have the pleasure of escorting you to the
  music-room, Mademoiselle?

MABEL CHILTERN (*looking very disappointed*) Delighted, Vicomte,
  quite delighted! (*Turning to Lord Goring*) Aren't you coming to the   280
  music-room?

LORD GORING Not if there is any music going on, Miss Mabel.

MABEL CHILTERN (*severely*) The music is in German. You would
  not understand it.

> Goes out with the Vicomte de Nanjac. Lord Caversham comes
> up to his son

LORD CAVERSHAM Well, sir! what are you doing here? Wasting your   285
  life as usual! You should be in bed, sir. You keep too late hours! I
  heard of you the other night at Lady Rufford's° dancing till four
  o'clock in the morning!

LORD GORING Only a quarter to four, father.

LORD CAVERSHAM Can't make out how you stand London Society.   290
  The thing has gone to the dogs, a lot of damned nobodies talking
  about nothing.

LORD GORING I love talking about nothing, father. It is the only
  thing I know anything about.

LORD CAVERSHAM You seem to me to be living entirely for pleasure.   295

LORD GORING What else is there to live for, father? Nothing ages like happiness.

LORD CAVERSHAM You are heartless, sir, very heartless!

LORD GORING I hope not, father. Good evening, Lady Basildon!

LADY BASILDON (*arching two pretty eyebrows*) Are you here? I had   300
no idea you ever came to political parties!

LORD GORING I adore political parties. They are the only place left to us where people don't talk politics.

LADY BASILDON I delight in talking politics. I talk them all day long. But I can't bear listening to them. I don't know how the   305
unfortunate men in the House stand these long debates.

LORD GORING By never listening.

LADY BASILDON Really?

LORD GORING (*in his most serious manner*) Of course. You see, it is a very dangerous thing to listen. If one listens one may be convinced;   310
and a man who allows himself to be convinced by an argument is a thoroughly unreasonable person.

LADY BASILDON Ah! that accounts for so much in men that I have never understood, and so much in women that their husbands never appreciate in them!   315

MRS MARCHMONT (*with a sigh*) Our husbands never appreciate anything in us. We have to go to others for that!

LADY BASILDON (*emphatically*) Yes, always to others, have we not?

LORD GORING (*smiling*) And those are the views of the two ladies who are known to have the most admirable husbands in London.   320

MRS MARCHMONT That is exactly what we can't stand. My Reginald is quite hopelessly faultless. He is really unendurably so, at times! There is not the smallest element of excitement in knowing him.

LORD GORING How terrible! Really, the thing should be more widely known!   325

LADY BASILDON Basildon is quite as bad; he is as domestic as if he was a bachelor.

MRS MARCHMONT (*pressing Lady Basildon's hand*) My poor Olivia! We have married perfect husbands, and we are well punished for it.   330

LORD GORING I should have thought it was the husbands who were punished.

MRS MARCHMONT (*drawing herself up*) Oh dear, no! They are as happy as possible! And as for trusting us, it is tragic how much they trust us.   335

LADY BASILDON Perfectly tragic!

LORD GORING Or comic, Lady Basildon?

LADY BASILDON Certainly not comic, Lord Goring. How unkind of you to suggest such a thing!

MRS MARCHMONT I am afraid Lord Goring is in the camp of the enemy, as usual. I saw him talking to that Mrs Cheveley when he came in.

LORD GORING Handsome woman, Mrs Cheveley!

LADY BASILDON (*stiffly*) Please don't praise other women in our presence. You might wait for us to do that!

LORD GORING I did wait.

MRS MARCHMONT Well, we are not going to praise her. I hear she went to the Opera on Monday night, and told Tommy Rufford at supper that, as far as she could see, London Society was entirely made up of dowdies and dandies.

LORD GORING She is quite right, too. The men are all dowdies and the women are all dandies, aren't they?

[*A pause*]

MRS MARCHMONT Oh! do you really think that is what Mrs Cheveley meant?

LORD GORING Of course. And a very sensible remark for Mrs Cheveley to make, too.

Enter Mabel Chiltern. She joins the group

MABEL CHILTERN Why are you talking about Mrs Cheveley? Everybody is talking about Mrs Cheveley! Lord Goring says—what did you say, Lord Goring, about Mrs Cheveley? Oh! I remember, that she was a genius in the daytime and a beauty at night.

LADY BASILDON What a horrid combination! So very unnatural!

MRS MARCHMONT (*in her most dreamy manner*) I like looking at geniuses, and listening to beautiful people.

LORD GORING Ah! that is morbid of you, Mrs Marchmont!

MRS MARCHMONT (*brightening to a look of real pleasure*) I am so glad to hear you say that. Marchmont and I have been married for seven years, and he has never once told me that I was morbid. Men are so painfully unobservant!

LADY BASILDON (*turning to her*) I have always said, dear Margaret, that you were the most morbid person in London.

MRS MARCHMONT Ah! but you are always sympathetic, Olivia!

MABEL CHILTERN Is it morbid to have a desire for food? I have a great desire for food. Lord Goring, will you give me some supper?

LORD GORING With pleasure, Miss Mabel.

Moves away with her

MABEL CHILTERN How horrid you have been! You have never 375
talked to me the whole evening!

LORD GORING How could I? You went away with the child-diplomatist.°

MABEL CHILTERN You might have followed us. Pursuit would have
been only polite. I don't think I like you at all this evening! 380

LORD GORING I like you immensely.

MABEL CHILTERN Well, I wish you'd show it in a more marked way!
They go downstairs°

MRS MARCHMONT Olivia, I have a curious feeling of absolute
faintness. I think I should like some supper very much. I know I
should like some supper. 385

LADY BASILDON I am positively dying for supper, Margaret!

MRS MARCHMONT Men are so horribly selfish, they never think of
these things.

LADY BASILDON Men are grossly material, grossly material!
The Vicomte de Nanjac enters from the music-room with [Mr
Montford and] some other guests. After having carefully exam-
ined all the people present, he approaches Lady Basildon

VICOMTE DE NANJAC May I have the honour of taking you down to 390
supper, Comtesse?

LADY BASILDON (*coldly*) I never take supper, thank you, Vicomte.
(*The Vicomte is about to retire. Lady Basildon, seeing this, rises at*
once and takes his arm) But I will come down with you with
pleasure. 395

VICOMTE DE NANJAC I am so fond of eating! I am very English in
all my tastes.

LADY BASILDON You look quite English, Vicomte, quite English.
They pass out. Mr Montford, a perfectly groomed young dandy,
approaches Mrs Marchmont

MR MONTFORD Like some supper, Mrs Marchmont?

MRS MARCHMONT (*languidly*) Thank you, Mr Montford, I never 400
touch supper. (*Rises hastily and takes his arm*) But I will sit beside
you, and watch you.

MR MONTFORD I don't know that I like being watched when I am
eating!

MRS MARCHMONT Then I will watch someone else. 405

MR MONTFORD I don't know that I should like that either.

MRS MARCHMONT (*severely*) Pray, Mr Montford, do not make these
painful scenes of jealousy in public!

*They go downstairs with the other guests, passing Sir Robert
Chiltern and Mrs Cheveley, who now enter*

SIR ROBERT CHILTERN And are you going to any of our country
houses before you leave England, Mrs Cheveley?   410

MRS CHEVELEY Oh, no! I can't stand your English house-parties. In
England people actually try to be brilliant at breakfast. That is so
dreadful of them! Only dull people are brilliant at breakfast. And
then the family skeleton is always reading family prayers.° My stay
in England really depends on you, Sir Robert. (*Sits down on the*   415
sofa)

SIR ROBERT CHILTERN (*taking a seat beside her*) Seriously?

MRS CHEVELEY Quite seriously. I want to talk to you about a great
political and financial scheme, about this Argentine Canal Company,° in fact.

SIR ROBERT CHILTERN What a tedious, practical subject for you to   420
talk about, Mrs Cheveley!

MRS CHEVELEY Oh, I like tedious, practical subjects. What I don't
like are tedious, practical people. There is a wide difference.
Besides, you are interested, I know, in International Canal
schemes. You were Lord Radley's secretary, weren't you, when the   425
Government bought the Suez Canal° shares?

SIR ROBERT CHILTERN Yes. But the Suez Canal was a very great
and splendid undertaking. It gave us our direct route to India. It
had imperial value. It was necessary that we should have control.
This Argentine scheme is a commonplace Stock Exchange   430
swindle.

MRS CHEVELEY A speculation, Sir Robert! A brilliant, daring speculation.

SIR ROBERT CHILTERN Believe me, Mrs Cheveley, it is a swindle.
Let us call things by their proper names. It makes matters simpler.   435
We have all the information about it at the Foreign Office. In fact,
I sent out a special Commission to inquire into the matter
privately, and they report that the works are hardly begun, and as
for the money already subscribed, no one seems to know what has
become of it. The whole thing is a second Panama, and with not   440
a quarter of the chance of success that miserable affair ever had. I
hope you have not invested in it. I am sure you are far too clever
to have done that.

MRS CHEVELEY I have invested very largely in it.

SIR ROBERT CHILTERN Who could have advised you to do such a   445
foolish thing?

MRS CHEVELEY Your old friend—and mine.

SIR ROBERT CHILTERN Who?

MRS CHEVELEY Baron Arnheim.

SIR ROBERT CHILTERN (*frowning*) Ah! yes. I remember hearing, at   450
the time of his death, that he had been mixed up in the whole
affair.

MRS CHEVELEY It was his last romance. His last but one, to do him
justice.

SIR ROBERT CHILTERN (*rising*) But you have not seen my Corots°   455
yet. They are in the music-room. Corots seem to go with music,
don't they? May I show them to you?

MRS CHEVELEY (*shaking her head*) I am not in a mood tonight for
silver twilights, or rose-pink dawns. I want to talk business.
   (*Motions to him with her fan to sit down again beside her*)

SIR ROBERT CHILTERN I fear I have no advice to give you, Mrs   460
Cheveley, except to interest yourself in something less dangerous.
The success of the Canal depends, of course, on the attitude of
England, and I am going to lay the report of the Commissioners
before the House tomorrow night.

MRS CHEVELEY That you must not do. In your own interests, Sir   465
Robert, to say nothing of mine, you must not do that.

SIR ROBERT CHILTERN (*looking at her in wonder*) In my own
interests? My dear Mrs Cheveley, what do you mean? (*Sits down
beside her*)

MRS CHEVELEY Sir Robert, I will be quite frank with you. I want
you to withdraw the report that you had intended to lay before   470
the House,° on the ground that you have reasons to believe that
the Commissioners have been prejudiced or misinformed, or
something. Then I want you to say a few words to the effect that
the Government is going to reconsider the question, and that
you have reason to believe that the Canal, if completed, will be   475
of great international value. You know the sort of things
ministers say in cases of this kind. A few ordinary platitudes
will do. In modern life nothing produces such an effect as a
good platitude. It makes the whole world kin.° Will you do that
for me?   480

SIR ROBERT CHILTERN Mrs Cheveley, you cannot be serious in
making me such a proposition!

MRS CHEVELEY I am quite serious.

SIR ROBERT CHILTERN (*coldly*) Pray allow me to believe that you
are not!   485

MRS CHEVELEY (*speaking with great deliberation and emphasis*) Ah! but I am. And if you do what I ask you, I . . . will pay you very handsomely!

SIR ROBERT CHILTERN Pay me!

MRS CHEVELEY Yes.

SIR ROBERT CHILTERN I am afraid I don't quite understand what you mean.

MRS CHEVELEY (*leaning back on the sofa and looking at him*) How very disappointing! And I have come all the way from Vienna in order that you should thoroughly understand me.

SIR ROBERT CHILTERN I fear I don't.

MRS CHEVELEY (*in her most nonchalant manner*) My dear Sir Robert, you are a man of the world, and you have your price, I suppose. Everybody has nowadays. The drawback is that most people are so dreadfully expensive. I know I am. I hope you will be more reasonable in your terms.

SIR ROBERT CHILTERN (*rises indignantly*) If you will allow me, I will call your carriage° for you. You have lived so long abroad, Mrs Cheveley, that you seem to be unable to realize that you are talking to an English gentleman.

MRS CHEVELEY (*detains him by touching his arm with her fan, and keeping it there while she is talking*) I realize that I am talking to a man who laid the foundation of his fortune by selling to a Stock Exchange speculator a Cabinet secret.

SIR ROBERT CHILTERN (*biting his lip*) What do you mean?

MRS CHEVELEY (*rising and facing him*) I mean that I know the real origin of your wealth and your career, and I have got your letter, too.

SIR ROBERT CHILTERN What letter?

MRS CHEVELEY (*contemptuously*) The letter you wrote to Baron Arnheim, when you were Lord Radley's secretary, telling the Baron to buy Suez Canal shares—a letter written three days before the Government announced its own purchase.

SIR ROBERT CHILTERN (*hoarsely*) It is not true.

MRS CHEVELEY You thought that letter had been destroyed. How foolish of you! It is in my possession.

SIR ROBERT CHILTERN The affair to which you allude was no more than a speculation. The House of Commons had not yet passed the bill; it might have been rejected.

MRS CHEVELEY It was a swindle, Sir Robert. Let us call things by their proper names. It makes everything simpler. And now I am

going to sell you that letter, and the price I ask for it is your public
support of the Argentine scheme. You made your own fortune out
of one canal. You must help me and my friends to make our
fortunes out of another!   530

SIR ROBERT CHILTERN It is infamous, what you propose—infamous!

MRS CHEVELEY Oh, no! This is the game of life as we all have to
play it, Sir Robert, sooner or later!

SIR ROBERT CHILTERN I cannot do what you ask me.   535

MRS CHEVELEY You mean you cannot help doing it. You know
you are standing on the edge of a precipice. And it is not for you
to make terms. It is for you to accept them. Supposing you
refuse—

SIR ROBERT CHILTERN What then?   540

MRS CHEVELEY My dear Sir Robert, what then? You are ruined, that
is all! Remember to what a point your Puritanism in England has
brought you. In old days nobody pretended to be a bit better than
his neighbours. In fact, to be a bit better than one's neighbour was
considered excessively vulgar and middle-class. Nowadays, with   545
our modern mania for morality, everyone has to pose as a paragon
of purity, incorruptibility, and all the other seven deadly virtues—
and what is the result? You all go over like ninepins—one after the
other. Not a year passes in England without somebody disappearing. Scandals used to lend charm, or at least interest, to a   550
man—now they crush him. And yours is a very nasty scandal. You
couldn't survive it. If it were known that as a young man, secretary
to a great and important minister, you sold a Cabinet secret for a
large sum of money, and that that was the origin of your wealth
and career, you would be hounded out of public life, you would   555
disappear completely. And after all, Sir Robert, why should you
sacrifice your entire future rather than deal diplomatically with
your enemy? For the moment I am your enemy. I admit it! And I
am much stronger than you are. The big battalions are on my side.
You have a splendid position, but it is your splendid position that 560
makes you so vulnerable. You can't defend it! And I am in attack.
Of course I have not talked morality to you. You must admit in
fairness that I have spared you that. Years ago you did a clever,
unscrupulous thing; it turned out a great success. You owe to it
your fortune and position. And now you have got to pay for it.   565
Sooner or later we all have to pay for what we do. You have to pay
now. Before I leave you tonight, you have got to promise me to

suppress your report, and to speak in the House in favour of this
scheme.

SIR ROBERT CHILTERN What you ask is impossible.   570

MRS CHEVELEY You must make it possible. You are going to make
it possible. Sir Robert, you know what your English newspapers
are like. Suppose that when I leave this house I drive down to some
newspaper office, and give them this scandal and the proofs of it!
Think of their loathsome joy, of the delight they would have in   575
dragging you down, of the mud and mire they would plunge you
in. Think of the hypocrite with his greasy smile penning his
leading article, and arranging the foulness of the public placard.°

SIR ROBERT CHILTERN Stop! You want me to withdraw the report
and to make a short speech stating that I believe there are   580
possibilities in the scheme?

MRS CHEVELEY (*sitting down on the sofa*) Those are my terms.

SIR ROBERT CHILTERN (*in a low voice*) I will give you any sum of
money you want.

MRS CHEVELEY Even you are not rich enough, Sir Robert, to buy   585
back your past. No man is.

SIR ROBERT CHILTERN I will not do what you ask me. I will not.

MRS CHEVELEY You have to. If you don't . . . (*Rises from the sofa*)

SIR ROBERT CHILTERN (*bewildered and unnerved*) Wait a moment!
What did you propose? You said that you would give me back my   590
letter, didn't you?

MRS CHEVELEY Yes. That is agreed. I will be in the Ladies' Gallery°
tomorrow night at half-past eleven. If by that time—and you will
have had heaps of opportunity—you have made an announcement
to the House in the terms I wish, I shall hand you back your letter   595
with the prettiest thanks, and the best, or at any rate the most
suitable, compliment I can think of. I intend to play quite fairly
with you. One should always play fairly . . . when one has the
winning cards. The Baron taught me that . . . amongst other
things.   600

SIR ROBERT CHILTERN You must let me have time to consider your
proposal.

MRS CHEVELEY No; you must settle now!

SIR ROBERT CHILTERN Give me a week—three days!

MRS CHEVELEY Impossible! I have got to telegraph to Vienna   605
tonight.

SIR ROBERT CHILTERN My God! what brought you into my life?

MRS CHEVELEY Circumstances.

Moves towards the door

SIR ROBERT CHILTERN Don't go. I consent. The report shall be
withdrawn. I will arrange for a question° to be put to me on the   610
subject.

MRS CHEVELEY Thank you. I knew we should come to an amicable
agreement. I understood your nature from the first. I analysed you,
though you did not adore me. And now you can get my carriage
for me, Sir Robert. I see the people coming up from supper, and   615
English men always get romantic after a meal, and that bores me
dreadfully.

> *Exit Sir Robert Chiltern. Enter Lady Chiltern, Lady Markby,*
> *Lord Caversham, Lady Basildon, Mrs Marchmont, Vicomte de*
> *Nanjac, Mr Montford [and other guests]*

LADY MARKBY Well, dear Mrs Cheveley, I hope you have enjoyed
yourself. Sir Robert is very entertaining, is he not?

MRS CHEVELEY Most entertaining! I have enjoyed my talk with him   620
immensely.

LADY MARKBY He has had a very interesting and brilliant career.
And he has married a most admirable wife. Lady Chiltern is a
woman of the very highest principles, I am glad to say. I am a little
too old now, myself, to trouble about setting a good example, but   625
I always admire people who do. And Lady Chiltern has a very
ennobling effect on life, though her dinner-parties are rather dull
sometimes. But one can't have everything, can one? And now I
must go, dear. Shall I call for you tomorrow?

MRS CHEVELEY Thanks.   630

LADY MARKBY We might drive in the Park° at five. Everything looks
so fresh in the Park now!

MRS CHEVELEY Except the people!

LADY MARKBY Perhaps the people are a little jaded. I have often
observed that the Season° as it goes on produces a kind of   635
softening of the brain. However, I think anything is better than
high intellectual pressure. That is the most unbecoming thing
there is. It makes the noses of the young girls so particularly large.
And there is nothing so difficult to marry as a large nose; men
don't like them. Good night, dear! (*To Lady Chiltern*) Good night,   640
Gertrude!

> *Goes out on Lord Caversham's arm*

MRS CHEVELEY What a charming house you have, Lady Chiltern! I
have spent a delightful evening. It has been so interesting getting
to know your husband.

LADY CHILTERN Why did you wish to meet my husband, Mrs   645
Cheveley?

MRS CHEVELEY Oh, I will tell you. I wanted to interest him in this
Argentine Canal scheme, of which I dare say you have heard. And
I found him most susceptible,—susceptible to reason, I mean. A
rare thing in a man. I converted him in ten minutes. He is going   650
to make a speech in the House tomorrow night in favour of the
idea. We must go to the Ladies' Gallery and hear him! It will be
a great occasion!

LADY CHILTERN There must be some mistake. That scheme could
never have my husband's support.   655

MRS CHEVELEY Oh, I assure you it's all settled. I don't regret my
tedious journey from Vienna now. It has been a great success. But,
of course, for the next twenty-four hours the whole thing is a dead
secret.

LADY CHILTERN (*gently*) A secret? Between whom?   660

MRS CHEVELEY (*with a flash of amusement in her eyes*) Between your
husband and myself.

       Enter Sir Robert Chiltern

SIR ROBERT CHILTERN Your carriage is here, Mrs Cheveley!

MRS CHEVELEY Thanks! Good evening, Lady Chiltern! Good night,
Lord Goring! I am at Claridge's.° Don't you think you might leave   665
a card?

LORD GORING If you wish, Mrs Cheveley!

MRS CHEVELEY Oh, don't be so solemn about it, or I shall be obliged
to leave a card on you. In England I suppose that would hardly be
considered *en règle*.° Abroad, we are more civilized. Will you see   670
me down, Sir Robert? Now that we have both the same interests
at heart we shall be great friends, I hope!

       *Sails out on Sir Robert Chiltern's arm. Lady Chiltern goes to
       the top of the staircase° and looks down at them as they descend.
       Her expression is troubled. After a little time she is joined by
       some of the guests, and passes with them into another reception-
       room*

MABEL CHILTERN What a horrid woman!

LORD GORING You should go to bed, Miss Mabel.

MABEL CHILTERN Lord Goring!   675

LORD GORING My father told me to go to bed an hour ago. I don't
see why I shouldn't give you the same advice. I always pass on
good advice. It is the only thing to do with it. It is never of any
use to oneself.

MABEL CHILTERN Lord Goring, you are always ordering me out of   680
the room. I think it most courageous of you. Especially as I am not
going to bed for hours. (*Goes over to the sofa*) You can come and
sit down if you like, and talk about anything in the world, except
the Royal Academy,° Mrs Cheveley, or novels in Scotch dialect.
They are not improving subjects. (*Catches sight of something that is*   685
lying on the sofa half hidden by the cushion) What is this? Someone
has dropped a diamond brooch!° Quite beautiful, isn't it? (*Shows*
it to him.) I wish it was mine, but Gertrude won't let me wear
anything but pearls, and I am thoroughly sick of pearls. They make
one look so plain, so good and so intellectual. I wonder whom the   690
brooch belongs to.

LORD GORING I wonder who dropped it.

MABEL CHILTERN It is a beautiful brooch.

LORD GORING It is a handsome bracelet.

MABEL CHILTERN It isn't a bracelet. It's a brooch.   695

LORD GORING It can be used as a bracelet.

> *Takes it from her, and pulling out a green letter-case,° puts the*
> *ornament carefully in it, and replaces the whole thing in his*
> *breast-pocket with the most perfect sangfroid*

MABEL CHILTERN What are you doing?

LORD GORING Miss Mabel, I am going to make a rather strange
request to you.

MABEL CHILTERN (*eagerly*) Oh, pray do! I have been waiting for it   700
all the evening.

LORD GORING (*is a little taken aback, but recovers himself*) Don't
mention to anybody that I have taken charge of this brooch.
Should anyone write and claim it, let me know at once.

MABEL CHILTERN That is a strange request.   705

LORD GORING Well, you see I gave this brooch to somebody once,
years ago.

MABEL CHILTERN You did?

LORD GORING Yes.

> *Lady Chiltern enters alone. The other guests have gone*

MABEL CHILTERN Then I shall certainly bid you good night. Good   710
night, Gertrude!

> *Exit*

LADY CHILTERN Good night, dear! (*To Lord Goring*) You saw whom
Lady Markby brought here tonight?

LORD GORING Yes. It was an unpleasant surprise. What did she
come here for?   715

LADY CHILTERN Apparently to try and lure Robert to uphold some fraudulent scheme in which she is interested. The Argentine Canal, in fact.

LORD GORING She has mistaken her man, hasn't she?

LADY CHILTERN She is incapable of understanding an upright   720
nature like my husband's!

LORD GORING Yes. I should fancy she came to grief if she tried to get Robert into her toils. It is extraordinary what astounding mistakes clever women make.

LADY CHILTERN I don't call women of that kind clever. I call them   725
stupid!

LORD GORING Same thing often. Good night, Lady Chiltern!

LADY CHILTERN Good night!
     Enter Sir Robert Chiltern

SIR ROBERT CHILTERN My dear Arthur, you are not going? Do stop a little!   730

LORD GORING Afraid I can't, thanks. I have promised to look in at the Hartlocks'. I believe they have got a mauve Hungarian band° that plays mauve Hungarian music. See you soon. Good-bye!
     Exit

SIR ROBERT CHILTERN How beautiful you look tonight, Gertrude!

LADY CHILTERN Robert, it is not true, is it? You are not going to   735
lend your support to this Argentine speculation? You couldn't!

SIR ROBERT CHILTERN (*starting*) Who told you I intended to do so?

LADY CHILTERN That woman who has just gone out, Mrs Cheveley, as she calls herself now. She seemed to taunt me with it. Robert,   740
I know this woman. You don't. We were at school together. She was untruthful, dishonest, an evil influence on everyone whose trust or friendship she could win. I hated, I despised her. She stole things,° she was a thief. She was sent away for being a thief. Why do you let her influence you?   745

SIR ROBERT CHILTERN Gertrude, what you tell me may be true, but it happened many years ago. It is best forgotten! Mrs Cheveley may have changed since then. No one should be entirely judged by their past.

LADY CHILTERN (*sadly*) One's past is what one is. It is the only way   750
by which people should be judged.

SIR ROBERT CHILTERN That is a hard saying, Gertrude!

LADY CHILTERN It is a true saying, Robert. And what did she mean by boasting that she had got you to lend your support, your name,

to a thing I have heard you describe as the most dishonest and   755
fraudulent scheme there has ever been in political life?

SIR ROBERT CHILTERN (*biting his lip*) I was mistaken in the view I
took. We all may make mistakes.

LADY CHILTERN But you told me yesterday that you had received
the report from the Commission, and that it entirely condemned   760
the whole thing.

SIR ROBERT CHILTERN (*walking up and down*) I have reasons now
to believe that the Commission was prejudiced, or, at any
rate, misinformed. Besides, Gertrude, public and private life are
different things. They have different laws, and move on different   765
lines.

LADY CHILTERN They should both represent man at his highest. I
see no difference between them.

SIR ROBERT CHILTERN (*stopping*) In the present case, on a matter of
practical politics, I have changed my mind. That is all.   770

LADY CHILTERN All!

SIR ROBERT CHILTERN (*sternly*) Yes!

LADY CHILTERN Robert! Oh! it is horrible that I should have to
ask you such a question—Robert, are you telling me the whole
truth?   775

SIR ROBERT CHILTERN Why do you ask me such a question?
   [*A pause*]

LADY CHILTERN Why do you not answer it?

SIR ROBERT CHILTERN (*sitting down*) Gertrude, truth is a very
complex thing, and politics is a very complex business. There are
wheels within wheels. One may be under certain obligations to   780
people that one must pay. Sooner or later in political life one has
to compromise. Everyone does.

LADY CHILTERN Compromise? Robert, why do you talk so differ-
ently tonight from the way I have always heard you talk? Why are
you changed?   785

SIR ROBERT CHILTERN I am not changed. But circumstances alter
things.

LADY CHILTERN Circumstances should never alter principles!

SIR ROBERT CHILTERN But if I told you—

LADY CHILTERN What?   790

SIR ROBERT CHILTERN That it was necessary, vitally necessary?

LADY CHILTERN It can never be necessary to do what is not
honourable. Or if it be necessary, then what is it that I have loved!
But it is not, Robert; tell me it is not. Why should it be? What

gain would you get? Money? We have no need of that! And money   795
that comes from a tainted source is a degradation. Power? But
power is nothing in itself. It is power to do good that is fine—that,
and that only. What is it, then? Robert, tell me why you are going
to do this dishonourable thing!

SIR ROBERT CHILTERN Gertrude, you have no right to use that   800
word. I told you it was a question of rational compromise. It is no
more than that.

LADY CHILTERN Robert, that is all very well for other men, for men
who treat life simply as a sordid speculation; but not for you,
Robert, not for you. You are different. All your life you have stood   805
apart from others. You have never let the world soil you. To the
world, as to myself, you have been an ideal always. Oh! be that
ideal still. That great inheritance throw not away—that tower of
ivory do not destroy. Robert, men can love what is beneath
them—things unworthy, stained, dishonoured. We women wor-   810
ship when we love; and when we lose our worship, we lose
everything. Oh! don't kill my love for you, don't kill that!

SIR ROBERT CHILTERN Gertrude!

LADY CHILTERN I know that there are men with horrible secrets in
their lives—men who have done some shameful thing, and who in   815
some critical moment have to pay for it, by doing some other act
of shame—oh! don't tell me you are such as they are! Robert, is
there in your life any secret dishonour or disgrace? Tell me, tell
me at once, that—

SIR ROBERT CHILTERN That what?   820

LADY CHILTERN (*speaking very slowly*) That our lives may drift
apart.

SIR ROBERT CHILTERN Drift apart?

LADY CHILTERN That they may be entirely separate. It would be
better for us both.   825

SIR ROBERT CHILTERN Gertrude, there is nothing in my past life
that you might not know.

LADY CHILTERN I was sure of it, Robert, I was sure of it. But why
did you say those dreadful things, things so unlike your real self?
Don't let us ever talk about the subject again. You will write, won't   830
you, to Mrs Cheveley, and tell her that you cannot support this
scandalous scheme of hers? If you have given her any promise you
must take it back, that is all!

SIR ROBERT CHILTERN Must I write and tell her that?

LADY CHILTERN Surely, Robert! What else is there to do?   835

SIR ROBERT CHILTERN I might see her personally. It would be better.

LADY CHILTERN You must never see her again, Robert. She is not a woman you should ever speak to. She is not worthy to talk to a man like you. No; you must write to her at once, now, this moment, and let your letter show her that your decision is quite irrevocable!

SIR ROBERT CHILTERN Write this moment!

LADY CHILTERN Yes.

SIR ROBERT CHILTERN But it is so late. It is close on twelve.

LADY CHILTERN That makes no matter. She must know at once that she has been mistaken in you—and that you are not a man to do anything base or underhand or dishonourable. Write here, Robert. Write that you decline to support this scheme of hers, as you hold it to be a dishonest scheme. Yes—write the word dishonest. She knows what that word means (*Sir Robert Chiltern sits down and writes a letter. His wife takes it up and reads it*) Yes; that will do. (*Rings bell*) And now the envelope. (*He writes the envelope slowly*)
        Enter Mason
Have this letter sent at once to Claridge's Hotel. There is no answer.
        Exit Mason. Lady Chiltern kneels down beside her husband and puts her arms round him
Robert, love gives one a sort of instinct to things. I feel tonight that I have saved you from something that might have been a danger to you, from something that might have made men honour you less than they do. I don't think you realize sufficiently, Robert, that you have brought into the political life of our time a nobler atmosphere, a finer attitude towards life, a freer air of purer aims and higher ideals—I know it, and for that I love you, Robert.

SIR ROBERT CHILTERN Oh, love me always, Gertrude, love me always!

LADY CHILTERN I will love you always, because you will always be worthy of love. We needs must love the highest° when we see it!
        Kisses him and rises and goes out. Sir Robert Chiltern walks up and down for a moment; then sits down and buries his face in his hands. The Servant enters and begins putting out the lights. Sir Robert Chiltern looks up

SIR ROBERT CHILTERN Put out the lights, Mason, put out the lights!°

*The Servant puts out the lights. The room becomes almost dark.
The only light there is comes from the great chandelier that hangs
over the staircase and illumines the tapestry of the Triumph of
Love*

ACT DROP

Second Act

Scene: Morning-room at Sir Robert Chiltern's house. Lord Goring, dressed in the height of fashion, is lounging in an armchair.° Sir Robert Chiltern is standing in front of the fireplace. He is evidently in a state of great mental excitement and distress. As the scene progresses he paces nervously up and down the room

LORD GORING My dear Robert, it's a very awkward business, very awkward indeed. You should have told your wife the whole thing. Secrets from other people's wives are a necessary luxury in modern life. So, at least, I am always told at the club by people who are bald enough° to know better. But no man should have a secret 5
from his own wife. She invariably finds it out. Women have a wonderful instinct about things. They can discover everything except the obvious.

SIR ROBERT CHILTERN Arthur, I couldn't tell my wife. When could I have told her? Not last night. It would have made a lifelong 10
separation between us, and I would have lost the love of the one woman in the world I worship, of the only woman who has ever stirred love within me. Last night it would have been quite impossible. She would have turned from me in horror . . . in horror and in contempt. 15

LORD GORING Is Lady Chiltern as perfect° as all that?

SIR ROBERT CHILTERN Yes, my wife is as perfect as all that.

LORD GORING (*taking off his left-hand glove*) What a pity! I beg your pardon, my dear fellow, I didn't quite mean that. But if what you tell me is true, I should like to have a serious talk about life with 20
Lady Chiltern.

SIR ROBERT CHILTERN It would be quite useless.

LORD GORING May I try?

SIR ROBERT CHILTERN Yes; but nothing could make her alter her views. 25

LORD GORING Well, at the worst it would simply be a psychological experiment.

SIR ROBERT CHILTERN All such experiments are terribly dangerous.

LORD GORING Everything is dangerous, my dear fellow. If it wasn't 30
so, life wouldn't be worth living . . . Well, I am bound to say that I think you should have told her years ago.

SIR ROBERT CHILTERN When? When we were engaged? Do you think she would have married me if she had known that the origin of my fortune is such as it is, the basis of my career such as it is, and that I had done a thing that I suppose most men would call shameful and dishonourable?

LORD GORING (*slowly*) Yes; most men would call it ugly names. There is no doubt of that.

SIR ROBERT CHILTERN (*bitterly*) Men who every day do something of the same kind themselves. Men who, each one of them, have worse secrets in their own lives.

LORD GORING That is the reason they are so pleased to find out other people's secrets. It distracts public attention from their own.

SIR ROBERT CHILTERN And, after all, whom did I wrong by what I did? No one.

LORD GORING (*looking at him steadily*) Except yourself, Robert.
        [*A pause*]

SIR ROBERT CHILTERN Of course I had private information about a certain transaction contemplated by the Government of the day, and I acted on it. Private information is practically the source of every large modern fortune.

LORD GORING (*tapping his boot with his cane*) And public scandal invariably the result.

SIR ROBERT CHILTERN (*pacing up and down the room*) Arthur, do you think that what I did nearly eighteen years ago should be brought up against me now? Do you think it fair that a man's whole career should be ruined for a fault done in one's boyhood almost? I was twenty-two at the time, and I had the double misfortune of being well-born and poor,° two unforgivable things nowadays. Is it fair that the folly, the sin of one's youth, if men choose to call it a sin, should wreck a life like mine, should place me in the pillory, should shatter all that I have worked for, all that I have built up? Is it fair, Arthur?

LORD GORING Life is never fair, Robert. And perhaps it is a good thing for most of us that it is not.

SIR ROBERT CHILTERN Every man of ambition has to fight his century with its own weapons. What this century worships is wealth. The god of this century is wealth. To succeed one must have wealth. At all costs one must have wealth.

LORD GORING You underrate yourself, Robert. Believe me, without wealth you could have succeeded just as well.

SIR ROBERT CHILTERN When I was old, perhaps. When I had lost my passion for power, or could not use it. When I was tired, worn

out, disappointed. I wanted my success when I was young. Youth
is the time for success. I couldn't wait.   75

LORD GORING Well, you certainly have had your success while you
are still young. No one in our day has had such a brilliant success.
Under-Secretary for Foreign Affairs at the age of forty—that's
good enough for anyone, I should think.

SIR ROBERT CHILTERN And if it is all taken away from me now? If   80
I lose everything over a horrible scandal? If I am hounded from
public life?

LORD GORING Robert, how could you have sold yourself for
money?

SIR ROBERT CHILTERN (*excitedly*) I did not sell myself for money.   85
I bought success at a great price. That is all.

LORD GORING (*gravely*) Yes; you certainly paid a great price for it.
But what first made you think of doing such a thing?

SIR ROBERT CHILTERN Baron Arnheim.

LORD GORING Damned scoundrel!   90

SIR ROBERT CHILTERN No; he was a man of a most subtle and
refined intellect.° A man of culture, charm, and distinction. One
of the most intellectual men I ever met.

LORD GORING Ah! I prefer a gentlemanly fool any day. There is
more to be said for stupidity than people imagine. Personally I   95
have a great admiration for stupidity. It is a sort of fellow-feeling,
I suppose. But how did he do it? Tell me the whole thing.

SIR ROBERT CHILTERN (*throws himself into an armchair by the
writing-table*) One night after dinner at Lord Radley's the Baron
began talking about success in modern life as something that one 100
could reduce to an absolutely definite science. With that wonderfully fascinating quiet voice of his he expounded to us the most
terrible of all philosophies,° the philosophy of power, preached to
us the most marvellous of all gospels, the gospel of gold. I think
he saw the effect he had produced on me, for some days afterwards 105
he wrote and asked me to come and see him. He was living then
in Park Lane,° in the house Lord Woolcomb has now. I remember
so well how, with a strange smile on his pale, curved lips, he led
me through his wonderful picture gallery, showed me his tapes-
tries, his enamels, his jewels, his carved ivories, made me wonder 110
at the strange loveliness of the luxury in which he lived; and then
told me that luxury was nothing but a background, a painted scene
in a play, and that power, power over other men, power over the
world, was the one thing worth having, the one supreme pleasure

worth knowing, the one joy one never tired of, and that in our   115
century only the rich possessed it.

LORD GORING (*with great deliberation*) A thoroughly shallow creed.

SIR ROBERT CHILTERN (*rising*) I didn't think so then. I don't think
so now. Wealth has given me enormous power. It gave me at the
very outset of my life freedom, and freedom is everything. You   120
have never been poor, and never known what ambition is. You
cannot understand what a wonderful chance the Baron gave me.
Such a chance as few men get.

LORD GORING Fortunately for them, if one is to judge by results.
But tell me definitely, how did the Baron finally persuade you   125
to—well, to do what you did?

SIR ROBERT CHILTERN When I was going away he said to me that
if I ever could give him any private information of real value he
would make me a very rich man. I was dazed at the prospect he
held out to me, and my ambition and my desire for power were at   130
that time boundless. Six weeks later certain private documents
passed through my hands.

LORD GORING (*keeping his eyes steadily fixed on the carpet*) State
documents?

SIR ROBERT CHILTERN Yes.   135

> Lord Goring sighs, then passes his hand across his forehead and
> looks up

LORD GORING I had no idea that you, of all men in the world, could
have been so weak, Robert, as to yield to such a temptation as
Baron Arnheim held out to you.

SIR ROBERT CHILTERN Weak? Oh, I am sick of hearing that phrase.
Sick of using it about others. Weak? Do you really think, Arthur,   140
that it is weakness that yields to temptation? I tell you that there
are terrible temptations that it requires strength, strength and
courage, to yield to. To stake all one's life on a single moment, to
risk everything on one throw, whether the stake be power or
pleasure, I care not—there is no weakness in that. There is a   145
horrible, a terrible courage. I had that courage. I sat down the same
afternoon and wrote Baron Arnheim the letter this woman now
holds. He made three-quarters of a million over the transaction.

LORD GORING And you?

SIR ROBERT CHILTERN I received from the Baron £110,000.   150

LORD GORING You were worth more, Robert.

SIR ROBERT CHILTERN No; that money gave me exactly what I
wanted, power over others. I went into the House immediately.

The Baron advised me in finance from time to time. Before five
years I had almost trebled my fortune. Since then everything that   155
I have touched has turned out a success. In all things connected
with money I have had a luck so extraordinary that sometimes it
has made me almost afraid. I remember having read somewhere,
in some strange book, that when the gods wish to punish us they
answer our prayers.   160

LORD GORING But tell me, Robert, did you never suffer any regret
for what you had done?

SIR ROBERT CHILTERN No. I felt that I had fought the century with
its own weapons, and won.

LORD GORING (*sadly*) You thought you had won?   165
      [*A long pause*]

SIR ROBERT CHILTERN I thought so. Arthur, do you despise me for
what I have told you?

LORD GORING (*with deep feeling in his voice*) I am very sorry for you,
Robert, very sorry indeed.

SIR ROBERT CHILTERN I don't say that I suffered any remorse. I   170
didn't. Not remorse in the ordinary, rather silly sense of the word.
But I have paid conscience money many times. I had a wild hope
that I might disarm destiny. The sum Baron Arnheim gave me I
have distributed twice over in public charities since then.

LORD GORING (*looking up*) In public charities? Dear me! what a lot   175
of harm you must have done, Robert!

SIR ROBERT CHILTERN Oh, don't say that, Arthur; don't talk like
that!

LORD GORING Never mind what I say, Robert. I am always saying
what I shouldn't say. In fact, I usually say what I really think. A   180
great mistake nowadays. It makes one so liable to be misunderstood. As regards this dreadful business, I will help you in
whatever way I can. Of course you know that.

SIR ROBERT CHILTERN Thank you, Arthur, thank you. But what is
to be done? What can be done?   185

LORD GORING (*leaning back with his hands in his pockets*) Well, the
English can't stand a man who is always saying he is in the right,
but they are very fond of a man who admits that he has been in
the wrong. It is one of the best things in them. However, in your
case, Robert, a confession would not do. The money, if you will   190
allow me to say so, is . . . awkward. Besides, if you did make a
clean breast of the whole affair, you would never be able to talk
morality again. And in England a man who can't talk morality

twice a week to a large, popular, immoral audience is quite over as a serious politician. There would be nothing left for him as a profession except Botany° or the Church. A confession would be of no use. It would ruin you.

SIR ROBERT CHILTERN It would ruin me. Arthur, the only thing for me to do now is to fight the thing out.

LORD GORING (*rising from his chair*)° I was waiting for you to say that, Robert. It is the only thing to do now. And you must begin by telling your wife the whole story.

SIR ROBERT CHILTERN That I will not do.

LORD GORING Robert, believe me, you are wrong.

SIR ROBERT CHILTERN I couldn't do it. It would kill her love for me. And now about this woman, this Mrs Cheveley. How can I defend myself against her? You knew her before, Arthur, apparently.

LORD GORING Yes.

SIR ROBERT CHILTERN Did you know her well?

LORD GORING (*arranging his necktie*) So little that I got engaged to be married° to her once, when I was staying at the Tenbys'. The affair lasted for three days . . . nearly.

SIR ROBERT CHILTERN Why was it broken off?

LORD GORING (*airily*) Oh, I forget. At least, it makes no matter. By the way, have you tried her with money? She used to be confoundedly fond of money.

SIR ROBERT CHILTERN I offered her any sum she wanted. She refused.

LORD GORING Then the marvellous gospel of gold breaks down sometimes. The rich can't do everything, after all.

SIR ROBERT CHILTERN Not everything. I suppose you are right. Arthur, I feel that public disgrace is in store for me. I feel certain of it. I never knew what terror was before. I know it now. It is as if a hand of ice were laid upon one's heart. It is as if one's heart were beating itself to death in some empty hollow.

LORD GORING (*striking the table*)° Robert, you must fight her. You must fight her.

SIR ROBERT CHILTERN But how?

LORD GORING I can't tell you how at present. I have not the smallest idea. But everyone has some weak point. There is some flaw in each one of us. (*Strolls over to the fireplace and looks at himself in the glass*) My father tells me that even I have faults. Perhaps I have. I don't know.

SIR ROBERT CHILTERN In defending myself against Mrs Cheveley,   235
I have a right to use any weapon I can find, have I not?

LORD GORING (*still looking in the glass*) In your place I don't think I
should have the smallest scruple in doing so. She is thoroughly
well able to take care of herself.

SIR ROBERT CHILTERN (*sits down at the table and takes a pen in his*   240
hand) Well, I shall send a cipher° telegram to the Embassy at
Vienna, to inquire if there is anything known against her. There
may be some secret scandal she might be afraid of.

LORD GORING (*settling his buttonhole*) Oh, I should fancy Mrs
Cheveley is one of those very modern women of our time who find   245
a new scandal as becoming as a new bonnet, and air them both in
the Park every afternoon at five-thirty. I am sure she adores
scandals, and that the sorrow of her life at present is that she can't
manage to have enough of them.

SIR ROBERT CHILTERN (*writing*) Why do you say that?   250

LORD GORING (*turning round*) Well, she wore far too much rouge last
night, and not quite enough clothes. That is always a sign of
despair in a woman.

SIR ROBERT CHILTERN (*striking a bell*) But it is worth while my
wiring to Vienna, is it not?   255

LORD GORING It is always worth while asking a question, though it
is not always worth while answering one.

    Enter Mason

SIR ROBERT CHILTERN Is Mr Trafford in his room?

MASON Yes, Sir Robert.

SIR ROBERT CHILTERN (*puts what he has written into an envelope,*   260
which he then carefully closes) Tell him to have this sent off in
cipher at once. There must not be a moment's delay.

MASON Yes, Sir Robert.

SIR ROBERT CHILTERN Oh! just give that back to me again.
    Writes something on the envelope. Mason then goes out with the
    letter

SIR ROBERT CHILTERN She must have had some curious hold over   265
Baron Arnheim. I wonder what it was.

LORD GORING (*smiling*) I wonder.

SIR ROBERT CHILTERN I will fight her to the death, as long as my
wife knows nothing.

LORD GORING (*strongly*) Oh, fight in any case—in any case.   270

SIR ROBERT CHILTERN (*with a gesture of despair*) If my wife found
out, there would be little left to fight for. Well, as soon as I hear

from Vienna, I shall let you know the result. It is a chance, just a chance, but I believe in it. And as I fought the age with its own weapons, I will fight her with her weapons. It is only fair, and she looks like a woman with a past, doesn't she?

LORD GORING Most pretty women do. But there is a fashion in pasts just as there is a fashion in frocks. Perhaps Mrs Cheveley's past is merely a slight *décolleté* ° one, and they are excessively popular nowadays. Besides, my dear Robert, I should not build too high hopes on frightening Mrs Cheveley. I should not fancy Mrs Cheveley is a woman who would be easily frightened. She has survived all her creditors, and she shows wonderful presence of mind.

SIR ROBERT CHILTERN Oh! I live on hopes now. I clutch at every chance. I feel like a man on a ship that is sinking. The water is round my feet, and the very air is bitter with storm. Hush! I hear my wife's voice.

Enter Lady Chiltern in walking dress°

LADY CHILTERN Good afternoon, Lord Goring!

LORD GORING Good afternoon, Lady Chiltern! Have you been in the Park?

LADY CHILTERN No; I have just come from the Woman's Liberal Association,° where, by the way, Robert, your name was received with loud applause, and now I have come in to have my tea. [*To Lord Goring*] You will wait and have some tea, won't you?

LORD GORING I'll wait for a short time, thanks.

LADY CHILTERN I will be back in a moment. I am only going to take my hat off.

LORD GORING (*in his most earnest manner*) Oh! please don't. It is so pretty. One of the prettiest hats I ever saw. I hope the Woman's Liberal Association received it with loud applause.

LADY CHILTERN (*with a smile*) We have much more important work to do than look at each other's bonnets, Lord Goring.

LORD GORING Really? What sort of work?

LADY CHILTERN Oh! dull, useful, delightful things,° Factory Acts, Female Inspectors, the Eight Hours' Bill, the Parliamentary Franchise.... Everything, in fact, that you would find thoroughly uninteresting.

LORD GORING And never bonnets?

LADY CHILTERN (*with mock indignation*) Never bonnets, never!

Lady Chiltern goes through the door leading to her boudoir

SIR ROBERT CHILTERN (*takes Lord Goring's hand*) You have been a
good friend to me, Arthur, a thoroughly good friend.

LORD GORING I don't know that I have been able to do much for
you, Robert, as yet. In fact, I have not been able to do anything   315
for you, as far as I can see. I am thoroughly disappointed with
myself.

SIR ROBERT CHILTERN You have enabled me to tell you the truth.
That is something. The truth has always stifled me.

LORD GORING Ah! the truth is a thing I get rid of as soon as   320
possible! Bad habit, by the way. Makes one very unpopular at the
club . . . with the older members. They call it being conceited.
Perhaps it is.

SIR ROBERT CHILTERN I would to God that I had been able to tell
the truth . . . to live the truth. Ah! that is the great thing in life, to   325
live the truth. (*Sighs, and goes towards the door*) I'll see you soon
again, Arthur, shan't I?

LORD GORING Certainly. Whenever you like. I'm going to look in at
the Bachelors' Ball° tonight, unless I find something better to do.
But I'll come round tomorrow morning. If you should want me   330
tonight by any chance, send round a note to Curzon Street.

SIR ROBERT CHILTERN Thank you.

    As he reaches the door, Lady Chiltern enters from her boudoir

LADY CHILTERN You are not going, Robert?

SIR ROBERT CHILTERN I have some letters to write, dear.

LADY CHILTERN (*going to him*) You work too hard, Robert. You   335
seem never to think of yourself, and you are looking so tired.

SIR ROBERT CHILTERN It is nothing, dear, nothing.

    He kisses her and goes out

LADY CHILTERN (*to Lord Goring*) Do sit down. I am so glad you
have called. I want to talk to you about . . . well, not about bonnets,
or the Woman's Liberal Association. You take far too much   340
interest in the first subject, and not nearly enough in the second.

LORD GORING You want to talk to me about Mrs Cheveley?

LADY CHILTERN Yes. You have guessed it. After you left last night
I found out that what she had said was really true. Of course I
made Robert write her a letter at once, withdrawing his promise.   345

LORD GORING So he gave me to understand.

LADY CHILTERN To have kept it would have been the first stain on
a career that has been stainless always. Robert must be above
reproach. He is not like other men. He cannot afford to do what
other men do. (*She looks at Lord Goring, who remains silent*) Don't   350

you agree with me? You are Robert's greatest friend. You are our greatest friend,° Lord Goring. No one, except myself, knows Robert better than you do. He has no secrets from me, and I don't think he has any from you.

LORD GORING He certainly has no secrets from me. At least I don't   355
think so.

LADY CHILTERN Then am I not right in my estimate of him? I know I am right. But speak to me frankly.

LORD GORING (*looking straight at her*) Quite frankly?

LADY CHILTERN Surely. You have nothing to conceal have you?   360

LORD GORING Nothing. But, my dear Lady Chiltern, I think, if you will allow me to say so, that in practical life—

LADY CHILTERN (*smiling*) Of which I know so little, Lord Goring—

LORD GORING Of which I know nothing by experience, though I   365
know something by observation. I think that in practical life there is something about success, actual success, that is a little unscrupulous, something about ambition that is unscrupulous always. Once a man has set his heart and soul on getting to a certain point, if he has to climb the crag, he climbs the crag; if he has to walk in   370
the mire—

LADY CHILTERN Well?

LORD GORING He walks in the mire. Of course I am only talking generally about life.

LADY CHILTERN (*gravely*) I hope so. Why do you look at me so   375
strangely, Lord Goring?

LORD GORING Lady Chiltern, I have sometimes thought that . . . perhaps you are a little hard in some of your views on life. I think that . . . often you don't make sufficient allowances. In every nature there are elements of weakness, or worse than weakness. Suppos-   380
ing, for instance, that—that any public man, my father, or Lord Merton, or Robert, say, had, years ago, written some foolish letter to someone . . .

LADY CHILTERN What do you mean by a foolish letter?

LORD GORING A letter gravely compromising one's position. I am   385
only putting an imaginary case.

LADY CHILTERN Robert is as incapable of doing a foolish thing as he is of doing a wrong thing.

[*A long pause*]

LORD GORING Nobody is incapable of doing a foolish thing. Nobody is incapable of doing a wrong thing.°   390

LADY CHILTERN Are you a Pessimist? What will the other dandies say? They will all have to go into mourning.

LORD GORING (*rising*) No, Lady Chiltern, I am not a Pessimist. Indeed I am not sure that I quite know what Pessimism really means. All I do know is that life cannot be understood without   395
much charity, cannot be lived without much charity. It is love, and not German philosophy, that is the true explanation of this world, whatever may be the explanation of the next. And if you are ever in trouble, Lady Chiltern, trust me absolutely, and I will help you in every way I can. If you ever want me, come to me for my   400
assistance, and you shall have it. Come at once to me.

LADY CHILTERN (*looking at him in surprise*) Lord Goring, you are talking quite seriously. I don't think I ever heard you talk seriously before.

LORD GORING (*laughing*) You must excuse me, Lady Chiltern. It   405
won't occur again, if I can help it.

LADY CHILTERN But I like you to be serious.

Enter Mabel Chiltern, in the most ravishing frock°

MABEL CHILTERN Dear Gertrude, don't say such a dreadful thing to Lord Goring. Seriousness would be very unbecoming to him. Good afternoon, Lord Goring!° Pray be as trivial as you can.   410

LORD GORING I should like to, Miss Mabel, but I am afraid I am . . . a little out of practice this morning; and besides, I have to be going now.

MABEL CHILTERN Just when I have come in! What dreadful manners you have! I am sure you were very badly brought up.   415

LORD GORING I was.

MABEL CHILTERN I wish I had brought you up!

LORD GORING I am so sorry you didn't.

MABEL CHILTERN It is too late now, I suppose?

LORD GORING (*smiling*) I am not so sure.   420

MABEL CHILTERN Will you ride tomorrow morning?

LORD GORING Yes, at ten.

MABEL CHILTERN Don't forget.

LORD GORING Of course I shan't. By the way, Lady Chiltern, there is no list of your guests in *The Morning Post*° of today. It has   425
apparently been crowded out by the County Council, or the Lambeth Conference, or something equally boring. Could you let me have a list? I have a particular reason for asking you.

LADY CHILTERN I am sure Mr Trafford will be able to give you one.

LORD GORING Thanks, so much.   430

MABEL CHILTERN Tommy is the most useful person in London.

LORD GORING (*turning to her*) And who is the most ornamental?

MABEL CHILTERN (*triumphantly*) I am.

LORD GORING How clever of you to guess it! (*Takes up his hat and cane*) Good-bye, Lady Chiltern! You will remember what I said to you, won't you?   435

LADY CHILTERN Yes; but I don't know why you said it to me.

LORD GORING I hardly know myself. Good-bye, Miss Mabel!

MABEL CHILTERN (*with a little moue° of disappointment*) I wish you were not going. I have had four wonderful adventures this morning; four and a half, in fact. You might stop and listen to some of them.   440

LORD GORING How very selfish of you to have four and a half! There won't be any left for me.

MABEL CHILTERN I don't want you to have any. They would not be good for you.   445

LORD GORING That is the first unkind thing you have ever said to me. How charmingly you said it! Ten tomorrow.

MABEL CHILTERN Sharp.

LORD GORING Quite sharp. But don't bring Mr Trafford.   450

MABEL CHILTERN (*with a little toss of the head*) Of course I shan't bring Tommy Trafford. Tommy Trafford is in great disgrace.

LORD GORING I am delighted to hear it.

> *Bows and goes out*

MABEL CHILTERN Gertrude,° I wish you would speak to Tommy Trafford.   455

LADY CHILTERN What has poor Mr Trafford done this time? Robert says he is the best secretary he has ever had.

MABEL CHILTERN Well, Tommy has proposed to me again. Tommy really does nothing but propose to me. He proposed to me last night in the music-room, when I was quite unprotected, as there was an elaborate trio going on. I didn't dare to make the smallest repartee, I need hardly tell you. If I had, it would have stopped the music at once. Musical people are so absurdly unreasonable. They always want one to be perfectly dumb at the very moment when one is longing to be absolutely deaf. Then he proposed to me in broad daylight this morning, in front of that dreadful statue° of Achilles. Really, the things that go on in front of that work of art are quite appalling. The police should interfere. At luncheon I saw by the glare in his eye that he was going to propose again, and I just managed to check him in time by assuring him that I was a   460   465   470 bimetallist. Fortunately I don't know what bimetallism° means. And I don't believe anybody else does either. But the observation crushed Tommy for ten minutes. He looked quite shocked. And then Tommy is so annoying in the way he proposes. If he proposed at the top of his voice, I should not mind so much. That might produce some effect on the public. But he does it in a horrid confidential way. When Tommy wants to be romantic he talks to one just like a doctor. I am very fond of Tommy, but his methods of proposing are quite out of date. I wish, Gertrude, you would speak to him, and tell him that once a week is quite often enough to propose to any one, and that it should always be done in a manner that attracts some attention.°

LADY CHILTERN Dear Mabel, don't talk like that. Besides, Robert thinks very highly of Mr Trafford. He believes he has a brilliant future before him.

MABEL CHILTERN Oh! I wouldn't marry a man with a future before him for anything under the sun.

LADY CHILTERN Mabel!

MABEL CHILTERN I know, dear.° You married a man with a future, didn't you? But then Robert was a genius, and you have a noble, self-sacrificing character. You can stand geniuses. I have no character at all, and Robert is the only genius I could ever bear. As a rule, I think they are quite impossible. Geniuses talk so much, don't they? Such a bad habit! And they are always thinking about themselves, when I want them to be thinking about me. I must go round now and rehearse at Lady Basildon's. You remember we are having *tableaux*,° don't you? The Triumph of something, I don't know what! I hope it will be triumph of me. Only triumph I am really interested in at present. (*Kisses Lady Chiltern and goes out; then comes running back*) Oh, Gertrude, do you know who is coming to see you? That dreadful Mrs Cheveley, in a most lovely gown. Did you ask her?

LADY CHILTERN (*rising*) Mrs Cheveley! Coming to see me? Impossible!

MABEL CHILTERN I assure you she is coming upstairs, as large as life and not nearly so natural.

LADY CHILTERN You need not wait, Mabel. Remember, Lady Basildon is expecting you.

MABEL CHILTERN Oh! I must shake hands with Lady Markby. She is delightful. I love being scolded by her.

    Enter Mason

MASON Lady Markby. Mrs Cheveley.

    Enter Lady Markby and Mrs Cheveley [Exit Mason]

LADY CHILTERN (*advancing to meet them*) Dear Lady Markby, how nice of you to come and see me! (*Shakes hands with her, and bows somewhat distantly° to Mrs Cheveley*) Won't you sit down, Mrs Cheveley?   515

MRS CHEVELEY Thanks. Isn't that Miss Chiltern? I should like so much to know her.

LADY CHILTERN Mabel, Mrs Cheveley wishes to know you.

    Mabel Chiltern gives a little nod

MRS CHEVELEY (*sitting down*) I thought your frock so charming last night, Miss Chiltern. So simple and . . . suitable.   520

MABEL CHILTERN Really? I must tell my dressmaker. It will be such a surprise to her. Good-bye, Lady Markby!

LADY MARKBY Going already?

MABEL CHILTERN I am so sorry but I am obliged to. I am just off to rehearsal. I have got to stand on my head in some *tableaux*.   525

LADY MARKBY On your head, child? Oh! I hope not. I believe it is most unhealthy. (*Takes a seat on the sofa next Lady Chiltern*)

MABEL CHILTERN But it is for an excellent charity: in aid of the Undeserving,° the only people I am really interested in. I am the secretary, and Tommy Trafford is treasurer.   530

MRS CHEVELEY And what is Lord Goring?

MABEL CHILTERN Oh! Lord Goring is president.

MRS CHEVELEY The post should suit him admirably, unless he has deteriorated since I knew him first.

LADY MARKBY (*reflecting*) You are remarkably modern, Mabel. A   535 little too modern, perhaps. Nothing is so dangerous as being too modern. One is apt to grow old-fashioned quite suddenly. I have known many instances of it.

MABEL CHILTERN What a dreadful prospect!

LADY MARKBY Ah! my dear, you need not be nervous. You will   40 always be as pretty as possible. That is the best fashion there is, and the only fashion that England succeeds in setting.

MABEL CHILTERN (*with a curtsey*) Thank you so much, Lady Markby, for England . . . and myself.

    Goes out

LADY MARKBY (*turning to Lady Chiltern*) Dear Gertrude, we   545 just called to know if Mrs Cheveley's diamond brooch has been found.

LADY CHILTERN Here?

MRS CHEVELEY Yes. I missed it when I got back to Claridge's, and
I thought I might possibly have dropped it here.   550

LADY CHILTERN I have heard nothing about it. But I will send for
the butler and ask. (*Touches the bell*)

MRS CHEVELEY Oh, pray don't trouble, Lady Chiltern. I dare say I
lost it at the Opera,° before we came on here.

LADY MARKBY Ah yes, I suppose it must have been at the Opera.   555
The fact is, we all scramble and jostle so much nowadays that I
wonder we have anything at all left on us at the end of an evening.
I know myself that, when I am coming back from the Drawing
Room,° I always feel as if I hadn't a shred on me, except a small
shred of decent reputation, just enough to prevent the lower classes 560
making painful observations through the windows of the carriage.
The fact is that our Society is terribly over-populated. Really,
someone should arrange a proper scheme of assisted emigration.°
It would do a great deal of good.

MRS CHEVELEY I quite agree with you, Lady Markby. It is nearly   565
six years since I have been in London for the Season, and I must
say Society has become dreadfully mixed. One sees the oddest
people everywhere.

LADY MARKBY That is quite true, dear. But one needn't know them.
I'm sure I don't know half the people who come to my house.   570
Indeed, from all I hear, I shouldn't like to.

   Enter Mason

LADY CHILTERN What sort of a brooch was it that you lost, Mrs
Cheveley?

MRS CHEVELEY A diamond snake-brooch with a ruby, a rather large
ruby.   575

LADY MARKBY I thought you said there was a sapphire on the head,
dear?

MRS CHEVELEY (*smiling*) No, Lady Markby—a ruby.

LADY MARKBY (*nodding her head*) And very becoming, I am quite
sure.   580

LADY CHILTERN Has a ruby and diamond brooch been found in any
of the rooms this morning, Mason?

MASON No, my lady.

MRS CHEVELEY It really is of no consequence, Lady Chiltern. I am
so sorry to have put you to any inconvenience.   585

LADY CHILTERN (*coldly*) Oh, it has been no inconvenience. That
will do, Mason. You can bring tea.

   Exit Mason

LADY MARKBY Well, I must say it is most annoying to lose anything. I remember once at Bath,° years ago, losing in the Pump Room an exceedingly handsome cameo bracelet that Sir John had given me.   590 I don't think he has ever given me anything since, I am sorry to say. He has sadly degenerated. Really, this horrid House of Commons quite ruins our husbands for us. I think the Lower House by far the greatest blow to a happy married life that there has been since that terrible thing called the Higher Education of   595 Women was invented.

LADY CHILTERN Ah! it is heresy to say that in this house, Lady Markby. Robert is a great champion of the Higher Education of Women, and so, I am afraid, am I.

MRS CHEVELEY The higher education of men is what I should like   600 to see. Men need it so sadly.

LADY MARKBY They do, dear. But I am afraid such a scheme would be quite unpractical. I don't think man has much capacity for development. He has got as far as he can, and that is not far, is it? With regard to women, well, dear Gertrude, you belong to the   605 younger generation, and I am sure it is all right if you approve of it. In my time, of course, we were taught not to understand anything. That was the old system, and wonderfully interesting it was. I assure you that the amount of things I and my poor dear sister were taught not to understand was quite extraordinary. But   610 modern women understand everything, I am told.

MRS CHEVELEY Except their husbands. That is the one thing the modern woman never understands.

LADY MARKBY And a very good thing too, dear, I dare say. It might break up many a happy home if they did. Not yours, I need hardly   615 say, Gertrude. You have married a pattern husband. I wish I could say as much for myself. But since Sir John has taken to attending the debates regularly, which he never used to do in the good old days, his language has become quite impossible. He always seems to think that he is addressing the House, and consequently   620 whenever he discusses the state of the agricultural labourer, or the Welsh Church,° or something quite improper of that kind, I am obliged to send all the servants out of the room. It is not pleasant to see one's own butler, who has been with one for twenty-three years, actually blushing at the side board, and the footmen making   625 contortions in corners like persons in circuses. I assure you my life will be quite ruined unless they send John at once to the Upper House.° He won't take any interest in politics then, will he? The

House of Lords is so sensible.° An assembly of gentlemen. But in
his present state, Sir John is really a great trial. Why, this morning   630
before breakfast was half over, he stood up on the hearthrug, put
his hands in his pockets, and appealed to the country at the top of
his voice. I left the table as soon as I had my second cup of tea, I
need hardly say. But his violent language could be heard all over
the house! I trust, Gertrude, that Sir Robert is not like that?   635

LADY CHILTERN But I am very much interested in politics, Lady
Markby. I love to hear Robert talk about them.

LADY MARKBY Well, I hope he is not as devoted to Blue Books° as
Sir John is. I don't think they can be quite improving reading for
anyone.   640

MRS CHEVELEY (*languidly*) I have never read a Blue Book. I prefer
books . . . in yellow covers.°

LADY MARKBY (*genially unconscious*) Yellow is a gayer colour, is it
not? I used to wear yellow a good deal in my early days, and would
do so now if Sir John was not so painfully personal in his   645
observations, and a man on the question of dress is always
ridiculous, is he not?

MRS CHEVELEY Oh, no! I think men are the only authorities on
dress.

LADY MARKBY Really? One wouldn't say so from the sort of hats   650
they wear, would one?

> *The butler enters,° followed by the footman. Tea is set on a small*
> *table close to Lady Chiltern*

LADY CHILTERN May I give you some tea, Mrs Cheveley?

MRS CHEVELEY Thanks.

> *The butler hands Mrs Cheveley a cup of tea on a salver*

LADY CHILTERN Some tea, Lady Markby?

LADY MARKBY No thanks, dear.   655

> *The servants go out.*

The fact is, I have promised to go round for ten minutes to see
poor Lady Brancaster, who is in very great trouble. Her daughter,
quite a well-brought-up girl, too, has actually become engaged to
be married to a curate in Shropshire. It is very sad, very sad
indeed. I can't understand this modern mania for curates. In my   660
time we girls saw them, of course, running about the place like
rabbits. But we never took any notice of them, I need hardly say.
But I am told that nowadays country society is quite honeycombed
with them. I think it most irreligious. And then the eldest son has
quarrelled with his father, and it is said that when they meet at the   665

club Lord Brancaster always hides himself behind the money article in *The Times*. However, I believe that is quite a common occurrence nowadays and that they have to take in extra copies of *The Times* at all the clubs in St James's Street; there are so many sons who won't have anything to do with their fathers, and so many fathers who won't speak to their sons. I think, myself, it is very much to be regretted.

MRS CHEVELEY So do I. Fathers have so much to learn from their sons nowadays.

LADY MARKBY Really, dear? What?

MRS CHEVELEY The art of living. The only really Fine Art we have produced in modern times.

LADY MARKBY (*shaking her head*) Ah! I am afraid Lord Brancaster knew a good deal about that. More than his poor wife ever did. (*Turning to Lady Chiltern*) You know Lady Brancaster, don't you, dear?

LADY CHILTERN Just slightly. She was staying at Langton last autumn, when we were there.

LADY MARKBY Well, like all stout women, she looks the very picture of happiness, as no doubt you noticed. But there are many tragedies in her family, besides this affair of the curate. Her own sister, Mrs Jekyll, had a most unhappy life; through no fault of her own, I am sorry to say. She ultimately was so broken-hearted that she went into a convent, or on to the operatic stage,° I forget which. No; I think it was decorative art-needlework she took up. I know she had lost all sense of pleasure in life. (*Rising*) And now, Gertrude, if you will allow me, I shall leave Mrs Cheveley in your charge and call back for her in a quarter of an hour. Or perhaps, dear Mrs Cheveley, you wouldn't mind waiting in the carriage while I am with Lady Brancaster. As I intend it to be a visit of condolence, I shan't stay long.

MRS CHEVELEY (*rising*) I don't mind waiting in the carriage at all, provided there is somebody to look at one.

LADY MARKBY Well, I hear the curate is always prowling about the house.

MRS CHEVELEY I am afraid I am not fond of girl friends.°

LADY CHILTERN (*rising*) Oh, I hope Mrs Cheveley will stay here a little. I should like to have a few minutes' conversation with her.

MRS CHEVELEY How very kind of you, Lady Chiltern! Believe me, nothing would give me greater pleasure.

LADY MARKBY Ah! no doubt you both have many pleasant reminis-
cences of your schooldays to talk over together. Good-bye, dear
Gertrude! Shall I see you at Lady Bonar's tonight? She has
discovered a wonderful new genius. He does . . . nothing at all, I   710
believe. That is a great comfort, is it not?

LADY CHILTERN Robert and I are dining at home by ourselves
tonight, and I don't think I shall go anywhere afterwards. Robert,
of course, will have to be in the House. But there is nothing
interesting on.   715

LADY MARKBY Dining at home by yourselves? Is that quite prudent?
Ah, I forgot, your husband is an exception. Mine is the general
rule, and nothing ages a woman so rapidly as having married the
general rule.

    Exit Lady Markby

MRS CHEVELEY Wonderful woman, Lady Markby, isn't she? Talks   720
more and says less than anybody I ever met. She is made to be a
public speaker. Much more so than her husband, though he is a
typical Englishman, always dull and usually violent.

LADY CHILTERN (*makes no answer, but remains standing. There is a
pause. Then the eyes of the two women meet. Lady Chiltern looks stern
and pale. Mrs Cheveley seems rather amused*) Mrs Cheveley, I   725
think it is right to tell you quite frankly that, had I known who
you really were, I should not have invited you to my house last
night.

MRS CHEVELEY (*with an impertinent smile*) Really?

LADY CHILTERN I could not have done so.   730

MRS CHEVELEY: I see that after all these years you have not changed
a bit, Gertrude.°

LADY CHILTERN I never change.

MRS CHEVELEY (*elevating her eyebrows*) Then life has taught you
nothing?   735

LADY CHILTERN It has taught me that a person who has once been
guilty of a dishonest and dishonourable action may be guilty of it
a second time, and should be shunned.

MRS CHEVELEY Would you apply that rule to everyone?

LADY CHILTERN Yes, to everyone, without exception.   740

MRS CHEVELEY Then I am sorry for you, Gertrude, very sorry for
you.

LADY CHILTERN You see now, I am sure, that for many reasons any
further acquaintance between us during your stay in London is
quite impossible?   745

MRS CHEVELEY (*leaning back in her chair*) Do you know, Gertrude, I don't mind your talking morality a bit. Morality is simply the attitude we adopt towards people whom we personally dislike. You dislike me. I am quite aware of that. And I have always detested you. And yet I have come here to do you a service.   750

LADY CHILTERN (*contemptuously*) Like the service you wished to render my husband last night, I suppose. Thank heaven, I saved him from that.

MRS CHEVELEY (*starting to her feet*) It was you who made him write that insolent letter to me? It was you who made him break his   755
promise?

LADY CHILTERN Yes.

MRS CHEVELEY Then you must make him keep it. I give you till tomorrow morning—no more. If by that time your husband does not solemnly bind himself to help me in this great scheme in which   760
I am interested—

LADY CHILTERN This fraudulent speculation—

MRS CHEVELEY Call it what you choose. I hold your husband in the hollow of my hand, and if you are wise you will make him do what I tell him.   765

LADY CHILTERN (*rising and going towards her*) You are impertinent. What has my husband to do with you? With a woman like you?

MRS CHEVELEY (*with a bitter laugh*) In this world like meets with like. It is because your husband is himself fraudulent and dishonest   770
that we pair so well together. Between you and him there are chasms. He and I are closer than friends. We are enemies linked together. The same sin binds us.

LADY CHILTERN How dare you class my husband with yourself? How dare you threaten him or me? Leave my house. You are unfit   775
to enter it.

> *Sir Robert Chiltern enters from behind.°* He hears his wife's last
> *words, and sees to whom they are addressed. He grows deadly*
> *pale*

MRS CHEVELEY Your house! A house bought with the price of dishonour. A house, everything in which has been paid for by fraud. (*Turns round and sees Sir Robert Chiltern*) Ask him what the origin of his fortune is! Get him to tell you how he sold to a   780
stockbroker a Cabinet secret. Learn from him to what you owe your position.

LADY CHILTERN It is not true! Robert! It is not true!

MRS CHEVELEY (*pointing at him with outstretched finger*) Look at him! Can he deny it? Does he dare to? 785

SIR ROBERT CHILTERN Go! Go at once. You have done your worst now.

MRS CHEVELEY My worst? I have not yet finished with you, with either of you. I give you both till tomorrow at noon. If by then you don't do what I bid you to do, the whole world shall know the 790 origin of Robert Chiltern.

Sir Robert Chiltern strikes the bell. Enter Mason°

SIR ROBERT CHILTERN Show Mrs Cheveley out.

Mrs Cheveley starts; then bows with somewhat exaggerated politeness to Lady Chiltern, who makes no sign of response. As she passes by Sir Robert Chiltern, who is standing close to the door, she pauses for a moment and looks him straight in the face. She then goes out, followed by the servant, who closes the door after him. The husband and wife are left alone. Lady Chiltern stands like someone in a dreadful dream. Then she turns round and looks at her husband. She looks at him with strange eyes, as though she was seeing him for the first time

LADY CHILTERN You sold a Cabinet secret for money! You began your life with fraud! You built up your career on dishonour! Oh, tell me it is not true! Lie to me! Lie to me! Tell me it is not true! 795

SIR ROBERT CHILTERN What this woman said is quite true. But, Gertrude, listen to me. You don't realize how I was tempted. Let me tell you the whole thing. (*Goes towards her*)

LADY CHILTERN Don't come near me. Don't touch me. I feel as if you had soiled me for ever. Oh! what a mask you have been 800 wearing all these years! A horrible painted mask! You sold yourself for money. Oh! a common thief were better. You put yourself up to sale to the highest bidder! You were bought in the market. You lie to the whole world. And yet you will not lie to me.

SIR ROBERT CHILTERN (*rushing towards her*) Gertrude! Gertrude! 805

LADY CHILTERN (*thrusting him back with outstretched hands*) No, don't speak! Say nothing! Your voice wakes terrible memories— memories of things that made me love you—memories of words that made me love you—memories that now are horrible to me. And how I worshipped you! You were to me something apart from 810 common life, a thing pure, noble, honest, without stain. The world seemed to me finer because you were in it, and goodness more real because you lived. And now—oh, when I think that I made of a man like you my ideal! the ideal of my life!

SIR ROBERT CHILTERN There was your mistake. There was your   815
error. The error all women commit. Why can't you women love
us, faults and all? Why do you place us on monstrous pedestals?
We have all feet of clay, women as well as men: but when we men
love women, we love them knowing their weaknesses, their follies,
their imperfections, love them all the more, it may be, for that   820
reason. It is not the perfect, but the imperfect, who have need of
love. It is when we are wounded by our own hands, or by the
hands of others, that love should come to cure us—else what use
is love at all? All sins, except a sin against itself, Love should
forgive. All lives, save loveless lives, true Love should pardon. A   825
man's love is like that. It is wider, larger, more human than a
woman's. Women think that they are making ideals of men. What
they are making of us are false idols merely. You made your false
idol of me, and I had not the courage to come down, show you my
wounds, tell you my weaknesses. I was afraid that I might lose your   830
love, as I have lost it now. And so, last night you ruined my life
for me—yes, ruined it! What this woman asked of me was nothing
compared to what she offered to me. She offered security, peace,
stability. The sin of my youth, that I had thought was buried, rose
up in front of me, hideous, horrible, with its hands at my throat.   835
I could have killed it for ever, sent it back into its tomb, destroyed
its record, burned the one witness against me. You prevented me.
No one but you, you know it. And now what is there before me
but public disgrace, ruin, terrible shame, the mockery of the world,
a lonely dishonoured life, a lonely dishonoured death, it maybe,   840
some day? Let women make no more ideals of men! let them not
put them on altars and bow before them, or they may ruin other
lives as completely as you—you whom I have so wildly loved—
have ruined mine!

> *He passes from the room.*° *Lady Chiltern rushes towards him,*
> *but the door is closed when she reaches it. Pale with anguish,*
> *bewildered, helpless, she sways like a plant in the water. Her*
> *hands, outstretched, seem to tremble in the air like blossoms in*
> *the wind. Then she flings herself down beside a sofa and buries*
> *her face. Her sobs are like the sobs of a child*

ACT DROP

Third Act

Scene: The Library in Lord Goring's house. An Adam room. On the right is the door leading into the hall. On the left, the door of the smoking-room. A pair of folding doors at the back open into the drawing-room. The fire is lit. Phipps, the Butler, is arranging some newspapers on the writing-table. The distinction of Phipps is his impassivity. He has been termed by enthusiasts the Ideal Butler. The Sphinx is not so incommunicable. He is a mask with a manner. Of his intellectual or emotional life, history knows nothing. He represents the dominance of form.

Enter Lord Goring° in evening dress with a buttonhole. He is wearing a silk hat and Inverness cape. White-gloved, he carries a Louis Seize cane. His are all the delicate fopperies of Fashion. One sees that he stands in immediate relation to modern life, makes it indeed, and so masters it. He is the first well-dressed philosopher in the history of thought

LORD GORING Got my second buttonhole for me, Phipps?

PHIPPS Yes, my lord.

Takes his hat, cane, and cape, and presents new buttonhole on salver

LORD GORING Rather distinguished thing, Phipps. I am the only person of the smallest importance in London at present who wears a buttonhole.   5

PHIPPS Yes, my lord. I have observed that.

LORD GORING (*taking out old buttonhole*) You see, Phipps, Fashion is what one wears oneself. What is unfashionable is what other people wear.

PHIPPS Yes, my lord.   10

LORD GORING Just as vulgarity is simply the conduct of other people.

PHIPPS Yes, my lord.

LORD GORING (*putting in new buttonhole*) And falsehoods the truths of other people.   15

PHIPPS Yes, my lord.

LORD GORING Other people are quite dreadful. The only possible society is oneself.

PHIPPS Yes, my lord.

LORD GORING To love oneself is the beginning of a lifelong   20
romance, Phipps.

PHIPPS Yes, my lord.

LORD GORING (*looking at himself in the glass*) Don't think I quite like
this buttonhole, Phipps. Makes me look a little too old. Makes me
almost in the prime of life, eh, Phipps?   25

PHIPPS I don't observe any alteration in your lordship's appearance.

LORD GORING You don't, Phipps?

PHIPPS No, my lord.

LORD GORING I am not quite sure. For the future a more trivial
buttonhole, Phipps, on Thursday evenings.   30

PHIPPS I will speak to the florist, my lord. She has had a loss in her
family lately, which perhaps accounts for the lack of triviality your
lordship complains of in the buttonhole.

LORD GORING Extraordinary thing about the lower class in England—they are always losing their relations.   35

PHIPPS Yes, my lord! They are extremely fortunate in that respect.

LORD GORING (*turns round and looks at him. Phipps remains impassive*)
Hum! Any letters, Phipps?

PHIPPS Three, my lord. (*Hands letters on a salver*)

LORD GORING (*takes letters*) Want my cab round in twenty minutes.   40

PHIPPS Yes, my lord.
        Goes towards door

LORD GORING (*holds up letter in pink envelope*)° Ahem! Phipps, when
did this letter arrive?

PHIPPS It was brought by hand just after your lordship went to the
Club.   45

LORD GORING That will do.
        Exit Phipps
Lady Chiltern's handwriting on Lady Chiltern's pink notepaper.
That is rather curious. I thought Robert was to write. Wonder
what Lady Chiltern has got to say to me? (*Sits at bureau, opens
letter, and reads it*) 'I want you. I trust you. I am coming to you.   50
Gertrude.' (*Puts down the letter with a puzzled look. Then takes it
up, and reads it again slowly*) 'I want you. I trust you. I am coming
to you.' So she has found out everything! Poor woman! Poor
woman! (*Pulls out watch and looks at it*) But what an hour to call!
Ten o'clock! I shall have to give up going to the Berkshires'.   55
However, it is always nice to be expected, and not to arrive. I am
not expected at the Bachelors', so I shall certainly go there. Well,
I will make her stand by her husband. That is the only thing for

her to do. That is the only thing for any woman to do. It is the
growth of the moral sense in women that makes marriage such a   60
hopeless, one-sided institution. Ten o'clock. She should be here
soon. I must tell Phipps I am not in to anyone else.
        Goes towards bell. Enter Phipps
PHIPPS Lord Caversham.°
LORD GORING Oh, why will parents always appear at the wrong
time? Some extraordinary mistake in nature, I suppose.   65
        Enter Lord Caversham
   Delighted to see you, my dear father.
        Goes to meet him
LORD CAVERSHAM Take my cloak off.
LORD GORING Is it worth while, father?
LORD CAVERSHAM Of course it is worth while, sir. Which is the
most comfortable chair?   70
LORD GORING This one, father. It is the chair I use myself, when I
have visitors.
LORD CAVERSHAM Thank ye. No draught, I hope, in this room?
LORD GORING No, father.
LORD CAVERSHAM (*sitting down*) Glad to hear it. Can't stand   75
draughts. No draughts at home.
LORD GORING Good many breezes,° father.
LORD CAVERSHAM Eh? Eh? Don't understand what you mean. Want
to have a serious conversation with you, sir.
LORD GORING My dear father! At this hour?   80
LORD CAVERSHAM Well, sir, it is only ten o'clock. What is your
objection to the hour? I think the hour is an admirable hour!
LORD GORING Well, the fact is, father, this is not my day for talking
seriously. I am very sorry, but it is not my day.
LORD CAVERSHAM What do you mean, sir?   85
LORD GORING During the Season, father, I only talk seriously on
the first Tuesday in every month, from four to seven.
LORD CAVERSHAM Well, make it Tuesday, sir, make it Tuesday.
LORD GORING But it is after seven, father, and my doctor says I
must not have any serious conversation after seven. It makes me   90
talk in my sleep.
LORD CAVERSHAM Talk in your sleep, sir? What does that matter?
You are not married.
LORD GORING No, father, I am not married.
LORD CAVERSHAM Hum! That is what I have come to talk to you   95
about, sir. You have got to get married, and at once. Why, when

I was your age, sir, I had been an inconsolable widower for three
months, and was already paying my addresses to your admirable
mother. Damme, sir, it is your duty to get married.° You can't be
always living for pleasure. Every man of position is married   100
nowadays. Bachelors are not fashionable any more. They are a
damaged lot. Too much is known about them. You must get a
wife, sir. Look where your friend Robert Chiltern has got to by
probity, hard work, and a sensible marriage with a good woman.
Why don't you imitate him, sir? Why don't you take him for your   105
model?

LORD GORING I think I shall, father.

LORD CAVERSHAM I wish you would, sir. Then I should be happy.
At present I make your mother's life miserable on your account.
You are heartless, sir, quite heartless.   110

LORD GORING I hope not, father.

LORD CAVERSHAM And it is high time for you to get married. You
are thirty-four years of age, sir.

LORD GORING Yes, father, but I only admit to thirty-two—thirty-
one and half when I have a really good buttonhole. This button-   115
hole is not . . . trivial enough.

LORD CAVERSHAM I tell you you are thirty-four, sir. And there is a
draught in your room, besides, which makes your conduct worse.
Why did you tell me there was no draught, sir? I feel a draught,
sir,° I feel it distinctly.   120

LORD GORING So do I, father. It is a dreadful draught. I will come
and see you tomorrow, father. We can talk over anything you like.
Let me help you on with your cloak, father.

LORD CAVERSHAM No, sir; I have called this evening for a definite
purpose, and I am going to see it through at all costs to my health   125
or yours. Put down my cloak, sir.

LORD GORING Certainly, father. But let us go into another room.
(*Rings bell*) There is a dreadful draught here.

    Enter Phipps

Phipps, is there a good fire in the smoking-room?

PHIPPS Yes, my lord.° [*Opens smoking-room door*]   130

LORD GORING Come in there, father. Your sneezes are quite heart-
rending.

LORD CAVERSHAM Well, sir, I suppose I have a right to sneeze when
I choose?

LORD GORING (*apologetically*) Quite so, father. I was merely expres-   135
sing sympathy.

LORD CAVERSHAM Oh, damn sympathy. There is a great deal too much of that sort of thing going on nowadays.

LORD GORING I quite agree with you, father. If there was less sympathy in the world there would be less trouble in the world. 140

LORD CAVERSHAM (*going towards the smoking-room*) That is a paradox, sir. I hate paradoxes.

LORD GORING So do I, father. Everybody one meets is a paradox nowadays. It is a great bore. It makes society so obvious.

LORD CAVERSHAM (*turning round, and looking at his son beneath his* 145 *bushy eyebrows*) Do you always really understand what you say, sir?

LORD GORING (*after some hesitation*) Yes, father, if I listen attentively.

LORD CAVERSHAM (*indignantly*) If you listen attentively! . . . Con- 150 ceited young puppy!

    Goes off grumbling into the smoking-room. Phipps [returns]

LORD GORING Phipps, there is a lady coming to see me this evening on particular business. Show her into the drawing-room when she arrives. You understand?

PHIPPS Yes, my lord. 155

LORD GORING It is a matter of the gravest importance, Phipps.

PHIPPS I understand, my lord.

LORD GORING No one else is to be admitted, under any circumstances.

PHIPPS I understand, my lord. 160

    Bell rings

LORD GORING Ah! that is probably the lady. I shall see her myself.

    Just as he is going towards the door Lord Caversham enters from the smoking-room

LORD CAVERSHAM Well, sir? am I to wait attendance on you?

LORD GORING (*considerably perplexed*) In a moment, father. Do excuse me. (*Lord Caversham goes back*) Well, remember my instructions, Phipps—into that room. 165

PHIPPS Yes, my lord.

    Lord Goring goes into the smoking-room. Harold, the footman, shows Mrs Cheveley in. Lamia-like,° she is in green and silver. She has a cloak of black satin, lined with dead rose-leaf silk

HAROLD What name, madam?

MRS CHEVELEY (*to Phipps, who advances towards her*) Is Lord Goring not here? I was told he was at home?

PHIPPS His lordship is engaged at present with Lord Caversham,   170
madam.

> *Turns a cold, glassy eye on Harold, who at once retires*

MRS CHEVELEY (*to herself*) How very filial!

PHIPPS His lordship told me to ask you, madam, to be kind enough
to wait in the drawing-room for him. His lordship will come to
you there.   175

MRS CHEVELEY (*with a look of surprise*) Lord Goring expects me?

PHIPPS Yes, madam.

MRS CHEVELEY Are you quite sure?

PHIPPS His lordship told me that if a lady called I was to ask her to
wait in the drawing-room.° (*Goes to the door of the drawing-room   180
and opens it*) His lordship's directions on the subject were very
precise.

MRS CHEVELEY (*to herself*) How thoughtful of him! To expect the
unexpected shows a thoroughly modern intellect. (*Goes towards the
drawing-room and looks in*) Ugh! How dreary a bachelor's drawing-   185
room always looks. I shall have to alter all this.° (*Phipps brings the
lamp from the writing-table*) No, I don't care for that lamp. It is far
too glaring. Light some candles.

PHIPPS (*replaces lamp*) Certainly, madam.

MRS CHEVELEY I hope the candles have very becoming shades.   190

PHIPPS We have had no complaints about them, madam, as yet.

> *Passes into the drawing-room and begins to light the*
> *candles.*

MRS CHEVELEY (*to herself*) I wonder what woman he is waiting for
tonight. It will be delightful to catch him. Men always look so silly
when they are caught. And they are always being caught. (*Looks
about room and approaches the writing-table*) What a very interesting   195
room! What a very interesting picture! Wonder what his correspondence is like. (*Takes up letters*) Oh, what a very uninteresting
correspondence! Bills and cards, debts and dowagers! Who on
earth writes to him on pink paper? How silly to write on pink
paper! It looks like the beginning of a middle-class romance.   200
Romance should never begin with sentiment. It should begin with
science and end with a settlement.° (*Puts letter down, then takes it
up again*) I know that handwriting.° That is Gertrude Chiltern's.
I remember it perfectly. The ten commandments in every stroke
of the pen, and the moral law all over the page. Wonder what   205
Gertrude is writing to him about? Something horrid about me, I
suppose. How I detest that woman! (*Reads it*) 'I trust you. I want

you. I am coming to you. Gertrude.' 'I trust you. I want you. I am coming to you.'

> *A look of triumph comes over her face. She is just about to steal the letter, when Phipps comes in*

PHIPPS The candles in the drawing-room are lit, madam, as you directed.   210

MRS CHEVELEY Thank you.

> *Rises hastily and slips the letter° under a large silver-cased blotting-book that is lying on the table*

PHIPPS I trust the shades will be to your liking, madam. They are the most becoming we have. They are the same as his lordship uses himself when he is dressing for dinner.   215

MRS CHEVELEY (*with a smile*) Then I am sure they will be perfectly right.

PHIPPS (*gravely*) Thank you, madam.

> *Mrs Cheveley goes into the drawing-room. Phipps closes the door and retires. The door is then slowly opened, and Mrs Cheveley comes out and creeps stealthily° towards the writing-table. Suddenly voices are heard from the smoking-room. Mrs Cheveley grows pale, and stops. The voices grow louder, and she goes back into the drawing-room, biting her lip.*
> *Enter Lord Goring and Lord Caversham*

LORD GORING (*expostulating*) My dear father, if I am to get married, surely you will allow me to choose the time, place, and person?   220
Particularly the person.

LORD CAVERSHAM (*testily*) That is a matter for me, sir. You would probably make a very poor choice. It is I who should be consulted, not you. There is property at stake. It is not a matter for affection. Affection comes later on in married life.   225

LORD GORING Yes. In married life affection comes when people thoroughly dislike each other, father, doesn't it?

> *Puts on Lord Caversham's cloak for him*

LORD CAVERSHAM Certainly, sir. I mean certainly not, sir. You are talking very foolishly tonight. What I say is that marriage is a matter for common sense.   230

LORD GORING But women who have common sense are so curiously plain, father, aren't they? Of course I only speak from hearsay.

LORD CAVERSHAM No woman, plain or pretty, has any common sense at all, sir. Common sense is the privilege of our sex.

LORD GORING Quite so. And we men are so self-sacrificing that we never use it, do we, father?   235

LORD CAVERSHAM I use it, sir. I use nothing else.

LORD GORING So my mother tells me.

LORD CAVERSHAM It is the secret of your mother's happiness. You
are very heartless, sir, very heartless.   240

LORD GORING I hope not, father.

> *Goes out for a moment.° Then returns, looking rather put out,*
> *with Sir Robert Chiltern*

SIR ROBERT CHILTERN My dear Arthur, what a piece of good luck
meeting you on the doorstep! Your servant had just told me you
were not at home. How extraordinary!

LORD GORING The fact is, I am horribly busy tonight, Robert, and   245
I gave orders I was not at home to anyone. Even my father had a
comparatively cold reception. He complained of a draught the
whole time.

SIR ROBERT CHILTERN Ah! you must be at home to me, Arthur.
You are my best friend. Perhaps by tomorrow you will be my only 250
friend. My wife has discovered everything.

LORD GORING Ah! I guessed as much!°

SIR ROBERT CHILTERN (*looking at him*) Really! How?

LORD GORING (*after some hesitation*) Oh merely by something in the
expression of your face as you came in. Who told her?   255

SIR ROBERT CHILTERN Mrs Cheveley herself. And the woman I
love knows that I began my career with an act of low dishonesty,
that I built up my life upon sands of shame—that I sold, like a
common huckster, the secret that had been intrusted to me as a
man of honour. I thank heaven poor Lord Radley died without   260
knowing that I betrayed him. I would to God I had died before I
had been so horribly tempted, or had fallen so low.

> *Burying his face in his hands.* [*A pause*]

LORD GORING You have heard nothing from Vienna yet, in answer
to your wire?

SIR ROBERT CHILTERN (*looking up*) Yes; I got a telegram from the 265
first secretary at eight o'clock tonight.

LORD GORING Well?

SIR ROBERT CHILTERN Nothing is absolutely known against her. On
the contrary, she occupies a rather high position in society. It is a
sort of open secret that Baron Arnheim left her the greater portion 270
of his immense fortune. Beyond that I can learn nothing.

LORD GORING She doesn't turn out to be a spy, then?

SIR ROBERT CHILTERN Oh! spies are of no use nowadays. Their
profession is over. The newspapers do their work instead.

LORD GORING And thunderingly° well they do it.   275

SIR ROBERT CHILTERN Arthur, I am parched with thirst. May I ring for something? Some hock and seltzer?°

LORD GORING Certainly. Let me.
        Rings the bell

SIR ROBERT CHILTERN Thanks! I don't know what to do, Arthur, I don't know what to do, and you are my only friend. But what a   280 friend you are—the one friend I can trust. I can trust you absolutely, can't I?
        Enter Phipps

LORD GORING My dear Robert, of course. Oh! (*To Phipps*) Bring some hock and seltzer.

PHIPPS Yes, my lord.   285

LORD GORING And Phipps!

PHIPPS Yes, my lord.

LORD GORING Will you excuse me for a moment, Robert? I want to give some directions° to my servant.

SIR ROBERT CHILTERN Certainly.   290

LORD GORING When that lady calls, tell her that I am not expected home this evening. Tell her that I have been suddenly called out of town. You understand?

PHIPPS The lady is in that room, my lord. You told me to show her into that room, my lord.   295

LORD GORING You did perfectly right.
        Exit Phipps
    What a mess I am in.° No; I think I shall get through it. I'll give her a lecture through the door. Awkward thing to manage, though.

SIR ROBERT CHILTERN Arthur, tell me what I should do. My life seems to have crumbled about me. I am a ship without a rudder   300 in a night without a star.

LORD GORING Robert, you love your wife, don't you?

SIR ROBERT CHILTERN I love her more than anything in the world. I used to think ambition the great thing. It is not. Love is the great thing in the world. There is nothing but love, and I love her. But   305 I am defamed in her eyes. I am ignoble in her eyes. There is a wide gulf between us now. She has found me out, Arthur, she has found me out.

LORD GORING Has she never in her life done some folly—some indiscretion—that she should not forgive your sin?   310

SIR ROBERT CHILTERN My wife! Never! She does not know what weakness or temptation is. I am of clay like other men. She stands

apart as good women do—pitiless in her perfection—cold and stern
and without mercy. But I love her, Arthur. We are childless, and
I have no one else to love, no one else to love me. Perhaps if God   315
had sent us children she might have been kinder to me. But God
has given us a lonely house. And she has cut my heart in two.
Don't let us talk of it. I was brutal to her this evening. But I
suppose when sinners talk to saints they are brutal always. I said
to her things that were hideously true, on my side, from my   320
standpoint, from the standpoint of men. But don't let us talk of
that.

LORD GORING Your wife will forgive you. Perhaps at this moment
she is forgiving you. She loves you, Robert. Why should she not
forgive?   325

SIR ROBERT CHILTERN God grant it! God grant it! (*Buries his face
in his hands*) But there is something more I have to tell you,
Arthur.

    Enter Phipps with drinks

PHIPPS (*hands hock and seltzer to Sir Robert Chiltern*) Hock and
seltzer, sir.   330

SIR ROBERT CHILTERN Thank you.

LORD GORING Is your carriage here, Robert?

SIR ROBERT CHILTERN No; I walked from the club.

LORD GORING Sir Robert will take my cab, Phipps.

PHIPPS Yes, my lord.   335

    Exit

LORD GORING Robert, you don't mind my sending you away?

SIR ROBERT CHILTERN Arthur, you must let me stay for five
minutes. I have made up my mind what I am going to do tonight
in the House. The debate on the Argentine Canal is to begin at
eleven. (*A chair falls in the drawing-room*)° What is that?   340

LORD GORING Nothing.

SIR ROBERT CHILTERN I heard a chair fall in the next room.
Someone has been listening.

LORD GORING No, no; there is no one there.

SIR ROBERT CHILTERN There is someone. There are lights in the   345
room, and the door is ajar. Someone has been listening to every
secret of my life. Arthur, what does this mean?

LORD GORING Robert, you are excited, unnerved. I tell you there is
no one in that room. Sit down, Robert.

SIR ROBERT CHILTERN Do you give me your word that there is no   350
one there?

LORD GORING Yes.

SIR ROBERT CHILTERN Your word of honour? (*Sits down*)

LORD GORING Yes.

SIR ROBERT CHILTERN (*rises*) Arthur, let me see for myself.   355

LORD GORING No, no.

SIR ROBERT CHILTERN If there is no one there why should I not look in that room? Arthur, you must let me go into that room and satisfy myself. Let me know that no eavesdropper has heard my life's secret. Arthur, you don't realize what I am going through.   360

LORD GORING Robert, this must stop. I have told you that there is no one in that room—that is enough.

SIR ROBERT CHILTERN (*rushes to the door of the room*) It is not enough. I insist on going into this room. You have told me there is no one there, so what reason can you have for refusing me?   365

LORD GORING For God's sake, don't! There is someone there. Someone whom you must not see.

SIR ROBERT CHILTERN Ah, I thought so!

LORD GORING I forbid you to enter that room.

SIR ROBERT CHILTERN Stand back. My life is at stake.° And I don't   370
care who is there. I will know who it is to whom I have told my secret and my shame.

> *Enters room*

LORD GORING Great Heavens! his own wife!

> *Sir Robert Chiltern comes back, with a look of scorn and anger on his face*

SIR ROBERT CHILTERN What explanation have you to give me for the presence of that woman here?   375

LORD GORING Robert, I swear to you on my honour that that lady is stainless and guiltless of all offence towards you.

SIR ROBERT CHILTERN She is a vile, an infamous thing!

LORD GORING Don't say that, Robert! It was for your sake she came here. It was to try and save you she came here. She loves you and   380
no one else.

SIR ROBERT CHILTERN You are mad. What have I to do with her intrigues with you? Let her remain your mistress! You are well suited to each other. She, corrupt and shameful—you, false as a friend, treacherous as an enemy even—   385

LORD GORING It is not true, Robert. Before heaven, it is not true. In her presence and in yours I will explain all.

SIR ROBERT CHILTERN Let me pass, sir. You have lied enough upon your word of honour.

*Sir Robert Chiltern goes out. Lord Goring rushes to the door of
the drawing-room, when Mrs Cheveley comes out, looking
radiant and much amused*

MRS CHEVELEY (*with a mock curtsey*) Good evening, Lord Goring!   390

LORD GORING Mrs Cheveley! Great heavens! . . . May I ask what
you were doing in my drawing-room?

MRS CHEVELEY Merely listening. I have a perfect passion for
listening through keyholes. One always hears such wonderful
things through them.   395

LORD GORING Doesn't that sound rather like tempting Providence?

MRS CHEVELEY Oh! surely Providence can resist temptation by this
time.

Makes a sign to him to take her cloak off, which he does°

LORD GORING I am glad you have called. I am going to give you
some good advice.   400

MRS CHEVELEY Oh! pray don't. One should never give a woman
anything that she can't wear in the evening.

LORD GORING I see you are quite as wilful as you used to be.

MRS CHEVELEY Far more! I have greatly improved. I have had more
experience.   405

LORD GORING Too much experience is a dangerous thing. Pray have
a cigarette. Half the pretty women in London smoke cigarettes.
Personally I prefer the other half.

MRS CHEVELEY Thanks. I never smoke. My dressmaker wouldn't
like it, and a woman's first duty in life is to her dressmaker, isn't   410
it? What the second duty is, no one has as yet discovered.

LORD GORING You have come here to sell me Robert Chiltern's
letter, haven't you?

MRS CHEVELEY To offer it to you on conditions. How did you guess
that?   415

LORD GORING Because you haven't mentioned the subject. Have
you got it with you?

MRS CHEVELEY (*sitting down*) Oh, no! A well-made dress has no
pockets.

LORD GORING What is your price for it?   420

MRS CHEVELEY How absurdly English you are! The English think
that a cheque-book can solve every problem in life. Why, my dear
Arthur, I have very much more money than you have, and quite
as much as Robert Chiltern has got hold of. Money is not what I
want.   425

LORD GORING What do you want then, Mrs Cheveley?

MRS CHEVELEY Why don't you call me Laura?°

LORD GORING I don't like the name.

MRS CHEVELEY You used to adore it.

LORD GORING Yes: that's why.   430

> *Mrs Cheveley motions to him to sit down beside her. He smiles, and does so*

MRS CHEVELEY Arthur, you loved me once.

LORD GORING Yes.

MRS CHEVELEY And you asked me to be your wife.

LORD GORING That was the natural result of my loving you.

MRS CHEVELEY And you threw me over because you saw, or said   435
you saw, poor old Lord Mortlake trying to have a violent flirtation°
with me in the conservatory at Tenby.

LORD GORING I am under the impression that my lawyer settled that
matter° with you on certain terms . . . dictated by yourself.

MRS CHEVELEY At the time I was poor; you were rich.   440

LORD GORING Quite so. That is why your pretended to love me.

MRS CHEVELEY (*shrugging her shoulders*) Poor old Lord Mortlake,
who had only two topics of conversation, his gout and his wife! I
never could quite make out which of the two he was talking about.
He used the most horrible language about them both. Well, you   445
were silly, Arthur. Why, Lord Mortlake was never anything more
to me than an amusement. One of those utterly tedious amusements one only finds at an English country house on an English
country Sunday. I don't think anyone at all morally responsible for
what he or she does at an English country house.   450

LORD GORING Yes. I know lots of people think that.

MRS CHEVELEY I loved you, Arthur.

LORD GORING My dear Mrs Cheveley, you have always been far too
clever to know anything about love.

MRS CHEVELEY I did love you. And you loved me. You know you   455
loved me; and love is a very wonderful thing. I suppose that when
a man has once loved a woman, he will do anything for her, except
continue to love her? (*Puts her hand on his*)°

LORD GORING (*taking his hand away quietly*) Yes: except that.

> [*A pause*]

MRS CHEVELEY I am tired of living abroad. I want to come back to   460
London. I want to have a charming house here. I want to have a
salon.° If one could only teach the English how to talk, and the
Irish how to listen, society here would be quite civilized. Besides,
I have arrived at the romantic stage. When I saw you last night at

the Chilterns', I knew you were the only person I had ever cared   465
for, if I ever have cared for anybody, Arthur. And so, on the
morning of the day you marry me, I will give you Robert
Chiltern's letter. That is my offer. I will give it to you now, if you
promise to marry me.

LORD GORING Now?   470

MRS CHEVELEY (*smiling*) Tomorrow.

LORD GORING Are you really serious?

MRS CHEVELEY Yes, quite serious.

LORD GORING I should make you a very bad husband.

MRS CHEVELEY I don't mind bad husbands. I have had two. They   475
amused me immensely.

LORD GORING You mean that you amused yourself immensely,
don't you?

MRS CHEVELEY What do you know about my married life?

LORD GORING Nothing: but I can read it like a book.   480

MRS CHEVELEY What book?

LORD GORING (*rising*) The Book of Numbers.°

MRS CHEVELEY Do you think it is quite charming of you to be so
rude to a woman in your own house?

LORD GORING In the case of very fascinating women, sex is a   485
challenge, not a defence.

MRS CHEVELEY I suppose that is meant for a compliment. My dear
Arthur, women are never disarmed by compliments. Men always
are. That is the difference between the two sexes.

LORD GORING Women are never disarmed by anything, as far as I   490
know them.

[*A pause*]

MRS CHEVELEY Then you are going to allow your greatest friend,
Robert Chiltern, to be ruined, rather than marry someone who
really has considerable attractions left. I thought you would have
risen to some great height of self-sacrifice, Arthur. I think you   495
should. And the rest of your life you could spend in contemplating
your own perfections.

LORD GORING Oh! I do that as it is. And self-sacrifice is a thing that
should be put down by law. It is so demoralizing to the people for
whom one sacrifices oneself. They always go to the bad.   500

MRS CHEVELEY As if anything could demoralize Robert Chiltern!
You seem to forget that I know his real character.

LORD GORING What you know about him is not his real character.
It was an act of folly done in his youth, dishonourable, I admit,

shameful, I admit, unworthy of him, I admit, and therefore . . . not   505
his true character.

MRS CHEVELEY How you men stand up for each other!

LORD GORING How you women war against each other!

MRS CHEVELEY (*bitterly*) I only war against one woman, against
Gertrude Chiltern. I hate her. I hate her now more than ever.   510

LORD GORING Because you have brought a real tragedy into her life,
I suppose.

MRS CHEVELEY (*with a sneer*) Oh, there is only one real tragedy in a
woman's life. The fact that her past is always her lover, and her
future invariably her husband.   515

LORD GORING Lady Chiltern knows nothing of the kind of life to
which you are alluding.

MRS CHEVELEY A woman whose size in gloves is seven and three-
quarters° never knows much about anything. You know Gertrude
has always worn seven and three-quarters? That is one of the   520
reasons why there was never any moral sympathy between us. . . .
Well, Arthur, I suppose this romantic interview may be regarded
as at an end. You admit it was romantic, don't you? For the
privilege of being your wife I was ready to surrender a great prize,
the climax of my diplomatic career. You decline. Very well. If Sir   525
Robert doesn't uphold my Argentine scheme, I expose him. *Voilà
tout.*°

LORD GORING You mustn't do that. It would be vile, horrible,
infamous.

MRS CHEVELEY (*shrugging her shoulders*) Oh! don't use big words.   530
They mean so little. It is a commercial transaction. That is all.
There is no good mixing sentimentality in it. I offered to sell
Robert Chiltern a certain thing. If he won't pay me my price, he
will have to pay the world a greater price. There is no more to be
said. I must go. Good-bye. Won't you shake hands?   535

LORD GORING With you? No. Your transaction with Robert Chiltern
may pass as a loathsome commercial transaction of a loathsome
commercial age; but you seem to have forgotten that you came her
tonight to talk of love, you whose lips desecrated the word love, you
to whom the thing is a book closely sealed, went this afternoon to   540
the house of one of the most noble and gentle women in the world
to degrade her husband in her eyes, to try and kill her love for him,
to put poison in her heart, and bitterness in her life, to break her
idol, and, it may be, spoil her soul. That I cannot forgive you. That
was horrible. For that there can be no forgiveness.   545

MRS CHEVELEY Arthur, you are unjust to me. Believe me, you are quite unjust to me. I didn't go to taunt Gertrude at all. I had no idea of doing anything of the kind when I entered. I called with Lady Markby simply to ask whether an ornament, a jewel, that I lost somewhere last night, had been found at the Chilterns'. If you don't believe me, you can ask Lady Markby. She will tell you it is true. The scene that occurred happened after Lady Markby had left, and was really forced on me by Gertrude's rudeness and sneers. I called, oh!—a little out of malice if you like—but really to ask if a diamond brooch of mine had been found. That was the origin of the whole thing.

LORD GORING A diamond snake-brooch with a ruby?

MRS CHEVELEY Yes. How do you know?

LORD GORING: Because it is found. In point of fact, I found it myself, and stupidly forgot to tell the butler anything about it as I was leaving. (*Goes over to the writing-table and pulls out the drawers*) It is in this drawer. No, that one. This is the brooch, isn't it?
    Holds up the brooch

MRS CHEVELEY Yes. I am so glad to get it back. It was . . . a present.

LORD GORING Won't you wear it?

MRS CHEVELEY Certainly, if you pin it in. (*Lord Goring suddenly clasps it on her arm*)° Why do you put it on as a bracelet? I never knew it could be worn as a bracelet.

LORD GORING Really?

MRS CHEVELEY (*holding out her handsome arm*) No; but it looks very well on me as a bracelet, doesn't it?

LORD GORING Yes; much better than when I saw it last.

MRS CHEVELEY When did you see it last?

LORD GORING (*calmly*) Oh, ten years ago, on Lady Berkshire, from whom you stole it.

MRS CHEVELEY (*starting*) What do you mean?

LORD GORING I mean that you stole that ornament from my cousin, Mary Berkshire,° to whom I gave it when she was married. Suspicion fell on a wretched servant, who was sent away in disgrace. I recognized it last night. I determined to say nothing about it till I had found the thief. I have found the thief now, and I have heard her own confession.

MRS CHEVELEY (*tossing her head*) It is not true.

LORD GORING You know it is true. Why, thief is written across your face at this moment.

MRS CHEVELEY I will deny the whole affair from beginning to end. I will say that I have never seen this wretched thing, that it was never in my possession.

> *Mrs Cheveley tries to get the bracelet off her arm, but fails. Lord*
> *Goring looks on amused. Her thin fingers tear at the jewel to no*
> *purpose. A curse breaks from her*

LORD GORING The drawback of stealing a thing, Mrs Cheveley, is
that one never knows how wonderful the thing that one steals is.
You can't get that bracelet off, unless you know where the spring   590
is. And I see you don't know where the spring is. It is rather
difficult to find.

MRS CHEVELEY You brute! You coward!
> *She tries again to unclasp the bracelet, but fails*

LORD GORING Oh! don't use big words. They mean so little.

MRS CHEVELEY (*again tears at the bracelet in a paroxysm of rage, with*   595
inarticulate sounds. Then stops, and looks at Lord Goring) What are
you going to do?

LORD GORING I am going to ring for my servant. He is an admirable
servant. Always comes in the moment one rings for him. When he
comes I will tell him to fetch the police.   600

MRS CHEVELEY (*trembling*) The police? What for?

LORD GORING Tomorrow the Berkshires will prosecute you. That is
what the police are for.

MRS CHEVELEY (*is now in an agony of physical terror. Her face is*
distorted. Her mouth awry. A mask has fallen from her. She is, for the
moment, dreadful to look at) Don't do that. I will do anything you   605
want. Anything in the world you want.

LORD GORING Give me Robert Chiltern's letter.

MRS CHEVELEY Stop! Stop! Let me have time to think.

LORD GORING Give me Robert Chiltern's letter.

MRS CHEVELEY I have not got it with me. I will give it to you   610
tomorrow.

LORD GORING You know you are lying. Give it to me at once. (*Mrs*
Cheveley pulls the letter out, and hands it to him. She is horribly pale)
This is it?

MRS CHEVELEY (*in a hoarse voice*) Yes.

LORD GORING (*takes the letter, examines it, sighs, and burns it over the*   615
lamp)° For so well-dressed a woman, Mrs Cheveley, you have
moments of admirable common sense. I congratulate you.

MRS CHEVELEY (*catches sight of Lady Chiltern's letter, the cover of*
which is just showing from under the blotting-book) Please get me a
glass of water.   620

LORD GORING Certainly.
> *Goes to the corner of the room and pours out a glass of water.*
> *While his back is turned Mrs Cheveley steals Lady Chiltern's*

> *letter. When Lord Goring returns with the glass she refuses it*
> *with a gesture*

MRS CHEVELEY Thank you. Will you help me on with my cloak?

LORD GORING With pleasure.

> *Puts her cloak on*

MRS CHEVELEY Thanks. I am never going to try to harm Robert
Chiltern again.   625

LORD GORING Fortunately you have not the chance, Mrs Cheveley.

MRS CHEVELEY Well, even if I had the chance, I wouldn't. On the
contrary, I am going to render him a great service.

LORD GORING I am charmed to hear it. It is a reformation.

MRS CHEVELEY Yes. I can't bear so upright a gentleman, so   630
honourable an English gentleman, being so shamefully deceived,
and so—

LORD GORING Well?

MRS CHEVELEY I find that somehow Gertrude Chiltern's dying
speech and confession has strayed into my pocket.   635

LORD GORING What do you mean?

MRS CHEVELEY (*with a bitter note of triumph in her voice*) I mean that
I am going to send Robert Chiltern the love letter his wife wrote
to you tonight.

LORD GORING Love letter?   640

MRS CHEVELEY (*laughing*) 'I want you. I trust you, I am coming to
you. Gertrude.'

> *Lord Goring rushes to the bureau and takes up the envelope,*
> *finds it empty, and turns round*

LORD GORING You wretched woman, must you always be thieving?
Give me back that letter. I'll take it from you by force. You shall
not leave my room till I have got it.   645

> *He rushes towards her, but Mrs Cheveley at once puts her hand*
> *on the electric bell that is on the table. The bell sounds with shrill*
> *reverberations,° and Phipps enters.* [*A pause*]

MRS CHEVELEY Lord Goring merely rang that you should show me
out. Good night, Lord Goring!

> *Goes out followed by Phipps. Her face is illumined with evil*
> *triumph. There is joy in her eyes. Youth seems to have come back*
> *to her. Her last glance is like a swift arrow. Lord Goring bites*
> *his lip, and lights a cigarette*

ACT DROP

Fourth Act

*Scene: Same as Act II. Lord Goring is standing by the fireplace
with his hands in his pockets. He is looking rather bored*

LORD GORING (*pulls out his watch, inspects it, and rings the bell*) It is
a great nuisance. I can't find anyone in this house to talk to. And
I am full of interesting information. I feel like the latest edition of
something or other.

Enter servant

JAMES Sir Robert is still at the Foreign Office, my lord. 5

LORD GORING Lady Chiltern not down yet?

JAMES Her ladyship has not yet left her room. Miss Chiltern has just
come in from riding.

LORD GORING (*to himself*) Ah! that is something.

JAMES Lord Caversham has been waiting some time in the library for 10
Sir Robert. I told him your lordship was here.

LORD GORING Thank you. Would you kindly tell him I've gone?

JAMES (*bowing*) I shall do so, my lord.

Exit servant

LORD GORING Really, I don't want to meet my father three days
running. It is a great deal too much excitement for any son. I hope 15
to goodness he won't come up. Fathers should be neither seen nor
heard. That is the only proper basis for family life. Mothers are
different. Mothers are darlings.

*Throws himself down into a chair, picks up a paper and begins
to read it. Enter Lord Caversham*

LORD CAVERSHAM Well, sir, what are you doing here? Wasting your
time as usual, I suppose? 20

LORD GORING (*throws down paper and rises*) My dear father, when
one pays a visit it is for the purpose of wasting other people's time,
not one's own.

LORD CAVERSHAM Have you been thinking over what I spoke to you
about last night? 25

LORD GORING I have been thinking about nothing else.

LORD CAVERSHAM Engaged to be married yet?

LORD GORING (*genially*) Not yet; but I hope to be before lunch-
time.

LORD CAVERSHAM (*caustically*) You can have till dinner-time if it 30
would be of any convenience to you.

LORD GORING Thanks awfully, but I think I'd sooner be engaged before lunch.

LORD CAVERSHAM Humph! Never know when you are serious or not.   35

LORD GORING Neither do I father.

A pause

LORD CAVERSHAM I suppose you have read *The Times*° this morning?

LORD GORING (*airily*): *The Times*? Certainly not. I only read *The Morning Post*. All that one should know about modern life is where   40 the Duchesses are; anything else is quite demoralizing.

LORD CAVERSHAM Do you mean to say you have not read *The Times* leading article on Robert Chiltern's career?

LORD GORING Good heavens! No. What does it say?

LORD CAVERSHAM What should it say, sir? Everything complimen-   45 tary, of course. Chiltern's speech last night on this Argentine Canal scheme was one of the finest pieces of oratory ever delivered in the House since Canning.°

LORD GORING Ah! Never heard of Canning. Never wanted to. And did . . . did Chiltern uphold the scheme?   50

LORD CAVERSHAM Uphold it, sir? How little you know him! Why, he denounced it roundly, and the whole system of modern political finance. This speech is the turning-point in his career, as *The Times* points out. You should read this article, sir. (*Opens The Times*) 'Sir Robert Chiltern . . . most rising of all our young   55 statesmen . . . Brilliant orator . . . Unblemished career . . . Well-known integrity of character . . . Represents what is best in English public life . . . Noble contrast to the lax morality so common among foreign politicians.' They will never say that of you, sir.

LORD GORING I sincerely hope not, father. However, I am delighted   60 at what you tell me about Robert, thoroughly delighted. It shows he has got pluck.

LORD CAVERSHAM He has got more than pluck, sir, he has got genius.

LORD GORING Ah! I prefer pluck. It is not so common, nowadays,   65 as genius is.

LORD CAVERSHAM I wish you would go into Parliament.

LORD GORING My dear father, only people who look dull ever get into the House of Commons, and only people who are dull ever succeed there.   70

LORD CAVERSHAM Why don't you try to do something useful in life?

231

LORD GORING I am far too young.°

LORD CAVERSHAM (*testily*) I hate this affectation of youth, sir. It is a great deal too prevalent nowadays.

LORD GORING Youth isn't an affectation. Youth is an art.   75

LORD CAVERSHAM Why don't you propose to that pretty Miss Chiltern?

LORD GORING I am of a very nervous disposition, especially in the morning.

LORD CAVERSHAM I don't suppose there is the smallest chance of   80
her accepting you.

LORD GORING I don't know how the betting° stands today.

LORD CAVERSHAM If she did accept you she would be the prettiest fool in England.

LORD GORING That is just what I should like to marry. A thorough-   85
ly sensible wife would reduce me to a condition of absolute idiocy in less then six months.

LORD CAVERSHAM You don't deserve her, sir.

LORD GORING My dear father, if we men married the women we deserved, we should have a very bad time of it.   90

Enter Mabel Chiltern

MABEL CHILTERN Oh! . . . How do you do, Lord Caversham? I hope Lady Caversham is quite well?

LORD CAVERSHAM Lady Caversham is as usual, as usual.

LORD GORING Good morning, Miss Mabel!

MABEL CHILTERN (*taking no notice at all of Lord Goring, and*   95
addressing herself exclusively to Lord Caversham) And Lady Caversham's bonnets . . . are they at all better?

LORD CAVERSHAM They have had a serious relapse,° I am sorry to say.

LORD GORING Good morning, Miss Mabel!   100

MABEL CHILTERN (*to Lord Caversham*) I hope an operation will not be necessary.

LORD CAVERSHAM (*smiling at her pertness*) If it is, we shall have to give Lady Caversham a narcotic. Otherwise she would never consent to have a feather touched.   105

LORD GORING (*with increased emphasis*) Good morning, Miss Mabel!

MABEL CHILTERN (*turning round with feigned surprise*) Oh, are you here? Of course you understand that after your breaking your appointment I am never going to speak to you again.

LORD GORING Oh, please don't say such a thing. You are the one   110
person in London I really like to have to listen to me.

MABEL CHILTERN Lord Goring, I never believe a single word that either you or I say to each other.

LORD CAVERSHAM You are quite right, my dear, quite right . . . as far as he is concerned, I mean. 115

MABEL CHILTERN Do you think you could possibly make your son behave a little better occasionally? Just as a change.

LORD CAVERSHAM I regret to say, Miss Chiltern, that I have no influence at all over my son. I wish I had. If I had, I know what I would make him do. 120

MABEL CHILTERN I am afraid that he has one of those terribly weak natures that are not susceptible to influence.

LORD CAVERSHAM He is very heartless, very heartless.

LORD GORING It seems to me that I am a little in the way here.

MABEL CHILTERN It is very good for you to be in the way, and to 125 know what people say of you behind your back.

LORD GORING I don't at all like knowing what people say of me behind my back. It makes me far too conceited.

LORD CAVERSHAM After that, my dear, I really must bid you good morning. 130

MABEL CHILTERN Oh! I hope you are not going to leave me all alone with Lord Goring? Especially at such an early hour in the day.

LORD CAVERSHAM I am afraid I can't take him with me to Downing Street.° It is not the Prime Minister's day for seeing the unem- ployed. 135

> *Shakes hands with Mabel Chiltern, takes up his hat and stick, and goes out, with a parting glare of indignation at Lord Goring*

MABEL CHILTERN (*takes up roses° and begins to arrange them in a bowl on the table*) People who don't keep their appointments in the Park are horrid.

LORD GORING Detestable.

MABEL CHILTERN I am glad you admit it. But I wish you wouldn't 140 look so pleased about it.

LORD GORING I can't help it. I always look pleased when I am with you.

MABEL CHILTERN (*sadly*) Then I suppose it is my duty to remain with you? 145

LORD GORING Of course it is.

MABEL CHILTERN Well, my duty is a thing I never do, on principle. It always depresses me. So I am afraid I must leave you.

LORD GORING Please don't, Miss Mabel. I have something very particular to say to you. 150

MABEL CHILTERN (*rapturously*) Oh, is it a proposal?°

LORD GORING (*somewhat taken aback*) Well, yes, it is—I am bound to say it is.

MABEL CHILTERN (*with a sigh of pleasure*) I am so glad. That makes the second today.   155

LORD GORING (*indignantly*) The second today? What conceited ass has been impertinent enough to dare to propose to you before I had proposed to you?

MABEL CHILTERN Tommy Trafford, of course. It is one of Tommy's day for proposing. He always proposes on Tuesdays and   160 Thursdays, during the season.

LORD GORING You didn't accept him, I hope?

MABEL CHILTERN I make it a rule never to accept Tommy. That is why he goes on proposing. Of course, as you didn't turn up this morning, I very nearly said yes. It would have been an excellent   165 lesson both for him and for you if I had. It would have taught you both better manners.

LORD GORING Oh! bother Tommy Trafford. Tommy is a silly little ass. I love you.

MABEL CHILTERN I know. And I think you might have mentioned   170 it before. I am sure I have given you heaps of opportunities.

LORD GORING Mabel, do be serious. Please be serious.

MABEL CHILTERN Ah! that is the sort of thing a man always says to a girl before he has been married to her. He never says it afterwards.   175

LORD GORING (*taking hold of her hand*) Mabel, I have told you that I love you. Can't you love me a little in return?

MABEL CHILTERN You silly Arthur! If you knew anything about . . . anything, which you don't, you would know that I adore you. Everyone in London knows it except you. It is a public scandal the   180 way I adore you. I have been going about for the last six months telling the whole of society that I adore you. I wonder you consent to have anything to say to me. I have no character left at all. At least, I feel so happy that I am quite sure I have no character left at all.   185

LORD GORING (*catches her in his arms° and kisses her. Then there is a pause of bliss*) Dear! Do you know I was awfully afraid of being refused!

MABEL CHILTERN (*looking up at him*) But you never have been refused yet by anybody, have you, Arthur? I can't imagine anyone   190 refusing you.

LORD GORING (*after kissing her again*) Of course I'm not nearly good enough for you, Mabel.

MABEL CHILTERN (*nestling close to him*) I am so glad, darling. I was afraid you were.   195

LORD GORING (*after some hesitation*) And I'm . . . I'm a little over thirty.

MABEL CHILTERN Dear, you look weeks younger than that.

LORD GORING (*enthusiastically*) How sweet of you to say so! . . . And it is only fair to tell you frankly that I am fearfully extravagant.   200

MABEL CHILTERN: But so am I, Arthur. So we're sure to agree. And now I must go and see Gertrude.

LORD GORING Must you really?

    Kisses her

MABEL CHILTERN Yes.

LORD GORING Then do tell her I want to talk to her particularly. I   205
have been waiting here all the morning to see either her or Robert.

MABEL CHILTERN Do you mean to say you didn't come here expressly to propose to me?

LORD GORING (*triumphantly*) No; that was a flash of genius.

MABEL CHILTERN Your first.   210

LORD GORING (*with determination*) My last.

MABEL CHILTERN I am delighted to hear it. Now don't stir. I'll be back in five minutes. And don't fall into any temptations while I am away.

LORD GORING Dear Mabel, while you are away, there are none. It   215
makes me horribly dependent on you.

    Enter Lady Chiltern

LADY CHILTERN Good morning, dear! How pretty you are looking!

MABEL CHILTERN How pale you are looking, Gertrude! It is most becoming!

LADY CHILTERN Good morning, Lord Goring!   220

LORD GORING (*bowing*) Good morning, Lady Chiltern.

MABEL CHILTERN (*aside to Lord Goring*) I shall be in the conservatory, under the second palm tree on the left.

LORD GORING Second on the left?

MABEL CHILTERN (*with a look of mock surprise*) Yes; the usual palm   225
tree.

    Blows a kiss to him, unobserved by Lady Chiltern, and goes out

LORD GORING Lady Chiltern, I have a certain amount of very good news to tell you. Mrs Cheveley gave me up Robert's letter last night, and I burned it. Robert is safe.

LADY CHILTERN (*sinking on the sofa*) Safe! Oh! I am so glad of that.   230
What a good friend you are to him—to us!

LORD GORING There is only one person now that could be said to
be in any danger.

LADY CHILTERN Who is that?

LORD GORING (*sitting down beside her*) Yourself.   235

LADY CHILTERN I! In danger? What do you mean?

LORD GORING Danger is too great a word. It is a word I should not
have used. But I admit I have something to tell you that may
distress you, that terribly distresses me. Yesterday evening you
wrote me a very beautiful, womanly letter, asking me for my help.   240
You wrote to me as one of your oldest friends, one of your
husband's oldest friends. Mrs Cheveley stole that letter from my
rooms.

LADY CHILTERN Well, what use is it to her? Why should she not
have it?   245

LORD GORING (*rising*) Lady Chiltern, I will be quite frank with you.
Mrs Cheveley puts a certain construction on that letter and
proposes to send it to your husband.

LADY CHILTERN But what construction could she put on it? . . . Oh!
not that!° not that! If I in—in trouble, and wanting your help,   250
trusting you, propose to come to you . . . that you may advise me
. . . assist me . . . Oh! are there women so horrible as that . . .? And
she proposes to send it to my husband? Tell me what happened.
Tell me all that happened.

LORD GORING Mrs Cheveley was concealed in a room adjoining my   255
library, without my knowledge. I thought that the person who was
waiting in that room to see me was yourself. Robert came in
unexpectedly. A chair or something fell in the room. He forced his
way in, and he discovered her. We had a terrible scene. I still
thought it was you. He left me in anger. At the end of everything   260
Mrs Cheveley got possession of your letter—she stole it, when or
how, I don't know.

LADY CHILTERN At what hour did this happen?

LORD GORING At half-past ten. And now I propose that we tell
Robert the whole thing at once.   265

LADY CHILTERN (*looking at him with amazement that is almost terror*)
You want me to tell Robert that the woman you expected was not
Mrs Cheveley, but myself? That it was I whom you thought was
concealed in a room in your house, at half-past ten o'clock at night?
You want me to tell him that?   270

LORD GORING I think it is better that he should know the exact truth.

LADY CHILTERN (*rising*) Oh, I couldn't, I couldn't!

LORD GORING May I do it?

LADY CHILTERN No.

LORD GORING (*gravely*) You are wrong, Lady Chiltern.   275

LADY CHILTERN No. The letter must be intercepted. That is all. But how can I do it? Letters arrive for him every moment of the day. His secretaries open them and hand them to him. I dare not ask the servants to bring me his letters. It would be impossible. Oh! why don't you tell me what to do?   280

LORD GORING Pray be calm, Lady Chiltern, and answer the questions I am going to put to you. You said his secretaries open his letters.

LADY CHILTERN Yes.

LORD GORING Who is with him today? Mr Trafford, isn't it?   285

LADY CHILTERN No. Mr Montford° I think.

LORD GORING You can trust him?

LADY CHILTERN (*with a gesture of despair*) Oh! how do I know?

LORD GORING He would do what you asked him, wouldn't he?

LADY CHILTERN I think so.   290

LORD GORING Your letter was on pink paper. He could recognize it without reading it, couldn't he? By the colour?

LADY CHILTERN I suppose so.

LORD GORING Is he in the house now?

LADY CHILTERN Yes.   295

LORD GORING Then I will go and see him myself, and tell him that a certain letter, written on pink paper, is to be forwarded to Robert today, and that at all costs it must not reach him. (*Goes to the door, and opens it*) Oh! Robert is coming upstairs with the letter in his hand. It has reached him already.   300

LADY CHILTERN (*with a cry of pain*) Oh! you have saved his life; what have you done with mine?

> *Enter Sir Robert Chiltern. He has the letter in his hand, and is reading it. He comes towards his wife, not noticing Lord Goring's presence*

SIR ROBERT CHILTERN 'I want you.° I trust you. I am coming to you. Gertrude.' Oh, my love! is this true? Do you indeed trust me, and want me? If so, it was for me to come to you, not for you to   305 write of coming to me. This letter of yours, Gertrude, makes me feel that nothing that the world may do can hurt me now. You want me, Gertrude?

*Lord Goring, unseen by Sir Robert Chiltern, makes an imploring
sign to Lady Chiltern to accept the situation and Sir Robert's
error*

LADY CHILTERN Yes.

SIR ROBERT CHILTERN You trust me, Gertrude?   310

LADY CHILTERN Yes.

SIR ROBERT CHILTERN Ah! why did you not add you loved me?

LADY CHILTERN (*taking his hand*) Because I loved you.

Lord Goring passes into the conservatory

SIR ROBERT CHILTERN (*kisses her*) Gertrude, you don't know what
I feel. When Montford passed me your letter across the table—he   315
had opened it by mistake, I suppose, without looking at the
handwriting on the envelope—and I read it—oh! I did not care
what disgrace or punishment was in store for me, I only thought
you loved me still.

LADY CHILTERN There is no disgrace in store for you, nor any   320
public shame. Mrs Cheveley has handed over to Lord Goring the
document that was in her possession, and he has destroyed it.

SIR ARTHUR CHILTERN Are you sure of this, Gertrude?

LADY CHILTERN Yes; Lord Goring has just told me.

SIR ROBERT CHILTERN Then I am safe! Oh! What a wonderful   325
thing to be safe! For two days I have been in terror. I am safe now.
How did Arthur destroy my letter? Tell me.

LADY CHILTERN He burned it.

SIR ROBERT CHILTERN I wish I had seen that one sin of my youth
burning to ashes. How many men there are in modern life who   330
would like to see their past burning to white ashes before them! Is
Arthur still here?

LADY CHILTERN Yes; he is in the conservatory.

SIR ROBERT CHILTERN I am so glad now I made that speech last
night in the House, so glad. I made it thinking that public disgrace 335
might be the result. But it has not been so.

LADY CHILTERN Public honour has been the result.

SIR ROBERT CHILTERN I think so. I fear so, almost. For although I
am safe from detection, although every proof against me is
destroyed, I suppose, Gertrude . . . I suppose I should retire from   340
public life?

He looks anxiously at his wife.

LADY CHILTERN (*eagerly*) Oh yes, Robert, you should do that. It is
your duty to do that.

SIR ROBERT CHILTERN It is much to surrender.

LADY CHILTERN No; it will be much to gain.   345

Sir Robert Chiltern walks up and down the room with a troubled expression. Then comes over to his wife, and puts his hand on her shoulder

SIR ROBERT CHILTERN And you would be happy living somewhere alone with me, abroad perhaps, or in the country away from London, away from public life? You would have no regrets?

LADY CHILTERN Oh! none, Robert.

SIR ROBERT CHILTERN (*sadly*) And your ambition for me? You used   350
to be ambitious for me.

LADY CHILTERN Oh, my ambition! I have none now, but that we two may love each other. It was your ambition that led you astray. Let us not talk about ambition.

Lord Goring returns from the conservatory, looking very pleased with himself, and with an entirely new buttonhole° that someone has made for him

SIR ROBERT CHILTERN (*going towards him*) Arthur, I have to thank   355
you for what you have done for me. I don't know how I can repay you. (*Shakes hands with him*)

LORD GORING My dear fellow, I'll tell you at once. At the present moment, under the usual palm tree . . . I mean in the conservatory . . .   360

Enter Mason

MASON Lord Caversham.

LORD GORING That admirable father of mine really makes a habit of turning up at the wrong moment. It is very heartless of him, very heartless indeed.

Enter Lord Caversham. Mason goes out

LORD CAVERSHAM Good morning, Lady Chiltern! Warmest congra-   365
tulations to you, Chiltern, on your brilliant speech last night. I have just left the Prime Minister, and you are to have the vacant seat in the Cabinet.

SIR ROBERT CHILTERN (*with a look of joy and triumph*) A seat in the Cabinet?   370

LORD CAVERSHAM Yes; here is the Prime Minister's letter. (*Hands letter*)

SIR ROBERT CHILTERN (*takes letter and reads it*) A seat in the Cabinet!

LORD CAVERSHAM Certainly, and you well deserve it too. You have got what we want so much in political life nowadays—high character, high moral tone, high principles. (*To Lord Goring*)   375
Everything that you have not got, sir, and never will have.

LORD GORING I don't like principles, father. I prefer prejudices.

Sir Robert Chiltern is on the brink of accepting the Prime

Minister's offer, when he sees his wife looking at him with her
clear, candid eyes. He then realizes that it is impossible

SIR ROBERT CHILTERN I cannot accept this offer, Lord Caversham.
I have made up my mind to decline it.

LORD CAVERSHAM Decline it, sir!   380

SIR ROBERT CHILTERN My intention is to retire at once from public
life.

LORD CAVERSHAM (*angrily*) Decline a seat in the Cabinet, and retire
from public life? Never heard such damned nonsense in the whole
course of my existence. I beg your pardon,° Lady Chiltern.   385
Chiltern, I beg your pardon. (*To Lord Goring*) Don't grin like that,
sir.

LORD GORING No, father.

LORD CAVERSHAM Lady Chiltern, you are a sensible woman, the
most sensible woman in London, the most sensible woman I   390
know. Will you kindly prevent your husband from making such
a . . . from talking such . . . Will you kindly do that, Lady Chiltern?

LADY CHILTERN I think my husband is right in his determination,
Lord Caversham. I approve of it.   395

LORD CAVERSHAM You approve of it? Good Heavens!

LADY CHILTERN (*taking her husband's hand*) I admire him for it. I
admire him immensely for it. I have never admired him so much
before. He is finer than even I thought him. (*To Sir Robert
Chiltern*) You will go and write your letter to the Prime Minister   400
now, won't you? Don't hesitate about it, Robert.

SIR ROBERT CHILTERN (*with a touch of bitterness*) I suppose I had
better write it at once. Such offers are not repeated. I will ask you
to excuse me for a moment, Lord Caversham.

LADY CHILTERN I may come with you, Robert, may I not?   405

SIR ROBERT CHILTERN Yes, Gertrude.

Lady Chiltern goes out with him

LORD CAVERSHAM What is the matter with the family? Something
wrong here, eh? (*Tapping his forehead*) Idiocy? Hereditary, I
suppose. Both of them, too. Wife as well as husband. Very sad.
Very sad indeed! And they are not an old family.° Can't under-   410
stand it.

LORD GORING It is not idiocy, father, I assure you.

LORD CAVERSHAM What is it then, sir?

LORD GORING (*after some hesitation*) Well, it is what is called
nowadays a high moral tone, father. That is all.   415

LORD CAVERSHAM Hate these new-fangled names. Same thing as we used to call idiocy fifty years ago. Shan't stay in this house any longer.

LORD GORING (*taking his arm*) Oh! just go in here for a moment, father. Second palm tree° to the left, the usual palm tree.   420

LORD CAVERSHAM What, sir?

LORD GORING I beg your pardon, father, I forgot. The conservatory, father, the conservatory—there is someone there I want you to talk to.

LORD CAVERSHAM What about, sir?   425

LORD GORING About me, father.

LORD CAVERSHAM (*grimly*) Not a subject on which much eloquence is possible.

LORD GORING No, father; but the lady is like me. She doesn't care much for eloquence in others. She thinks it a little loud.   430

> Lord Caversham goes into the conservatory. Lady Chiltern enters

LORD GORING Lady Chiltern, why are you playing Mrs Cheveley's cards?°

LADY CHILTERN (*startled*) I don't understand you.

LORD GORING Mrs Cheveley made an attempt to ruin your husband. Either to drive him from public life, or to make him adopt a   435 dishonourable position. From the latter tragedy you saved him. The former you are now thrusting on him. Why should you do him the wrong Mrs Cheveley tried to do and failed?

LADY CHILTERN Lord Goring?

LORD GORING (*pulling himself together for a great effort, and showing*   440 *the philosopher° that underlies the dandy*) Lady Chiltern, allow me. You wrote me a letter last night in which you said you trusted me and wanted my help. Now is the moment when you really want my help, now is the time when you have got to trust me, to trust in my counsel and judgement. You love Robert. Do you   445 want to kill his love for you? What sort of existence will he have if you rob him of the fruits of his ambition, if you take him from the splendour of a great political career, if you close the doors of public life against him, if you condemn him to sterile failure, he who was made for triumph and success? Women are not meant   450 to judge us, but to forgive us when we need forgiveness. Pardon, not punishment, is their mission. Why should you scourge him with rods for a sin done in his youth, before he knew you, before he knew himself? A man's life is of more value than a woman's.

It has larger issues, wider scope, greater ambitions. A woman's   455
life revolves in curves of emotions. It is upon lines of intellect
that a man's life progress. Don't make any terrible mistake, Lady
Chiltern. A woman who can keep a man's love, and love him in
return, has done all the world wants of women, or should want
of them.   460

LADY CHILTERN (*troubled and hesitating*) But it is my husband
himself who wishes to retire from public life. He feels it is his
duty. It was he who first said so.

LORD GORING Rather than lose your love, Robert would do anything, wreck his whole career, as he is on the brink of doing now.   465
He is making for you a terrible sacrifice. Take my advice, Lady
Chiltern, and do not accept a sacrifice so great. If you do you will
live to repent it bitterly. We men and women are not made to
accept such sacrifices from each other. We are not worthy of them.
Besides, Robert has been punished enough.   470

LADY CHILTERN We have both been punished. I set him up too
high.

LORD GORING (*with deep feeling in his voice*) Do not for that reason
set him down now too low. If he has fallen from his altar, do not
thrust him into the mire. Failure to Robert would be the very mire   475
of shame. Power is his passion. He would lose everything, even his
power to feel love. Your husband's life is at this moment in your
hands, your husband's love is in your hands. Don't mar both for
him.

      Enter Sir Robert Chiltern

SIR ROBERT CHILTERN Gertrude, here is the draft of my letter.   480
Shall I read it to you?

LADY CHILTERN Let me see it.

      Sir Robert hands her the letter. She reads it, and then, with a
      gesture of passion, tears it up

SIR ROBERT CHILTERN What are you doing?

LADY CHILTERN A man's life° is of more value than a woman's. It
has larger issues, wider scope, greater ambitions. Our lives revolve   485
in curves of emotions. It is upon lines of intellect that a man's life
progresses. I have just learnt this, and much else with it, from
Lord Goring. And I will not spoil your life for you, nor see you
spoil it as a sacrifice to me, a useless sacrifice!

SIR ROBERT CHILTERN Gertrude! Gertrude!   490

LADY CHILTERN You can forget. Men easily forget. And I forgive.
That is how women help the world. I see that now.

SIR ROBERT CHILTERN (*deeply overcome by emotion, embraces her*)
My wife! my wife! (*To Lord Goring*) Arthur, it seems that I am
always to be in your debt.   495

LORD GORING Oh dear no, Robert. Your debt is to Lady Chiltern,
not to me!

SIR ROBERT CHILTERN I owe you much. And now tell me what you
were going to ask me just now as Lord Caversham came in.

LORD GORING Robert, you are your sister's guardian,° and I want   500
your consent to my marriage with her. That is all.

LADY CHILTERN Oh, I am so glad! I am so glad!
          Shakes hands with Lord Goring

LORD GORING Thank you, Lady Chiltern.

SIR ROBERT CHILTERN (*with a troubled look*) My sister to be your
wife?   505

LORD GORING Yes.

SIR ROBERT CHILTERN (*speaking with great firmness*). Arthur, I am
very sorry, but the thing is quite out of the question. I have to
think of Mabel's future happiness. And I don't think her happiness
would be safe in your hands. And I cannot have her sacrificed!   510

LORD GORING Sacrificed!

SIR ROBERT CHILTERN Yes, utterly sacrificed. Loveless marriages
are horrible. But there is one thing worse than an absolutely
loveless marriage. A marriage in which there is love, but on one
side only; faith, but on one side only; devotion, but on one side   515
only, and in which of the two hearts one is sure to be broken.

LORD GORING But I love Mabel. No other woman has any place in
my life.

LADY CHILTERN Robert, if they love each other, why should they
not be married?   520

SIR ROBERT CHILTERN Arthur cannot bring Mabel the love that she
deserves.

LORD GORING What reason have you for saying that?
          [*A pause*]

SIR ROBERT CHILTERN Do you really require me to tell you?

LORD GORING Certainly I do.   525

SIR ROBERT CHILTERN As you choose. When I called on you
yesterday evening I found Mrs Cheveley concealed in your rooms.
It was between ten and eleven o'clock at night. I do not wish to
say anything more. Your relations with Mrs Cheveley have, as I
said to you last night, nothing whatsoever to do with me. I know   530
you were engaged to be married to her once. The fascination she

exercised over you then seems to have returned. You spoke to me last night of her as of a woman pure and stainless, a woman whom you respected and honoured. That may be so. But I cannot give my sister's life into your hands. It would be wrong of me. It would be unjust, infamously unjust to her.   535

LORD GORING I have nothing more to say.

LADY CHILTERN Robert, it was not Mrs Cheveley whom Lord Goring expected last night.

SIR ROBERT CHILTERN Not Mrs Cheveley! Who was it then?   540

LORD GORING Lady Chiltern!

LADY CHILTERN It was your own wife. Robert, yesterday afternoon Lord Goring told me that if ever I was in trouble I could come to him for help, as he was our oldest and best friend. Later on, after that terrible scene in this room, I wrote to him telling him that I   545 trusted him, that I had need of him, that I was coming to him for help and advice. (*Sir Robert Chiltern takes the letter out of his pocket*) Yes, that letter. I didn't go to Lord Goring's, after all. I felt that it is from ourselves alone that help can come. Pride made me think that. Mrs Cheveley went. She stole my letter and sent it anony-   550 mously to you this morning, that you should think . . . Oh! Robert, I cannot tell you what she wished you to think . . .

SIR ROBERT CHILTERN What! Had I fallen so low in your eyes that you thought that even for a moment I could have doubted your goodness? Gertrude, Gertrude, you are to me the white image of   555 all good things, and sin can never touch you. Arthur, you can go to Mabel, and you have my best wishes! Oh! stop a moment. There is no name at the beginning of this letter. The brilliant Mrs Cheveley does not seem to have noticed that. There should be a name.   560

LADY CHILTERN Let me write yours. It is you I trust and need. You and none else.

LORD GORING Well, really, Lady Chiltern, I think I should have back my own letter.

LADY CHILTERN (*smiling*) No; you shall have Mabel. (*Takes the letter*   565 *and writes her husband's name on it*)

LORD GORING Well, I hope she hasn't changed her mind. It's nearly twenty minutes since I saw her last.

    Enter Mabel Chiltern and Lord Caversham

MABEL CHILTERN Lord Goring, I think your father's conversation much more improving than yours. I am only going to talk to Lord Caversham in the future, and always under the usual palm tree.   570

LORD GORING Darling!
 Kisses her

LORD CAVERSHAM (*considerably taken aback*) What does this mean, sir? You don't mean to say that this charming, clever young lady has been so foolish as to accept you?

LORD GORING Certainly, father! And Chiltern's been wise enough 575
to accept the seat in the Cabinet.

LORD CAVERSHAM I am very glad to hear that, Chiltern . . . I congratulate you, sir. If the country doesn't go to the dogs or the Radicals,° we shall have you Prime Minister, some day.
 Enter Mason

MASON Luncheon is on the table, my Lady! 580
 Mason goes out

MABEL CHILTERN You'll stop to luncheon, Lord Caversham, won't you?

LORD CAVERSHAM With pleasure, and I'll drive you down to Downing Street afterwards, Chiltern. You have a great future before you, a great future. (*To Lord Goring*) Wish I could say the 585
same for you, sir. But your career will have to be entirely domestic.

LORD GORING Yes, father, I prefer it domestic.

LORD CAVERSHAM And if you don't make this young lady an ideal husband,° I'll cut you off with a shilling.

MABEL CHILTERN An ideal husband! Oh, I don't think I should like 590
that. It sounds like something in the next world.

LORD CAVERSHAM What do you want him to be then, dear?

MABEL CHILTERN He can be what he chooses. All I want is to be . . to be . . . oh! a real wife to him.

LORD CAVERSHAM Upon my word, there is a good deal of common 595
sense in that, Lady Chiltern.
 They all go out except Sir Robert Chiltern. He sinks into a chair, wrapt in thought. After a little time Lady Chiltern returns to look for him

LADY CHILTERN (*leaning over the back of the chair*) Aren't you coming in, Robert?

SIR ROBERT CHILTERN (*taking her hand*) Gertrude, is it love you feel for me, or is it pity merely? 600

LADY CHILTERN (*kisses him*) It is love, Robert. Love, and only love. For both of us a new life is beginning.

CURTAIN°

THE
IMPORTANCE OF BEING
EARNEST
A Trivial Comedy for Serious People

To
ROBERT BALDWIN ROSS
in Appreciation
in Affection

THE PERSONS OF THE PLAY

The play was first staged at St James's Theatre, London, 14 February 1895.

John Worthing, JP	*Mr George Alexander*
Algernon Moncrieff	*Mr Allan Aynesworth*
Revd Canon Chasuble, DD	*Mr H. H. Vincent*
Merriman (Butler)	*Mr Frank Dyall*
Lane (Manservant)	*Mr F. Kinsey Peile*
Lady Bracknell	*Miss Rose Leclercq*
Hon. Gwendolen Fairfax	*Miss Irene Vanbrugh*
Cecily Cardew	*Miss Evelyn Millard*
Miss Prism (Governess)	*Mrs George Canninge*

THE SCENES OF THE PLAY

Act 1
Algernon Moncrieff's flat in Half-Moon Street, W.

Act 2
The garden at the Manor House, Woolton

Act 3
Drawing-room at the Manor House, Woolton

Time
The Present

First Act

Scene: Morning-room in Algernon's flat in Half-Moon Street. The room is luxuriously and artistically furnished. The sound of a piano is heard in the adjoining room. Lane is arranging afternoon tea on the table and, after the music has ceased, Algernon enters [from music-room]

ALERGNON Did you hear what I was playing, Lane?

LANE I didn't think it polite to listen, sir.

ALGERNON I'm sorry for that, for your sake. I don't play accurately—anyone can play accurately—but I play with wonderful expression. As far as the piano is concerned, sentiment is my forte. 5
I keep science for Life.

LANE Yes, sir.

ALGERNON And, speaking of the science of Life, have you got the cucumber sandwiches cut for Lady Bracknell?

LANE Yes, sir. (*Hands them on a salver*)° 10

ALGERNON (*inspects them, takes two, and sits down on the sofa*) Oh!
. . . by the way, Lane, I see from your book that on Thursday night, when Lord Shoreham° and Mr Worthing were dining with me, eight bottles of champagne are entered as having been consumed. 15

LANE Yes, sir; eight bottles and a pint.

ALGERNON Why is it that at a bachelor's establishment the servants invariably drink the champagne? I ask merely for information.

LANE I attribute it to the superior quality of the wine, sir. I have often observed that in married households the champagne is rarely 20
of a first-rate brand.

ALGERNON Good heavens! Is marriage so demoralizing as that?

LANE I believe it *is* a very pleasant state, sir. I have had very little experience of it myself up to the present. I have only been married once. That was in consequence of a misunderstanding° between 25
myself and a young person.

ALGERNON (*languidly*) I don't know that I am much interested in your family life, Lane.

LANE No, sir; it is not a very interesting subject. I never think of it myself. 30

ALGERNON Very natural, I am sure. That will do, Lane, thank you.

LANE Thank you, sir.

Lane goes out

ALGERNON Lane's views on marriage seem somewhat lax. Really, if
the lower orders don't set us a good example, what on earth is the
use of them? They seem, as a class, to have absolutely no sense of   35
moral responsibility.

Enter Lane

LANE Mr Ernest Worthing.

Enter Jack.° Lane goes out

ALGERNON How are you, my dear Ernest? What brings you up to
town?

JACK Oh, pleasure, pleasure!° What else should bring one anywhere?   40
Eating as usual, I see, Algy!

ALGERNON (*stiffly*) I believe it is customary in good society to take
some slight refreshment° at five o'clock. Where have you been
since last Thursday?

JACK (*sitting down on the sofa*) In the country.   45

ALGERNON What on earth do you do there?

JACK (*pulling off his gloves*) When one is in town one amuses oneself.
When one is in the country one amuses other people. It is
excessively boring.

ALGERNON And who are the people you amuse?   50

JACK (*airily*) Oh, neighbours, neighbours.

ALGERNON Got nice neighbours in your part of Shropshire?°

JACK Perfectly horrid! Never speak to one of them.

ALGERNON How immensely you must amuse them! (*Goes over and
takes sandwich*) By the way, Shropshire is your county, is it not?   55

JACK Eh? Shropshire? Yes, of course. Hallo! Why all these cups?
Why cucumber sandwiches? Why such reckless extravagance in
one so young? Who is coming to tea?

ALGERNON Oh! merely Aunt Augusta and Gwendolen.

JACK How perfectly delightful!   60

ALGERNON Yes, that is all very well; but I am afraid Aunt Augusta
won't quite approve of your being here.

JACK May I ask why?

ALGERNON My dear fellow, the way you flirt with Gwendolen is
perfectly disgraceful. It is almost as bad as the way Gwendolen   65
flirts with you.

JACK I am in love with Gwendolen. I have come up to town
expressly to propose to her.

ALGERNON I thought you had come up for pleasure? . . . I call that
business.   70

JACK How utterly unromantic you are!

ALGERNON I really don't see anything romantic in proposing. It is very romantic to be in love. But there is nothing romantic about a definite proposal. Why, one may be accepted. One usually is, I believe. Then the excitement is all over. The very essence of romance is uncertainty. If ever I get married, I'll certainly try to forget the fact.

JACK I have no doubt about that, dear Algy. The Divorce Court was specially invented for people whose memories are so curiously constituted.

ALGERNON Oh! there is no use speculating on that subject. Divorces are made in Heaven—(*Jack puts out his hand to take a sandwich. Algernon at once interferes*)° Please don't touch the cucumber sandwiches. They are ordered specially for Aunt Augusta. (*Takes one and eats it*)

JACK Well, you have been eating them all the time.

ALGERNON That is quite a different matter. She is my aunt. (*Takes plate from below*)° Have some bread and butter. The bread and butter is for Gwendolen. Gwendolen is devoted to bread and butter.

JACK (*advancing to table and helping himself*) And very good bread and butter it is too.

ALGERNON Well, my dear fellow, you need not eat as if you were going to eat it all. You behave as if you were married to her already. You are not married to her already, and I don't think you ever will be.

JACK Why on earth do you say that?

ALGERNON Well, in the first place, girls never marry the men they flirt with. Girls don't think it right.

JACK Oh, that is nonsense!

ALGERNON It isn't. It is a great truth. It accounts for the extraordinary number of bachelors that one sees all over the place. In the second place, I don't give my consent.

JACK Your consent!

ALGERNON My dear fellow, Gwendolen is my first cousin. And before I allow you to marry her, you will have to clear up the whole question of Cecily. (*Rings bell*)

JACK Cecily! What on earth do you mean? What do you mean, Algy, by Cecily? I don't know anyone of the name of Cecily.

Enter Lane

ALGERNON Bring me that cigarette case Mr Worthing left in the smoking-room the last time he dined here.

LANE Yes, sir.

Lane goes out

JACK Do you mean to say you have had my cigarette case all this time? I wish to goodness you had let me know. I have been writing frantic letters to Scotland Yard° about it. I was very nearly offering a large reward.   115

ALGERNON Well, I wish you would offer one. I happen to be more than usually hard up.

JACK There is no good offering a large reward now that the thing is found.

> *Enter Lane with the cigarette case on a salver.° Algernon takes it at once. Lane goes out*

ALGERNON I think that is rather mean of you, Ernest, I must say.   120
(*Opens case and examines it*) However, it makes no matter, for, now that I look at the inscription inside, I find that the thing isn't yours after all.

JACK Of course it's mine. (*Moving to him*) You have seen me with it a hundred times, and you have no right whatsoever to read what   125
is written inside. It is a very ungentlemanly thing to read a private cigarette case.

ALGERNON Oh! it is absurd to have a hard and fast rule about what one should read and what one shouldn't. More than half of modern culture depends on what one shouldn't read.   130

JACK I am quite aware of the fact, and I don't propose to discuss modern culture. It isn't the sort of thing one should talk of in private. I simply want my cigarette case back.

ALGERNON Yes; but this isn't your cigarette case. This cigarette case is a present from someone of the name of Cecily, and you said you   135
didn't know anyone of that name.

JACK Well, if you want to know, Cecily happens to be my aunt.

ALGERNON Your aunt!

JACK Yes. Charming old lady she is, too. Lives at Tunbridge Wells.°
Just give it back to me, Algy.   140

ALGERNON (*retreating to back of sofa*) But why does she call herself little Cecily if she is your aunt and lives at Tunbridge Wells?
(*Reading*) 'From little Cecily with her fondest love.'

JACK (*moving to sofa and kneeling upon it*) My dear fellow, what on earth is there in that? Some aunts are tall, some aunts are not   145
tall. That is a matter that surely an aunt may be allowed to decide for herself. You seem to think that every aunt should be exactly like your aunt! That is absurd! For Heaven's sake give me back my cigarette case. (*Follows Algernon round the room*)

ALGERNON Yes. But why does your aunt call you her uncle? 'From   150
little Cecily, with her fondest love to her dear Uncle Jack.' There
is no objection, I admit, to an aunt being a small aunt, but why an
aunt, no matter what her size may be, should call her own nephew
her uncle, I can't quite make out. Besides, your name isn't Jack at
all; it is Ernest.   155

JACK It isn't Ernest; it's Jack.

ALGERNON You have always told me it was Ernest. I have introduced you to every one as Ernest. You answer to the name of
Ernest. You look as if your name was Ernest. You are the most
earnest looking person I ever saw in my life. It is perfectly absurd   160
your saying that your name isn't Ernest. It's on your cards. Here
is one of them. (*Taking it from case*) 'Mr Ernest Worthing, B.4,
The Albany.'° I'll keep this as a proof that your name is Ernest if
ever you attempt to deny it to me, or to Gwendolen, or to anyone
else. (*Puts the card in his pocket*)   165

JACK Well, my name is Ernest in town and Jack in the country, and
the cigarette case was given to me in the country.

ALGERNON Yes, but that does not account for the fact that your
small Aunt Cecily, who lives at Tunbridge Wells, calls you her
dear uncle. Come, old boy, you had much better have the thing   170
out at once.

JACK My dear Algy, you talk exactly as if you were a dentist. It is
very vulgar to talk like a dentist when one isn't a dentist. It
produces a false impression.

ALGERNON Well, that is exactly what dentists always do. Now, go   175
on! Tell me the whole thing. I may mention that I have always
suspected you of being a confirmed and secret Bunburyist; and I
am quite sure of it now.

JACK Bunburyist? What on earth do you mean by a Bunburyist?

ALGERNON I'll reveal to you the meaning of that incomparable   180
expression as soon as you are kind enough to inform me why you
are Ernest in town and Jack in the country.

JACK Well, produce my cigarette case first.

ALGERNON Here it is. (*Hands cigarette case*)° Now produce your
explanation, and pray make it improbable. (*Sits on sofa*)°   185

JACK My dear fellow, there is nothing improbable about my explanation at all. In fact it's perfectly ordinary. Old Mr Thomas
Cardew, who adopted me when I was a little boy, made me in his
will guardian to his granddaughter, Miss Cecily Cardew. Cecily,
who addresses me as her uncle from motives of respect that you   190

could not possibly appreciate, lives at my place in the country under the charge of her admirable governess, Miss Prism.

ALGERNON Where is that place in the country, by the way?

JACK That is nothing to you, dear boy. You are not going to be invited. . . . I may tell you candidly that the place is not in Shropshire.

ALGERNON I suspected that, my dear fellow! I have Bunburyed all over Shropshire on two separate occasions. Now, go on. Why are you Ernest in town and Jack in the country?

JACK My dear Algy, I don't know whether you will be able to understand my real motives. You are hardly serious enough. When one is placed in the position of guardian, one has to adopt a very high moral tone on all subjects. It's one's duty to do so. And as a high moral tone can hardly be said to conduce very much to either one's health or one's happiness, in order to get up to town I have always pretended to have a younger brother of the name of Ernest, who lives in the Albany, and gets into the most dreadful scrapes. That, my dear Algy, is the whole truth pure and simple.

ALGERNON The truth is rarely pure and never simple. Modern life would be very tedious if it were either, and modern literature a complete impossibility!

JACK That wouldn't be at all a bad thing.

ALGERNON Literary criticism is not your forte, my dear fellow. Don't try it. You should leave that to people who haven't been at a University. They do it so well in the daily papers. What you really are is a Bunburyist. I was quite right in saying you were a Bunburyist. You are one of the most advanced Bunburyists I know.

JACK What on earth do you mean?

ALGERNON You have invented a very useful younger brother called Ernest, in order that you may be able to come up to town as often as you like. I have invented an invaluable permanent invalid called Bunbury,° in order that I may be able to go down into the country whenever I choose. Bunbury is perfectly invaluable. If it wasn't for Bunbury's extraordinary bad health, for instance, I wouldn't be able to dine with you at Willis's° tonight, for I have been really engaged to Aunt Augusta for more than a week.

JACK I haven't asked you to dine with me anywhere tonight.

ALGERNON I know. You are absurdly careless about sending out invitations. It is very foolish of you. Nothing annoys people so much as not receiving invitations.

JACK You had much better dine with your Aunt Augusta.

ALGERNON I haven't the smallest intention of doing anything of the kind. To begin with, I dined there on Monday, and once a week is quite enough to dine with one's own relations. In the second place, whenever I do dine there I am always treated as a member of the family, and sent down° with either no woman at all, or two. In the third place, I know perfectly well whom she will place me next to, tonight. She will place me next Mary Farquhar, who always flirts with her own husband across the dinner-table. That is not very pleasant. Indeed, it is not even decent . . . and that sort of thing is enormously on the increase. The amount of women in London who flirt with their own husbands is perfectly scandalous. It looks so bad. It is simply washing one's clean linen in public. Besides, now that I know you to be a confirmed Bunburyist I naturally want to talk to you about Bunburying. I want to tell you the rules.

JACK I'm not a Bunburyist at all. If Gwendolen accepts me, I am going to kill my brother, indeed I think I'll kill him in any case. Cecily is a little too much interested in him. It is rather a bore. So I am going to get rid of Ernest. And I strongly advise you to do the same with Mr . . . with your invalid friend who has the absurd name.

ALGERNON Nothing will induce me to part with Bunbury, and if you ever get married, which seems to me extremely problematic, you will be very glad to know Bunbury. A man who marries without knowing Bunbury has a very tedious time of it.

JACK That is nonsense. If I marry a charming girl like Gwendolen, and she is the only girl I ever saw in my life that I would marry, I certainly won't want to know Bunbury.

ALGERNON Then your wife will. You don't seem to realize, that in married life three is company and two is none.

JACK (*sententiously*) That, my dear young friend, is the theory that the corrupt French Drama° has been propounding for the last fifty years.

ALGERNON Yes; and that the happy English home has proved in half the time.

JACK For heaven's sake, don't try to be cynical. It's perfectly easy to be cynical.

ALGERNON My dear fellow, it isn't easy to be anything nowadays. There's such a lot of beastly competition about. (*The sound of an electric bell is heard*) Ah! that must be Aunt Augusta. Only

relatives, or creditors,° ever ring in that Wagnerian° manner. Now, if I get her out of the way for ten minutes, so that you can have an opportunity for proposing to Gwendolen, may I dine with you   275
tonight at Willis's?

JACK I suppose so, if you want to.

ALGERNON Yes, but you must be serious about it. I hate people who are not serious about meals. It is so shallow of them.

Enter Lane

LANE Lady Bracknell and Miss Fairfax.   280

Algernon goes forward to meet them. Enter Lady Bracknell and Gwendolen

LADY BRACKNELL Good afternoon, dear Algernon,° I hope you are behaving very well.

ALGERNON I'm feeling very well, Aunt Augusta.

LADY BRACKNELL That's not quite the same thing. In fact the two things rarely go together. (*Sees Jack and bows to him with icy   285
coldness*)

ALGERNON (*to Gwendolen*) Dear me, you are smart!

GWENDOLEN I am always smart! Aren't I, Mr Worthing?

JACK You're quite perfect, Miss Fairfax.

GWENDOLEN Oh! I hope I am not that. It would leave no room for developments, and I intend to develop in many directions. (*Gwen-   290
dolen and Jack sit down together in the corner*)

LADY BRACKNELL I'm sorry if we are a little late, Algernon, but I was obliged to call on dear Lady Harbury.° I hadn't been there since her poor husband's death. I never saw a woman so altered; she looks quite twenty years younger. And now I'll have a cup of tea, and one of those nice cucumber sandwiches you promised me.   295

ALGERNON Certainly, Aunt Augusta. (*Goes over to tea-table*)

LADY BRACKNELL Won't you come and sit here, Gwendolen?

GWENDOLEN Thanks, mamma, I'm quite comfortable where I am.°

ALGERNON (*picking up empty plate in horror*) Good heavens! Lane! Why are there no cucumber sandwiches? I ordered them spe-   300
cially.

LANE (*gravely*) There were no cucumbers in the market this morn-ing, sir. I went down twice.°

ALGERNON No cucumbers!

LANE No, sir. Not even for ready money.   305

ALGERNON That will do, Lane, thank you.

LANE Thank you, sir.

Goes out

ALGERNON I am greatly distressed, Aunt Augusta, about there being no cucumbers, not even for ready money.

LADY BRACKNELL It really makes no matter, Algernon. I had some 310 crumpets with Lady Harbury, who seems to me to be living entirely for pleasure now.

ALGERNON I hear her hair has turned quite gold from grief.

LADY BRACKNELL It certainly has changed its colour. From what cause I, of course, cannot say. (*Algernon crosses and hands tea*)° 315 Thank you. I've quite a treat for you tonight, Algernon. I am going to send you down with Mary Farquhar. She is such a nice woman, and so attentive to her husband. It's delightful to watch them.

ALGERNON I am afraid, Aunt Augusta, I shall have to give up the pleasure of dining with you tonight after all. 320

LADY BRACKNELL (*frowning*) I hope not, Algernon. It would put my table completely out.° Your uncle would have to dine upstairs. Fortunately he is accustomed to that.

ALGERNON It is a great bore, and, I need hardly say, a terrible disappointment to me, but the fact is I have just had a telegram to 325 say that my poor friend Bunbury is very ill again. (*Exchanges glances with Jack*) They seem to think I should be with him.

LADY BRACKNELL It is very strange. This Mr Bunbury seems to suffer from curiously bad health.

ALGERNON Yes; poor Bunbury is a dreadful invalid. 330

LADY BRACKNELL Well, I must say, Algernon, that I think it is high time that Mr Bunbury made up his mind whether he was going to live or to die. This shilly-shallying with the question is absurd. Nor do I in any way approve of the modern sympathy with invalids. I consider it morbid. Illness of any kind° is hardly a thing 335 to be encouraged in others. Health is the primary duty of life. I am always telling that to your poor uncle, but he never seems to take much notice . . . as far as any improvement in his ailments goes. I should be much obliged if you would ask Mr Bunbury, from me, to be kind enough not to have a relapse on Saturday, for 340 I rely on you to arrange my music for me. It is my last reception,° and one wants something that will encourage conversation, particularly at the end of the season when everyone has practically said whatever they had to say, which, in most cases, was probably not much. 345

ALGERNON I'll speak to Bunbury, Aunt Augusta, if he is still conscious, and I think I can promise you he'll be all right by Saturday. Of course the music is a great difficulty. You see, if one

plays good music, people don't listen, and if one plays bad music
people don't talk. But I'll run over the programme I've drawn out,   350
if you will kindly come into the next room for a moment.

LADY BRACKNELL Thank you, Algernon. It is very thoughtful of
you. (*Rising, and following Algernon*) I'm sure the programme will
be delightful, after a few expurgations. French songs° I cannot
possibly allow. People always seem to think that they are improper,   355
and either look shocked, which is vulgar, or laugh, which is worse.
But German sounds a thoroughly respectable language,° and
indeed I believe is so. Gwendolen, you will accompany me.

GWENDOLEN Certainly, mamma.

> *Lady Bracknell and Algernon go into the music-room, Gwen-
> dolen remains behind*

JACK Charming day it has been, Miss Fairfax.   360

GWENDOLEN Pray don't talk to me about the weather,° Mr Worthing. Whenever people talk to me about the weather, I always feel
quite certain that they mean something else. And that makes me
so nervous.

JACK I do mean something else.   365

GWENDOLEN I thought so. In fact, I am never wrong.

JACK And I would like to be allowed to take advantage of Lady
Bracknell's temporary absence. . . .

GWENDOLEN I would certainly advise you to do so. Mamma has a
way of coming back suddenly into a room that I have often had to   370
speak to her about.

JACK (*nervously*) Miss Fairfax, ever since I met you I have admired
you more than any girl . . . I have ever met since . . . I met you.

GWENDOLEN Yes, I am quite aware of the fact. And I often wish that
in public, at any rate, you had been more demonstrative. For me   375
you have always had an irresistible fascination. Even before I met
you I was far from indifferent to you. (*Jack looks at her in
amazement*) We live, as I hope you know, Mr Worthing, in an age
of ideals. The fact is constantly mentioned in the more expensive
monthly magazines, and has reached the provincial pulpits I am   380
told; and my ideal has always been to love someone of the name
of Ernest. There is something in that name that inspires absolute
confidence. The moment Algernon first mentioned to me that he
had a friend called Ernest, I knew I was destined to love you.

JACK You really love me, Gwendolen?°   385

GWENDOLEN Passionately!

JACK Darling! You don't know how happy you've made me.

GWENDOLEN My own Ernest!

JACK But you don't really mean to say that you couldn't love me if
my name wasn't Ernest?   390

GWENDOLEN But your name is Ernest.

JACK Yes, I know it is. But supposing it was something else? Do you
mean to say you couldn't love me then?

GWENDOLEN (*glibly*) Ah! that is clearly a metaphysical speculation,
and like most metaphysical speculations has very little reference at   395
all to the actual facts of real life, as we know them.

JACK Personally, darling, to speak quite candidly, I don't much care
about the name of Ernest. . . . I don't think the name suits me at
all.

GWENDOLEN It suits you perfectly. It is a divine name. It has music   400
of its own. It produces vibrations.

JACK Well, really, Gwendolen, I must say that I think there are lots
of other much nicer names. I think Jack, for instance, a charming
name.

GWENDOLEN Jack? . . . No, there is very little music in the name   405
Jack, if any at all, indeed. It does not thrill. It produces absolutely
no vibrations. . . . I have known several Jacks, and they all, without
exception, were more than usually plain. Besides, Jack is a
notorious domesticity for John! And I pity any woman who is
married to a man called John. She would probably never be   410
allowed to know the entrancing pleasure of a single moment's
solitude. The only really safe name is Ernest.

JACK Gwendolen, I must get christened at once—I mean we must
get married at once. There is no time to be lost.

GWENDOLEN Married, Mr Worthing?°   415

JACK (*astounded*) Well . . . surely. You know that I love you, and you
led me to believe, Miss Fairfax, that you were not absolutely
indifferent to me.

GWENDOLEN I adore you. But you haven't proposed to me yet.
Nothing has been said at all about marriage. The subject has not   420
even been touched on.

JACK Well . . . may I propose to you now?

GWENDOLEN I think it would be an admirable opportunity. And to
spare you any possible disappointment, Mr Worthing, I think it
only fair to tell you quite frankly beforehand that I am fully   425
determined to accept you.

JACK Gwendolen!

GWENDOLEN Yes, Mr Worthing, what have you got to say to me?

JACK You know what I have got to say to you.

GWENDOLEN Yes, but you don't say it.   430

JACK Gwendolen, will you marry me? (*Goes on his knees*)

GWENDOLEN Of course I will, darling. How long you have been about it! I am afraid you have had very little experience in how to propose.

JACK My own one, I have never loved anyone in the world but you.   435

GWENDOLEN Yes, but men often propose for practice. I know my brother Gerald does. All my girl-friends tell me so. What wonderfully blue eyes° you have, Ernest! They are quite, quite, blue. I hope you will always look at me just like that, especially when there are other people present.   440

> *Enter Lady Bracknell*

LADY BRACKNELL Mr Worthing! Rise, sir, from this semi-recumbent posture. It is most indecorous.

GWENDOLEN Mamma! (*He tries to rise; she restrains him*) I must beg you to retire. This is no place for you. Besides, Mr Worthing has not quite finished yet.   445

LADY BRACKNELL Finished what, may I ask?

GWENDOLEN I am engaged to Mr Worthing, mamma. (*They rise together*)

LADY BRACKNELL Pardon me, you are not engaged to anyone. When you do become engaged to someone, I, or your father, should his health permit him, will inform you of the fact. An   450
engagement should come on a young girl as a surprise, pleasant° or unpleasant, as the case may be. It is hardly a matter that she could be allowed to arrange for herself. . . . And now I have a few questions to put to you, Mr Worthing. While I am making these inquiries, you, Gwendolen, will wait for me below in the   455
carriage.

GWENDOLEN (*reproachfully*) Mamma!

LADY BRACKNELL In the carriage, Gwendolen!

> *Gwendolen goes to the door. She and Jack blow kisses to each other behind Lady Bracknell's back. Lady Bracknell looks vaguely about as if she could not understand what the noise was. Finally turns round*

Gwendolen, the carriage!

GWENDOLEN Yes, mamma.   460

> *Goes out, looking back at Jack*

LADY BRACKNELL (*sitting down*) You can take a seat, Mr Worthing. (*Looks in her pocket for note-book and pencil*)°

JACK Thank you, Lady Bracknell, I prefer standing.

LADY BRACKNELL (*pencil and note-book in hand*). I feel bound to tell you that you are not down on my list of eligible young men, although I have the same list as the dear Duchess of Bolton has. We work together, in fact. However, I am quite ready to enter your name, should your answers be what a really affectionate mother requires. Do you smoke?

JACK Well, yes, I must admit I smoke.

LADY BRACKNELL I am glad to hear it. A man should always have an occupation of some kind. There are far too many idle men in London as it is. How old are you?

JACK Twenty-nine.

LADY BRACKNELL A very good age to be married at. I have always been of opinion that a man who desires to get married should know either everything or nothing. Which do you know?

JACK (*after some hesitation*) I know nothing, Lady Bracknell.

LADY BRACKNELL I am pleased to hear it. I do not approve of anything that tampers with natural ignorance. Ignorance is like a delicate exotic fruit; touch it and the bloom is gone. The whole theory of modern education is radically unsound. Fortunately in England, at any rate, education produces no effect whatsoever. If it did, it would prove a serious danger to the upper classes, and probably lead to acts of violence in Grosvenor Square. What is your income?

JACK Between seven and eight thousand a year.

LADY BRACKNELL (*makes a note in her book*) In land, or in investments?

JACK In investments, chiefly.

LADY BRACKNELL That is satisfactory. What between the duties expected of one during one's lifetime, and the duties exacted from one after one's death,° land has ceased to be either a profit or a pleasure. It gives one position, and prevents one from keeping it up. That's all that can be said about land.

JACK I have a country house with some land, of course, attached to it, about fifteen hundred acres, I believe; but I don't depend on that for my real income. In fact, as far as I can make out, the poachers are the only people who make anything out of it.

LADY BRACKNELL A country house! How many bedrooms? Well, that point can be cleared up afterwards. You have a town house, I hope? A girl with a simple, unspoiled nature, like Gwendolen, could hardly be expected to reside in the country.

JACK Well, I own a house in Belgrave Square,° but it is let by the
year to Lady Bloxham. Of course, I can get it back whenever I like,
at six months' notice.   505

LADY BRACKNELL Lady Bloxham?° I don't know her.

JACK Oh, she goes about very little. She is a lady considerably
advanced in years.

LADY BRACKNELL Ah, nowadays that is no guarantee of respectability of character. What number in Belgrave Square?   510

JACK 149.

LADY BRACKNELL (shaking her head) The unfashionable side. I
thought there was something. However, that could easily be
altered.

JACK Do you mean the fashion, or the side?   515

LADY BRACKNELL (sternly) Both, if necessary, I presume. What are
your politics?

JACK Well, I am afraid I really have none. I am a Liberal Unionist.°

LADY BRACKNELL Oh, they count as Tories. They dine with us. Or   520
come in the evening, at any rate. Now to minor matters. Are your
parents living?

JACK I have lost both my parents.

LADY BRACKNELL Both? . . . That seems like carelessness.° Who
was your father? He was evidently a man of some wealth. Was he   525
born in what the Radical papers call the purple of commerce, or
did he rise from the ranks of the aristocracy?

JACK I am afraid I really don't know. The fact is, Lady Bracknell, I
said I had lost my parents. It would be nearer the truth to say that
my parents seem to have lost me. . . . I don't actually know who I   530
am by birth. I was . . . well, I was found.

LADY BRACKNELL Found!

JACK The late Mr Thomas Cardew, an old gentleman of a very
charitable and kindly disposition, found me, and gave me the name
of Worthing, because he happened to have a first-class ticket for   535
Worthing in his pocket at the time. Worthing is a place in Sussex.
It is a seaside resort.

LADY BRACKNELL Where did the charitable gentleman who had a
first-class ticket for this seaside resort find you?

JACK (gravely) In a hand-bag.   540

LADY BRACKNELL A hand-bag?°

JACK (very seriously) Yes, Lady Bracknell. I was in a hand-bag—a somewhat large, black leather hand-bag, with handles to it—an ordinary hand-bag in fact.

LADY BRACKNELL In what locality did this Mr James, or Thomas, 545
Cardew come across this ordinary hand-bag?

JACK In the cloak-room° at Victoria Station. It was given to him in mistake for his own.

LADY BRACKNELL The cloak-room at Victoria Station?

JACK Yes. The Brighton line.° 550

LADY BRACKNELL The line is immaterial.° Mr Worthing, I confess I feel somewhat bewildered by what you have just told me. To be born, or at any rate bred, in a hand-bag, whether it had handles or not, seems to me to display a contempt for the ordinary decencies of family life that reminds° one of the worst excesses of the French 555
Revolution. And I presume you know what that unfortunate movement led to? As for the particular locality in which the hand-bag was found, a cloak-room at a railway station might serve to conceal a social indiscretion°—has probably, indeed, been used for that purpose before now—but it could hardly be regarded as 560
an assured basis for a recognized position in good society.

JACK May I ask you then what you would advise me to do? I need hardly say I would do anything in the world to ensure Gwendolen's happiness.

LADY BRACKNELL I would strongly advise you, Mr Worthing, to try 565
and acquire some relations as soon as possible, and to make a definite effort to produce at any rate one parent, of either sex, before the season° is quite over.

JACK Well, I don't see how I could possibly manage to do that. I can produce the hand-bag at any moment. It is in my dressing-room 570
at home. I really think that should satisfy you, Lady Bracknell.

LADY BRACKNELL Me, sir! What has it to do with me? You can hardly imagine that I and Lord Bracknell would dream of allowing our only daughter—a girl brought up with the utmost care—to marry into a cloak-room, and form an alliance with a parcel? Good 575
morning, Mr Worthing!°

Lady Bracknell sweeps out in majestic indignation

JACK Good morning! (*Algernon, from the other room, strikes up the Wedding March.° Jack looks perfectly furious, and goes to the door*)
For goodness' sake don't play that ghastly tune, Algy! How idiotic you are! 580

The music stops and Algernon enters cheerily

ALGERNON Didn't it go off all right, old boy? You don't mean to say
Gwendolen refused you? I know it is a way she has. She is always
refusing people. I think it is most ill-natured of her.

JACK Oh, Gwendolen is as right as a trivet. As far as she is
concerned, we are engaged. Her mother is perfectly unbearable.   585
Never met such a Gorgon.° . . . I don't really know what a Gorgon
is like, but I am quite sure that Lady Bracknell is one. In any case,
she is a monster, without being a myth, which is rather unfair. . . .
I beg your pardon, Algy, I suppose I shouldn't talk about your own
aunt in that way before you.   590

ALGERNON My dear boy,° I love hearing my relations abused. It is
the only thing that makes me put up with them at all. Relations
are simply a tedious pack of people, who haven't got the remotest
knowledge of how to live, nor the smallest instinct about when to
die.   595

JACK Oh, that is nonsense!

ALGERNON It isn't!

JACK Well, I won't argue about the matter. You always want to argue
about things.

ALGERNON That is exactly what things were originally made for.   600

JACK Upon my word, if I thought that, I'd shoot myself. . . . (A
pause) You don't think there is any chance of Gwendolen becoming like her mother in about a hundred and fifty years, do you
Algy?

ALGERNON All women become like their mothers. That is their   605
tragedy. No man does. That's his.

JACK Is that clever?

ALGERNON It is perfectly phrased! and quite as true as any observation in civilized life should be.

JACK I am sick to death of cleverness. Everybody is clever nowadays. 610
You can't go anywhere without meeting clever people. The thing
has become an absolute public nuisance. I wish to goodness we had
a few fools left.

ALGERNON We have.

JACK I should extremely like to meet them. What do they talk about? 615

ALGERNON The fools? Oh! about the clever people, of course.

JACK What fools!

ALGERNON By the way, did you tell Gwendolen the truth about your
being Ernest in town, and Jack in the country?

JACK (in a very patronizing manner) My dear fellow, the truth isn't 620
quite the sort of thing one tells to a nice sweet refined girl. What
extraordinary ideas you have about the way to behave to a woman!

ALGERNON The only way to behave to a woman is to make love° to her, if she is pretty, and to someone else if she is plain.

JACK Oh, that is nonsense.   625

ALGERNON What about your brother? What about the profligate Ernest?

JACK Oh, before the end of the week I shall have got rid of him. I'll say he died in Paris of apoplexy. Lots of people die of apoplexy, quite suddenly, don't they?   630

ALGERNON Yes, but it's hereditary, my dear fellow. It's a sort of thing that runs in families. You had much better say a severe chill.

JACK You are sure a severe chill isn't hereditary, or anything of that kind?

ALGERNON Of course it isn't!   635

JACK Very well, then. My poor brother Ernest is carried off suddenly in Paris, by a severe chill. That gets rid of him.

ALGERNON But I thought you said that . . . Miss Cardew was a little too much interested in your poor brother Ernest? Won't she feel his loss a good deal?   640

JACK Oh, that is all right. Cecily is not a silly romantic girl, I am glad to say. She has got a capital appetite, goes long walks, and pays no attention at all to her lessons.

ALGERNON I would rather like to see Cecily.

JACK I will take very good care you never do. She is excessively   645
pretty, and she is only just eighteen.°

ALGERNON Have you told Gwendolen yet that you have an excessively pretty ward who is only just eighteen?

JACK Oh! one doesn't blurt these things out to people. Cecily and Gwendolen are perfectly certain to be extremely great friends. I'll   650
bet you anything you like that half an hour after they have met, they will be calling each other sister.

ALGERNON Women only do that when they have called each other a lot of other things first. Now, my dear boy, if we want to get a good table at Willis's, we really must go and dress.° Do you know   655
it is nearly seven?

JACK (irritably) Oh! it always is nearly seven.

ALGERNON Well, I'm hungry.

JACK I never knew you when you weren't. . . .

ALGERNON What shall we do after dinner? Go to a theatre?   660

JACK Oh no! I loathe listening.

ALGERNON Well, let us go to the Club?°

JACK Oh, no! I hate talking.

ALGERNON Well, we might trot round to the Empire° at ten?

JACK Oh, no! I can't bear looking at things. It is so silly.   665

ALGERNON Well, what shall we do?

JACK Nothing!

ALGERNON It is awfully hard work doing nothing. However, I don't mind hard work where there is no definite object of any kind.

> *Enter Lane*

LANE Miss Fairfax.   670

> *Enter Gwendolen. Lane goes out*

ALGERNON Gwendolen, upon my word!

GWENDOLEN Algy, kindly turn your back.° I have something very particular to say to Mr Worthing.

ALGERNON Really, Gwendolen, I don't think I can allow this at   675
all.°

GWENDOLEN Algy, you always adopt a strictly immoral attitude towards life. You are not quite old enough to do that. (*Algernon retires to the fireplace*)

JACK My own darling!

GWENDOLEN Ernest, we may never be married. From the expression on mamma's face I fear we never shall. Few parents nowadays pay   680
any regard to what their children say to them. The old-fashioned respect for the young is fast dying out. Whatever influence I ever had over mamma, I lost at the age of three. But although she may prevent us from becoming man and wife, and I may marry someone else, and marry often, nothing that she can possibly do   685
can alter my eternal devotion to you.

JACK Dear Gwendolen!

GWENDOLEN The story of your romantic origin, as related to me by mamma, with unpleasing comments, has naturally stirred the deeper fibres of my nature. Your Christian name has an irresistible   690
fascination. The simplicity of your character makes you exquisitely incomprehensible to me. Your town address at the Albany I have. What is your address in the country?

JACK The Manor House, Woolton, Hertfordshire.°

> *Algernon, who has been carefully listening, smiles to himself, and writes the address on his shirt-cuff. Then picks up the Railway Guide*

GWENDOLEN There is a good postal service, I suppose? It may be   695
necessary to do something desperate. That of course will require serious consideration. I will communicate with you daily.

JACK My own one!

GWENDOLEN How long do you remain in town?

JACK Till Monday.   700
GWENDOLEN Good! Algy, you may turn round now.
ALGERNON Thanks, I've turned round already.
GWENDOLEN You may also ring the bell.
         [Algernon rings bell]
JACK You will let me see you to your carriage, my own darling?
GWENDOLEN Certainly.   705
         [Enter Lane]°
JACK I will see Miss Fairfax out.
LANE Yes, sir.
         Jack and Gwendolen go off. Lane presents several letters on a
         salver, to Algernon. It is to be surmised that they are bills, as
         Algernon, after looking at the envelopes, tears them up
ALGERNON A glass of sherry, Lane.
LANE Yes, sir.
ALGERNON Tomorrow, Lane, I'm going Bunburying.   710
LANE Yes, sir.
ALGERNON I shall probably not be back till Monday. You can put
   up° my dress clothes, my smoking jacket°, and all the Bunbury
   suits . . .
LANE Yes, sir. (*Handing sherry*)   715
ALGERNON I hope tomorrow will be a fine day, Lane.
LANE It never is, sir.
ALGERNON Lane, you're a perfect pessimist.
LANE I do my best to give satisfaction, sir.
         Enter Jack. Lane goes off
JACK There's a sensible, intellectual girl! the only girl I ever cared   720
   for in my life. (*Algernon is laughing immoderately*) What on earth
   are you so amused at?
ALGERNON Oh, I'm a little anxious about poor Bunbury, that is all.
JACK If you don't take care, your friend Bunbury will get you into a
   serious scrape some day.   725
ALGERNON I love scrapes. They are the only things that are never
   serious.
JACK Oh, that's nonsense, Algy. You never talk anything but nonsense.
ALGERNON Nobody ever does.   730
         Jack looks indignantly at him, and leaves the room. Algernon
         lights a cigarette, reads his shirt-cuff,° and smiles.

   ACT DROP

Second Act

Scene: Garden at the Manor House. A flight of grey stone steps leads up to the house. The garden, an old-fashioned one, full of roses. Time of year, July. Basket chairs, and a table covered with books, are set under a large yew-tree. Miss Prism discovered seated at the table. Cecily is at the back, watering flowers

MISS PRISM (*calling*) Cecily, Cecily! Surely such a utilitarian occupation as the watering of flowers is rather Moulton's duty° than yours? Especially at a moment when intellectual pleasures await you. Your German grammar is on the table. Pray open it at page fifteen. We will repeat yesterday's lesson. 5

CECILY (*coming over very slowly*) But I don't like German. It isn't at all a becoming language. I know perfectly well that I look quite plain after my German lesson.

MISS PRISM Child, you know how anxious your guardian is that you should improve yourself in every way. He laid particular stress on 10 your German, as he was leaving for town yesterday. Indeed, he always lays stress on your German when he is leaving for town.

CECILY Dear Uncle Jack is so very serious! Sometimes he is so serious that I think he cannot be quite well.°

MISS PRISM (*drawing herself up*) Your guardian enjoys the best of 15 health, and his gravity of demeanour is especially to be commended in one so comparatively young as he is. I know no one who has a higher sense of duty and responsibility.

CECILY I suppose that is why he often looks a little bored when we three are together. 20

MISS PRISM Cecily! I am surprised at you. Mr Worthing has many troubles in his life. Idle merriment and triviality would be out of place in his conversation. You must remember his constant anxiety about that unfortunate young man his brother.

CECILY I wish Uncle Jack would allow that unfortunate young man, 25 his brother, to come down here sometimes. We might have a good influence over him, Miss Prism. I am sure you certainly would. You know German, and geology, and things of that kind influence a man very much. (*Cecily begins to write in her diary*)°

MISS PRISM (*shaking her head*) I do not think that even I could 30 produce any effect on a character that according to his own brother's admission is irretrievably weak and vacillating. Indeed I am not sure that I would desire to reclaim him. I am not in favour of this modern mania for turning bad people into good people at a moment's notice. As a man sows so let him reap. You must put away your diary, Cecily. I really don't see why you should keep a diary at all.

CECILY I keep a diary in order to enter the wonderful secrets of my life. If I didn't write them down I should probably forget all about them.

MISS PRISM Memory, my dear Cecily, is the diary that we all carry about with us.

CECILY Yes, but it usually chronicles the things that have never happened, and couldn't possibly have happened. I believe that Memory is responsible for nearly all the three-volume novels that Mudie° sends us.

MISS PRISM Do not speak slightingly of the three-volume novel, Cecily. I wrote one myself in earlier days.

CECILY Did you really, Miss Prism? How wonderfully clever you are! I hope it did not end happily? I don't like novels that end happily. They depress me so much.

MISS PRISM The good ended happily, and the bad unhappily. That is what Fiction means.

CECILY I suppose so. But it seems very unfair. And was your novel ever published?

MISS PRISM Alas! no. The manuscript unfortunately was abandoned.° (*Cecily starts*) I used the word in the sense of lost or mislaid. To your work, child, these speculations are profitless.

CECILY (*smiling*) But I see dear Dr Chasuble coming up through the garden.

MISS PRISM (*rising and advancing*) Dr Chasuble! This is indeed a pleasure.

Enter Canon Chasuble

CHASUBLE And how are we this morning?° Miss Prism, you are, I trust, well?

CECILY Miss Prism has just been complaining of a slight headache. I think it would do her so much good to have a short stroll with you in the Park, Dr Chasuble.

MISS PRISM Cecily, I have not mentioned anything about a headache.°

CECILY No, dear Miss Prism, I know that, but I felt instinctively that you had a headache. Indeed I was thinking about that, and not about my German lesson, when the Rector came in.

CHASUBLE I hope, Cecily, you are not inattentive.

CECILY Oh, I am afraid I am.

CHASUBLE That is strange. Were I fortunate enough to be Miss 75
Prism's pupil, I would hang upon her lips. [*Miss Prism glares*] I
spoke metaphorically.—My metaphor was drawn from bees.
Ahem! Mr Worthing, I suppose, has not returned from town yet?

MISS PRISM We do not expect him till Monday afternoon.

CHASUBLE Ah yes, he usually likes to spend his Sunday in London. 80
He is not one of those whose sole aim is enjoyment, as, by all
accounts, that unfortunate young man his brother seems to be. But
I must not disturb Egeria° and her pupil any longer.

MISS PRISM Egeria? My name is Laetitia, Doctor.

CHASUBLE (*bowing*) A classical allusion merely, drawn from the 85
Pagan authors. I shall see you both no doubt at Evensong?

MISS PRISM I think, dear Doctor, I will have a stroll with you. I find
I have a headache after all, and a walk might do it good.

CHASUBLE With pleasure, Miss Prism, with pleasure. We might go
as far as the schools and back. 90

MISS PRISM That would be delightful. Cecily, you will read your
Political Economy in my absence. The chapter on the Fall of the
Rupee° you may omit. It is somewhat too sensational. Even these
metallic problems have their melodramatic side.

> *Goes down the garden with Dr Chasuble*

CECILY (*picks up books and throws them back on table*) Horrid Political 95
Economy! Horrid Geography! Horrid, horrid German!

> *Enter Merriman with a card on a salver*

MERRIMAN Mr Ernest Worthing has just driven over from the
station. He has brought his luggage with him.°

CECILY (*takes the card and reads it*) 'Mr Ernest Worthing, B.4 The
Albany, W.'° Uncle Jack's brother! Did you tell him Mr Worthing 100
was in town?

MERRIMAN Yes, Miss. He seemed very much disappointed. I mentioned that you and Miss Prism were in the garden. He said he
was anxious to speak to you privately for a moment.

CECILY Ask Mr Ernest Worthing to come here. I suppose you had 105
better talk to the housekeeper about a room° for him.

MERRIMAN Yes, Miss.

> *Merriman goes off*

CECILY I have never met any really wicked person before. I feel
rather frightened. I am so afraid he will look just like everyone else.

> *Enter Algernon,° very gay and debonair*

He does!   110

ALGERNON (*raising his hat*) You are my little cousin Cecily, I'm sure.

CECILY You are under some strange mistake. I am not little. In fact,
I believe I am more than usually tall for my age. (*Algernon is rather
taken aback*) But I am your cousin Cecily. You, I see from your
card, are Uncle Jack's brother, my cousin Ernest, my wicked   115
cousin Ernest.

ALGERNON Oh! I am not really wicked at all, cousin Cecily. You
mustn't think that I am wicked.

CECILY If you are not, then you have certainly been deceiving us all
in a very inexcusable manner. I hope you have not been leading a   120
double life, pretending to be wicked and being really good all the
time. That would be hypocrisy.

ALGERNON (*looks at her in amazement*) Oh! Of course I have been
rather reckless.

CECILY I am glad to hear it.°   125

ALGERNON In fact, now you mention the subject, I have been very
bad in my own small way.

CECILY I don't think you should be so proud of that, though I am
sure it must have been very pleasant.

ALGERNON It is much pleasanter being here with you.   130

CECILY I can't understand how you are here at all. Uncle Jack won't
be back till Monday afternoon.

ALGERNON That is a great disappointment.° I am obliged to go up
by the first train on Monday morning. I have a business appointment that I am anxious. . . . to miss!   135

CECILY Couldn't you miss it anywhere but in London?

ALGERNON No: the appointment is in London.

CECILY Well, I know, of course, how important it is not to keep a
business engagement, if one wants to retain any sense of the beauty
of life, but still I think you had better wait till Uncle Jack arrives.   140
I know he wants to speak to you about your emigrating.

ALGERNON About my what?

CECILY Your emigrating. He has gone up to buy your outfit.

ALGERNON I certainly wouldn't let Jack buy my outfit. He has no
taste in neckties at all.   145

CECILY I don't think you will require neckties. Uncle Jack is sending
you to Australia.

ALGERNON Australia! I'd sooner die.

CECILY Well, he said at dinner on Wednesday night, that you would
have to choose between this world, the next world, and Australia.   150

ALGERNON Oh, well! The accounts I have received of Australia and
the next world are not particularly encouraging. This world is good
enough for me, cousin Cecily.

CECILY Yes, but are you good enough for it?

ALGERNON I'm afraid I'm not that. That is why I want you to   155
reform me. You might make that your mission, if you don't mind,
cousin Cecily.

CECILY I'm afraid I've no time, this afternoon.

ALGERNON Well, would you mind my reforming myself this afternoon?   160

CECILY It is rather Quixotic° of you. But I think you should try.

ALGERNON I will. I feel better already.

CECILY You are looking a little worse.

ALGERNON That is because I am hungry.

CECILY How thoughtless of me. I should have remembered that   165
when one is going to lead an entirely new life, one requires regular
and wholesome meals. Won't you come in?

ALGERNON Thank you. Might I have a buttonhole first? I have never
any appetite unless I have a buttonhole first.

CECILY A Maréchal Niel?° (*Picks up scissors*)   170

ALGERNON No, I'd sooner have a pink rose.

CECILY Why? (*Cuts a flower*)

ALGERNON Because you are like a pink rose, cousin Cecily.

CECILY I don't think it can be right for you to talk to me like that.
Miss Prism never says such things to me.   175

ALGERNON Then Miss Prism is a short-sighted old lady. (*Cecily puts
the rose in his buttonhole*) You are the prettiest girl I ever saw.

CECILY Miss Prism says that all good looks are a snare.

ALGERNON They are a snare that every sensible man would like to
be caught in.   180

CECILY Oh! I don't think I would care to catch a sensible man. I
shouldn't know what to talk to him about.

They pass into the house. Miss Prism and Dr Chasuble return°

MISS PRISM You are too much alone, dear Dr Chasuble. You should
get married. A misanthrope I can understand—a womanthrope,°
never!   185

CHASUBLE (*with a scholar's shudder*) Believe me, I do not deserve so
neologistic° a phrase. The precept as well as the practice of the
Primitive° Church was distinctly against matrimony.

MISS PRISM (*sententiously*) That is obviously the reason why the
Primitive Church has not lasted up to the present day. And you   190
do not seem to realize, dear Doctor, that by persistently remaining

single, a man converts himself into a permanent public temptation.
Men should be more careful; this very celibacy leads weaker vessels
astray.

CHASUBLE But is a man not equally attractive when married?   195

MISS PRISM No married man is ever attractive except to his wife.

CHASUBLE And often, I've been told, not even to her.°

MISS PRISM That depends on the intellectual sympathies of the
woman. Maturity can always be depended on. Ripeness can be
trusted. Young women are green. (*Dr Chasuble starts*)° I spoke   200
horticulturally. My metaphor was drawn from fruits. But where is
Cecily?

CHASUBLE Perhaps she followed us to the schools.

*Enter Jack slowly° from the back of the garden. He is dressed in
the deepest mourning, with crape hatband and black gloves*

MISS PRISM Mr Worthing!

CHASUBLE Mr Worthing?   205

MISS PRISM This is indeed a surprise. We did not look for you till
Monday afternoon.

JACK (*shakes Miss Prism's hand in a tragic manner*) I have returned
sooner than I expected. Dr Chasuble, I hope you are well?

CHASUBLE Dear Mr Worthing, I trust this garb of woe does not   210
betoken some terrible calamity?

JACK My brother.

MISS PRISM More shameful debts and extravagance?

CHASUBLE Still leading his life of pleasure?

JACK (*shaking his head*) Dead!   215

CHASUBLE Your brother Ernest dead?

JACK Quite dead.

MISS PRISM What a lesson for him! I trust he will profit by it.

CHASUBLE Mr Worthing, I offer you my sincere condolence. You
have at least the consolation of knowing that you are always the   220
most generous and forgiving of brothers.

JACK Poor Ernest!° He had many faults, but it is a sad, sad blow.

CHASUBLE Very sad indeed. Were you with him at the end?

JACK No. He died abroad; in Paris, in fact. I had a telegram last night
from the manager of the Grand Hotel.°   225

CHASUBLE Was the cause of death mentioned?

JACK A severe chill, it seems.

MISS PRISM As a man sows, so shall he reap.

CHASUBLE (*raising his hand*) Charity, dear Miss Prism, charity! None
of us are perfect. I myself am peculiarly susceptible to draughts.   230
Will the interment take place here?

277

JACK No. He seems to have expressed a desire to be buried in Paris.

CHASUBLE In Paris! (*Shakes his head*) I fear that hardly points to any
very serious state of mind at the last. You would no doubt wish
me to make some slight allusion to this tragic domestic affliction   235
next Sunday. (*Jack presses his hand convulsively*) My sermon on
the meaning of the manna° in the wilderness can be adapted to
almost any occasion, joyful, or, as in the present case, distressing.
(*All sigh*) I have preached it at harvest celebrations, christenings,
confirmations, on days of humiliation and festal days. The last time   240
I delivered it was in the Cathedral, as a charity sermon on behalf
of the Society for the Prevention of Discontent among the Upper
Orders. The Bishop, who was present, was much struck by some
of the analogies I drew.

JACK Ah! that reminds me, you mentioned christenings I think, Dr   245
Chasuble? I suppose you know how to christen all right? (*Dr
Chasuble looks astounded*) I mean, of course, you are continually
christening, aren't you?

MISS PRISM It is, I regret to say, one of the Rector's most constant
duties in this parish. I have often spoken to the poorer classes on   250
the subject. But they don't seem to know what thrift° is.

CHASUBLE But is there any particular infant in whom you are
interested, Mr Worthing? Your brother was, I believe, unmarried,
was he not?

JACK Oh yes.   255

MISS PRISM (*bitterly*) People who live entirely for pleasure usually are.

JACK But it is not for any child, dear Doctor. I am very fond of
children. No! the fact is, I would like to be christened myself, this
afternoon, if you have nothing better to do.

CHASUBLE But surely, Mr Worthing, you have been christened   260
already?

JACK I don't remember anything about it.

CHASUBLE But have you any grave doubts on the subject?

JACK I certainly intend to have. Of course I don't know if the thing
would bother you in any way, or if you think I am a little too old   265
now.

CHASUBLE Not at all. The sprinkling,° and, indeed, the immersion
of adults is a perfectly canonical practice.

JACK Immersion!

CHASUBLE You need have no apprehensions. Sprinkling is all that is   270
necessary, or indeed I think advisable. Our weather is so changeable. At what hour would you wish the ceremony performed?

JACK Oh, I might trot round about five if that would suit you.

CHASUBLE Perfectly, perfectly! In fact I have two similar ceremonies
to perform at that time. A case of twins that occurred recently in   275
one of the outlying cottages on your own estate. Poor Jenkins the
carter, a most hard-working man.

JACK Oh! I don't see much fun in being christened along with other
babies. It would be childish. Would half-past five do?

CHASUBLE Admirably! Admirably! (*Takes out watch*) And now, dear   280
Mr Worthing, I will not intrude any longer into a house of sorrow.
I would merely beg you not to be too much bowed down by grief.
What seem to us bitter trials are often blessings in disguise.

MISS PRISM This seems to me a blessing of an extremely obvious
kind.   285

>   *Enter Cecily from the house*

CECILY Uncle Jack! Oh, I am pleased to see you back. But what
horrid clothes you have got on. Do go and change them.

MISS PRISM Cecily!

CHASUBLE My child! my child.

>   *Cecily goes towards Jack; he kisses her brow in a melancholy
>   manner*

CECILY What is the matter, Uncle Jack? Do look happy! You look as   290
if you had toothache, and I have got such a surprise for you. Who
do you think is in the dining-room? Your brother!

JACK Who?

CECILY Your brother Ernest. He arrived about half an hour ago.

JACK What nonsense! I haven't got a brother.   295

CECILY Oh, don't say that. However badly he may have behaved to
you in the past he is still your brother. You couldn't be so heartless
as to disown him. I'll tell him to come out. And you will shake
hands with him, won't you, Uncle Jack?

>   *Runs back into the house*

CHASUBLE These are very joyful tidings.   300

MISS PRISM After we had all been resigned to his loss, his sudden
return seems to me peculiarly distressing.

JACK My brother is in the dining-room? I don't know what it all
means. I think it is perfectly absurd.

>   *Enter Algernon and Cecily hand in hand. They come slowly up
>   to Jack*

JACK Good heavens! (*Motions Algernon away*)   305

ALGERNON Brother John, I have come down from town to tell you
that I am very sorry for all the trouble I have given you, and that

I intend to lead a better life in the future. (*Jack glares at him and does not take his hand*)

CECILY Uncle Jack, you are not going to refuse your own brother's hand? 310

JACK Nothing will induce me to take his hand. I think his coming down here disgraceful. He knows perfectly well why.

CECILY Uncle Jack, do be nice. There is some good in everyone. Ernest has just been telling me about his poor invalid friend Mr Bunbury whom he goes to visit so often. And surely there must be 315 much good in one who is kind to an invalid, and leaves the pleasures of London to sit by a bed of pain.

JACK Oh! he has been talking about Bunbury, has he?

CECILY Yes, he has told me all about poor Mr Bunbury, and his terrible state of health. 320

JACK Bunbury! Well, I won't have him talk to you about Bunbury or about anything else. It is enough to drive one perfectly frantic.

ALGERNON Of course I admit that the faults were all on my side. But I must say that I think that Brother John's coldness to me is peculiarly painful. I expected a more enthusiastic welcome, espe- 325 cially considering it is the first time I have come here.

CECILY Uncle Jack,° if you don't shake hands with Ernest I will never forgive you.

JACK Never forgive me?

CECILY Never, never, never! 330

JACK Well, this is the last time I shall ever do it. (*Shakes hands with Algernon and glares*)

CHASUBLE It's pleasant, is it not, to see so perfect a reconciliation? I think we might leave the two brothers together.

MISS PRISM Cecily, you will come with us.

CECILY Certainly, Miss Prism. My little task of reconciliation is 335 over.

CHASUBLE You have done a beautiful action today, dear child.

MISS PRISM We must not be premature in our judgements.

CECILY I feel very happy.°

They all go off except Jack and Algernon

JACK You young scoundrel, Algy, you must get out of this place as 340 soon as possible. I don't allow any Bunburying here.

Enter Merriman

MERRIMAN I have put Mr Ernest's things in the room next to yours, sir. I suppose that is all right?

JACK What?

MERRIMAN Mr Ernest's luggage, sir. I have unpacked it and put it   345
in the room next to your own.

JACK His luggage?

MERRIMAN Yes, sir. Three portmanteaus, a dressing-case,° two
hat-boxes, and a large luncheon-basket.

ALGERNON I am afraid I can't stay more than a week° this time.   350

JACK Merriman, order the dog-cart° at once. Mr Ernest has been
suddenly called back to town.

MERRIMAN Yes, sir.

    Goes back into the house

ALGERNON What a fearful liar you are, Jack. I have not been called
back to town at all.   355

JACK Yes, you have.

ALGERNON I haven't heard anyone call me.

JACK Your duty as a gentleman calls you back.

ALGERNON My duty as a gentleman has never interfered with my
pleasures in the smallest degree.   360

JACK I can quite understand that.

ALGERNON Well, Cecily is a darling.

JACK You are not to talk of Miss Cardew like that. I don't like it.

ALGERNON Well, I don't like your clothes. You look perfectly
ridiculous in them. Why on earth don't you go up and change? It   365
is perfectly childish to be in deep mourning for a man who is
actually staying for a whole week with you in your house as a guest.
I call it grotesque.

JACK You are certainly not staying with me for a whole week as a
guest or anything else. You have got to leave . . . by the four-five   370
train.°

ALGERNON I certainly won't leave you so long as you are in
mourning. It would be most unfriendly. If I were in mourning you
would stay with me, I suppose. I should think it very unkind if
you didn't.   375

JACK Well, will you go if I change my clothes?

ALGERNON Yes, if you are not too long. I never saw anybody take
so long to dress, and with such little result.

JACK Well, at any rate, that is better than being always over-dressed
as you are.   380

ALGERNON If I am occasionally a little over-dressed, I make up for
it by being always immensely over-educated.

JACK Your vanity is ridiculous, your conduct an outrage, and your
presence in my garden utterly absurd. However, you have got to

catch the four-five, and I hope you will have a pleasant journey 385
back to town. This Bunburying, as you call it, has not been a great
success for you.

    Goes into the house

ALGERNON I think it has been a great success. I'm in love with
Cecily, and that is everything.

    Enter Cecily at the back of the garden. She picks up the can and
    begins to water the flowers

But I must see her before I go, and make arrangements for another 390
Bunbury. Ah, there she is.

CECILY Oh, I merely came back to water the roses. I thought you
were with Uncle Jack.

ALGERNON He's gone to order the dog-cart for me.

CECILY Oh, is he going to take you for a nice drive? 395

ALGERNON He's going to send me away.

CECILY Then have we got to part?

ALGERNON I am afraid so. It's a very painful parting.

CECILY It is always painful to part from people whom one has known
for a very brief space of time. The absence of old friends one can 400
endure with equanimity. But even a momentary separation from
anyone to whom one has just been introduced is almost unbearable.

ALGERNON Thank you.

    Enter Merriman

MERRIMAN The dog-cart is at the door, sir. 405

    Algernon looks appealingly° at Cecily

CECILY It can wait, Merriman . . . for . . . five minutes.

MERRIMAN Yes, miss.

    Exit Merriman

ALGERNON I hope, Cecily, I shall not offend you if I state quite
frankly and openly that you seem to me to be in every way the
visible personification of absolute perfection. 410

CECILY I think your frankness does you great credit, Ernest. If you
will allow me, I will copy your remarks into my diary. (*Goes over
to table and begins writing in diary*)

ALGERNON Do you really keep a diary? I'd give anything to look at
it. May I?

CECILY Oh no. (*Puts her hand over it*) You see, it is simply a very 415
young girl's record of her own thoughts and impressions, and
consequently meant for publication. When it appears in volume
form I hope you will order a copy. But pray, Ernest, don't stop. I

delight in taking down from dictation. I have reached 'absolute
perfection.' You can go on. I am quite ready for more.   420
ALGERNON (*somewhat taken aback*) Ahem! Ahem!
CECILY Oh, don't cough, Ernest. When one is dictating one should
speak fluently and not cough. Besides, I don't know how to spell
a cough. (*Writes as Algernon speaks*)
ALGERNON (*speaking very rapidly*) Cecily, ever since I first looked   425
upon your wonderful and incomparable beauty, I have dared to
love you wildly, passionately, devotedly, hopelessly.
CECILY I don't think that you should tell me that you love me wildly,
passionately, devotedly, hopelessly. Hopelessly doesn't seem to
make much sense, does it?   430
ALGERNON Cecily!
    Enter Merriman
MERRIMAN The dog-cart is waiting, sir.
ALGERNON Tell it to come round next week, at the same hour.
MERRIMAN (*looks at Cecily, who makes no sign*) Yes, sir.
    Merriman retires
CECILY Uncle Jack would be very much annoyed if he knew you   435
were staying on till next week, at the same hour.
ALGERNON Oh, I don't care about Jack. I don't care for anybody in
the whole world but you. I love you, Cecily. You will marry me,
won't you?
CECILY You silly boy! Of course. Why, we have been engaged for   440
the last three months.
ALGERNON For the last three months?
CECILY Yes, it will be exactly three months on Thursday.
ALGERNON But how did we become engaged?
CECILY Well, ever since dear Uncle Jack first confessed to us that he   445
had a younger brother who was very wicked and bad, you of course
have formed the chief topic of conversation between myself and
Miss Prism. And of course a man who is much talked about is
always very attractive. One feels there must be something in him
after all. I daresay it was foolish of me, but I fell in love with you,   450
Ernest.
ALGERNON Darling! And when was the engagement actually settled?
CECILY On the 14th of February° last. Worn out by your entire
ignorance of my existence, I determined to end the matter one way   455
or the other, and after a long struggle with myself I accepted you
under this dear old tree here.° The next day I bought this little

ring in your name, and this is the little bangle with the true lovers' knot I promised you always to wear.

ALGERNON Did I give you this? It's very pretty, isn't it? 460

CECILY Yes, you've wonderfully good taste, Ernest. It's the excuse I've always given for your leading such a bad life. And this is the box in which I keep all your dear letters. (*Kneels at table, opens box, and produces letters tied up with blue ribbon*)

ALGERNON My letters! But my own sweet Cecily, I have never written you any letters. 465

CECILY You need hardly remind me of that, Ernest. I remember only too well that I was forced to write your letters for you. I wrote always three times a week, and sometimes oftener.

ALGERNON Oh, do let me read them, Cecily!

CECILY Oh, I couldn't possibly. They would make you far too 470 conceited. (*Replaces box*) The three you wrote me after I had broken off the engagement are so beautiful, and so badly spelled, that even now I can hardly read them without crying a little.

ALGERNON But was our engagement ever broken off?

CECILY Of course it was. On the 22nd of last March. You can see 475 the entry if you like. (*Shows diary*) 'Today I broke off my engagement with Ernest. I feel it is better to do so. The weather still continues charming.'

ALGERNON But why on earth did you break it off? What had I done? I had done nothing at all. Cecily, I am very much hurt indeed to 480 hear you broke it off. Particularly when the weather was so charming.

CECILY It would hardly have been a really serious engagement if it hadn't been broken off at least once. But I forgave you before the week was out. 485

ALGERNON (*crossing to her, and kneeling*) What a perfect angel you are, Cecily.

CECILY You dear romantic boy. (*He kisses her, she puts her fingers through his hair*) I hope your hair curls naturally, does it?

ALGERNON Yes, darling, with a little help from others. 490

CECILY I am so glad.

ALGERNON You'll never break off our engagement again, Cecily?

CECILY I don't think I could break it off now that I have actually met you. Besides, of course, there is the question of your name.

ALGERNON (*nervously*) —Yes, of course. 495

CECILY You must not laugh at me, darling, but it had always been a girlish dream of mine to love someone whose name was Ernest.

(*Algernon rises, Cecily also*) There is something in that name that seems to inspire absolute confidence. I pity any poor married woman whose husband is not called Ernest.   500

ALGERNON But, my dear child, do you mean to say you could not love me if I had some other name?

CECILY But what name?

ALGERNON Oh, any name you like—Algernon—for instance . . .

CECILY But I don't like the name of Algernon.   505

ALGERNON Well, my own dear, sweet, loving little darling, I really can't see why you should object to the name of Algernon. It is not at all a bad name. In fact, it is rather an aristocratic name. Half of the chaps who get into the Bankruptcy Court° are called Algernon. But seriously, Cecily . . . (*moving to her*) if my name was Algy,   510 couldn't you love me?

CECILY (*rising*) I might respect you, Ernest, I might admire your character, but I fear that I should not be able to give you my undivided attention.

ALGERNON Ahem! Cecily! (*Picking up hat*) Your Rector here is, I   515 suppose, thoroughly experienced in the practice of all the rites and ceremonials of the Church?

CECILY Oh, yes. Dr Chasuble is a most learned man. He has never written a single book, so you can imagine how much he knows.   520

ALGERNON I must see him at once on a most important christening—I mean on most important business.

CECILY Oh!

ALGERNON I shan't be away more than half an hour.

CECILY Considering that we have been engaged since February the   525 14th, and that I only met you today for the first time, I think it is rather hard that you should leave me for so long a period as half an hour. Couldn't you make it twenty minutes?

ALGERNON I'll be back in no time.

Kisses her and rushes down the garden

CECILY What an impetuous boy he is! I like his hair so much. I must   530 enter his proposal in my diary.

Enter Merriman

MERRIMAN A Miss Fairfax has just called to see Mr Worthing. On very important business, Miss Fairfax states.

CECILY Isn't Mr Worthing in his library?

MERRIMAN Mr Worthing went over in the direction of the Rectory   535 some time ago.

CECILY Pray ask the lady to come out here; Mr Worthing is sure to
be back soon. And you can bring tea.

MERRIMAN Yes, Miss.

Goes out

CECILY Miss Fairfax! I suppose one of the many good elderly women   540
who are associated with Uncle Jack in some of his philanthropic
work in London. I don't quite like women who are interested in
philanthropic work. I think it is so forward of them.

Enter Merriman

MERRIMAN Miss Fairfax.

Enter Gwendolen.° Exit Merriman

CECILY (*advancing to meet her*) Pray let me introduce myself to you.   545
My name is Cecily Cardew.

GWENDOLEN Cecily Cardew? (*Moving to her and shaking hands*)
What a very sweet name! Something tells me that we are going to
be great friends. I like you already more than I can say. My first
impressions of people are never wrong.   550

CECILY How nice of you to like me so much after we have known
each other such a comparatively short time. Pray sit down.

GWENDOLEN (*still standing up*) I may call you Cecily, may I not?

CECILY With pleasure!

GWENDOLEN And you will always call me Gwendolen, won't you?   555

CECILY If you wish.

GWENDOLEN Then that is all quite settled, is it not?

CECILY I hope so.

A pause. They both sit down together°

GWENDOLEN Perhaps this might be a favourable opportunity for my
mentioning who I am. My father is Lord Bracknell. You have   560
never heard of papa, I suppose?

CECILY I don't think so.

GWENDOLEN Outside the family circle, papa, I am glad to say, is
entirely unknown. I think that is quite as it should be. The home
seems to me to be the proper sphere for the man. And certainly   565
once a man begins to neglect his domestic duties he becomes
painfully effeminate, does he not? And I don't like that. It makes
men so very attractive. Cecily, mamma, whose views on education
are remarkably strict, has brought me up to be extremely short-
sighted; it is part of her system; so do you mind my looking at you   570
through my glasses?

CECILY Oh! not at all, Gwendolen. I am very fond of being looked
at.

GWENDOLEN (*after examining Cecily carefully through a lorgnette*)
You are here on a short visit I suppose.   575

CECILY Oh no! I live here.

GWENDOLEN (*severely*) Really? Your mother, no doubt, or some
female relative of advanced years, resides here also?

CECILY Oh no! I have no mother, nor, in fact, any relations.

GWENDOLEN Indeed?   580

CECILY My dear guardian, with the assistance of Miss Prism, has the
arduous task of looking after me.

GWENDOLEN Your guardian?

CECILY Yes, I am Mr Worthing's ward.

GWENDOLEN Oh! It is strange he never mentioned to me that he had   585
a ward. How secretive of him! He grows more interesting hourly.
I am not sure, however, that the news inspires me with feelings of
unmixed delight. (*Rising and going to her*) I am very fond of you,
Cecily; I have liked you ever since I met you! But I am bound to
state that now that I know that you are Mr Worthing's ward, I   590
cannot help expressing a wish you were—well just a little older
than you seem to be—and not quite so very alluring in appearance.
In fact, if I may speak candidly—

CECILY Pray do! I think that whenever one has anything unpleasant
to say, one should always be quite candid.   595

GWENDOLEN Well, to speak with perfect candour, Cecily, I wish
that you were fully forty-two, and more than usually plain for your
age. Ernest has a strong upright nature. He is the very soul of truth
and honour. Disloyalty would be as impossible to him as deception. But even men of the noblest possible moral character are   600
extremely susceptible to the influence of the physical charms of
others. Modern, no less than Ancient History, supplies us with
many most painful examples of what I refer to. If it were not so,
indeed, History would be quite unreadable.

CECILY I beg your pardon, Gwendolen, did you say Ernest?   605

GWENDOLEN Yes.

CECILY Oh, but it is not Mr Ernest Worthing who is my guardian.
It is his brother—his elder brother.

GWENDOLEN (*sitting down again*) Ernest never mentioned to me that
he had a brother.   610

CECILY I am sorry to say they have not been on good terms for a
long time.

GWENDOLEN Ah! that accounts for it. And now that I think of it I
have never heard any man mention his brother. The subject seems

distasteful to most men. Cecily, you have lifted a load from my   615
mind. I was growing almost anxious. It would have been terrible
if any cloud had come across a friendship like ours, would it not?
Of course you are quite, quite sure that it is not Mr Ernest
Worthing who is your guardian?

CECILY Quite sure. (*A pause*) In fact, I am going to be his.   620

GWENDOLEN (*enquiringly*) I beg your pardon?

CECILY (*rather shy and confidingly*) Dearest Gwendolen, there is no
reason why I should make a secret of it to you. Our little county
newspaper is sure to chronicle the fact next week. Mr Ernest
Worthing and I are engaged to be married.   625

GWENDOLEN (*quite politely, rising*) My darling Cecily, I think there
must be some slight error. Mr Ernest Worthing is engaged to me.
The announcement will appear in the *Morning Post*° on Saturday
at the latest.

CECILY (*very politely, rising*) I am afraid you must be under some   630
misconception. Ernest proposed to me exactly ten minutes ago.
(*Shows diary*)

GWENDOLEN (*examines diary through her lorgnette carefully*) It is very
curious, for he asked me to be his wife yesterday afternoon at 5.30.
If you would care to verify the incident, pray do so. (*Produces diary
of her own*) I never travel without my diary. One should always   635
have something sensational to read in the train. I am so sorry, dear
Cecily, if it is any disappointment to you, but I am afraid *I* have
the prior claim.

CECILY It would distress me more than I can tell you, dear Gwendolen, if it caused you any mental or physical anguish, but I feel   640
bound to point out that since Ernest proposed to you he clearly
has changed his mind.

GWENDOLEN (*meditatively*) If the poor fellow has been entrapped
into any foolish promise I shall consider it my duty to rescue him
at once, and with a firm hand.   645

CECILY (*thoughtfully and sadly*) Whatever unfortunate entanglement
my dear boy may have got into, I will never reproach him with it
after we are married.

GWENDOLEN Do you allude to me, Miss Cardew, as an entanglement? You are presumptuous. On an occasion of this kind it   650
becomes more than a moral duty to speak one's mind. It becomes
a pleasure.

CECILY Do you suggest, Miss Fairfax, that I entrapped Ernest into
an engagement? How dare you? This is no time for wearing the
shallow mask of manners. When I see a spade I call it a spade.   655

GWENDOLEN (*satirically*) I am glad to say that I have never seen a
spade. It is obvious that our social spheres have been widely
different.

> *Enter Merriman,° followed by the footman. He carries a salver,
> table cloth, and plate stand. Cecily is about to retort. The
> presence of the servants exercises a restraining influence, under
> which both girls chafe*

MERRIMAN Shall I lay tea here as usual, Miss?

CECILY (*sternly, in a calm voice*) Yes, as usual.   660

> *Merriman begins to clear table and lay cloth. A long pause.
> Cecily and Gwendolen glare at each other.*

GWENDOLEN Are there many interesting walks in the vicinity, Miss
Cardew?

CECILY Oh! yes! a great many. From the top of one of the hills quite
close one can see five counties.

GWENDOLEN Five counties! I don't think I should like that; I hate   665
crowds.

CECILY (*sweetly*) I suppose that is why you live in town?

> *Gwendolen bites her lip, and beats her foot nervously with her
> parasol*

GWENDOLEN (*looking around*) Quite a well-kept garden this is, Miss
Cardew.

CECILY So glad you like it, Miss Fairfax.   670

GWENDOLEN I had no idea there were any flowers in the country.

CECILY Oh, flowers are as common here, Miss Fairfax, as people are
in London.°

GWENDOLEN Personally I cannot understand how anybody manages
to exist in the country, if anybody who is anybody does. The   675
country always bores me to death.

CECILY Ah! This is what the newspapers call agricultural depression,
is it not? I believe the aristocracy are suffering very much from it
just at present. It is almost an epidemic amongst them, I have been
told. May I offer you some tea, Miss Fairfax?   680

GWENDOLEN (*with elaborate politeness*) Thank you. (*Aside*) Detestable girl! But I require tea!

CECILY (*sweetly*) Sugar?

GWENDOLEN (*superciliously*) No, thank you. Sugar is not fashionable
any more. (*Cecily looks angrily at her, takes up the tongs and puts* 685
four lumps of sugar into the cup)

CECILY (*severely*) Cake or bread and butter?

GWENDOLEN (*in a bored manner*) Bread and butter, please. Cake is
rarely seen at the best houses nowadays.

CECILY (*cuts a very large slice of cake and puts it on the tray*) Hand
that to Miss Fairfax.   690

> *Merriman does so, and goes out with footman. Gwendolen drinks*
> *the tea and makes a grimace. Puts down cup at once, reaches out*
> *her hand to the bread and butter, looks at it, and finds it is cake.*
> *Rises in indignation*

GWENDOLEN You have filled my tea° with lumps of sugar, and
though I asked most distinctly for bread and butter, you have given
me cake. I am known for the gentleness of my disposition, and the
extraordinary sweetness of my nature, but I warn you, Miss
Cardew, you may go too far.   695

CECILY (*rising*) To save my poor, innocent, trusting boy from the
machinations of any other girl there are no lengths to which I
would not go.

GWENDOLEN From the moment I saw you I distrusted you. I felt
that you were false and deceitful. I am never deceived in such   700
matters. My first impressions of people are invariably right.

CECILY It seems to me, Miss Fairfax, that I am trespassing on your
valuable time. No doubt you have many other calls of a similar
character to make in the neighbourhood.

> *Enter Jack°*

GWENDOLEN (*catching sight of him*) Ernest! My own Ernest!   705

JACK Gwendolen! Darling! (*Offers to kiss her*)

GWENDOLEN (*drawing back*) A moment! May I ask if you are
engaged to be married to this young lady? (*Points to Cecily*)

JACK (*laughing*) To dear little Cecily! Of course not! What could have
put such an idea into your pretty little head?   710

GWENDOLEN Thank you. You may! (*Offers her cheek*)

CECILY (*very sweetly*) I knew there must be some misunderstanding,
Miss Fairfax. The gentleman whose arm is at present round your
waist is my dear guardian, Mr John Worthing.

GWENDOLEN I beg your pardon?   715

CECILY This is Uncle Jack.

GWENDOLEN (*receding*) Jack! Oh!

> *Enter Algernon*

CECILY Here is Ernest.

ALGERNON (*goes straight over to Cecily without noticing anyone else*)
My own love! (*Offers to kiss her*)   720

CECILY (*drawing back*) A moment, Ernest! May I ask you—are you
engaged to be married to this young lady?

ALGERNON (*looking round*) To what young lady? Good heavens!
Gwendolen!

CECILY Yes! to good heavens, Gwendolen, I mean to Gwendolen.   725

ALGERNON (*laughing*) Of course not! What could have put such an idea into your pretty little head?

CECILY Thank you. (*Presenting her cheek to be kissed*)   You may. (*Algernon kisses her*)

GWENDOLEN I felt there was some slight error, Miss Cardew. The gentleman who is now embracing you is my cousin, Mr Algernon   730
Moncrieff.

CECILY (*breaking away from Algernon*) Algernon Moncrieff! Oh!°
> *The two girls move towards each other and put their arms round each other's waists as if for protection*

CECILY Are you called Algernon?

ALGERNON I cannot deny it.

CECILY Oh!   735

GWENDOLEN Is your name really John?

JACK (*standing rather proudly*) I could deny it if I liked. I could deny anything if I liked. But my name certainly is John. It has been John for years.

CECILY (*to Gwendolen*) A gross deception has been practised on both   740
of us.

GWENDOLEN My poor wounded Cecily!

CECILY My sweet wronged Gwendolen!

GWENDOLEN (*slowly and seriously*) You will call me sister, will you not?   745
> *They embrace. Jack and Algernon groan and walk up and down*

CECILY (*rather brightly*) There is just one question I would like to be allowed to ask my guardian.

GWENDOLEN An admirable idea! Mr Worthing, there is just one question I would like to be permitted to put to you. Where is your brother Ernest? We are both engaged to be married to your brother   750
Ernest, so it is a matter of some importance to us to know where your brother Ernest is at present.

JACK (*slowly and hesitatingly*) Gwendolen—Cecily—it is very painful for me to be forced to speak the truth. It is the first time in my life that I have ever been reduced to such a painful position, and   755
I am really quite inexperienced in doing anything of the kind. However, I will tell you quite frankly that I have no brother Ernest. I have no brother at all. I never had a brother in my life, and I certainly have not the smallest intention of ever having one in the future.   760

CECILY (*surprised*) No brother at all?

JACK (*cheerily*) None!

GWENDOLEN (*severely*) Had you never a brother of any kind?

JACK (*pleasantly*) Never. Not even of any kind.

GWENDOLEN I am afraid it is quite clear, Cecily, that neither of us   765
is engaged to be married to anyone.

CECILY It is not a very pleasant position for a young girl suddenly
to find herself in. Is it?

GWENDOLEN Let us go into the house. They will hardly venture to
come after us there.   770

CECILY No, men are so cowardly, aren't they?

They retire into the house° with scornful looks

JACK This ghastly state of things is what you call Bunburying, I
suppose?

ALGERNON Yes, and a perfectly wonderful Bunbury it is. The most
wonderful Bunbury I have ever had in my life.   775

JACK Well, you've no right whatsoever to Bunbury here.

ALGERNON That is absurd. One has a right to Bunbury anywhere
one chooses. Every serious Bunburyist knows that.

JACK Serious Bunburyist! Good heavens!

ALGERNON Well, one must be serious about something, if one wants   780
to have any amusement in life. I happen to be serious about
Bunburying. What on earth you are serious about I haven't got the
remotest idea. About everything, I should fancy. You have such an
absolutely trivial nature.

JACK Well, the only small satisfaction I have in the whole of this   785
wretched business is that your friend Bunbury is quite exploded.
You won't be able to run down to the country quite so often as
you used to do, dear Algy. And a very good thing too.

ALGERNON Your brother is a little off colour, isn't he, dear Jack?
You won't be able to disappear to London quite so frequently as   790
your wicked custom was. And not a bad thing either.

JACK As for your conduct towards Miss Cardew, I must say that your
taking in a sweet, simple, innocent girl like that is quite inexcusable. To say nothing of the fact that she is my ward.

ALGERNON I can see no possible defence at all for your deceiving a   795
brilliant, clever, thoroughly experienced young lady like Miss
Fairfax. To say nothing of the fact that she is my cousin.

JACK I wanted to be engaged to Gwendolen, that is all. I love her.

ALGERNON Well, I simply wanted to be engaged to Cecily. I adore
her.   800

JACK There is certainly no chance of your marrying Miss Cardew.

ALGERNON I don't think there is much likelihood, Jack, of you and
Miss Fairfax being united.

JACK Well, that is no business of yours.

ALGERNON If it was my business, I wouldn't talk about it. (*Begins to* 805
eat muffins) It is very vulgar to talk about one's business. Only
people like stockbrokers do that, and then merely at dinner parties.

JACK How you can sit there, calmly eating muffins when we are in
this horrible trouble, I can't make out. You seem to me to be
perfectly heartless. 810

ALGERNON Well, I can't eat muffins in an agitated manner. The
butter would probably get on my cuffs. One should always eat
muffins quite calmly. It is the only way to eat them.

JACK I say it's perfectly heartless your eating muffins at all, under
the circumstances. 815

ALGERNON When I am in trouble, eating is the only thing that
consoles me. Indeed, when I am in really great trouble, as anyone
who knows me intimately will tell you, I refuse everything except
food and drink. At the present moment I am eating muffins
because I am unhappy. Besides, I am particularly fond of muffins. 820
(*Rising*)

JACK (*rising*) Well, there is no reason why you should eat them all in
that greedy way. (*Takes muffins from Algernon*)

ALGERNON (*offering tea-cake*) I wish you would have tea-cake instead. I don't like tea-cake.

JACK Good heavens! I suppose a man may eat his own muffins in his 825
own garden.

ALGERNON But you have just said it was perfectly heartless to eat
muffins.

JACK I said it was perfectly heartless of you, under the circumstances.
That is a very different thing. 830

ALGERNON That may be. But the muffins are the same. (*He seizes
the muffin-dish from Jack*)

JACK Algy, I wish to goodness you would go.

ALGERNON You can't possibly ask me to go without having some
dinner. It's absurd. I never go without my dinner. No one ever
does, except vegetarians and people like that. Besides I have just 835
made arrangements with Dr Chasuble to be christened at a quarter
to six under the name of Ernest.

JACK My dear fellow, the sooner you give up that nonsense the
better. I made arrangements this morning° with Dr Chasuble to
be christened myself at 5.30, and I naturally will take the name of 840
Ernest. Gwendolen would wish it. We cannot both be christened
Ernest. It's absurd. Besides, I have a perfect right to be christened if I like. There is no evidence at all that I have ever been

christened by anybody. I should think it extremely probable I
never was, and so does Dr Chasuble. It is entirely different in your   845
case. You have been christened already.

ALGERNON   Yes, but I have not been christened for years.

JACK   Yes, but you have been christened. That is the important thing.

ALGERNON   Quite so. So I know my constitution can stand it. If you
are not quite sure about your ever having been christened, I must   850
say I think it rather dangerous your venturing on it now. It might
make you very unwell. You can hardly have forgotten that
someone very closely connected with you was very nearly carried
off this week in Paris by a severe chill.

JACK   Yes, but you said yourself that a severe chill was not hereditary.   855

ALGERNON   It usen't to be, I know—but I daresay it is now. Science
is always making wonderful improvements in things.

JACK (*picking up the muffin-dish*) Oh, that is nonsense; you are always
talking nonsense.

ALGERNON   Jack, you are at the muffins again! I wish you wouldn't.   860
There are only two left. (*Takes them*) I told you I was particularly
fond of muffins.

JACK   But I hate tea-cake.

ALGERNON   Why on earth then do you allow tea-cake to be served
up for your guests? What ideas you have of hospitality!   865

JACK   Algernon! I have already told you to go. I don't want you here.
Why don't you go!

ALGERNON   I haven't quite finished my tea yet! and there is still one
muffin left.

> *Jack groans, and sinks into a chair. Algernon still continues
> eating*

ACT DROP

Third Act

*Scene: Morning-room at the Manor House. Gwendolen and
Cecily are at the window, looking out into the garden.*

GWENDOLEN The fact that they did not follow us at once into the
house, as anyone else would have done, seems to me to show that
they have some sense of shame left.

CECILY They have been eating muffins. That looks like repentance.
[*A pause*]

GWENDOLEN They don't seem to notice us at all. Couldn't you 5
cough?

CECILY But I haven't got a cough.

GWENDOLEN They're looking at us. What effrontery!

CECILY They're approaching. That's very forward of them.

GWENDOLEN Let us preserve a dignified silence. 10

CECILY Certainly. It's the only thing to do now.
*Enter Jack followed by Algernon. They whistle some dreadful
popular air° from a British Opera*

GWENDOLEN This dignified silence seems to produce an unpleasant
effect.

CECILY A most distasteful one.

GWENDOLEN But we will not be the first to speak. 15

CECILY Certainly not.

GWENDOLEN Mr Worthing, I have something very particular to ask
you. Much depends on your reply.

CECILY Gwendolen, your common sense is invaluable. Mr Moncrieff, kindly answer me the following question. Why did you 20
pretend to be my guardian's brother?

ALGERNON In order that I might have an opportunity of meeting you.

CECILY (*to Gwendolen*) That certainly seems a satisfactory explanation, does it not?

GWENDOLEN Yes, dear, if you can believe him. 25

CECILY I don't. But that does not affect the wonderful beauty of his
answer.

GWENDOLEN True. In matters of grave importance, style, not
sincerity, is the vital thing. Mr Worthing, what explanation can
you offer to me for pretending to have a brother? Was it in order 30
that you might have an opportunity of coming up to town to see
me as often as possible?

JACK Can you doubt it, Miss Fairfax?°

GWENDOLEN I have the gravest doubts upon the subject. But I intend to crush them. This is not the moment for German scepticism. (*Moving to Cecily*) Their explanations appear to be quite satisfactory, especially Mr Worthing's. That seems to me to have the stamp of truth upon it.

CECILY I am more than content with what Mr Moncrieff said. His voice alone inspires one with absolute credulity.

GWENDOLEN Then you think we should forgive them?

CECILY Yes. I mean no.

GWENDOLEN True! I had forgotten. There are principles at stake that one cannot surrender. Which of us should tell them? The task is not a pleasant one.

CECILY Could we not both speak at the same time?

GWENDOLEN An excellent idea! I nearly always speak at the same time as other people. Will you take the time from me?

CECILY Certainly. (*Gwendolen beats time with uplifted finger*)

GWENDOLEN and CECILY (*speaking together*)° Your Christian names are still an insuperable barrier. That is all!

JACK and ALGERNON (*speaking together*) Our Christian names! Is that all? But we are going to be christened this afternoon.

GWENDOLEN (*to Jack*) For my sake you are prepared to do this terrible thing?

JACK I am.

CECILY (*to Algernon*) To please me you are ready to face this fearful ordeal?

ALGERNON I am!

GWENDOLEN How absurd to talk of the equality of the sexes! Where questions of self-sacrifice are concerned, men are infinitely beyond us.

JACK We are! (*Clasps hands with Algernon*)

CECILY They have moments of physical courage of which we women know absolutely nothing.

GWENDOLEN (*to Jack*) Darling!

ALGERNON (*to Cecily*) Darling! (*They fall into each other's arms*)
      Enter Merriman. When he enters he coughs loudly, seeing the situation

MERRIMAN Ahem! Ahem! Lady Bracknell.

JACK Good heavens!
      Enter Lady Bracknell. The couples separate, in alarm. Exit Merriman

LADY BRACKNELL Gwendolen! What does this mean?   70

GWENDOLEN Merely that I am engaged to be married to Mr Worthing, mamma.

LADY BRACKNELL Come here. Sit down. Sit down immediately. Hesitation of any kind is a sign of mental decay in the young, of physical weakness in the old. (*Turns to Jack*) Apprised, sir, of my   75
daughter's sudden flight by her trusty maid, whose confidence I purchased by means of a small coin, I followed her at once by a luggage train.° Her unhappy father is, I am glad to say, under the impression that she is attending a more than usually lengthy lecture by the University Extension Scheme on the Influence of a   80
permanent income on Thought. I do not propose to undeceive him. Indeed I have never undeceived him on any question. I would consider it wrong. But of course, you will clearly understand that all communication between yourself and my daughter must cease immediately from this moment. On this point, as indeed on all   85
points, I am firm.

JACK I am engaged to be married to Gwendolen, Lady Bracknell!

LADY BRACKNELL You are nothing of the kind, sir. And now as regards Algernon! . . . Algernon!

ALGERNON Yes, Aunt Augusta.   90

LADY BRACKNELL May I ask if it is in this house that your invalid friend Mr Bunbury resides?

ALGERNON (*stammering*) Oh! No! Bunbury doesn't live here. Bunbury is somewhere else at present. In fact, Bunbury is dead.

LADY BRACKNELL Dead! When did Mr Bunbury die? His death   95
must have been extremely sudden.

ALGERNON (*airily*) Oh! I killed Bunbury this afternoon. I mean poor Bunbury died this afternoon.

LADY BRACKNELL What did he die of?

ALGERNON Bunbury? Oh, he was quite exploded.   100

LADY BRACKNELL Exploded! Was he the victim of a revolutionary outrage? I was not aware that Mr Bunbury was interested in social legislation. If so, he is well punished for his morbidity.

ALGERNON My dear Aunt Augusta, I mean he was found out! The doctors found out that Bunbury could not live, that is what I   105
mean—so Bunbury died.

LADY BRACKNELL He seems to have had great confidence in the opinion of his physicians. I am glad, however, that he made up his mind at the last to some definite course of action, and acted under proper medical advice. And now that we have finally got rid of this   110

Mr Bunbury, may I ask, Mr Worthing, who is that young person whose hand my nephew Algernon is now holding in what seems to me a peculiarly unnecessary manner?

JACK That lady is Miss Cecily Cardew, my ward. (*Lady Bracknell bows coldly to Cecily*) 115

ALGERNON I am engaged to be married to Cecily, Aunt Augusta.

LADY BRACKNELL I beg your pardon?

CECILY Mr Moncrieff and I are engaged to be married, Lady Bracknell.

LADY BRACKNELL (*with a shiver, crossing to the sofa and sitting down*) 120
I do not know whether there is anything peculiarly exciting in the air of this particular part of Hertfordshire, but the number of engagements that go on seems to me considerably above the proper average that statistics have laid down for our guidance. I think some preliminary enquiry on my part would not be out of place. 125
Mr Worthing, is Miss Cardew at all connected with any of the larger railway stations in London? I merely desire information. Until yesterday I had no idea that there were any families or persons whose origin was a Terminus. (*Jack looks perfectly furious, but restrains himself*)

JACK (*in a clear, cold voice*) Miss Cardew is the granddaughter of the 130
late Mr Thomas Cardew of 149 Belgrave Square, S.W.; Gervase Park, Dorking, Surrey; and the Sporran, Fifeshire, N.B.°

LADY BRACKNELL That sounds not unsatisfactory. Three addresses always inspire confidence, even in tradesmen. But what proof have I of their authenticity? 135

JACK I have carefully preserved the Court Guides of the period. They are open to your inspection, Lady Bracknell.

LADY BRACKNELL (*grimly*) I have known strange errors in that publication.

JACK Miss Cardew's family solicitors are Messrs Markby, Markby, 140
and Markby.

LADY BRACKNELL Markby, Markby, and Markby? A firm of the very highest position in their profession. Indeed I am told that one of the Mr Markbys is occasionally to be seen at dinner parties. So far I am satisfied. 145

JACK (*very irritably*) How extremely kind of you, Lady Bracknell! I have also in my possession, you will be pleased to hear, certificates of Miss Cardew's birth, baptism, whooping cough, registration, vaccination, confirmation, and the measles; both the German and the English variety. 150

LADY BRACKNELL Ah! A life crowded with incident, I see; though perhaps somewhat too exciting for a young girl. I am not myself in favour of premature experiences. (*Rises, looks at her watch*) Gwendolen! the time approaches for our departure. We have not a moment to lose. As a matter of form, Mr Worthing, I had better ask you if Miss Cardew has any little fortune?

JACK Oh! about a hundred and thirty thousand pounds in the Funds.° That is all. Good-bye, Lady Bracknell. So pleased to have seen you.

LADY BRACKNELL (*sitting down again*) A moment, Mr Worthing. A hundred and thirty thousand pounds! And in the Funds! Miss Cardew seems to me a most attractive young lady, now that I look at her. Few girls of the present day have any really solid qualities, any of the qualities that last, and improve with time. We live, I regret to say, in an age of surfaces. (*To Cecily*) Come over here, dear. (*Cecily goes across*) Pretty child! your dress is sadly simple, and your hair seems almost as Nature might have left it. But we can soon alter all that. A thoroughly experienced French maid produces a really marvellous result in a very brief space of time. I remember recommending one to young Lady Lancing,° and after three months her own husband did not know her.

JACK And after six months nobody knew her.

LADY BRACKNELL (*glares at Jack for a few moments. Then bends, with a practised smile, to Cecily*) Kindly turn round, sweet child. (*Cecily turns completely round*) No, the side view is what I want. (*Cecily presents her profile*) Yes, quite as I expected. There are distinct social possibilities in your profile. The two weak points in our age are its want of principle and its want of profile. The chin a little higher, dear. Style largely depends on the way the chin is worn. They are worn very high,° just at present, Algernon!

ALGERNON Yes, Aunt Augusta!

LADY BRACKNELL There are distinct social possibilities in Miss Cardew's profile.

ALGERNON Cecily is the sweetest, dearest, prettiest girl in the whole world. And I don't care twopence about social possibilities.

LADY BRACKNELL Never speak disrespectfully of Society, Algernon. Only people who can't get into it do that. (*To Cecily*) Dear child, of course you know that Algernon has nothing but his debts to depend upon. But I do not approve of mercenary marriages. When I married Lord Bracknell I had no fortune of any kind. But I never

dreamed for a moment of allowing that to stand in my way. Well,
I suppose I must give my consent.

ALGERNON Thank you, Aunt Augusta.

LADY BRACKNELL Cecily, you may kiss me!   195

CECILY (*kisses her*) Thank you, Lady Bracknell.

LADY BRACKNELL You may also address me as Aunt Augusta for
the future.

CECILY Thank you, Aunt Augusta.

LADY BRACKNELL The marriage, I think, had better take place quite   200
soon.

ALGERNON Thank you, Aunt Augusta.

CECILY Thank you, Aunt Augusta.

LADY BRACKNELL To speak frankly, I am not in favour of long
engagements. They give people the opportunity of finding out each   205
other's character before marriage, which I think is never advisable.

JACK I beg your pardon for interrupting you, Lady Bracknell, but
this engagement is quite out of the question. I am Miss Cardew's
guardian, and she cannot marry without my consent until she
comes of age. That consent I absolutely decline to give.   210

LADY BRACKNELL Upon what grounds may I ask? Algernon is an
extremely, I may almost say an ostentatiously, eligible young man.
He has nothing, but he looks everything. What more can one
desire?

JACK It pains me very much to have to speak frankly to you, Lady   215
Bracknell, about your nephew, but the fact is that I do not approve
at all of his moral character. I suspect him of being untruthful.

Algernon and Cecily look at him in indignant amazement

LADY BRACKNELL Untruthful! My nephew Algernon? Impossible!
He is an Oxonian.°

JACK I fear there can be no possible doubt about the matter. This   220
afternoon during my temporary absence in London on an important question of romance, he obtained admission to my house by
means of the false pretence of being my brother. Under an
assumed name he drank, I've just been informed by my butler, an
entire pint bottle of my Perrier-Jouet, Brut, '89;° a wine I was   225
specially reserving for myself. Continuing his disgraceful deception, he succeeded in the course of the afternoon in alienating the
affections of my only ward. He subsequently stayed to tea, and
devoured every single muffin. And what makes his conduct all the
more heartless is, that he was perfectly well aware from the first   230
that I have no brother, that I never had a brother, and that I don't

intend to have a brother, not even of any kind. I distinctly told him so myself yesterday afternoon.

LADY BRACKNELL Ahem! Mr Worthing, after careful consideration I have decided entirely to overlook my nephew's conduct to you.   235

JACK That is very generous of you, Lady Bracknell. My own decision, however, is unalterable. I decline to give my consent.

LADY BRACKNELL (*to Cecily*) Come here, sweet child. (*Cecily goes over*) How old are you, dear?

CECILY Well, I am really only eighteen, but I always admit to twenty   240
when I go to evening parties.

LADY BRACKNELL You are perfectly right in making some slight alteration. Indeed, no woman should ever be quite accurate about her age. It looks so calculating. . . . (*In a meditative manner*) Eighteen, but admitting to twenty at evening parties. Well, it will   245
not be very long before you are of age and free from the restraints of tutelage. So I don't think your guardian's consent is, after all, a matter of any importance.

JACK Pray excuse me, Lady Bracknell, for interrupting you again, but it is only fair to tell you that according to the terms of her   250
grandfather's will Miss Cardew does not come legally of age till she is thirty-five.°

LADY BRACKNELL That does not seem to me to be a grave objection. Thirty-five is a very attractive age. London society is full of women of the very highest birth who have, of their own free   255
choice, remained thirty-five for years. Lady Dumbleton is an instance in point. To my own knowledge she has been thirty-five ever since she arrived at the age of forty, which was many years ago now. I see no reason why our dear Cecily should not be even still more attractive at the age you mention than she is at present.   260
There will be a large accumulation of property.

CECILY Algy, could you wait for me till I was thirty-five?

ALGERNON Of course I could, Cecily. You know I could.

CECILY Yes, I felt it instinctively, but I couldn't wait all that time. I hate waiting even five minutes for anybody. It always makes me   265
rather cross. I am not punctual myself, I know, but I do like punctuality in others, and waiting, even to be married, is quite out of the question.

ALGERNON Then what is to be done, Cecily?

CECILY I don't know, Mr Moncrieff.°   270

LADY BRACKNELL My dear Mr Worthing, as Miss Cardew states positively that she cannot wait till she is thirty-five—a remark

which I am bound to say seems to me to show a somewhat
impatient nature—I would beg of you to reconsider your decision.

JACK But my dear Lady Bracknell, the matter is entirely in your own   275
hands. The moment you consent to my marriage with Gwendolen,
I will most gladly allow your nephew to form an alliance with my
ward.

LADY BRACKNELL (*rising and drawing herself up*) You must be quite
aware that what you propose is out of the question.   280

JACK Then a passionate celibacy° is all that any of us can look
forward to.

LADY BRACKNELL That is not the destiny I propose for Gwendolen.
Algernon, of course, can choose for himself. (*Pulls out her watch*)
Come, dear (*Gwendolen rises*), we have already missed five, if not   285
six, trains. To miss any more might expose us to comment on the
platform.

Enter Dr Chasuble

CHASUBLE Everything is quite ready for the christenings.

LADY BRACKNELL The christenings, sir! Is not that somewhat
premature?   290

CHASUBLE (*looking rather puzzled, and pointing to Jack and Algernon*)
Both these gentlemen have expressed a desire for immediate
baptism.

LADY BRACKNELL At their age? The idea is grotesque and irreligious! Algernon, I forbid you to be baptized. I will not hear of   295
such excesses. Lord Bracknell would be highly displeased if he
learned that that was the way in which you wasted your time and
money.

CHASUBLE Am I to understand then that there are to be no
christenings at all this afternoon?   300

JACK I don't think that, as things are now, it would be of much
practical value to either of us, Dr Chasuble.

CHASUBLE I am grieved to hear such sentiments from you, Mr
Worthing. They savour of the heretical views of the Anabap-
tists,° views that I have completely refuted in four of my unpub-   305
lished sermons. However, as your present mood seems to be one
peculiarly secular, I will return to the church at once. Indeed, I
have just been informed by the pew-opener° that for the last hour
and a half Miss Prism has been waiting for me in the vestry.

LADY BRACKNELL (*starting*) Miss Prism! Did I hear you mention a   310
Miss Prism?

CHASUBLE Yes, Lady Bracknell. I am on my way to join her.

LADY BRACKNELL Pray allow me to detain you for a moment. This matter may prove to be one of vital importance to Lord Bracknell and myself. Is this Miss Prism a female of repellent aspect, 315 remotely connected with education?

CHASUBLE (*somewhat indignantly*) She is the most cultivated of ladies, and the very picture of respectability.

LADY BRACKNELL It is obviously the same person.° May I ask what position she holds in your household? 320

CHASUBLE (*severely*) I am a celibate,° madam.

JACK (*interposing*) Miss Prism, Lady Bracknell, has been for the last three years Miss Cardew's esteemed governess and valued companion.

LADY BRACKNELL In spite of what I hear of her, I must see her at 325 once. Let her be sent for.

CHASUBLE (*looking off*) She approaches; she is nigh.

> *Enter Miss Prism hurriedly*

MISS PRISM I was told you expected me in the vestry, dear Canon. I have been waiting for you there for an hour and three quarters. (*Catches sight of Lady Bracknell who has fixed her with a stony glare. Miss Prism grows pale and quails. She looks anxiously round as if desirous to escape*)

LADY BRACKNELL (*in a severe, judicial voice*). Prism! (*Miss Prism bows* 330 *her head in shame*) Come here, Prism! (*Miss Prism approaches in a humble manner*) Prism! Where is that baby? (*General consternation. The Canon starts back in horror. Algernon and Jack pretend to be anxious to shield° Cecily and Gwendolen from hearing the details of a terrible public scandal*) Twenty-eight years ago, Prism, you left Lord Bracknell's house, Number 104, Upper Grosvenor Square,° in charge of a perambulator that contained a baby, of the male sex. 335 You never returned. A few weeks later, through the elaborate investigations of the Metropolitan police, the perambulator was discovered at midnight standing by itself in a remote corner of Bayswater. It contained the manuscript of a three-volume novel of more than usually revolting sentimentality. (*Miss Prism starts in* 340 *involuntary indignation*) But the baby was not there. (*Everyone looks at Miss Prism*) Prism! Where is that baby?

> *A pause.*

MISS PRISM Lady Bracknell, I admit with shame that I do not know. I only wish I did. The plain facts of the case are these. On the morning of the day you mention, a day that is for ever branded on 345 my memory, I prepared as usual to take the baby out in its perambulator. I had also with me a somewhat old, but capacious hand-bag in which I had intended to place the manuscript of a work of fiction that I had written during my few unoccupied hours. In a moment of mental abstraction, for which I can never forgive myself, I deposited the manuscript in the bassinette° and placed the baby in the hand-bag.

JACK (*who had been listening attentively*) But where did you deposit the hand-bag?

MISS PRISM Do not ask me, Mr Worthing.

JACK Miss Prism, this is a matter of no small importance to me. I insist on knowing where you deposited the hand-bag that contained that infant.

MISS PRISM I left it in the cloak-room of one of the larger railway stations in London.

JACK What railway station?

MISS PRISM (*quite crushed*) Victoria. The Brighton line. (*Sinks into a chair*)

JACK I must retire to my room for a moment. Gwendolen, wait here for me.

GWENDOLEN If you are not too long, I will wait here for you all my life.

   Exit Jack in great excitement

CHASUBLE What do you think this means, Lady Bracknell?

LADY BRACKNELL I dare not even suspect, Dr Chasuble. I need hardly tell you that in families of high position strange coincidences are not supposed to occur. They are hardly considered the thing.

   Noises heard overhead as if some one was throwing trunks about.
   Everyone looks up

CECILY Uncle Jack seems strangely agitated.

CHASUBLE Your guardian has a very emotional nature.

LADY BRACKNELL This noise is extremely unpleasant. It sounds as if he was having an argument. I dislike arguments of any kind. They are always vulgar, and often convincing.

CHASUBLE (*looking up*) It has stopped now. (*The noise is redoubled*)

LADY BRACKNELL I wish he would arrive at some conclusion.

GWENDOLEN This suspense is terrible. I hope it will last.

   Enter Jack with a hand-bag of black leather in his hand

JACK (*rushing over to Miss Prism*) Is this the hand-bag, Miss Prism? Examine it carefully before you speak. The happiness of more than one life depends on your answer.

MISS PRISM (*calmly*)° It seems to be mine. Yes, here is the injury it received through the upsetting of a Gower Street° omnibus in

younger and happier days. Here is the stain on the lining caused
by the explosion of a temperance beverage,° an incident that   385
occurred at Leamington.° And here, on the lock, are my initials. I
had forgotten that in an extravagant mood I had had them placed
there. The bag is undoubtedly mine. I am delighted to have it so
unexpectedly restored to me. It has been a great inconvenience
being without it all these years.   390

JACK (*in a pathetic voice*) Miss Prism, more is restored to you than
this hand-bag. I was the baby you placed in it.

MISS PRISM (*amazed*) You?

JACK (*embracing her*). Yes—mother!

MISS PRISM (*recoiling in indignant astonishment*) Mr Worthing! I am   395
unmarried!

JACK Unmarried! I do not deny that is a serious blow. But after all,
who has the right to cast a stone° against one who has suffered?
Cannot repentance wipe out an act of folly? Why should there be
one law for men, and another for women? Mother, I forgive   400
you.° (*Tries to embrace her again*)

MISS PRISM (*still more indignant*) Mr Worthing, there is some error.
(*Pointing to Lady Bracknell*) There is the lady who can tell you
who you really are.

[*A pause*]

JACK Lady Bracknell, I hate to seem inquisitive, but would you   405
kindly inform me who I am?

LADY BRACKNELL I am afraid that the news I have to give you will
not altogether please you. You are the son of my poor sister, Mrs
Moncrieff, and consequently Algernon's elder brother.

JACK Algy's elder brother! Then I have a brother after all. I knew I   410
had a brother! I always said I had a brother! Cecily—how could
you have ever doubted that I had a brother. (*Seizes hold of
Algernon*) Dr Chasuble, my unfortunate brother. Miss Prism, my
unfortunate brother. Gwendolen, my unfortunate brother. Algy,
you young scoundrel, you will have to treat me with more respect   415
in the future. You have never behaved to me like a brother in all
your life.

ALGERNON Well, not till today, old boy, I admit. I did my best,
however, though I was out of practice.

Shakes hands

GWENDOLEN (*to Jack*) My own! But what own are you? What is   420
your Christian name, now that you have become someone else?

JACK Good heavens!—I had quite forgotten that point. Your decision
on the subject of my name is irrevocable, I suppose?

GWENDOLEN I never change, except in my affections.

CECILY What a noble nature you have, Gwendolen!   425

JACK Then the question had better be cleared up at once. Aunt Augusta, a moment. At the time when Miss Prism left me in the hand-bag, had I been christened already?

LADY BRACKNELL Every luxury that money could buy, including christening, had been lavished on you by your fond and doting   430 parents.

JACK Then I was christened! That is settled. Now, what name was I given? Let me know the worst.

LADY BRACKNELL Being the eldest son you were naturally christened after your father.   435

JACK (*irritably*) Yes, but what was my father's Christian name?

LADY BRACKNELL (*meditatively*) I cannot at the present moment recall what the General's Christian name was. But I have no doubt he had one. He was eccentric, I admit. But only in later years. And that was the result of the Indian climate, and marriage, and   440 indigestion, and other things of that kind.

JACK Algy! Can't you recollect what our father's Christian name was?

ALGERNON My dear boy, we were never even on speaking terms. He died before I was a year old.

JACK His name would appear in the Army Lists of the period, I   445 suppose, Aunt Augusta?

LADY BRACKNELL The General was essentially a man of peace, except in his domestic life. But I have no doubt his name would appear in any military directory.

JACK The Army Lists of the last forty years are here. These   450 delightful records should have been my constant study. (*Rushes to bookcase and tears the books out*) M. Generals . . . Mallam, Maxbohm,° Magley—what ghastly names they have—Markby, Migsby, Mobbs, Moncrieff! Lieutenant 1840, Captain, Lieutenant-Colonel, Colonel, General 1869, Christian names, Ernest John.   455 (*Puts book very quietly down and speaks quite calmly*) I always told you, Gwendolen, my name was Ernest, didn't I? Well, it is Ernest after all. I mean it naturally is Ernest.

LADY BRACKNELL Yes, I remember now that the General was called Ernest. I knew I had some particular reason for disliking the name.   460

GWENDOLEN Ernest! My own Ernest! I felt from the first that you could have no other name!

JACK Gwendolen, it is a terrible thing for a man to find out suddenly that all his life he has been speaking nothing but the truth. Can you forgive me?   465

GWENDOLEN I can. For I feel that you are sure to change.

JACK My own one!

CHASUBLE (*to Miss Prism*) Laetitia! (*Embraces her*)

MISS PRISM (*enthusiastically*) Frederick! At last!

ALGERNON Cecily! (*Embraces her*) At last!   470

JACK Gwendolen! (*Embraces her*) At last!

LADY BRACKNELL My nephew, you seem to be displaying signs of
triviality.

JACK On the contrary, Aunt Augusta, I've now realized for the first
time in my life the vital Importance of Being Earnest.   475

TABLEAU°

CURTAIN

APPENDIX

The First Scenario of *The Importance of Being Earnest*

THIS first scenario of *The Importance of Being Earnest* has been lost for many years. It is reproduced from a typescript in the William Andrews Clark Memorial Library, Los Angeles, by permission of the library and of Mr Merlin Holland. It has previously been published in full in the *Times Literary Supplement* (20 Dec. 1991) and in Ian Small, *Oscar Wilde Revalued* (1993); it appears in part in *The Letters of Oscar Wilde*, p. 359.

Wilde wrote it in July 1894, at a time when complete plays and royalties were clearly no longer sufficient to keep his precarious finances buoyant. Alexander, the producer of Wilde's first theatrical success, *Lady Windermere's Fan*, had expressed an interest in a new comedy. Wilde rapidly composed the scenario to secure an advance, before going to Worthing, initially to spend a holiday with his family, but also to work on the play. Having received the advance, he began to backtrack, suggesting the play was too farcical for Alexander and offering him a more suitable and 'strong' outline, which eventually became, in Frank Harris's hands, *Mr and Mrs Daventry*.

The scenario clearly forms the skeleton of the play which became *The Importance of Being Earnest*, though Miss Prism alone of the prototype roles bears the same name as her eventual character. Several names come from previous plays or drafts (as was Wilde's habit in working versions): most notably, Lord Alfred Rufford, whose style inevitably suggests Lord Alfred Douglas, Wilde's constant companion at this period. The 'double life' features strongly, as does the arrest for debts, which survived only in the four-act version. Miss Prism is clearly destined to act as the *dea ex machina*, though Wilde has not worked out how she will 'set all right'. Wilde had as yet not travelled down to Worthing on the Brighton line from Victoria station; and at this point, the emphasis seems to be on Bertram/George Ashton as the guardian, rather than on Jack/Ernest as the orphan or foundling.

16, Tite Street,
My dear Aleck,   S.W.

Thanks for your letter. There really is nothing more to tell you about the comedy beyond what I said already. I mean that the real charm of the play, if it is to have charm, must be in the dialogue. The plot is slight, but, I think, adequate.

Act I. Evening party. 10 p.m.

Lord Alfred Rufford's rooms in Mayfair. Arrives from country Bertram Ashton his friend: a man of 25 or 30 years of age: his great friend.

Rufford asks him about his life. He tells him that he has a ward, etc. very young and pretty. That in the country he has to be serious, etc. that he comes to town to enjoy himself, and has invented a fictitious younger brother of the name of George—to whom all his misdeeds are put down. Rufford is deeply interested about the ward.

Guests arrive: the Duchess of Selby and her daughter, Lady Maud Rufford, with whom the guardian is in love—fin-de-siecle talk, a lot of guests—the guardian proposes to Lady Maud on his knees—enter Duchess—

Lady Maud. 'Mamma, this is no place for you.'

Scene: Duchess enquires for *her son Lord Alfred Rufford*: servant comes in with note to say that Lord Alfred has been suddenly called away to the country. Lady Maud vows eternal fidelity to the guardian whom she only knows under the name of *George* Ashton.

(P.S. The disclosure of the guardian of his double life is occasioned by Lord Alfred saying to him 'You left your handkerchief here the last time you were up' (or cigarette case). The guardian takes it—the Lord A. says but 'why, dear George, is it marked Bertram—who is Bertram Ashton?' Guardian discloses plot.)

Act II. The guardian's home—pretty cottage. Mabel Harbord, his ward, and her governess, Miss Prism, Governess of course dragon of propriety. Talk about the profligate George: maid comes in to say 'Mr. George Ashton'.—governess protests against his admission. Mabel insists. Enter Lord Alfred. Falls in love with ward at once. He is reproached with his bad life, etc. Expressed great repentance. They go to garden.

Enter guardian: Mabel comes in: 'I have a great surprise for you—your brother is here'—Guardian, of course, denies having a brother. Mabel says 'You cannot disown your own brother, whatever he has done.'—and brings in Lord Alfred. Scene: also scene between two men alone. Finally Lord Alfred arrested for debts contracted by guardian: guardian delighted: Mabel, however, makes him forgive his brother and pay up. Guardian looks over bills and scolds Lord Alfred for profligacy.

Miss Prism backs the guardian up. Guardian then orders his brother out of the house. Mabel intercedes, and brother remains. Miss Prism has designs on the guardian—matrimonial—she is 40 at least—she believes he is proposing to her and accepts him—his consternation.

Act III. Mabel and the false brother. He proposes, and is accepted.

When Mabel is alone, Lady Maud, who only knows the guardian under the name of George, arrives alone. She tells Mabel she is engaged to George—scene naturally. Mabel retires: enter George, he kisses his sister naturally. Enter Mabel and sees them. Explanations, of course. Mabel breaks off the match on the ground that there is nothing to reform in George: she only consented to marry him because she thought he was bad and wanted guidance—He promises to be a bad husband—so as to give her an opportunity of making him a better man; she is a little mollified.

Enter guardian: he is reproached also by Lady Maud for his respectable life in the country: a J. P.: a county-councillor: a churchwarden: a philanthropist: a good example. He appeals to his life in London: she is mollified, on condition that he never lives in the country: the country is demoralising: it makes you respectable. 'The simple fare at the Savoy: the quiet life in Piccadilly: the solitude of Mayfair is what you need, etc.'

Enter Duchess in pursuit of her daughter—objects to both matches. Miss Prism, who had in early days been governess to the Duchess, sets it all right, without intending to do so—everything ends happily.

Result   Curtain

Author called.

Cigarette called.

Manager called.

Royalties for a year for author.

Manager credited with writing the play. He consoles himself for the slander with bags of red gold.

Fireworks

Of course this scenario is open to alterations: the third act, after entrance of Duchess, will have to be elaborated: also, the local doctor, or clergyman, must be brought in, in the play, for Prism.

Well, I think an amusing thing with lots of fun and wit might be made. If you think so, too, and care to have the refusal of it—do let me know—and send me £150. If, when the play is finished, you think it too slight—not serious enough—of course you have the £150 back—I want to go away and write it—and it could be ready in October—as I have nothing else to do—and Palmer is anxious to have a play from me for the States 'with no real serious interest'—just a comedy.

In the meanwhile, my dear Aleck, I am so pressed for money, that I don't know what to do. Of course I am extravagant, but a great deal of my worries comes from the fact that I have had for three years to keep up two establishments—my dear Mother's as well as my own—like many Irish ladies she never gets her jointure paid—small though it is—and naturally it falls on me—this is of course *quite private* but for these years I have had two houses on my shoulders—and of course, am extravagant besides—you have always been a good wise friend to me—so think what you can do.

Kind regards to Mrs. Aleck.

Ever,

OSCAR

EXPLANATORY NOTES

Lady Windermere's Fan

Dedication. Robert Bulwer, the first Earl of Lytton (1831–91), was the son of Bulwer Lytton, and a poet and diplomat. Wilde enlisted his support in obtaining a Civil List Pension for Lady Wilde.

The Persons of the Play. There is usually a reason behind Wilde's choice of names. For his more important characters, he tended to choose place-names, often drawn from areas he had stayed in while writing the play: he began *Lady Windermere's Fan* in the Lake District and travelled through Selby, in Yorkshire (the name of the Windermeres' country house), on the same trip. (He also often reused names from previous works—a Lady Windermere featured in *Lord Arthur Savile's Crime*, a source also for the names Jedburgh and Plymdale.) Wilde is precise about rank and forms of address: 'Lady Agatha' is the daughter, and 'Lord Augustus' the younger son, of a duke. He was careful to avoid extant titles, but seldom employed names which would seem blatantly unrealistic. Even his 'comic' names are relatively restrained—the well-bred but intellectually limited Dumby, for example, or the Australian Hopper. In the Clark MS version, there are a number of age indications, including 'middle-aged' (Dumby), 'young—masher'—a dedicated lady-killer—(Graham), and 'young—30' (Lady Plymdale). Lady Jedburgh ('old') is Graham's aunt.

Cast. George Alexander: a fine actor who was trained under Irving at the Lyceum. He became manager of the St James's Theatre in 1891 and actively encouraged new work by English playwrights. It was Wilde's good fortune to have so accomplished and perceptive a man as producer of two of his comedies.

Ben Webster: as Cecil Graham wore a green carnation as a button-hole—as did Graham Robertson and other friends of Wilde in the first-night audience. This dandiacal touch was echoed by Wilde himself when he made his notorious curtain-speech. According to Henry James, the 'unspeakable one' appeared 'with a metallic blue carnation in his button-hole and a cigarette in his fingers'. A green flower was apparently used as a code of recognition by Paris homosexuals, though most of the London audience would not have known this.

Francis Adolphus Vane-Tempest: an actor who had the right credentials for Dumby: Harrow and Oxford, and two failures to be elected to Parliament.

Lily Hanbury: a cousin of Julia Neilson (the first Hester Worsley in *A Woman of No Importance*). She appeared later in Pinero's *Amazons*.

Marion Terry: a sister of Ellen Terry. An accomplished and elegant actress, she worked for some time with the Bancrofts at the Prince of Wales's Theatre. Wilde originally offered the part of a woman with a grown-up illegitimate daughter to Lily Langtry, who responded: 'My dear Oscar, am I old enough to have a grown-up daughter of any description?' (See Wilde's use of this remark, Act IV, lines 236–7.)

Settings. Wilde originally envisaged four different settings: Lord Windermere's Library for Act I, the Drawing-room for Act II, Lord Darlington's rooms for Act III, and Lady Windermere's Boudoir for Act IV. During rehearsals, he learnt that Alexander was planning to use the Library for Act IV. 'If through pressure of time, or for reasons of economy, you are unable to give the play its full scenic mounting, the scene that has to be repeated should be *the second, not the first*. Lady Windermere *may* be in her drawing-room in the fourth act. *She should not be in her husband's library*. This is a very important point' (*More Letters*, 110). The shift to the neutral Morning-room was an acceptable compromise. Lady Windermere would normally have received afternoon visitors in her drawing-room, but it was being prepared for the dance.

1 *Carlton House Terrace*: a real address, between Pall Mall and The Mall, denoting political power and solid integrity, near the Foreign Office and within easy walking distance of the more prestigious London clubs.

The *Bureau R* is Lord Windermere's territory, balanced by Lady Windermere's *Sofa and tea-table L*. The table R with the roses forms a third focal point. Stage directions in earlier drafts draw attention to the fan lying on that table, 'long shaped cardboard box for fan' (Clark MS), highlighted by the dialogue at l. 15. The fan is a conspicuous, feathered object.

terrace L. The use of an off-stage space, in this case the terrace, is characteristic of Wilde—it becomes crucial in Act II. Here it is used to protect Lady Agatha from overhearing scandal.

There is also a table upstage L (with a photograph album on it). In the Clark MS there is a chair by the bureau, one either side of the table R, and a chair to the R of the tea-table, but Wilde makes this last chair redundant by the S.D. at l. 32.

Arranging the roses provides an image of the natural and simple, an indication of Lady Windermere's character, and a reference to the Windermeres' life outside London.

1 *at home*: the butler asks whether Lady Windermere wishes to receive visitors. (If she didn't, or was genuinely not at home, the visitor would leave a calling card.) The very fact of Parker's enquiry signals the slight sense of strain. Social calls were customarily made between 3 p.m. and

6 p.m.—the later in the afternoon, the closer the acquaintance. A visit from a man on his own was a little unusual, hence Lady Windermere's hesitation in receiving him.

5 *anyone*: in early drafts, 'anyone' is underlined, indicating that, from Lady Windermere's point of view, this is not a private or indiscreet visit.

12 *I can't shake hands*: the offered hand, on the part of the man, instead of a bow, indicates a claim of friendship; Lady Windermere's rejection, perfectly polite, is also significant. A photograph of the first production shows Darlington, hand in pocket, gazing intently at Lady Windermere, whose own eyes are occupied on her flower-arranging.

13 *They came up from Selby*: the roses arrived by train from Selby, in Yorkshire, the Windermeres' country house.

20 *of age*: it is Lady Windermere's twenty-first birthday, when her education, in the wider sense, may be assumed complete.

22 *Do sit down*: The table was very small, and the invitation to sit helps to defuse an intimate and highly charged position by creating some distance between Lady Windermere and Lord Darlington.

25 *flowers for you to walk on*: Wilde threw an armful of lilies at the feet of Sarah Bernhardt when he met her at Folkestone in 1879. Lord Darlington's presumption, and its coded message, are emphasized by the short pause which follows.

28 *at the Foreign Office*: a public reception at the Foreign Office—a social, not a political, occasion.

30 *Put it there, Parker. That will do*: 'there' is on the tea-table L. Lady Windermere then tells Parker he need not stay (i.e. to help with passing teacups etc.). This is a very public play: a servant is frequently present in the background or may enter at any moment. The private exchange has been interrupted by the arrival of Parker and the Footman.

31 *Won't you come over?*: Lady Windermere is on the sofa, protected by the tea things in front of her. Lord Darlington has to bring a chair across. It would be inappropriate for him to sit beside her, as the Duchess of Berwick does later. The s.d. '*takes chair and goes across L.C.*' only makes sense if there is no other chair by the tea-table.

48 *what most other men are*: Lady Windermere is signalling both her recognition of Lord Darlington's suppressed declaration of love, and her rejection of it.

68 *great friends*: the repetition of 'friend' stresses its possible meaning of 'lover'. A photograph shows Darlington leaning forward, cup in hand, while Lady Windermere avoids his gaze.

76 *Puritan*: a common term with Wilde, applied also to Hester Worsley in *A Woman of No Importance*. The connotations are of old-fashioned

morality, purity, and sacrifice, as opposed to modern immorality and the ruthless, speculative acquisition of power and property.

78 *My mother died*: this misleading information was, originally, not to have been clarified until Fourth Act. See note to l. 523.

94 S.D. *Enter Parker*: Parker's entrance punctuates the increasingly intimate conversation.

104 *intimate friend of a woman*: Lord Darlington's oblique reference is the first in a sequence of three explanations about Mrs Erlynne, each one false, which gives a sense of formal patterning to the play, a technique taken even further in *Salome*.

107 *console*: euphemism for taking a lover.

119 *charming or tedious*: Lord Darlington expounds the 'morality' of the dandy.

122 *Don't stir*: Lady Windermere's movement may indicate momentarily to Lord Darlington that she is about to ask him to leave, annoyed by his compliment. Again, she controls the situation.

151 S.D. *looking at her*: The Clark MS adds a move for Darlington, 'goes L', which clears the centre of the stage for the Duchess's entrance.

155 *Margaret*: the use of Lady Windermere's first name indicates close friendship. 'Duchess falls back, Agatha advances & shakes hands with Lady W, Duchess Xs behind Agatha to Lord D. L & shakes hands' (Clark MS).

163 *this is Lord Darlington*: Darlington shakes hands with Lady Agatha. 'Agatha & Lord D talk together' (Clark MS).

165 S.D. *sits on sofa*: from this position the Duchess is in command of the stage.

167 *Her own son-in-law supplies it*: the Duchess disparages as a matter of course any connection between the aristocracy and 'trade', in ironic contrast to her interest in Mr Hopper's wealth.

171 *small and early*: the dance is to be formal but private, not large enough to be described as a ball, and one from which the guests would be expected to leave relatively early. At a dance 'the number of the guests varies from eighty to two hundred; at a ball they vary from two hundred to five hundred' (*Manners and Rules of Good Society, or Solecisms to be Avoided*, by a Member of the Aristocracy, numerous editions).

173 *very select*: Darlington's gloss is not just a compliment. He draws attention to the very high reputation of the Windermeres' social circle. To be received in their house would guarantee Mrs Erlynne's social acceptability.

194 *all the honours*: the honours are the court cards. To hold all the honours is to have a very strong hand at bridge or whist. Darlington is again hinting at Windermere's supposed infidelity.

215 S.D. *standing up stage*: With the Duchess and her daughter downstage, Lady Windermere and Lord Darlington are isolated by the central doors for this more intimate farewell exchange. French adds 'sunset effect starts'—see l. 247.

224 S.D. *Crosses to sofa*: There is radical stage repositioning for the Duchess's revelations. Their inherent seriousness is counterpointed by the comic form of her speech and the manipulation of Lady Agatha.

257 *Windermere*: the use of Windermere without the title indicates social superiority and familiarity.

262 *not at home to anyone*: Mrs Erlynne's conduct contrasts sharply with Lady Windermere's reception of Lord Darlington.

272 *Curzon Street*: this location in Mayfair, off Park Lane, was expensive as well as respectable. The implication is that Lord Windermere has set up his mistress at considerable cost.

281 *the Park*: to drive in Hyde Park was part of the socially accepted way of spending the day.

287 *to Homburg or to Aix*: it was fashionable to stay in such German spa towns, as Wilde himself did, to recuperate from too much eating and drinking during the London season; but going abroad was also a way of avoiding social embarrassment.

302 *Oxford*: Wilde's private joke recalls his own conduct at University, the memory of which had been revived by his recent acquaintance with Lord Alfred Douglas, an Oxford undergraduate.

315 *without a character*: the Duchess did not provide her with a written reference of good character, thus ensuring that she was not re-employed.

319 *dining out*: they are dining at someone else's house, before coming on to the dance.

340 *sending a card*: Lady Windermere has sent an invitation card to Mr Hopper at the Duchess's suggestion.

347 *every season*: the London season was the traditional time for launching daughters into society and, if possible, securing satisfactory marriages for them.

356 *I will find out*: This awkward soliloquy betrays Wilde's relative lack of theatre experience. But the symbolism—the locked male notebook—and the actions—cutting open the cover—are powerful, while the use of the bureau introduces a hitherto unexplored area of the stage. The action highlights the question of a woman's legal and moral rights, and the way in which women had been excluded from whole areas of

life. The landmark Married Women's Property Act of 1882 had given women legal control over their property and income for the first time.

364 S.D. *Throws book on floor*: the Clark MS expands: 'Throws book on floor C. and goes down L.'; Windermere at l. 370 'puts book on Desk R & returns to C.'.

389 S.D. *Sits on sofa*: Lady Windermere retreats to the sofa, drawing Lord Windermere across at l. 394.

435 *I want you to send her an invitation*: the card would read 'Lady Windermere—At Home' with the addition of 'dancing', and would be in the name of the hostess, with the guest's name in the hostess's handwriting.

442 *to receive her once*: to be seen being received by so upright a hostess as Lady Windermere would make Mrs Erlynne socially respectable and accepted by the most fastidious—however bizarre it may seem, this was how English society functioned. Even so, a double standard is indicated, with a distinction between unreserved acceptance and what society was prepared to accept.

451 *I beg of you*: the Clark MS indicates 'Moves to her to take her hand, she X's to C'.

454 *Arthur*: the use of Windermere's first name hints at Lady Windermere's growing sense of power and autonomy.

456 *I have friends*: the Clark typescript has an interesting variation, 'I have friends, one friend at any rate', emphasizing Lady Windermere's impulse to turn to Lord Darlington.

481 S.D. *writes card*: Mrs Erlynne will, of course, realize the implication when she sees that her invitation is in Lord Windermere's handwriting.

487 *No. 84A*: the number did not exist.

493 *Child*: the patronizing word emphasizes Lady Windermere's youthfulness (and naïvety), and perhaps reflects Torvald's treatment of Nora in Ibsen's *A Doll's House*, which Wilde had seen.

499 S.D. *Rings bell*: the stage direction, present in the Licensing Copy, was omitted from the first edition.

504 *my own room*: the Windermeres have separate bedrooms, as was customary at that time among the upper classes. Other texts (i.e. the Licensing Copy) include an instruction from Lady Windermere to Parker: 'And hand me that fan', so that she is holding it while she makes the point about pronouncing the names distinctly. Perhaps Wilde judged this to be over-emphatic.

506 *pronounce the names*: the guests' names would be announced by the butler as they arrived at the dance.

523 *who this woman really is*: Lord Windermere supplies the first strong hint as to the relationship between Lady Windermere and Mrs Erlynne. Wilde finally, if reluctantly, accepted Alexander's advice that the audience should be informed about this at an earlier point in the play, rather than through the conventional delayed, melodramatic revelation which he had planned. After the first night, the relationship was unveiled at the close of the First Act. Wilde's letter to the Editor of the *St James's Gazette* was published on 27 February: 'all my friends, without exception, were of opinion that the psychological interest of the second act would be greatly increased by the disclosure of the actual relationship existing between Lady Windermere and Mrs Erlynne—an opinion, I may add, that had been strongly held and urged by Mr Alexander. As to those of us who do not look upon a play as a mere question of pantomime and clowning, psychological interest is everything. I determined consequently to make a change in the precise moment of revelation.' Wilde also wrote to Alexander at length about the point (*Selected Letters*, 102–4). Wilde's final choice of words is subtler than the explicit alternatives used in early performances, for instance, 'I can't tell her that that woman is her own Mother!' (Clark typescript).

2 This scene expanded through successive drafts, and Wilde added non-speaking roles. While not quite on the scale of the reception in *An Ideal Husband*, it represents something considerably grander than the 'small and early' dance of Lady Windermere's description. Most drafts specify 'Style Louis Seize. White walls. Red and gold furniture.' There must be at least one sofa. Clark MS s.d. places a large three-sectioned ottoman R.C., which is used as one focal point, balanced by a sofa U.L., and adds, as hand properties, 'Pen, ink, writing paper, a blotting pad on desk R.' This desk, or bureau, where Lady Windermere writes her near-fatal letter at l. 451, which Mrs Erlynne reads at l. 469, must be in a relatively prominent position (D.S.R. in French). Wilde employs two off-stage locations, the ballroom, where the public life of the guests continues, and the terrace, the place for private assignations. Parker, in evening dress, announces the arrivals. Even when Lord Windermere appears, his wife is left to greet the guests, as customary.

5 *your card*: each woman is provided with a card, on which the dances are listed; and a gentleman would ask if his name could be entered in advance for one or more dances.

9 *such particularly younger sons!*: younger sons were undesirable partners because they would inherit little.

10 s.d. *Enter . . . Lady Plymdale*: Mr Dumby is clearly identified as Lady Plymdale's companion, if not lover. He calls her 'my dear Laura' at l. 226.

38 *on the map*: At rehearsal, Wilde noted that Fanny Coleman, playing the Duchess of Berwick, had left out 'Agatha has found Australia on the map. What a curious shape it is!' The words, he complained to Alexander, 'give the point to the remark about the young country. To omit them is to leave out the point of the climax' (*More Letters*, 113). In fact, in this letter Wilde omits the additional phrase 'Just like a large packing case.' This is a typical example of how the final printed text has expanded.

65 *Demmed*: this usage, like 'Egad!', places Lord Augustus as humorously old-fashioned, as well as something of a roué—but, like Lady Bracknell, he demands to know a prospective wife's pedigree.

90 *Would you introduce her to your wife?*: the coded question asks: is she your mistress?

94 *Mrs Erlynne has received a card*: Lord Windermere is punctilious about the truth, though the distinction is lost on Lord Augustus.

97 s.d. *Lady Agatha and Mr Hopper cross*: Lord Augustus's pursuit of Mrs Erlynne is counterpointed by his niece's courting.

101 *Why don't you ask me how I am?*: Cecil Graham defines himself as a dandy. Again, Wilde records an instance of how this scene changed in rehearsal: 'With regard to yourself, when Cecil Graham bores you with his chatter you broke off last night by saying "How amusing!", or some word like that. I think it would be better to say "Excuse me for a moment", as I suggested. Lord W. is terribly agitated about Mrs Erlynne's coming, and the dandy's chatter bores him, does not please him. He has no taste for it' (*More Letters*, 113). The use of Lord Augustus to deflect Graham's attention is a more economical solution.

116 s.d. *Moves away R.*: Clark typescript adds 'Band'.

129 *Will you . . . Lord Darlington?*: the fan is used as a sexual invitation to Lord Darlington, as well as a reminder of the threat to strike Mrs Erlynne.

147 s.d. *Mrs Erlynne enters*: Wilde has prepared on-stage (and off-stage) audiences for the last of the guests. Mrs Erlynne's beautiful dress and dignified manner are crucial—she has exquisite taste. 'We must not make Mrs E. look like a cocotte. She is an adventuress, not a cocotte' (*More Letters*, 113). The expected melodramatic gesture does not materialize.

166 *Come out on the terrace*: the terrace is established as a place for the private and the secret. For the next speech, Clark MS adds 'L arm on Lord D's R—she speaks over her shoulder to Parker', increasing the intimacy.

169 *Prince Doria's*: 'Prince Alfonzo Doria-Pamphili had married into the English nobility. His Palazzo Doria is one of the finest palaces in Rome'

(Isobel Murray (ed.), *The Writings of Oscar Wilde* (1989)). This is a rare instance of Wilde citing a contemporary: Mrs Erlynne is name-dropping on an international scale.

172 *I should so much like to know her*: once securely established as 'respectable' in the Windermere house, Mrs Erlynne brilliantly exploits the opportunity, using the men to gain an entrée with the women. She breaks etiquette by forcing an introduction to someone of higher rank. At this point, the Clark typescript adds 'Band stops'.

198 *wicked French novel*: France was the traditional source, from a Victorian and English perspective, of immorality, and French novels were published in a distinctive yellow cover. But Dumby's description suggests something especially decadent and luxurious.

204 *I'll dance with you first*: by taking the initiative in the decision to dance, Mrs Erlynne demonstrates her power over Lord Windermere.

216 *my bouquet*: Mrs Erlynne's bouquet is used as a counterpoint to the fan, but with comic effect.

220 *Delighted!*: the Clark typescript adds 'Band'; French specifies a waltz.

229 *That woman*: Wilde noted to Alexander: 'Also, would you remind Lady Plymdale to say "That woman!" not "That *dreadful* woman" ' (*More Letters*, 113—see l. 147).

241 *just the thing for him*: Mrs Erlynne will divert Lord Plymdale, and so leave his wife free to pursue her own affairs.

249 S.D. *They pass into the ball-room*. It is clear that the drawing-room has completely emptied for the current dance— 'stage quite clear' (Clark typescript). Wilde advised Alexander: 'I think also that C. Graham should not take his aunt into the ballroom—young dandies dislike their aged relatives—at least rarely pay them attention. Lady J. should have a debutante in tow' (*More Letters*, 115). The Clark MS adds: 'Lord D helps her off with her cloak and puts it on sofa up L.'

324 S.D. *A pause*: the Clark MS adds: 'both standing close together, she looking in his face'.

325 *You break my heart!*: the melodramatic intensity is only partly moderated by the simplicity of the phrasing. This whole sequence is reminiscent of a French *drame*, by Sardou or Dumas *fils*. Wilde's revisions show he was conscious of the heightened rhetoric: for instance, he deleted 'Goodbye . . . my love' (Clark typescript).

331 S.D. *The music stops*. Wilde commented to Alexander: 'Details in life are of no importance, but in art details are vital.

'In the comedy scenes people should speak out more, be more assertive. Every *word* of a comedy dialogue should reach the ears of the audience. This applies especially to the Duchess, who should be larger in assertion. The chatter that drowned her speech in *Act* 2 about Mrs

Erlynne and the Saville girls might be *before* her entrance, and the guests pass chattering on to the terrace, leaving two on the sofa at back, and two on the seat at entrance' (*More Letters*, 112). Wilde is not just being protective of his dialogue: the juxtaposition of Lord Darlington's farewell and the Duchess's comic reversal of her previous piece of scandal is an example of Wilde's playful shifts of tone—which itself leads in to the comedy of Hopper's proposal to Lady Agatha, an ironic contrast to the previous declaration of love, and no less hypocritical for being funny.

357 *James!*: the Duchess swiftly shifts Hopper to first-name status.

367 *Grosvenor Square*: an eminently respectable and aristocratic address.

371 *you can take Agatha down*: now that the deed is done, Agatha can be packed off home.

374 *have a chat with the Duke*: strictly, Hopper should ask the Duke's permission to marry his daughter; but the Duchess's approval is clearly the deciding factor.

379 *love*: the speech recalls Lady Windermere's statement that she married for love, in contrast to the Duchess's hard-headed campaign to find a wealthy husband for her daughter before the end of the season.

395 *almost modern*: Dumby suggests that to be modern is to be deceitful: he assumes that Mrs Erlynne is Windermere's mistress.

407 *The last time I saw her*: Wilde further clarifies Mrs Erlynne's relationship to Lady Windermere.

411 S.D. *Exit*. Again, the drawing-room empties, another of Wilde's contrasts in the organization of the act.

424 *settlement*: after establishing Mrs Erlynne as respectable, Lord Windermere is now expected to settle money on her.

446 S.D. *Music strikes up*: the music serves as an ironic counterpoint to Lady Windermere's decision to leave her husband.

454 S.D. *Exit*: Lady Windermere leaves the same way as her departing guests.

464 S.D. *The music . . . stops*: the silence gives weight to Mrs Erlynne's crucial speech of revelation. Parker has given orders to the band, presumably on Lady Windermere's instruction. (In French, he also lowers the lights.)

482 S.D. *Drops letter*: the mother's dropped letter echoes the daughter's dropped fan.

488 S.D. *takes the letter*: the Clark MS adds: 'puts letter in bosom of dress'.

497 S.D. *Enter Lord Augustus*: Lord Augustus's entrance with the bouquet in itself is comic, puncturing the preceding tension.

511 *Well, really*: this downbeat ending was clearly Alexander's suggestion. 'With regard to the speech of Mrs Erlynne at the end of Act II, you must remember that until Wednesday night Mrs Erlynne rushed off the stage leaving Lord Augustus in a state of bewilderment. Such are the stage directions in the play. When the alteration in the business was made I don't know, but I should have been informed at once . . . I don't in any degree object to it. It is a different effect, that is all . . . I want Mrs Erlynne's whole scene with Lord Augustus to be a "tornado" scene, and the thing to go as quickly as possible' (*Selected Letters*, 102). French has a complex routine for the close: Mrs Erlynne exits, Lord Augustus rushes after her, meets Parker in door, drops flowers and exits; Parker picks them up and goes off. This may reflect early stage practice.

3 The sombre masculinity of the setting is in sharp contrast to the splendour of the previous scene. Darlington's rooms have all the paraphernalia of the male world: writing-table, smoking and drinking accessories. A Tantalus frame holds bottles of spirits which are visible, but contained within a locked frame. The fire is lit. (For Gielgud's 1945 production, Cecil Beaton designed 'green-shadowed bachelor quarters'.) The Licensing Copy contains interesting variations: it specifies the Library: 'Cairene screen. Door at back of stage. Ordinary door L.C. with leather screen near it. Room Oriental and luxurious.' The screen was perhaps a conscious echo of *The School for Scandal*. For Lady Windermere to arrive at a man's rooms on her own, at night, is in itself a cause for scandal (compare Lady Chiltern in *An Ideal Husband*).

2 *Why doesn't he come?*: the extreme length of this soliloquy is something Wilde learnt to avoid in his later comedies.

22 S.D. *puts on her cloak*: this emphasizes Lady Windermere's decision to return to her husband (in the Second Act she had asked for it to be sent out to her when she accompanied Darlington on to the terrace).

37 S.D. *throws off her cloak*: again, the gesture with the cloak clarifies the reversal of her previous decision.

81 S.D. *throws it into the fire*: Wilde's frequent use of letters reflects the stock-in-trade of the well-made play; the melodramatic burning was used by Ibsen in *Hedda Gabler*, which Wilde saw twice in April 1891, at the Vaudeville Theatre, with Elizabeth Robins as Hedda.

127 *Arthur*: unconsciously, Mrs Erlynne uses the Christian name—Windermere is, after all, her son-in-law—but to Lady Windermere it is evidence of a liaison.

137 S.D. *does not dare to touch her*: Mrs Erlynne repeatedly shows that she longs to touch and embrace her daughter; throughout this scene, Wilde suggests that the revelation may be about to happen, but circumvents

it. A physical text of gesture and movement accompanies and points up the verbal.

158 *child*: the repetitions emphasize the suppressed relationship, and increase audience expectation that it will be revealed, giving an added dimension to what otherwise might seem sentimental. Contrast Wilde's comic use of the revelation about Ernest's mother at the end of *The Importance of Being Earnest*.

173 S.D. *look of wonderful joy*: Mrs Erlynne helps her daughter into the cloak and is close to her only for seconds.

178 *Save me!*: the Clark MS adds: 'Lady W Xs from L of Mrs E to R of her, clinging to her'—another fleeting physical contact.

179 S.D. *Voices outside*: the Licensing Copy includes a specific line for Lord Windermere, 'I don't think I can come in.'

185 *Nonsense, dear Windermere*: Lord Augustus is doggedly carrying out Mrs Erlynne's orders; but for Mrs Erlynne to be found by him in Darlington's rooms means the end of her prospects of marriage. Clark MS adds after 'Lord Augustus!' 'Pause standing C then speaks sadly'.

187 S.D. *door R.*: the door Right leads to the rest of Darlington's apartment, the interior rooms, placing Mrs Erlynne in a thoroughly compromising position.

188 *out of the club*: the men have presumably walked the short distance from the club, whereas Mrs Erlynne has come by carriage. 'All men without coats except Lord W—Dumby carries coat which he puts on chair up L. C. All men with hats—' (Clark MS). Lord Augustus has an old-fashioned opera hat which he closes and puts on the table. Wilde commented to Alexander after a rehearsal: 'Act 3 Lord A's coat is too horsy: also he should take it off. He wants to make a night of it.'

202 *no business of yours*: the gulf between Lord Windermere's and Graham's morality is emphasized by their separation on the stage—Windermere with Lord Augustus, Graham allied to Dumby, Darlington tactfully distracting Graham temporarily with the offer of a drink. This sequence portrays a male school for scandal, orchestrated by Graham, in which Mrs Erlynne is anatomized, and Lord Augustus baited. The conversation is punctuated by puffs of cigar smoke and fuelled by whisky (a modern drink) and brandy and soda (traditional).

230 *Wiesbaden*: a fashionable German spa.

238 *Our grandmothers . . . wind for them*: to 'throw your cap over a windmill' signifies ambition. Mill suggests industrial mills, hence marrying into a fortune. To 'raise the wind' is to acquire wealth. (*Raising the Wind* was a popular early nineteenth-century farce by Kenny; but its protagonist was an initially penniless male adventurer.)

252 S.D. *puts his hands on his shoulders*: Graham is very active in this scene, moving from person to person, whispering, touching. His extreme youth makes gestures like this one even more presumptuous.

265 *men who are not their husbands*: Dumby's comment is an insult to Lord Augustus, but it is also highly offensive to Lord Windermere, widely assumed to have a liaison with Mrs Erlynne. The rise in emotional temperature, diverted in the next sequence, prepares for the confrontation between Windermere and Darlington at the end of the act.

278 *Nonconformist*: in this context, morally strict and puritanical.

294 *drink again*: the Clark MS adds 'Drinks his B & S'. The broad comedy provides a contrast to the following sequence.

307 *we are all in the gutter*: Darlington, a dandy until his declaration of love for Lady Windermere, betrays his new status of lover by his seriousness. This unguarded revelation, repeated by Dumby, catches Graham's attention. He leaves Lord Augustus to concentrate on Darlington, preparing for the mischief-making with the fan.

316 *a good woman*: the play's sub-title is introduced and explored in preparation for Mrs Erlynne's defining action.

324 *middle-class education*: Wilde plays with a quotation from Steele, 'To love her is a liberal education' (*The Tatler*, No. 49).

364 S.D. *Sees Lady Windermere's fan*: the fan, of course, has been visible to the audience throughout. Haddon Chambers had used the same device in *The Idler*, produced by Alexander at the St James's Theatre in 1891 (as reviewers mentioned). But the mislaid object—fan, jewellery, handkerchief—is standard. As often, Wilde makes use of the traditional in a novel way.

380 *some woman*: the coarse phrase underlines the oppressive gender warfare.

410 *Hands off, Cecil*: Windermere is about to attack Darlington physically—the counterpart to his wife's threat to strike Mrs Erlynne.

419 *I'll—*: Wilde's revisions shift the tone an inch or two from the brink of melodrama. The Clark typescript completes the line, '—shoot you like a dog', to be answered by Darlington: 'Send your seconds to me tomorrow and you will get the explanation customary amongst gentlemen.' (Melodramatic or not, this kind of language permeates the Wilde/Queensberry/Douglas fracas.)

424 S.D. *enters behind R*: Mrs Erlynne enters from the interior of the apartment to confront the male world, in a superbly timed theatrical gesture. Gielgud's 1945 production offered a memorable interpretation: 'By ingeniously wearing her cloak loosely thrown over one shoulder, Isabel Jeans conveys so much that Wilde left unsaid. By making a

daring cross-stage exit with one bare shoulder turned towards the male guests, she heightens the situation enormously, for her casual appearance obviously gives the impression that she has been in the next room some time, possibly expecting Darlington to join her in a tête-a-tête supper' (*Theatre World*, Oct. 1945).

4 Wilde seems to have overcome his misgivings about using the same setting as in the First Act. Cecil Beaton's design for Gielgud's 1945 production originally reused the Second Act ballroom setting for economy; after the play had toured, he put in a 'small gilded cage of a boudoir' of yellow silk, which accords with Wilde's direction in the Licensing Copy. It does seem that Wilde intended four settings, and the shift to a personal room of Lady Windermere's would have reflected the exploration of her understanding and her growing authority; note also the use of her personal maid, Rosalie, at the opening. The Licensing Copy specifies: 'White woodwork. Panels of crushed strawberry silk. Green carpet. Louis Seize furniture. Silver-framed mirror on table.'

15 *I told him*: Rosalie's intervention underlines both the formality of upper-class life and the high-profile role of servants.

28 *I would have publicly disgraced her*. Wilde emphasizes the parallel functions of the two public middle acts, framed by the outer acts which are each organized around a series of more intimate conversations.

45 *Let us go away*: Wilde echoes the opening of Act I, with the reference to the Windermeres' country house at Selby, in contrast to the pressures of the London season, now drawing to a close.

70 *the good and the bad*: in this key speech, Lady Windermere reverses her previous moral dicta, preparing for her insistence on receiving Mrs Erlynne, in opposition to her husband.

90 s.d. *Lady Windermere's fan*: the arrival of the fan prevents the confession which its discovery the night before had almost forced.

106 s.d. *Enter Mrs Erlynne*: Cecil Beaton designed a japonica pink morning ensemble for Isabel Jeans—'a shade of overstress in the colouring suggesting a woman not accepted by London society, an outcast compelled to live on the Continent, as penance for past transgressions' (*Theatre World*, Oct. 1945).

115 s.d. *sits down beside her*: this position recalls the First Act stage arrangement, when the Duchess of Berwick first informed Lady Windermere about Mrs Erlynne.

120 *fogs and—serious people*: Mrs Erlynne reverts to her dandiacal tone of the Second Act.

123 *Club Train*: a special express train to the Continent will take Mrs Erlynne (like Lord Darlington) into exile, at a safe distance from the moral hypocrisy of England.

150 *Lady Windermere . . . Mrs Erlynne*: the names accentuate the formality of the social relationship, in contrast to the suppressed intimacy.

190 S.D. *rising*: the Clark MS expands: 'Mrs E rises—strong—looking in his eyes'.

202 *blackmailing*: Windermere becomes increasingly moralistic and strident during this sequence, highlighting the impossible position in which society placed women like Mrs Erlynne.

220 *innocent-looking girl*: the word-picture contrasts with Mrs Erlynne's sophisticated appearance.

240 *pink shades*: these create a softer, more flattering light.

245 *a heart doesn't suit me*: Mrs Erlynne reverts to the hard adventuress she has become.

253 *in real life we don't do such things*: this may be an echo, as Katharine Worth suggests, of Judge Brack at the end of *Hedda Gabler*, 'People don't do such things.'

258 *to do that*: Wilde has suppressed a resonant line which appears in the Clark MS: 'My dear Windermere, nothing matters in the nineteenth century except want of money.' ('Nineteenth' was amended to 'present'.)

261 *fatal mistake*: the line comes from a stage world of absolutes; but the new morality is expressed by Mrs Erlynne's reply. To achieve her aim, Mrs Erlynne is prepared to exploit the language of melodrama, as at l. 272, a language which corresponds to the black and white simplistic views of Lord Windermere.

285 *my secret*: in Wilde's world, the women have secrets, and so the moral power.

339 *Then pay your debt by silence*: the alliance between the two women is emphasized by a Clark s.d.: 'Ladies hands in hands, & hold hands until Lord W enters'.

358 *Shrewsbury and Talbot*: a superior kind of cab.

370 S.D. *Shakes hands*: the friendly handshake contrasts with the distant cold bow of the Second Act, and the unfulfilled embrace of the Third Act.

382 *carry the fan*: Lord Augustus, in carrying the fan, echoes his action with the bouquet of the Second Act.

404 S.D. *sits on sofa*: the Windermeres sit, holding hands, and embrace after 'We were never separated' (Clark MS).

410 *roses are white and red*: a verbal reprise of the roses of the First Act, but a hint, too, at simple moral values, in preparation for the momentary shock of Lord Augustus's 'Arthur, she has explained everything'.

430 *a very good woman!*: the use of the play's sub-title in the last line is conventional. As in the Second Act, Wilde exploits Lord Augustus to

lighten the tone. Lady Windermere, appropriately, corrects her husband and has the last word.

Salome

Dedication. Wilde's wording contrives to obscure his bitter disappointment with Douglas over his inept translation, which he had been forced to rework himself.

This text, apparently so different in style to the four comedies, is exceptional as the only one of these plays for which Wilde did not have the benefit of a production. The text itself, a 'translation' from the French, is not even the one which Sarah Bernhardt began to rehearse in London in June 1892. As a result, Wilde has written very few stage directions, since these usually developed during the later drafts of his plays while they were nearing the rehearsal process or were later reflections of stage performance.

The Persons of the Play. Wilde bases his characters, and the outline of the action, on biblical accounts, but constantly alters and moulds the narrative into the pattern of his own myth. The Gospel accounts also clearly influence the style and rhythm of the language. See Matthew 3: 1–17 and 14: 1–12; Mark 1: 1–11 and 6: 14–28; and Luke 3: 1–20.

Herod Antipas: one of three sons of Herod the Great, he was Tetrarch (ruler) of Galilee and Peraea from 4 BC to AD 39. He ruled with the consent and overall control of the Roman Emperor. He divorced his wife in order to marry his niece, Herodias, for which he was censured by John the Baptist.

Iokanaan: the Hebrew form of John (used also by Flaubert in *Hérodias*). John the Baptist preached *c.* AD 27 on the banks of the river Jordan, calling on his hearers to repent and be baptized in view of the imminence of the Kingdom of God. He baptized Jesus and recognized him as the Messiah. According to the historian Josephus, he was imprisoned and put to death in the fortress of Machaerus. Wilde's use of 'Iokanaan', with a soft 'Yo', may be an attempt to distance the character from the biblical John.

Cappadocian: an inhabitant of Cappadocia, which was a Roman Province in Asia Minor, annexed in AD 17.

Nubian: an inhabitant of Nubia, which was a kingdom in north-east Africa.

Nazarenes: a term used for early Christians, who believed that Jesus was the Messiah. The Nazarenes identify with Iokanaan: they kneel to pray after his execution, l. 1008 s.d.

Herodias: according to the accounts of Mark and Matthew, Herodias had persuaded Herod to imprison John, for denouncing her marriage as unlawful.

Salome: the daughter of Herodias by her first husband. Josephus identified her as the unnamed 'daughter of Herodias' who danced before Herod on his birthday.

Scene. Salome was written between *Lady Windermere's Fan* and *A Woman of No Importance*, both plays which make use of a terrace: it seems the essential Wilde location, artificial yet with the natural impinging on it. (Wilde is echoing the opening of Flaubert's *Hérodias*.) The staircase and the cistern (another detail from Flaubert) provide two opposing focal points. In Terence Gray's production at the Festival Theatre, Cambridge (1929-31), the staircase dominated the set: there was a 'huge tin tea-tray' moon, and the cistern was a down-stage trap, through which Iokanaan's masked head protruded. In Steven Berkoff's 1989 staging, his black, grey, and white Art Deco approach represented the cistern by a square of light.

The moon passes through three phases during the course of the play: white, red, and black. Colour, however interpreted, is dominant. Wilde, according to Graham Robertson, declared at one point that everyone on stage should be in yellow. 'It was a good idea and I saw its possibilities at once—every costume of some shade of yellow from clearest lemon to deep orange, with here and there just a hint of black—yes, you must have that—and all upon a pale ivory terrace against a great empty sky of deepest violet.

' "A violet sky," repeated Oscar Wilde slowly. "Yes—I never thought of that. Certainly a violet sky and then, in place of an orchestra, braziers of perfume. Think—the scented clouds rising and partly veiling the stage from time to time—a new perfume for each emotion!" ' (W. Graham Robertson, *Time Was* (1931), 244).

Charles Ricketts was approached by Wilde with a view to designing the Lugné-Poe production in Paris (the commission did not materialize). 'I proposed a black floor, upon which Salomé's feet could move like white doves; this was said to capture the author. The sky was to be a rich turquoise green, cut by the perpendicular fall of gilded strips of Japanese matting forming an aerial tent above the terraces. Did Wilde suggest the division of the actors into separate masses of colour? To-day I cannot decide. The Jews were to be in yellow, John in white, and Herod and Herodias in blood-red. Over Salomé the discussions were endless; should she be clothed in black—like the night, in silver like the moon or—the suggestion was Wilde's—green like a curious poisonous lizard?' (*Self-Portrait: Letters and Journals of Charles Ricketts*, ed. Cecil Lewis (1939), 137).

In Ricketts's production for the Literary Theatre Society at the King's Hall on 10 June 1906, he 'placed dim cypress-like curtains against a star-lit sky; the players were clothed in every shade of blue, deepening into dark violet and green, the general harmony of blue on blue being relieved by the red lances of the soldiers' (Charles Ricketts, *Pages on Art* (1913), 244).

In a synopsis Ricketts wrote for Robert Ross, he suggested: 'Salome, dressed in a mist rising by moonlight, with a train of blue and black moths. Herodias, in a peacock train of Dahlias and a horned tiara. Herod is robed in silver and blue lined with flame decorated with griffons, sphinxes and angels. The scene is all blue on blue.'

Max Beerbohm commented that *Salome*, in construction, was very like a Greek play. Berkoff recognized this by organizing the minor roles into a chorus. Terence Gray's approach to the play is revealing: 'I produce it for sound and movement, and not at all for character.'

The figure of Naaman, the executioner, is present throughout. Whatever the stage arrangement, the banqueting-hall is obviously visible from the terrace.

16 *Pharisees*: the leading Jewish religious party, who upheld a legalistic Judaism.

17 *Sadducees*: a Jewish politico-religious sect, opposed to the Pharisees. They rejected the Pharisees' belief in resurrection and in the existence of angels.

42 *Samothrace*: an island in the Aegean.

Caesar: Tiberius, Roman Emperor AD 14–37.

44 *Cyprus*: the island of Cyprus, rather than 'a town', would seem more logical. Possibly the 'town' arose from a misreading by the French printer of 'ville' for 'ile', which Wilde allowed to stand because it provided variation.

54 *The Romans have driven them out*: Cappadocia was a Hittite and later Persian kingdom, annexed by the Romans in AD 17.

65 *After me shall come another*: Iokanaan's prophecy of the coming of Jesus is based on the Gospel accounts and draws also on Isaiah, for instance, 11: 6–8 and 35: 1.

81 *locusts and wild honey*: see Matthew 3: 4.

100 *Tetrarch's brother*: this is an invention of Wilde's: Philip died in AD 34. Historically, Philip was Salome's husband.

132 *Smyrna*: a prosperous seaport in Asia Minor, modern Turkey.

170 *Elias*: the New Testament form of Elijah, the great prophet whose return would herald the restoration of Israel.

212 *cover of this well*: it is unclear precisely where the cover of the well is: Salome has looked down into the cistern at l. 218, presumably through some kind of grating. Wilde may be recalling Flaubert's description, in

which bronze lids were set between paving-stones to cover the cisterns. This is the kind of discrepancy which would have been clarified in rehearsal: it also helps to explain why the most successful productions have been non-representational.

215 *little green flower*: in his essay 'Pen, Pencil, and Poison', a 'study in green' (1889), Wilde wrote that Thomas Griffiths Wainewright had 'that curious love of green, which in individuals is always the sign of a subtle artistic temperament, and in nations is said to denote a laxity, if not a decadence of morals'. Wilde uses the idea of a green flower almost as a private code.

241 *land of Chaldaea?*: this and the following speech of Iokanaan are based on Ezekiel 23, in which the prophet compares the faithlessness of Samaria and Jerusalem to the whoredoms of two women with the Assyrians and the Babylonians, associated with Chaldaea. In Flaubert, Herodias appears wearing an Assyrian mitre.

246 *baldricks*: belts or girdles.

255 *fan of the Lord*: a winnowing-fan, as in Matthew 3: 12: 'Whose fan is in his hand, and he will throughly cleanse his threshing-floor.'

291 *Daughter of Sodom*: Sodom was one of the cities God destroyed (see Genesis 18 and 19), and, like Babylon, a byword for immorality.

293 *Son of Man*: a title of the Messiah, used of Jesus in the New Testament.

297 *beating of the wings of the angel of death*: Wilde derives this from John Bright, speaking in the House of Commons on the Crimean War on 23 Feb. 1855: 'The angel of death has been abroad throughout the land; you may almost hear the beating of his wings.'

304 *Thy body is white*: Wilde draws on many biblical sources here, and extensively on the Song of Songs.

323 *Edom*: a one-time neighbouring country to Israel, with Petra as its capital.

348 *Moab*: another neighbouring kingdom, east of the Dead Sea.

361 S.D. *He kills himself*: significantly, Salome does not react.

382 *remission of thy sins*: John baptized people in Jordan, after they had confessed their sins: there may be an allusion to 'the woman who was a sinner', Luke 7.

398 *ever very low*: Wilde echoes Lear, speaking of Cordelia, *King Lear*, V. iii. 274–5: 'Her voice was ever soft, | Gentle and low, an excellent thing in woman.'

404 S.D. *all the Court*: this forms an impressive entrance. Tigellinus is the chief Roman ambassador. Line 421 suggests there is at least one more. Herod identifies three slaves by name (ll. 418 and 1059). Five Jews are

indicated, of whom one may be a Sadducee and one a Pharisee. Salome's slaves may be present throughout. Depending upon the style of the production, there may also be on-stage musicians, cup-bearers, etc.

418 *lay carpets there*: apart from the implications of this and further orders, there are minimal stage directions for the disposition of the Court. It is clear that some kind of seating must be brought in for Herod and Herodias, and arguably for Tigellinus.

440 *Stoics*: an austere school of philosophers, founded by Zeno, who were opposed by Nero and his successors.

457 S.D. *They take away the body*: it would be appropriate for it to be the soldiers who take away their Captain's body, before returning to the stage.

524 *Gentiles*: biblical term for non-Jews.

565 *Messias*: Jesus, the Messiah.

573 *water into wine*: John 2: 1–10 describes the marriage at Cana.

580 *talking with angels*: the reference is to Jesus's transfiguration, as described in Matthew 17: 1–13.

591 *daughter of Jairus*: see Mark 5: 35–43.

606 *Samaria*: the Jews were consistently hostile to Samaria, situated west of the Jordan between Galilee and Judaea.

654 *like unripe figs*: Wilde imitates apocalyptic language—as, for instance, that of the Revelation of St John the Divine 6: 13.

679 *veil of the sanctuary*: Herod the Great began the rebuilding of the Temple: it was completed in AD 64 (and destroyed in AD 70). The veil, a screen of fine coloured linen, hung between the Holy Place and the innermost sanctuary, the Holy of Holies.

709 *you shall be eaten of worms*: this fate befell Herod Agrippa, Acts of the Apostles 12: 23.

768 *The flowers are like fire*: there is an intentional parallel between Herod's garland of roses and Jesus's crown of thorns.

797 *seven veils*: this is Wilde's invention. The words 'et les sept voiles' were added by Wilde in pencil to the page proofs of the French text. It is simpler (though less realistic) if Salome's slaves do not go off and return with perfume, veils, etc.

804 *Thou hast waded deep enough in it*: compare *Macbeth*, III. iv. 136–7.

817 *who cometh from Edom*: Wilde is drawing on Isaiah 60: 1–2.

830 S.D. *dance of the seven veils*: the most critical moment in the play remains the most elusive, as with Yeats's dance plays. Salomé's dance forms the climax to Flaubert's *Hérodias*: there Salome dances on her hands, as she does on the thirteenth-century tympanum on Rouen

cathedral. Wilde reportedly offered the part to a Romanian acrobat whom he had seen dancing on her hands at the Moulin Rouge. Lisa Munte, the first Salomé in Lugné-Poe's Paris production of 1896, for which Lautrec supplied a poster, seems to have represented, or indicated, the wilder, erotic interpretation: she was described in *La Plume* as 'souple et féline à souhait' [supple and feline to perfection] and this emphasis has been developed in productions of Strauss's opera. English Salomes have tended to be more controlled, either because of inhibition, or because of a less representational interpretation. William Archer suggested that the company should have been sent by special train to Berlin before attempting such a play; even then Miss Darragh would have been an impossible Salome, executing the dance with all the propriety of an English governess. Max Beerbohm had similar complaints about the irredeemably polite actress: 'To think that a young English lady in the twentieth century could have been so badly brought up as to behave in so outrageous a manner!' (*Saturday Review*, 13 May 1905). There is a characteristic straining for reticence on the part of English reviewers and audiences. Beatrix Lehmann, at the Cambridge Festival Theatre, acted 'with minute control: the dance was, happily, not a "performance" ' (*Granta*, 28 Nov. 1931)—though choreographed by Ninette de Valois. Even in the Berkoff production, the dance became a mimed strip-tease, and the focus therefore shifted to Herod, as though the most important image was inside his head. The difficulty stems from the duality of Wilde's conception, imagining Salome as both powerfully sexual and at the same time intensely pure. The dance is an expression of total self-absorption and self-expression: in Yeats's phrase, 'self-delighting'. There is no indication about music.

837 *charger*: dish (as in Mark 6: 25).

956 *chrysolites*: a chrysolite is a semi-precious stone, like chrysoprase, sardonyx, chalcedony, etc. Wilde used them as much for their sound as their meaning, like the list of jewels in chapter 11 of *The Picture of Dorian Gray*, itself modelled on passages in Huysmans's *A Rebours*.

972 *land of the Seres*: China.

978 *veil of the sanctuary*: Herod's offering is the supreme act of sacrilege. Behind this passage lies, perhaps, the stealing of the veil in chapter 5 of Flaubert's *Salammbô*.

1055 *I am well pleased with my daughter*: Herodias's words recall the voice from heaven, Luke 3: 22: 'Thou art my beloved Son; in thee I am well pleased.'

1062 s.d. *The stage becomes quite dark*: Salome's final act, the kissing of the severed head, and her last speech, apparently take place in darkness: a rare and dangerous piece of staging, but in keeping with Wilde's experiment with 'total theatre' techniques. Beerbohm recorded that the first English Salome 'brought the head briskly down to the footlights, and in that glare delivered to it all her words and kisses', thereby destroying 'all our illusion'.

1069 *Kill that woman!*: like the dance, this climactic moment relies on precise physical interpretation. The death throes of the characters in which Sarah Bernhardt specialized (such as Tosca or Cléopâtre) tended to be protracted and spectacular. This ending is Wilde's invention.

A Woman of No Importance

Dedication. The Countess de Grey had previously been married to the Earl of Lonsdale. She was a famous society beauty and a friend of Wilde since 1880.

The Persons of the Play. Lord Illingworth: the name may have been suggested by a character in Hawthorne's *Scarlet Letter*, Chillingworth.

Lord Alfred Rufford: the form of the title indicates that he is the younger son of a duke or marquess. In Philip Prowse's 1991 production for the Royal Shakespeare Company, he was played as an an exquisite Oxford undergraduate. Wilde's choice of name must be a private reference to Lord Alfred Douglas.

The Ven. Archdeacon Daubeny, DD: 'Ven.' is an abbreviation for Venerable, the courtesy title given to an Archdeacon, next in rank to a Bishop in the Anglican Church. 'DD' is 'Doctor of Divinity'. A Dr Daubeny had been a fellow of Wilde's Oxford college and had left in his will a bust of Augustus Caesar, to be given to the first member of Magdalen College 'after my decease who shall gain the Newdigate Prize'. Wilde duly inherited the bust.

Lady Hunstanton: Hunstanton is a small seaside resort in Norfolk, not far from where Wilde was staying when he wrote the play.

Lady Caroline Pontefract: the form 'Lady Caroline' indicates that she is the daughter of an earl.

Lady Stutfield: Wilde gave some specific character notes to his New York agent: 'Lady Stutfield is very serious and romantic—she must play as if she was playing the heroine of a romance. Lady Hunstanton is genial, loveable, and kind: Lady Caroline hard and bitter: the girl simple and direct: the boy must be charming and young . . . Lord Illingworth requires great distinction' (*More Letters*, 120).

Hester Worsley: Wilde tried various names for his American Puritan. She was Mabel in early drafts. A note on one draft reads: 'Ruth: some nice New England name—Mary'. Hester may derive from Hester Prynne, heroine of *The Scarlet Letter*, who was 'forced to stand in public with her illegitimate child and wearing the letter "A" (for adulteress) embroidered on her dress. It is probably no accident that

Mrs Arbuthnot's name begins with A' (Katharine Worth, *Oscar Wilde* (1983), 110).

Cast: *Tree*: Herbert Beerbohm Tree, the actor-manager, had all the elegance and style to play Lord Illingworth, in spite of Wilde's initial reluctance: 'As Herod in my *Salome* you would be admirable. As a peer of the realm in my latest dramatic device, pray forgive me if I do not see you.' Wilde described Illingworth: 'He is certainly not natural. He is a figure of art. Indeed, if you can bear the truth, he is MYSELF.' At rehearsals, Wilde tried to make Tree less theatrical, commenting: 'Ah, every day Herbert becomes *de plus en plus Oscarisé*. It is a wonderful case of Nature imitating Art' (Hesketh Pearson, *Beerbohm Tree: His Life and Laughter* (1956), 65 and 71).

Terry: Fred Terry and Julia Neilson (Gerald Arbuthnot and Hester Worsley) were husband and wife. Fred Terry wanted to make Gerald a man of the world, and again Wilde strove to modify his interpretation.

Rose Leclercq: she subsequently played Lady Bracknell, who shares something of Lady Hunstanton's style and idiosyncracies.

Mrs Bernard Beere: Mrs Beere as Mrs Arbuthnot 'looked magnificent in her black robe and Magdalen-red hair'.

The Scenes. Wilde included his favourite setting of a terrace (as in *Salome*) and used four separate locations, with the play moving from the grand scale of Hunstanton Chase to the provincial and domestic confinement of Mrs Arbuthnot's sitting-room in a 'third-rate English town'. The play also moves between two gardens, the open lawns and formal terracing of the great house and the enclosed haven at Mrs Arbuthnot's. (Note Lord Illingworth's comment: 'I was twenty-one, I believe, when the whole thing began in your father's garden' (2. 555–6). Prowse, who designed a formal setting backed by a semi-classical landscape painting, with a fountain like a stuffed ottoman, all in Grosvenor Gallery greenery-yallery colours, began the scene with a dreamlike sequence in which Lord Alfred, barefoot and in white, practised his croquet shots. There was the occasional cry of a peacock, in keeping with the human display which follows.

The Shires: literally, these are the English counties whose names end in -shire; the term also refers to the Midland counties noted for fox-hunting (see Lord Illingworth's definition of health, I. 280–2.).

1 This is one of Wilde's most ambitious settings—terrace, lawn, yew-tree, the perfect image of the English country house-party; apparently idyllic, but poisoned and corrupt. It is reminiscent of the opening of Henry James's *The Portrait of a Lady*. (Wilde returns to the outdoor setting, and the yew-tree, in *The Importance of Being Earnest*.) The

submerged reference to the Garden of Eden is picked up at ll. 513–14, 'The Book of Life begins with a man and a woman in a garden.'

19 *little lax*: the notion of social respectability, and acceptability, central to *Lady Windermere's Fan*, is equally important in this play; as often, Wilde introduces the theme via a comic character, who is none the less formidable.

24 *One*: the impersonal third person—characteristic of the old-fashioned upper class.

28 *I dislike Mrs Allonby*: Wilde swiftly establishes Hester as truthful and transparent, a contrast to the masks assumed by the English characters.

41 *worked for their living*: Lady Caroline formulates the astonishingly hypocritical but still surviving English distinction between inherited and earned wealth, 'old' and 'new' money.

52 S.D. *Footman*: the Footman serves to build up Lady Hunstanton's entrance; the season is, perhaps, early autumn, as the shooting season has begun. (Lady Hunstanton has a brace of partridge placed in the Archdeacon's carriage.) The shawls and wraps enhance the autumnal feeling, almost Chekhovian, and visually point the contrast between the old and middle-aged, and the young, which is part of the play's structure. The servants, and the fetching and carrying, emphasize the Victorian upper classes' ability to transfer their indoor world outside. Presumably, the Footman has also brought a writing-case (see l. 71). Wilde referred to Act I as the perfect act, since it contained 'absolutely no action at all'.

60 *Shetland*: a type of wool.

79 *Are you very pleased about it?*: Hester's silence has already indicated her disapproval.

86 *offered Vienna*: the post of ambassador at Vienna—then one of the key European (and world) posts.

114 *before Eleanor came out*: before her daughter Eleanor was presented at court, and so introduced into adult society.

123 S.D. *Enter Mrs Allonby*: 'Mrs Tree [Mrs Allonby] as she stood on the terrace . . . seemed a dainty figure sketched by Lancret. Her dress, pure Louis XV, was of white silk chine, with roses of every tint—a silk that reminded one of old-fashioned chintz. Her quaintly cut cloak of willow-green, open from throat to hem, with short pelerine, was edged with sable, and had a silk lining of a still softer shade; a branch of mauve orchids held in her hand gave the finishing touch of colour to the pretty picture' (*The Sketch*, 26 Apr. 1893). The elaborate description suggests how strong a contrast Wilde was making between the female dandy and the comparative simplicity of Hester and Mrs Arbuthnot. Mrs Allonby and Lady Stutfield carry parasols.

127 *Quite, quite wonderful*: Wilde, following tradition, endows his comic characters with verbal mannerisms and obsessions.

140 *young women*: in devising the women characters, Wilde plays with the full range of age and sexual status: the dowagers Lady Caroline and Lady Hunstanton, the young, married but apparently available women, Mrs Allonby and Lady Stutfield (in two drafts, it is clear that Lady Stutfield is a widow), the pretty unmarried 'widow' in black, and the *ingénue* Hester dominate the play.

167 *I think not, John*: Sir John has obviously seated himself next to Lady Stutfield, pursuing the traditional English country house-party pastime of flirtation.

189 S.D. *Enter Lord Illingworth*: illustrations show Lord Illingworth with hat, stick, and gloves.

212 *These American girls*: like Virginia Otis in Wilde's story 'The Canterville Ghost', who marries the Duke of Cheshire.

221 *orphan*: Hester, like Gerald (and John Worthing), is fatherless.

225 *American dry goods*: the joke appears also in chapter 3 of Wilde's 'decadent' novel *The Picture of Dorian Gray*—there are many verbal echoes and parallels between the two works. (*The Picture of Dorian Gray* first appeared in 1890 and, in a revised and extended form, in Apr. 1891.)

263 *East End*: the poorest district of London.

273 *Blankets and coals*: often distributed by the clergy on behalf of some local charity.

282 *The English country gentleman . . . the uneatable*: while this is one of the play's best known epigrams, it is quite in character for the fastidious peer to despise the hearty, coarse country gentleman. Lord Illingworth succeeded to the title because of his elder brother's death in the hunting-field (2. 407). His comment softens the previous snub to Kelvil.

290 *Vulgar habit*: Lord Illingworth has been sitting beside Mrs Allonby— the two most dandiacal characters in the play gravitate to each other's company.

306 *orchid*: archetypal cultivated, exotic, and decadent flower.

333 *our English home-life*: the grand setting gives added irony to this piece of hypocrisy.

345 *You a married man, Mr Kettle?*: Lady Caroline unerringly finds a way of making Kelvil unattractive to Lady Stutfield.

360 *cigarettes*: the connotation of a cigarette (especially a gold-tipped one) is of something modern, even decadent. Wilde develops this motif relentlessly in *The Importance of Being Earnest*.

382 *Yellow Drawing-room*: clearly Hunstanton Chase offers a choice of drawing-rooms.

385 *your nephew*: Lord Alfred Rufford.

388 S.D. *Exeunt*. The cross entrance and exit allow Mrs Allonby the opportunity to comment on the Pontefracts. Wilde completes this act, after the gradual build-up of characters to the full complement of the house-party, with a more detailed coda, featuring initially the two couples, and two contrasting moral codes.

414 *everyone*: with the exception of Hester.

442 *decidedly pretty*: a sexual challenge, taken up by Mrs Allonby at l. 459.

526 *A woman of no importance*: the phrase sets up the pattern which is completed by the last speech of the Fourth Act, spoken by the woman in question, Mrs Arbuthnot; but, taken in conjunction with the smile to the current Mrs A, Mrs Allonby, it serves to question the integrity of Lord Illingworth, until this point the most entertaining character.

2 This scene above all establishes *A Woman of No Importance* as a women's play. For two-thirds of the act, the five women—six with the arrival of Mrs Arbuthnot—have priority, and their conversation and physical presence set the agenda. Mrs Allonby and Lady Stutfield might sit together on one sofa; the two older women, Lady Hunstanton and Lady Caroline, on another. Hester is apart and to one side, in her 'nice little corner' (l. 227), probably a little up-stage. Hester, the silent listener, thus creates a second focus on the stage. In the first production, Hester's dress 'of white satin, was entirely veiled by silver-spangled tulle. In itself the dress, glistening and shimmering with every movement, was pretty, but somehow seemed hardly suited to the stately, puritanical Hester Worsley' (*Sketch*, 26 Apr. 1893). It would, however, ensure that Hester was kept within the audience's eye.

9 *breathing space*: the custom was for the women to leave the dining-room after the dessert wine had been passed round once, to take coffee on their own, while the men were left with the port. (Contrast Ibsen's handling of this moment in the opening sequence of *The Wild Duck*.)

34 *married women's property*: this is both a general reference to topical debate, and also specifically to the Married Women's Property Acts. The important 1882 legislation was extended and refined in 1893.

51 *Hunstanton*: correct, but imposingly dismissive, way of referring to her dead husband.

53 *promissory note*: a legal document which obliges someone to pay a sum of money on a stated day (and perhaps a suppressed reference to sexual obligation).

57 *only had one husband*: Wilde's ironic commentary on the ideals of married life is conveyed adroitly by the pattern of relationships: Lady

Caroline is the only woman we see with her husband. Not only is he her fourth, but he is forever pursuing other women. Mrs Allonby has an absent husband; the other women are widowed or unmarried, while the off-stage wife of the Archdeacon is a chronic invalid and 'happiest alone'.

86 *mauvais quart d'heure*: an unpleasant quarter of an hour.

88 *very, very wrong*: Lady Stutfield 'innocently' pursues the 'wrong thing' Mr Allonby did—the sub-text, presumably, is that he was both sexually and romantically inexperienced.

124 *middle classes*: they are treated as a race quite as remote as, and distinctly less welcome than, the lower classes. Many of them would, of course, be present in the theatre audience, at least after the opening night.

151 *The Ideal Man*: Lady Stutfield's phrase points towards Wilde's next play, *An Ideal Husband*, while Mrs Allonby's definitions look forward to the tone, at least, of *The Importance of Being Earnest*. She is speaking with an authority that matches Lord Illingworth's pronouncements; and these speeches are balanced by Hester's alternative values expressed later in the scene.

209 *never surrender*: again, the sexual connotations become more noticeable, prompting Lady Hunstanton's concern about the impact on Hester.

235 S.D. *continuing*: Hester clearly speaks loudly enough to be heard by the other guests, should they choose to do so (as do Mrs Allonby and Lady Stutfield at ll. 249–50).

260 S.D. *Gets up*: the move gives Hester greater prominence for her key speech at ll. 263 ff.

262 *iron Exhibition*: the International Exhibition at Chicago, May to Nov. 1893.

278 *leper in purple*: this phrase and the succeeding sentence were presumed to give particular offence to some members of the audience and were omitted from later performances.

285 *Lord Henry Weston*: his name echoes that of the corrupting Lord Henry Wotton in *The Picture of Dorian Gray*.

293 *Let all women who have sinned be punished*: the moral absolute is reminiscent of Lady Windermere's initial attitude. Hester, who has before been used as an on-stage audience, becomes the protagonist, while Mrs Arbuthnot, in penitential black with lace trimmings, is compelled to listen to her judgement. Mrs Arbuthnot, like Hester, stands out against 'the brilliant dresses of the butterfly women' (*Sketch*, 26 Apr. 1893). However, the *Daily Telegraph*'s description of Mrs Arbuthnot's entrance suggests an ambiguity in the image: Mrs Beere 'dressed in close-fitting black velvet, glides into the room' (20 Apr. 1893).

303 *pillar of fire*: see Exodus 13: 21. Hester shares Mrs Arbuthnot's range of biblical reference.

306 *my cotton*: Lady Caroline has some kind of needlework with her, as in the First Act. The comic intervention also serves to shift the women's attention to Mrs Arbuthnot.

308 *I didn't hear you announced*: conventionally, Mrs Arbuthnot's arrival would have been announced by a servant.

310 *party*: other texts add a S.D.: 'Hester hands a reel of cotton to Lady C, who bows'.

325 *Mrs Arbuthnot's things*: in the Prowse production, Mrs Arbuthnot brought her embroidery with her (see 3. 150). Other texts indicate that Lady Hunstanton takes Mrs Arbuthnot to sit on a sofa at this point.

336 *Now, do come*: the arrival of Mrs Arbuthnot demands that the grouping changes, aligning Hester and Mrs Arbuthnot, and preparing for Mrs Allonby's barb at l. 348. Mrs Allonby and Lady Stutfield remain in the room as a visual counterpoint.

367 *he does nothing*: the occupation of the dandy.

395 *straws in his hair*: a traditional emblem of lunacy. In nineteenth-century productions, Ophelia appeared with straws in her hair in her mad scene.

402 *a very good match for her*: the daughter of a Duchess would be expected to marry someone much higher in rank than a mere baronet. Significantly, it is Lady Cecilia who tried to 'buy off' Rachel (l. 562), whereas Lord Illingworth's father told him it was his duty to marry her (l. 567).

409 *George came in for everything*: the younger son's unexpected inheritance is the moment of realization for Mrs Arbuthnot.

421 S.D. *Enter Sir John*: earlier texts have an entrance for Mr Kelvil here, with the other men.

433 S.D. *Sir John goes over*: Wilde's stage direction should indicate that Lord Illingworth enters at this point, as Sir John Pontefract crosses obediently back to his wife. In the Prowse production, he entered at l. 429.

461 *All women . . . That is his*: Wilde reworked this for Algernon in *The Importance of Being Earnest*. The conjunction of a flippantly witty exchange with the tension of the imminent recognition is characteristic of Wilde's method.

472 *for the moment*: although Mrs Arbuthnot is habitually solemn, Wilde gives her an occasional cutting edge, as in this concluding flick. She also avoids addressing Lord Illingworth directly in this first speech, which has been prompted by Gerald. Stage directions in some versions have 'Mrs Arbuthnot puts hand on Gerald', which would create a

resonant stage-picture when Lord Illingworth repeats the gesture at l. 473.

498 *in black velvet*: Mrs Allonby deliberately depersonalizes Mrs Arbuthnot, while emphasizing her beauty.

524 *John!*. The shift to the music-room gives Pontefract a fresh opportunity to pursue Lady Stutfield.

526 S.D. *Sound of violin*: the violin continues under the following exchange; the Second Act repeats the pattern of the First Act, with a key private dialogue placed after large-scale public conversations. Realistically, there will be a few moments before the music begins, and it seems appropriate to have a pause before Lord Illingworth speaks.

527 *Rachel!*: Lord Illingworth immediately becomes more intimate, with his use of her Christian name, but his repetitions become progressively condescending.

531 *no right*: no legal right.

562 *six hundred a year*: this was a considerable sum. Paradoxically, while the women are made to suffer by 'society', Wilde makes women responsible for perpetuating society's 'values'.

615 *Children begin by loving their parents*: Lord Illingworth's three statements are played back to him by Mrs Arbuthnot at Act IV, ll. 465–7.

617 *George*: the personal plea is emphasized by the use of the first name, framing the speech. The biblical references, which are in keeping with Mrs Arbuthnot's role, are broadly pertinent—the little vineyard refers to Ahab's seizure of Naboth's vineyard (1 Kings 21), and the ewe lamb to David's possession of Bathsheba (2 Samuel 11–12).

3 The portraits emphasize the notion of family, ancestry, and inherited wealth (as in Ibsen's *Rosmersholm*). The fateful terrace is again in evidence. The men are clearly smoking (see l. 137). Lord Illingworth's posture is significant. The male-dominated stage picture contrasts with the opening image of the Second Act.

26 S.D. *puts his hand on Gerald's shoulder*: Wilde echoes the pattern of gesture of 2. 473 (and that between mother and daughter in the Third Act of *Lady Windermere's Fan*).

63 *A well-tied tie . . . in life*: in the Prowse production, Lord Illingworth retied Gerald's bow-tie at this point.

74 *that is all*: following this line, other texts indicate: 'Servants bring on a tray with lemonade, etc., on it and place it on table RC.'

84 *Women are pictures*: Lord Illingworth alludes to the picture-gallery setting.

102 *plain and the coloured*: this extends the picture references: prints for toy theatres were issued in two versions, plain (a penny) and coloured

(twopence). Illingworth's 'lesson' on the nature of women is the counterpart to Mrs Allonby's on the Ideal Man.

128 *Peerage*: *Burke's Peerage, Baronetage and Knightage* (the recognized authority on Britain's aristocracy and their family pedigrees) or some similar publication.

132 S.D. *appears on terrace behind*: Mrs Arbuthnot acts as a visual qualification to Lord Illingworth's declaration.

154 *Dorcas*: Dorcas (Acts of the Apostles 9: 39) made 'coats and garments' for widows—hence a 'Dorcas Society', providing clothes for charity.

155 *tambour frame*: a wooden frame for embroidery.

166 *Humane Society*: 'a society for the rescue of drowning persons' (*OED*).

173 *every saint has a past*: Lord Illingworth makes a coded and cruel reference to Mrs Arbuthnot.

183 *have you seen John anywhere?*: Wilde constantly undercuts the serious debate about Gerald's future with these comic interventions, which make the melodramatic ending of the act the more startling.

208 *Bimetallism*: the theory of a fixed ratio between gold and silver coinage, a contemporary topic both inexhaustible and insoluble, and seemingly beyond Lady Stutfield's understanding. Like 'Patagonia', it seems to imply flirtation, or at least attempted flirtation.

212 *Patagonia*: the inference is that Sir John's commentary on South American mores has been mildly improper.

248 S.D. *Moves . . . back of stage*: again, Wilde places Mrs Arbuthnot where she offers a visual commentary on the rest of society, especially during the patterned definitions of 'the secret of life'.

282 *Memory in a woman*: the reference for the audience is to the silent figure of Mrs Arbuthnot.

287 *Doctor Daubeny's carriage!*: the Archdeacon's carriage has arrived at a pre-arranged time, signalling the end of the formal part of the evening.

298 *beautiful moon tonight*: with the departure of the Archdeacon, Mrs Allonby initiates the darker side of the evening.

312 *India*: the Indian Empire was a crucial sphere of political influence and offers a plausible destination for Lord Illingworth, as well as a powerful attraction to Gerald. The idea of emigration, or of living abroad, is a recurrent theme in Wilde.

339 *sins of the parents*: as in Ibsen's *Ghosts*, the reference is to the Old Testament law (Exodus 20: 5).

341 S.D. *Moves away to fireplace*: the S.D. here in other texts is: 'Looks away and wipes her eyes with her handkerchief'.

360 *He won't come*: the Licensing Copy indicates 'wipes her eyes with her handkerchief'.

437 S.D. *sits down beside his mother*: Wilde is moving into dangerously sentimental territory with this stage position; but the mood is partly controlled by Gerald's reaction, and rejection, 'No nice girl would'.

481 *purest thing on God's earth*: arguably, someone as naïve as Gerald might well fall back on the language of melodrama; but the following sequence must strain the ingenuity of any director, actor, or actress. William Archer's criticism of this moment is quoted in the introduction. The s.d. in the Licensing Copy (and other texts) is marginally less effective, since it does not relate to previous act endings: 'Mrs Arbuthnot sinks on her knees and bows her head. Hester with a look of pain glides from the room. Lord Illingworth bites his lip, hesitates for a moment, and then goes off. Gerald forces his mother back, and with a look of horror and amazement, gazes into her face.' It's a very fine margin. Prowse handled the moment by suppressing some of the lines, though stretching social conventions by setting the kiss on-stage, and so in public, with the shadowy figure of Mrs Allonby in the background.

4 This is the only small-scale domestic setting in Wilde's four comedies: a sitting-room, not a drawing-room, morning-room, or library; 'nice and old-fashioned' (ll. 15–16), not modern. The garden is an integral part of the stage-picture: a beautiful 'Cotman-like landscape, seen through the bay window' (*Echo*, 20 Apr. 1893).

18 *happy English home*: the concept has been discussed theoretically in the previous acts: Mrs Allonby's visit to this rarity prepares for Lord Illingworth's.

32 *Fresh natural flowers*: this is a most un-Wildean combination, but Lady Hunstanton's description emphasizes the significance Wilde placed on physical surroundings in his plays.

42 *Divorce Court*: presumably Lord Ashton was charged with adultery and cited as a co-respondent in a divorce suit.

76 *When a man says that*: Mrs Allonby, having encouraged Lord Illingworth to attempt to corrupt Hester, now begins to turn her attention to Gerald.

83 *she has a bad headache*: this is a slight rebuff to Lady Hunstanton, underlined by Gerald's subsequent comment.

90 *But mothers are so weak*: Lady Hunstanton is clearly annoyed that her plan for Gerald has not materialized.

99 *What name can I sign?*: only in writing to his father would the name be a problem—this lends added weight to the advice directed at Gerald through the French window in the following speeches. There is also a link with a sequence in the Third Act, surviving in two drafts but later

deleted, in which Lord Illingworth persuades Gerald to write his name as Gerald Harford, on the pretext that he needs to inspect his handwriting if he is to be his secretary.

> GERALD Yes, I wish our name had been Harford.

> LORD ILLINGWORTH Oh, Arbuthnot is a very—a very useful name.—Your handwriting is excellent, Gerald. It has not got the slightest trace of the ledger or the bank about it. It is the handwriting of a gentleman. . . .

In those versions this serves to explain Lord Illingworth's recognition of Gerald's handwriting at l. 415, though he might be assumed to know it already.

105 *bring me back something nice*: Mrs Allonby's is the voice of temptation, characteristically expressed as a joke.

137 *I will not marry Lord Illingworth*: the rejection is not just of Lord Illingworth, but of the most traditional kind of conclusion in a *drame* or well-made play.

183 S.D. *Enter Hester behind*: Hester's position repeats the entrances of Mrs Arbuthnot in the Second and Third Acts. She is about to assume Mrs Arbuthnot's moral values.

217 *when you were naked*: Mrs Arbuthnot's speech is laden with biblical references to, for example, Matthew 25: 35–6, and the cadences of the Book of Common Prayer.

221 *Not Hannah*: see 1 Samuel 1–2.

225 *to man's estate*: echoing Feste's song at the end of Shakespeare's *Twelfth Night*.

291 S.D. *kneels down*: before this action, Gerald has to decide to make his sacrifice—of his 'name', of legitimacy. To shame her, is to insist on her marrying Lord Illingworth; to save her, is to accept her as 'my mother and my father all in one'.

304 S.D. *flings himself sobbing on a sofa*: the actions, positions, gestures dominate the sequence; it is as though we are seeing a series of animated Victorian narrative paintings (which themselves drew heavily on the theatre for subject-matter and style). It is only in the context of Wilde's urbane comic control that such a melodramatic scene seems surprising.

332 S.D. *starts*: the presence of the servant delays Mrs Arbuthnot's first question.

359 *entailed*: the property is legally tied to the holder of the title, and so not in Lord Illingworth's gift. Gerald will receive a country house, a shooting lodge, and a town house—enough for even the most demanding English gentleman. All of Lord Illingworth's arrangements are concerned with property and money.

383 *you are not necessary*: Hester is an heiress. Significantly, money has not been mentioned by her.

403 S.D. *A pause*: Wilde uses the pause effectively (as at l. 474). In two drafts, Lord Illingworth takes out a cigarette, and is rebuked by Mrs Arbuthnot—'My son has never smoked in this room.'

420 S.D. *reads it slowly*: Wilde deliberately slows the pace of the act at this point; the letter of revelation and clarification is a standard dramatic convention, traditionally initiating a resolution. Wilde makes use of the convention before exploding it.

473 *What fin-de-siècle person?*: the person capable of such an act should be intensely end-of-the-century, modern, a creator of taste and morality: that it is the Puritan who rejected his advances cuts Lord Illingworth deeply. The *Pall Mall Gazette* (20 Apr. 1893) praised Tree's dexterity in suggesting 'a sudden uncomfortable feeling of old age coming over the brilliant sinner—an old age that betrayed itself in mere hints of speech and gait, and that contrasted grimly with the elaborate youth-fulness of dress.'

474 S.D. *begins putting it on*: the putting on of one glove is a process which, for a dandy, takes some time.

490 *and one's——*: Mrs Arbuthnot has been unmoved by his insults to her and acts only to prevent the word 'bastard'.

499 S.D. *picks it up*: the final image pointedly places the two women together, while Gerald holds the last relic of his father, a single glove.

An Ideal Husband

Dedication. Frank Harris (1856–1931) was a journalist, a lively if factually unreliable writer, and a generous friend to Wilde. He bought the rights to a Wilde scenario, which he turned into the play *Mr and Mrs Daventry*.

The Persons of the Play. *Caversham*: Wilde has given his characters high social ranking. The Earl of Caversham is a Knight of the Garter, the highest order of knighthood in England and an honour in the sovereign's gift.

Goring: Wilde was living at Goring-on-Thames between June and October 1893, while working on the play.

Chiltern: the Chiltern hills run close to Goring. A member of Parliament who needs to resign may apply for the 'Chiltern Hundreds'. A Lord Chiltern has a minor part in Trollope's Palliser novel *The Eustace Diamonds* (1871–3). Lady Chiltern's first name, Gertrude, may derive from Gertrude Pearce, who was tutoring Vyvyan Wilde that summer.

De Nanjac: the name of a character in a play by Dumas *fils*, *Le Demi-Monde* (1885)

Markby: the name occurs twice in *The Importance of Being Earnest*, as John Worthing's solicitor, and as a General in the Army list.

Lady Basildon: Lady Basildon is a countess, as wife of an earl.

Mrs Cheveley: Wilde may have taken the name from Rosina Bulwer's novel, lampooning her husband, *Cheveley, or the Man of Honour* (1839).

Cast. Charles Hawtrey: he had impersonated Wilde in Brookfield's play; he also agitated against Wilde in the libel case.

Lewis Waller: good-looking, and with a vibrant voice, as actor-manager he took the leading male role of Sir Robert Chiltern. Wilde reportedly commented: 'He would make an admirable D'Artagnan' (Hesketh Pearson, *The Last Actor-Managers* (1950), 43).

C. H. Brookfield: Brookfield had written and appeared in a burlesque on Wilde, *The Poet and the Puppets*, in 1892. He disliked Wilde and searched for evidence to support Queensberry in the imminent libel case.

Julia Neilson: Miss Neilson had played the strait-laced Hester in *A Woman of No Importance*. She was initially uneasy in her role; she thought Lady Chiltern 'an impossible prig'—'I hated her.' She went to tea with Wilde and his wife, recalling later that 'his very tall, heavy figure was always about the theatre' (*This For Remembrance* (1940), 139). Wilde wrote to her husband: 'Let me assure you that it is what I believe is called the part of the "leading lady"; it is the important part, and the only sympathetic part. Indeed the other woman does not appear in the last act at all' (*More Letters*, 127). (The 'other woman' is Mrs Cheveley, the role of Mabel Chiltern being thought subsidiary.)

The Scenes of the Play. Grosvenor Square and Curzon Street place the action at the centre of power, political and social, in contemporary London. Among the most distinctive designs for this play are Rex Whistler's, done in his army tent for the 1943 Westminster Theatre production: 'the combination of ceremonious Georgian rooms with absurd Victorian furnishings caught the style and wit of the dramatist' (James Agate, 'Oscar Wilde and the Theatre', *The Masque*, 3 (1949)).

1 *An Ideal Husband* has the fullest, most detailed of Wilde's directions for settings, as he deliberately strives to create a word-picture for his readers. By contrast, the typescript of 10 Mar. 1894, states only: 'Lady Chiltern is receiving her guests. The room is brilliantly lighted, and full of people.' Earlier drafts place this act in the drawing-room. The shift to the grander Octagon Room, with the tapestry in the background, the series of reception rooms, and the number of non-speaking actors (the copy prepared for Frohman has movements for forty) indicate the lavish scale of the opening stage-picture, reflecting Chiltern's position and wealth. Carl Toms's opulent setting for the 1992 Globe Theatre

production showed the guests actually ascending the staircase to be received by Lady Chiltern. The paintings and large-scale decorative work of Boucher (1703–1770) mirrored the elegance of French society in the period which ended with Louis XVI (Seize) and the French Revolution. Watteau (1684–1721), an exquisite colourist, was praised by Wilde's mentor, Walter Pater. In the opening chapter of *Sybil* (1845), a novel which has several points of contact with Wilde's play, Disraeli refers to 'the scenes of Watteau and Boucher that sparkled on the medallions over the lofty doors'. The lavish concept was largely conveyed by the clothes. Julia Neilson's 1895 costume was, according to her, an 'astonishing creation'—'of cream brocaded silk, with a bodice decked with chiffon and strewn with Neapolitan violets; and it had bunches of violets round the skirt and on the shoulders' (*This For Remembrance*, 140).

1   *Going on*: it was common society practice to visit several houses during the evening—dinner at one, a reception (such as this, with classical music provided as entertainment) at another, and a dance at a third. The string quartet is mildly 'serious', in keeping with the political atmosphere. The 1899 text has 'Margaret' for 'Olivia': as Isobel Murray has pointed out, the women are interchangeable.

17 *trivial*: the word looks forward to *The Importance of Being Earnest*—in fact, the tone adopted by these two 'exquisite' women strongly resembles that of Wilde's next play.

23 s.d. *known for his neckties*: the Vicomte's interest in neckties anticipates Lord Goring's. Wilde uses a minor dandy to set off his more detailed study.

25 S.D. *the Garter*: the order of the Garter marks Lord Caversham as one of the Victorian great and good. Wilde assumes his audience will recognize such emblems. 'Whig' is the eighteenth-century term for the political party more usually known in Wilde's time as the Liberals, or for a representative of that party's more moderate, less radical, wing. Wilde is writing during a Liberal administration. Sir Thomas Lawrence (1769–1830) was the leading portrait painter of his time: he was commissioned to paint the heads of state and military leaders after the defeat of Napoleon.

30 S.D. *English type of prettiness*: as opposed to the French fragility of Watteau.

    Tanagra: third century BC Greek terracotta statuette, characteristically of a draped woman.

33 *the Row*: Rotten Row, in Hyde Park.

41 *at home on Wednesdays*: the Chilterns regularly entertain on Wednesday during the London season.

58 S.D. *à la marquise*: the style comes from the period of Louis XV. Mrs

Cheveley's appearance defines her, as Lord Goring's buttonholes define him. 'Venetian red' suggests flamboyance and adventure; 'heliotrope' is purple. The comparison of a luxurious, hot-house orchid contrasts with the apple-blossom fragrance of Mabel Chiltern. 'Tawny-haired, red-cheeked, white-shouldered' was the critic William Archer's description. James Agate thought Martita Hunt in the 1943 production 'looked like a Sargent and displayed inimitable breeding'.

80 *at the Foreign Office*: Wilde gave Sir Robert various offices in different drafts, settling finally on Under-Secretary of State for Foreign Affairs. The arrangement echoes contemporary politics: when Wilde wrote the play, Sir Edward Grey was Under-Secretary, speaking on foreign affairs in the House of Commons, while Lord Rosebery was Foreign Secretary. When Rosebery succeeded Gladstone as Prime Minister, Lord Kimberley took over the Foreign Office, with Grey remaining in office, the position at the time of the play's opening. (If Chiltern had been Foreign Secretary, he would have already had a seat in the Cabinet by right, as offered to him at 4. 371.)

81 *Vienna*: Mrs Cheveley's city lay at the centre of European politics.

84 S.D. *Moves away*: the Frohman script has a s.d. 'music off' at line 70, to help prepare for the relatively empty stage which must accompany the conversation between Sir Robert and Mrs Cheveley. The movement pattern of the act is rather fluid. It is not clear, for example, at what point Lady Chiltern leaves: possibly at line 409, with the other guests.

92 *butter me*: he means 'butter me up'.

96 S.D. *Sir Robert Chiltern*: as Russell Jackson points out, 'the idealised picture of Sir Robert owes more to Wilde's private imagery than to the actor's appearance' (*Two Society Comedies: A Woman of No Importance, An Ideal Husband*, ed. Ian Small and Russell Jackson (1983)), Waller being known for conventionally robust good looks. Here Wilde seems to be writing pointedly for the reader's imagination, rather than recalling stage practice. The romantic expression in the deep-set eyes and the pale, thin, pointed hands suggest the artist, not the politician. Sir Anthony Van Dyck (1599–1641), the Flemish painter, ended his career in England at the court of Charles I.

97 *Good evening, Lady Markby!*: Frohman notes that Sir Robert shakes Lady Markby's hand, a sign of familiarity.

116 *good chef*: Lady Markby assumes an automatic invitation to dinner.

151 *blue spectacles*: the modern equivalent would be dark glasses (as opposed to rose-tinted).

187 S.D. *Drops her fan*: the action makes Sir Robert stoop at Mrs Cheveley's request. Mrs Cheveley uses her fan as a weapon later in the scene, at ll. 459 and 506.

205 *Baron Arnheim*: the name and the Vienna connection indicate that the Baron was Austrian or German. Wilde may be recalling Baron Reinach, a German Jewish banker implicated in the Panama Canal scheme scandal. See note to l. 419.

216 *old Greek*: Sir Robert refers to the wanderings and adventures of Odysseus; Mrs Cheveley's comment about Penelope, Odysseus's faithful wife, suggests that she herself played the role of the seductive Calypso.

219 S.D. *Enter Lord Goring*: The following description provides the classic definition of the Wildean dandy, an idealized self-portrait. Some modern productions make Lord Goring resemble Wilde, as, for example, in Martin Shaw's performance (Globe Theatre, 1992).

232 *Boodle's Club*: Boodle's in St James's is one of the oldest and most distinguished London clubs.

270 *dragon of good taste*: this must be a malapropism for 'paragon'. The funny foreigner who makes linguistic mistakes is an uncharacteristically laboured joke on Wilde's part.

287 *Lady Rufford's*: the name occurs in both *Lady Windermere's Fan* and *A Woman of No Importance*.

378 *child-diplomatist*: the Vicomte de Nanjac. (In the British Library typescript, 'dreadful little Frenchman', with MS correction to 'affected'—presumably, Wilde thought better of committing a gratuitous insult against the French to print.)

382 S.D. (*They go downstairs*): the reception rooms are on the first floor, the dining-room on the ground floor.

414 *family prayers*: some English households retained the habit of holding family prayers each morning.

419 *Argentine Canal Company*: the fictional scheme is modelled on the French Panama Canal project, which collapsed in 1889. The scandal broke in 1892, and encompassed the probable suicide of Reinach, the resignation of the French Cabinet, and the imprisonment of Lesseps and Eiffel.

426 *Suez Canal*: the shares were bought on Disraeli's advice in 1875. Baron Rothschild provided the finance and, conceivably, the vital information.

455 *my Corots*: to collect the landscapes of the French painter Corot (1796–1875) suggests both taste and wealth—and the connection is that Baron Arnheim provided the means to buy the paintings, as well as the lesson in taste.

471 *the House*: the House of Commons

479 *It makes the whole world kin*: *Troilus and Cressida*, III. iii. 171: 'One touch of nature makes the whole world kin.'

503 *I will call your carriage*: this is the diplomatic way of dismissing someone. Once a servant has announced that the carriage is ready, it should be socially impossible to remain (a convention defied by Algernon in *The Importance of Being Earnest*).

578 *public placard*: this would display the lurid headlines, as Wilde would shortly experience. He may here have been recalling the fate of Parnell.

592 *Ladies' Gallery*: there was a separate Ladies' Gallery at the House of Commons.

610 *I will arrange for a question*: this would be a 'planted' question, put for his convenience by a member of Sir Robert's political party.

631 *the Park*: specifically Hyde Park.

635 *the Season*: the London social season.

665 *Claridge's*: staying at Claridge's hotel in Mayfair indicates Mrs Cheveley's wealth, but also her isolation—she has no friends to stay with.

670 *en règle*: it would not be within the normal social conventions for a single woman to leave a calling card for an unmarried man.

672 S.D. *top of the staircase*: Wilde makes effective use of the key, and central, position at the head of the staircase.

684 *except the Royal Academy*: this is a standard Wilde barb—the Royal Academy was notorious for conservatism in art.

687 *diamond brooch!*: the device of the diamond brooch/bracelet was a relatively late addition to the plot. In early versions, it was simply an excuse for Mrs Cheveley's social call in the Second Act, and was a diamond star.

696 S.D. *green letter-case*: a small case or wallet to put letters in (like other of Goring's accessories, it sounds like one of Wilde's possessions).

732 *mauve Hungarian band*: dressed, presumably, in mauve, a rather laboured aesthetic joke (in recognition that these were the 'mauve' Nineties, mauve, with green and yellow, being the characteristic colours of the decade).

744 *She stole things*: Mrs Cheveley's crimes, and their discovery, passed through a number of versions. Lady Chiltern echoes the rigid moral statements of Lady Windermere and Hester Worsley.

866 *We needs must love the highest*: Lady Chiltern quotes Tennyson, the Poet Laureate (whom Wilde despised). The words are those of Queen Guinevere, in reference to Arthur, *Guinevere*, (1859) l. 651.

869 *Put out the lights!*: an echo of *Othello*, V. ii. 7 ('Put out the light, and then put out the light:'), and a prelude to the grand and ironic effect as the Triumph of Love tapestry is illuminated. The effect seems a little too subtle for effective stage realization in the 1890s and may be intended more for the reader.

2 S.D. *lounging in an armchair*: Lord Goring's relaxed position recalls Lord Illingworth's in the Third Act of *A Woman of No Importance*. His gestures—taking off a glove, tapping his boot with his cane, leaning back with hands in pockets, arranging his necktie, settling his button-hole—contrast throughout with Sir Robert Chiltern's nervous pacing, throwing himself into an armchair, etc., as do his pace and manner of speech.

5 *bald enough*: the phrase means 'old enough', but carries the added suggestion that hair has fallen out through worry, and is a further glance at the recurrent Wildean cult of youth.

16 *perfect*: Lord Goring's question, his comment at l. 18, 'What a pity!', and his witty objectivity throughout, prevent the scene from becoming too solemn.

59 *well-born and poor*: the combination was an obsession with Wilde, who seems to have regarded himself in a similar light: well-born, poor, and brilliant.

92 *most subtle and refined intellect*: Wilde reverses the expected attitudes: 'damned scoundrel' is more the tone of the Chilterns, while the dandiacal Goring would seem more likely to appreciate a subtle intellect.

103 *he expounded to us the most terrible of all philosophies*: compare the fatal influence of Lord Henry Wotton on Dorian Gray, and the deadly impact of the poisonous book.

107 *Park Lane*: in Mayfair, another fashionable and expensive address.

196 *Botany*: Wilde cites botany as a harmless—and, by inference, point-less—occupation. He substituted it for bimetallism (Clark typescript), which he uses later for Mabel Chiltern instead of the more shocking socialism.

200 S.D. *rising from his chair*: the action punctuates the moral decision.

212 *engaged to be married*: a crucial revelation, not just for the main plot, but because it gives added weight to Sir Robert's stance in the Fourth Act about Lord Goring's engagement to Mabel.

227 S.D. *striking the table*: the gesture is the more significant because it is uncharacteristic. Lord Goring immediately reverts to the elegant dandy after this melodramatic slip.

241 *cipher*: in code.

279 *decolleté*: her past is like a low-cut, revealing dress, such as Mrs Cheveley had worn at the reception. In the Clark typescript Mrs Cheveley's past was 'merely one from Paris'.

288 S.D. *walking dress*: a dress suitable for being outside (i.e. in Hyde Park) or for public engagements.

293 *Woman's Liberal Association*: founded in 1886. Women were becoming active in political organizations, even though they were still deprived of the vote.

306 *dull, useful, delightful things*: issues which formed part of the Liberal Party's 1892 manifesto—the Female Inspectors were for factories; the Eight Hours' Bill concerned the hours of the working day. Wilde is concerned to make the background references contemporary and authentic.

329 *Bachelors' Ball*: a Charity Ball, one of many in the London season.

352 *You are our greatest friend*: the addition of 'our' makes Lord Goring a family friend. In *Lady Windermere's Fan*, Lord Darlington gives the term a more intimate nuance, in the First Act, l. 68.

390 *Nobody is incapable of doing a wrong thing*: the statement lies at the centre of the play; it is Lord Goring's serious manner which is so startling to Lady Chiltern—he corrects himself at l. 405.

407 S.D. *most ravishing frock*: Mabel Chiltern's appearance acts as a visual bridge from the serious to the 'trivial'.

410 *Good afternoon, Lord Goring!*: the BL typescript has a MS s.d. 'shakes hands'.

425 *The Morning Post . . . Conference*: the *Morning Post* habitually printed lists of guests at private functions. *County Council*—the London County Council; *Lambeth Conference*—Conference of Church of England Bishops at the Archbishop of Canterbury's London home, Lambeth Palace. (There had been one in 1888.)

439 S.D. *moue*: pout.

454 *Gertrude*: the BL typescript adds a MS s.d. 'putting arm round waist'.

466 *dreadful statue*: the statue of Achilles in Hyde Park was 'dreadful', presumably, because naked.

471 *bimetallism*: the theory of the system was to introduce a fixed ratio between gold and silver currencies. A debate in the House of Commons on 28 Feb. 1893 'caused schism amongst both parties'. See *A Woman of No Importance*, 3. 208 and note.

482 *attracts some attention*, 489 *I know, dear*: s.d.s on other scripts indicate 'on arm of sofa' and 'sits on arm of Lady C's chair' at these points. Mabel's behaviour is spontaneous, warm, intimate, unconventional.

497 *tableaux*: based on famous paintings, these were the Victorian equivalent of the Charity fashion show. There is a glance, too, at the tapestry 'The Triumph of Love' in the First Act.

514 S.D. *bows somewhat distantly*: the coldly formal greetings of Lady Chiltern and Mabel Chiltern are significant. By social convention, Mrs

Cheveley needs to be introduced before she can speak directly to Mabel.

529 *Undeserving*: Mabel's imaginary charity defines her as a dandy. The Victorians tended to confine their good works to the 'deserving poor', who looked for work and were properly grateful and respectful.

554 *at the Opera*: this took place earlier in the evening of the Chilterns' reception.

559 *Drawing Room*: a formal occasion at Court, when titled women such as Lady Markby presented débutantes to the Queen.

563 *assisted emigration*: emigration from England and Wales ran at an annual average of over 100,000 during the 1890s, mostly to the United States. Even so, the net increase in population was a quarter of a million.

589 *Bath*: a fashionable spa town of an earlier era.

622 *agricultural labourer, or the Welsh Church*: agriculture was in a state of acute depression and frequently debated. A Welsh Disestablishment Bill was introduced in April 1894, but withdrawn after heated discussion.

628 *Upper House*: the House of Lords.

629 *The House of Lords is so sensible*: the constitutional position of the Lords was a current issue, the tension increased by having a massively Conservative Upper House and a Liberal Government.

638 *Blue Books*: government reports were published in blue covers.

642 *in yellow covers*: French novels.

651 S.D. *The butler enters*: the presence and movements of the servants lend an ironic touch to Lady Markby's indiscreet gossip.

689 *she went into a convent, or on to the operatic stage*: Lady Markby exploits the same kind of comic alternatives Wilde has already used for Lady Hunstanton in *A Woman of No Importance*, 1. 135.

701 *I am not fond of girl friends*: this seems a rather demeaning barb—Mrs Cheveley is never given the consistency and discrimination of, say, Mrs Erlynne; but it may also be aimed at her previous relationship with Lady Chiltern.

732 *Gertrude*: the use of the first name is presumptuous, helping to prompt the dangerously absolute 'I never change'.

776 S.D. *enters from behind*: Wilde makes effective use of the 'unseen' entrance, as in Mrs Arbuthnot's entrance from the terrace in *A Woman of No Importance*, 2. 294. Mrs Cheveley's comment about the house and its contents motivates her turn at l. 779.

791 S.D. *Enter Mason*: the intervention of the servant, before whom Mrs Cheveley must maintain propriety, leaves her no alternative.

844 S.D. *He passes from the room*: this stage direction was added at proof stage, but may be a memory of the first production—'the door is closed when she reaches it' suggests a visualized stage performance.

3 The location of the rooms is important. Wilde establishes three distinct areas, in addition to the central space of the Library: the hall (and beyond the hall the street) to the right; to the left, the male preserve of the smoking-room; at the back, the drawing-room. The Library is in the eighteenth-century classical style of the Scottish architect Adam. A diagram on a typescript dated 16 Jan. 1894, shows the table centre stage, a chair stage right, and a bureau downstage left (described in the published text as a writing-table). Lord Goring, the first well-dressed philosopher in the history of thought, is echoed by the Ideal Butler, Phipps—not just reflections of modern life, but masters of it. (In specifying an Inverness cape and a Louis XVI cane, Wilde is listing his own personal accessories.) This combination of taste and elegance, both of setting, dress and manners, becomes the context for a pattern of action which has all the hallmarks and rhythms of a boulevard farce.

S.D. *Enter Lord Goring*: Lord Goring opens each of the last three acts and is used by Wilde to set the dominant tone.

42 S.D. *pink envelope*: the pink envelope and notepaper mark it as a woman's, and also make it more conspicuous for an audience, as its precise physical position becomes important later in the act.

63 *Lord Caversham*: the first instance of the unexpected, heightened by the impassivity of Phipps, who acts as a kind of stage-manager to the comings and goings.

77 *breezes*: colloquial for 'brisk disagreements'.

99 *it is your duty to get married*: Lord Caversham shares Lady Caroline Pontefract's views on the duty of men to be married (*A Woman of No Importance*, 2. 24), but he expresses them in a more generous way. His affectionate relationship with Lord Goring, while essentially comic, is the only positive father/son relationship in Wilde's comedies.

120 *I feel a draught, sir*: a sneeze (the first of several) seems indicated.

130 *Yes, my lord*: Phipps presumably moves to the door of the smoking-room, ushers Lord Caversham in, and closes the door behind him for the private instructions at l. 152.

166 S.D. *Lamia-like*: the Lamia was a female demon, with the body of a serpent—as in Keats's poem *Lamia* (1820). Mrs Cheveley is dressed to kill. She avoids giving her name.

180 *drawing-room*: the drawing-room, the inner room, must be visible, and its lighting changes as Phipps lights the candles, while Mrs Cheveley prowls around the Library. In the Frohman text, there are stage directions: 'lights down in drawing-room' when Phipps opens the

door, and appropriate changes as the candles are lit and the shades fitted.

186 *I shall have to alter all this*: Mrs Cheveley plans to marry Lord Goring and so re-establish herself in London society.

202 *settlement*: a financial marriage settlement.

203 *I know that handwriting*: Gertrude Chiltern's handwriting reflects her Old Testament, rigid morality, but the message is, apparently, uncharacteristic.

212 S.D. *slips the letter*: the Frohman text has a more specific s.d.: 'places pink letter on table and closes the lid of the blotter over it, down stage, so as to hide it, the pink envelope is left on corner of table below blotter'.

218 S.D. *creeps stealthily*: this attempt to steal the letter may appear melodramatic: it is also comic. In one text Wilde added a speech for Mrs Cheveley: 'I should like to have that letter! It might be useful when Lady Chiltern arrives. (*Hears voices and retreats*) I can't! What a disappointment!' The reliance on action alone lightens the tone and is much more manageable in terms of staging.

241 S.D. *Goes out for a moment*: Lord Goring accompanies his father to the front door. Chiltern is the third unexpected visitor of the evening, and the most potentially embarrassing—the only person expected, of course, does not come. It would be unconventional, and *risqué*, for any unaccompanied woman to call on a single man after dinner. In the Licensing Copy, Goring comments on Lady Chiltern's announcement, 'But what an hour to call. Upon my word these immaculate people do very foolish things sometimes. I'll give her a good lecture when she arrives, make her stand by her husband and send her home.'

252 *I guessed as much!*: Frohman indicates that Lord Goring notices the tell-tale envelope at this point and puts it in his pocket.

275 *thunderingly*: *The Times* was known as the Thunderer.

277 *hock and seltzer?*: white wine and soda water—a favourite drink of Wilde and of Dorian Gray.

289 *some directions*: Lord Goring's instructions are not heard by Sir Robert.

297 *What a mess I am in*: this speech is, of course, an aside. In Peter Hall's 1992 production, Lord Goring went to open slightly the drawing-room door at this point, so that Mrs Cheveley should not miss his 'lecture'.

340 S.D. *A chair falls in the drawing-room*: apparently one of Wilde's rare clumsy touches in this act—commented on by reviewers. But if Mrs Cheveley intentionally knocks the chair over, as her eventual appearance 'radiant and much amused' may suggest, the intervention is at least motivated, even if the precise motivation is not clear. In the early version, Chiltern has in his hand a 'fatal confession' made by Mrs

Cheveley when her theft of Lady Berkshire's jewellery was discovered, prompting some deliberate off-stage reaction. In Peter Hall's production, the door swung open a little further at Sir Robert's revelation, 'I have made up my mind what I am going to do tonight in the House.'

370 *My life is at stake*: the melodramatic tone begins to dominate, but is strongly qualified by the audience's constant awareness of Mrs Cheveley's presence, and so contributes to the comic impact.

398 S.D. *Makes a sign . . . he does*: taking off the cloak echoes the previous action with Lord Caversham.

427 *Why don't you call me Laura?*: Lord Goring maintains formality even with Mabel Chiltern, calling her Miss Mabel until she has accepted his proposal. Mrs Cheveley's suggestion that Lord Goring call her Laura is a reminder that they were once engaged.

436 *violent flirtation*: in the Clark typescript the expression is stronger and given to Lord Goring: 'I found you sitting on the knees of a married man, kissing him.'

439 *my lawyer settled that matter*: the breaking off of an engagement could be claimed, in law, to be a breach of promise—hence the financial settlement.

458 S.D. *Puts her hand on his*: this reflective sequence gives some reality to the past relationship.

462 *I want to have a salon*: Mrs Cheveley imagines herself as a London society hostess, the centre of an artistic and intellectual circle.

482 *Numbers*: a heavy reference to the Old Testament book implying promiscuity.

519 *seven and three-quarters*: the size suggests large and inelegant hands.

527 *Voilà tout*: a late textual change from 'That is all.'

566 S.D. *clasps it on her arm*: the device is reminiscent of French Romantic drama.

577 *my cousin, Mary Berkshire*: The cluster of coincidences is excessive. The bracelet was a relatively last-minute addition to the plot, which may account for the slightly shorthand nature of these details.

616 S.D. *burns it over the lamp*: Lord Goring must also release Mrs Cheveley from the bracelet at this point, as the Frohman text indicates.

645 S.D. *shrill reverberations*: Mrs Cheveley keeps her hand on the bell for longer than normal, a sound of apparent triumph at the close of the act. She speaks because Lord Goring refuses to do so. The presence of Phipps protects her.

4 Lord Goring occupies the same position as Sir Robert in the Second Act. (Other texts place this act in Lady Chiltern's boudoir.)

37 *The Times*: a 'serious' paper; *The Morning Post* contained the society news.

48 *Canning*: (1770–1827), renowned as an orator. He was a brilliant foreign minister and, briefly, Prime Minister.

72 *too young*: Lord Goring's age, 34 in the final version, varied from draft to draft.

82 *betting*: Lord Goring implies that the possible engagement is current gossip.

98 *serious relapse*: Lord Caversham responds to Mabel's pretence of ignoring his son.

134 *Downing Street*: Lord Caversham has an appointment at 10 Downing Street, to see the Prime Minister. Unemployment was an urgent contemporary issue.

136 S.D. *takes up roses*: Wilde used the same action at the opening of *Lady Windermere's Fan*.

151 *Oh, is it a proposal?*: like Cecily and Gwendolen in comparable circumstances in *The Importance of Being Earnest*, Mabel takes the initiative.

186 S.D. *catches her in his arms*. The placing of this scene, with its intimacy and momentary sincerity, is important, since it enables Wilde to devote the closing image to the Chilterns. It is also, of course, a false dénouement, since it is threatened (if not too seriously) by Sir Robert's knowledge of Mrs Cheveley's intimacy with Lord Goring. The lightness of the scene makes a sharp contrast with the earnestness that is to follow. In the Clark typescript, this scene takes place in Lord Caversham's presence, and he refuses to allow the marriage on the grounds of idiocy in the family: 'The girl accepts you, and her brother refuses a seat in the Cabinet.'

250 *Oh! not that!*: the s.d. in the Frohman text reads: 'they look fixedly at each other a moment. Lady C. falls back on chair horrified'.

286 *Mr Montford*: the first edition has 'Montfort', presumably a misprint for the 'perfectly groomed young dandy' of the First Act.

303 *I want you*: the misunderstanding has a comic dimension, which is surely intentional, when coupled with Lord Goring's signals behind Sir Robert's back.

354 S.D. *entirely new buttonhole*: the buttonholes have been given sufficient attention for the change to be noticed by an audience.

385 *I beg your pardon*: he apologizes for swearing. Lord Caversham's role, and Lord Goring's commentary, vocal and visual, maintain the comic tone.

410 *not an old family*: the assumption is that most old English families were riddled with inherited idiocy.

420 *Second palm tree*: the first edition has 'Third palm tree', but that must be a slip deriving from an earlier version, where the palm tree joke is extended by Mabel after she has been kept waiting by Lord Goring—'The third palm tree to the left. Not the usual palm tree.'

432 *playing Mrs Cheveley's cards?*: playing Mrs Cheveley's cards for her, to enable her to win the game.

441 S.D. *philosopher*: another serious speech from the supposedly trivial Lord Goring. It is clear that he is being sincere, though he is propounding principles which he himself would never follow.

484 *A man's life*: Lady Chiltern's word for word repetition has a comic impact, and Lord Goring is present as stage-manager of the resolution.

500 *your sister's guardian*: Wilde, as often, postpones or qualifies the simple ending which the plot seems to suggest.

579 *Radicals*: the more extreme section of the Liberal party.

589 *ideal husband*: ironically, the 'ideal husband' is Sir Robert; the crucial distinction is between 'ideal' and 'real'.

Curtain: Wilde experimented with a number of endings. In the Frohman version, the last s.d. is: 'Exit Caversham—Goring and Sir Robert meet C. shaking hands as Curtain falls', following a last line spoken by Lord Goring. Russell Jackson suggests that this may well have been the practice of the first production. Wilde had originally closed the play on a line for Lady Chiltern, 'There is love in it, and that is better'. In the Clark typescript, Lady Chiltern's 'Ah, there is love, and that is everything' is given to Lord Goring, and the word 'father' added, which is what appears in the Licensing Copy. Wilde's more prolonged and sentimental ending is harder to achieve, but is, perhaps, subtler than the more conventional ensemble conclusion.

The Importance of Being Earnest

Dedication: Robert Ross (1869–1918) was Wilde's most faithful friend and his literary executor.

The Persons of the Play. This set of names incorporates more allusions and connotations than usual, even by Wilde's standards.

Worthing: the seaside town in Sussex where Wilde was staying when he wrote much of the play, and an appropriately upright name for a Justice of the Peace. (The play's working title, *Lady Lancing*, and the reference to Lord Shoreham (1. 13), commemorate other Sussex seaside resorts.)

Algernon Moncrieff: in the first scenario, the comparable character was 'Lord Alfred Rufford', perhaps too blatant an echo of Lord Alfred Douglas.

Chasuble: a chasuble is a vestment worn by priests when celebrating the Eucharist, a practice of the early Church revived in the nineteenth century by the Oxford Movement. (Wilde had been drawn to High Church Anglican ceremonial at Oxford.) Like the Archdeacon in *A Woman of No Importance*, Chasuble is a Doctor of Divinity. The name suggests chastity.

Merriman, Lane: according to Max Beerbohm, Wilde threatened to name the two butlers Mathews and Lane, after his publishers at the Bodley Head, Elkin Mathews and John Lane, with whom he was at odds—they had announced the splitting of their partnership in Sept. 1894. 'The name Merriman is, I suppose, a token of forgiveness.' (Written in Max Beerbohm's copy, owned by Sir Rupert Hart-Davis.)

Lady Bracknell: Bracknell was where the Marchioness of Queensberry, Lord Alfred Douglas's mother, lived.

Hon. Gwendolen Fairfax: Gwendolen has the courtesy title of Honourable, as daughter of a baron or viscount.

Cecily Cardew: the Cardews were friends of Wilde; their daughter, Cicely, was born in May 1893, and Wilde reportedly promised to name the heroine of his next play after her. In the 1993 Aldwych production, 'Cecily' was pronounced 'Cicely', in the late Victorian style.

Prism: this wonderfully apposite name belonged to the governess from the first scenario, with connotations of geometry and also of elocution, deriving from Mrs General in Dickens's *Little Dorrit*: 'Papa, potatoes, poultry, prunes, and prism, are all very good words for the lips: especially prunes and prism.' A 'Miss Prunes and Prism' is someone very affected and precise.

Cast. Apart from Alexander, only two of the cast had appeared in a Wilde comedy before: Vincent (who was Lord Augustus Lorton in *Lady Windermere's Fan*), and Rose Leclerq (Lady Hunstanton in *A Woman of No Importance*). Violet Lyster took over the part of Cecily Cardew for some later performances.

1 Half-Moon Street is one side of a rough rectangle, together with Piccadilly, Park Lane, and Curzon Street. The '*artistically*' signifies 'in good taste', not necessarily an accompaniment to '*luxuriously*'. Wilde gives no description of the furniture arrangement; there must be a sofa, at least two chairs, and a place for the sherry decanter and glasses, in addition to a table for the tea and a tiered cake-stand. Two doors are indicated, one to the adjoining music-room, one to the rest of the house. What Algernon is playing, and how, is important. In Donald Sinden's 1987 production, Ken Wynne as Lane underwent 'aesthetic torture when obliged to listen to Algernon playing the piano with more expression than accuracy' (Francis King, *Sunday Telegraph*). In the Talawa Theatre production (1989), Lane sang a different tune to the

one Algernon was tinkling off-stage. The Asquith film script stipulates Chopin's C sharp minor Waltz, played with more spirit than accuracy.

10 S.D. *Hands them on a salver*: this action sets the play's tone: the heightened, almost absurd, decorum, immediately exploded by the nonchalant, even ruthless, satisfaction of appetite.

13 *Shoreham*: the 1899 edition has 'Shoreman', but earlier drafts read Shoreham, which must be correct.

25 *misunderstanding*: presumably the marriage was undertaken because of an implied promise, though 'misunderstanding' also seems to function as a euphemism like Lady Bracknell's 'social indiscretion', l. 558.

37 S.D. *Enter Jack*: Jack brings hat, stick, and gloves with him, and shakes hands with Algernon (Alexander's s.d.), indicating the intention, at least, of a short visit. Jack and Algernon are subtly differentiated, by age, appearance, and manner: Algernon is established as younger than Jack (l. 58). Reviewing the 1982 National Theatre production, Michael Billington (*Guardian*) drew attention to the contrast between the dry formality of Martin Jarvis's whey-faced Jack, with his 'wing collar, cruel specs and severe swept back hair', and Nigel Havers's 'floppy-cravatted, curly-haired, insouciant' Algernon. In the 1989 Talawa production Ben Thomas as Algernon was 'a smooth aesthete done out in a crisp moustache and cream suit' (Nicholas de Jongh, *Guardian*).

40 *Oh, pleasure, pleasure!*: French adds 'putting hat on table', the first of a series of gestures implying a more extended call.

43 *slight refreshment*: sandwiches, bread and butter, crumpets, muffins, even, in the country, cake (2. 686), might accompany the tea which was served around five o'clock. The Victorian upper classes ate steadily. Dinner might not be until 8.30 p.m.

52 *Shropshire?*: a county in the west Midlands, some distance from London.

83 S.D. *interferes*: more specifically, 'Algy takes up plate and puts it on his knees' (Alexander). The obsession with food reflects Wilde's own habits. Theodore Wratislaw, staying with Wilde at Goring, recorded a bizarre 'exhibition of wrath' over a plate of biscuits, and Wilde's enormous consumption of sausages.

87 S.D. *from below*: the plates are on a tiered stand.

114 *Scotland Yard*: the Metropolitan police headquarters.

119 S.D. *Enter Lane . . . salver*: Alexander expands: 'Algy and Jack both try to take it. Algy takes it and moves down R.'

139 *Tunbridge Wells*: a spa town in Kent, traditional residence for respectable old aunts.

163 *B.4, The Albany*: Wilde originally wrote E.4, but changed the address to an unoccupied apartment. E.4 was the apartment of the homosexual

George Ives, at which Wilde met Jack Bloxam, the founder of a one-issue Oxford magazine, *The Chameleon*, which was cited during Wilde's trials. Albany, as it is usually referred to, at the other end of Piccadilly from Half-Moon Street, next to the Royal Academy, had sets of 'bachelor chambers'. Built in 1802–3, it had slightly lost its exclusive reputation by the end of the century.

184 s.d. *Hands cigarette case*: Alexander's notes indicate that Algernon helps himself to a cigarette before handing it over; Jack also takes one. They light them at significant moments—Algernon after his crucial question at l. 199, Jack as he completes his reply at l. 208.

185 s.d. *Sits on sofa*: after Jack's pursuit of Algernon, Wilde introduces a stiller stage position for Jack's explanation.

223 *Bunbury*: Wilde had a friend from Trinity College, Dublin, Henry S. Bunbury. The assonance with Bumbury makes the name vaguely disconcerting, an effect which Wilde promotes by repetition.

226 *Willis's*: this fashionable restaurant in King Street, near the St James's Theatre, famous for its cuisine, scarlet leather seats and yellow candle shades, was patronized by Wilde and Lord Alfred Douglas. Some of the audience would dine there after the performance, as Wilde's friend Ada Leverson did on the first night of *Earnest*.

237 *sent down*: guests assembled before dinner in the drawing-room, up-stairs. A man would be partnered with a woman, whom he would escort downstairs to the dining-room and then sit beside.

264 *French Drama*: like the French novel, French drama was thought of by the English as potentially corrupting, with frequent instances of adultery and infidelity, as in the plays of Dumas *fils*. In reality, English dramatists (including Wilde) borrowed extensively from French models, though tending to dilute the more explicit and sensational facts.

273 *creditors*: in earlier versions, Algernon's creditors hounded him through the play.

Wagnerian: when Wilde's first child was born, he commented that its style was essentially Wagnerian.

281 *Good afternoon, dear Algernon*: various editions (e.g. French) indicate that Lady Bracknell shakes hands with Algernon, while Gwendolen kisses her hand to Jack behind her mother's back.

292 *Lady Harbury*: at this point, Lane enters with a teapot (Alexander)—otherwise, the tea would be stewed—and pours a cup for Lady Bracknell. Algernon adds milk before handing it to her at l. 315. There are many variations in the s.d.s of early versions.

298 *where I am*: Gwendolen is swiftly established as having a mind of her own (as at l. 290). As the Asquith script comments, Gwendolen,

'although young and pretty, has something of her mother's air and carriage'.

303 *I went down twice*: Lane is the perfect complement to Algernon, lying with elegant aplomb. He must take the empty plate from Algernon at this point.

315 S.D. *hands tea*: Alexander adds a s.d. for Jack and Gwendolen—Gwendolen 'pours out two cups, they both drink and talk'.

322 *completely out*: Algernon's absence would create uneven numbers. An equal number of ladies and gentlemen might be invited, but it was customary to invite two additional gentlemen 'in order that the married ladies should not be obliged to go in to dinner with each other's husbands only' (*Manners and Rules of Good Society* (1924), 103).

335 *Illness of any kind . . .* : Lady Bracknell echoes the short shrift given to invalids in Samuel Butler's *Erewhon* (1872).

341 *my last reception*: Lady Bracknell has arranged a number of receptions during the current London season.

353 *French songs*: morally suspect, like French novels and plays.

357 *German sounds a thoroughly respectable language*: the respectability of German was guaranteed by the blood ties and frequent contacts between the English and German royal families.

361 *Pray don't talk to me about the weather*: 'Gwendolen comes down right, throws wrap over back of sofa then sits down-stage' (Alexander). Even her speech carries a hint of Lady Bracknell.

385 *Gwendolen?*: Jack's use of 'Gwendolen' for the first time is a declaration of love in itself. (Compare Lord Goring and Miss Mabel in *An Ideal Husband*.) Alexander adds more details—at 'Passionately!', Gwendolen puts her arms round Jack's neck. At l. 386, they embrace. In the National Theatre production of 1982, Zoe Wanamaker pronounced 'Passionately' 'in a voice of throaty sexiness' (Billington, *Guardian*).

415 *Married, Mr Worthing?*: Gwendolen reacts crisply to Jack's presumption about getting married by returning to the formality of 'Mr Worthing', which he echoes at l. 417. French adds s.d., 'They both rise'.

438 *What wonderfully blue eyes*: Gwendolen, a modern woman, assumes the initiative, even taking over the traditionally male expressions. Alexander's stage directions extend the reversal with physical gestures: Lady Bracknell repeats 'Mr Worthing!' at l. 441, but Gwendolen restrains Jack—'pushes him down with her hands on his shoulders'—and at l. 447—'I am engaged to Mr Worthing, mamma'—'lifts Jack up by placing her hand underneath his elbows'.

451 *pleasant*: after 'pleasant', Alexander points the alternative with a s.d.: 'stares at Jack, then goes L. a little, turns'.

461 S.D. *note-book and pencil*: Lady Bracknell makes notes of Jack's answers to her questions (not just as directed at l. 487). In Nicholas Hytner's 1993 Aldwych production, Maggie Smith developed the note-taking into a superb, if extended, comic routine. The MS draft indicates that Jack pulls out his cigarette case, replacing it at a glare from Lady Bracknell.

492 *after one's death*: death duties were a tax on inherited capital, introduced by the Liberal Government in the 1894 Budget to the dismay of the propertied class.

503 *Belgrave Square*: just south of Hyde Park Corner.

506 *Lady Bloxham?*: French adds '(severely)'.

519 *Liberal Unionist*: Lady Bracknell would not have entertained a Liberal. Liberal Unionists voted against Gladstone's proposals for Home Rule for Ireland. Led by Joseph Chamberlain, they helped form the Conservative Government which came to power in 1895.

524 *Both? . . . That seems like carelessness*: in earlier texts, the line reads: 'Both? To lose one parent may be regarded as a misfortune—to lose *both* seems like carelessness.' Robert Ross's edition of 1908–9, which makes some slight changes to the 1899 text, reads: 'To lose one parent, Mr Worthing, may be regarded as a misfortune; to lose both looks like carelessness.' The longer versions have subsequent theatrical tradition to support them.

541 *A hand-bag?*: Edith Evans's majestic interpretation of Lady Bracknell—her 'great essay in dragonhood'—captured on film, television, and radio, must have seemed a formidable obstacle to succeeding actresses. Her rendering of this line, equally unforgettable, has entered folklore, giving rise to innumerable ghastly imitations. She herself grew to dislike the role: 'I've played her everywhere except on ice and under water' (Bryan Forbes, *Ned's Girl* (1977), 195). James Agate (*Sunday Times*, 5 Feb. 1939) wrote: 'As long as Miss Evans is on the stage one has no doubt about anything except the relative grandeur of Lady Bracknell's upholstery, and those two hats in one of which swans nest while in the other all the fowls of Rostand's "Chantecleer" come to roost.' Irene Handl (Greenwich Theatre, 1975) avoided comparisons by making Lady Bracknell of German extraction. The first Lady Bracknell, Rose Leclercq, established the strong physical presence of the character: 'The handkerchief she used, the long bottle of eau-de-Cologne, the way she sat—such details marked her as the blue-blooded lady she portrayed' (Irene Vanbrugh, *To Tell My Story* (1948)—Vanbrugh was the original Gwendolen). Judi Dench's brilliant Lady Bracknell at the National Theatre, 1982, presented a much younger woman, in her forties. Michael Billington saw her as 'a woman prey to quicksilver feelings. Thus she starts the famous interview with Mr

Worthing with a voracious, note-taking delight in his financial prospects: even the news that he inhabits the unfashionable side of Belgrave Square elicits nothing more than a mercurial giggle. . . . But the shattering news of his origins is greeted not with a sub-Evans swoop but with a very slow, incredulous removal of her glasses and a sotto voce rendering of "A handbag?" in thunderous disbelief. Ostentatiously tearing up her notes, she conducts the rest of the interrogation with the hurried politeness of someone anxious to catch a train' (Billington, *Guardian*).

547 *cloak-room*: the left luggage office.

550 *The Brighton line*: some of these details may have been suggested to Wilde through his friendship with Mr Philip Cardew, as well as by his own excursions. Philip's brother Christopher, who died in Oct. 1893, was a director of the London, Brighton, and South Coast Railway, which shared the terminus of Victoria station with the London, Chatham, and Dover Railway.

551 *The line is immaterial*: French notes that Lady Bracknell rises.

555 *reminds*: the 1899 text has 'remind'.

559 *social indiscretion*: Lady Bracknell implies, of course, that the baby was illegitimate, the product of a liaison between a 'gentleman' and someone of lower rank (a situation Wilde had already explored in *A Woman of No Importance*). Lost babies are a stock motif of comedy and melodrama, but this is also a link with the reality of Victorian society.

568 *the season*: the London season was, for 'society', the traditional period for engagements.

576 *Good morning, Mr Worthing!*: so in 1899 edition, but logically 'Good afternoon'.

577 s.d. *Wedding March*: Mendelssohn's Wedding March for *A Midsummer Night's Dream*.

586 *Gorgon*: Greek monster, with serpents in place of hair.

591 *My dear boy*: stage tradition often has Algernon settling himself on a sofa with his feet up for this speech.

623 *make love*: as usual at this period, verbally only.

646 *only just eighteen*: girls from the upper classes 'came out' into society at 18, after which they were considered marriageable.

655 *go and dress*: people put on evening dress, even when dining at a smart restaurant, or when attending a play or opera in a box or the 'dress circle'.

662 *the Club?*: this would be one of the exclusively male clubs such as White's or Boodle's, near the St James's Theatre.

664 *the Empire*: famous music-hall in Leicester Square, whose promenade had been a notorious rendezvous for prostitutes. Mrs Ormiston Chant of the Britishwoman's Temperance Association had objected to the renewal of the Empire's licence in the autumn of 1894. If Algernon and Jack arrived at ten, they would have seen the 'Grand Ballet' featuring the *première danseuse* Helene Cornalba in 'Round the Town'.

672 *turn your back*: French has a s.d. for Gwendolen, 'turning him round'.

675 *I don't think I can allow this at all*: Algernon, who breaks all the rules when it suits him, is suggesting that he should not leave Gwendolen 'alone' with Jack, unchaperoned, even by just turning his back.

694 *The Manor House, Woolton, Hertfordshire*: a contemporary photograph in the *Sketch*, 20 Feb. 1895, shows Irene Vanbrugh as Gwendolen noting the address in her diary.

705 S.D. *Enter Lane*: Alexander has a s.d.: 'As Lane enters Jack and Gwendolen are kissing R.U. As Jack looks up he turns his back and stands below door R.U.'

713 *put up*: pack.

smoking jacket: indoor jacket, often of velvet.

730 S.D. *reads his shirt-cuff*: Algernon reads Jack's address from his shirt cuff. In his copy of the first edition, Max Beerbohm adds a last comment for Algernon: 'And besides, I *love* nonsense!' This agrees with the four-act version. The Alexander text reads: 'Nobody ever does. Besides I love nonsense!', and continues with the address read aloud from the shirt cuff, together with the s.d. 'Drinking as curtain falls'. Beerbohm comments: 'I have a good verbal and visual memory, and I can still hear Allen Aynesworth saying these words, and see him raising his glass of sherry as he said them and as the curtain fell. I don't see why Oscar cut them from the printed version; for they surely are just right.'

2 This is a rather more detailed outdoor setting than the First Act of *A Woman of No Importance*. The opening action lightly illustrates the Wildean tension between pleasure and duty. The roses are an integral part of the setting. In the National Theatre production, this was the most commented upon of John Bury's settings. Billington reported that the designs hinted at the play's topsy-turvy, Gilbertian quality in their faint stylization: 'The second-act garden, for instance, has a glassy, reflecting surface, sporadic rose-trees (again a hint of Alice?) [*Alice in Wonderland*] and a silhouetted village background' (*Guardian*).

2 *Moulton's duty*: the gardener Moulton appeared on stage in the original draft.

14 *quite well*: French indicates that Cecily puts down her watering-can at this point.

29 S.D. *diary*: this is a highly literary play, full of references to manuscripts and books, the triumph of art. In addition to Cecily's and Gwendolen's diaries, there are Lady Bracknell's note-book and Miss Prism's three-volume novel, as well as the Railway Guides and Army Lists. Cecily must sit just before this action.

46 *Mudie*: a London circulating library.

57 *abandoned*: this almost submerged *double-entendre* (lost or mislaid/licentious) leads on to Chasuble's 'hang upon her lips' at l. 76, and his reference to the Pagan authors, establishing an undercurrent of licence bubbling beneath the surface decorum.

63 *And how are we this morning?*: Chasuble shakes hands with Miss Prism (French).

69 *headache*: Miss Prism sits, followed by Chasuble at l. 73. He rises at l. 83, and Miss Prism immediately after (French).

83 *Egeria*: the nymph who instructed Numa Pompilius, the second King of Rome, and so any wise adviser. Laetitia (l. 84) is the Latin for 'joy, happiness'.

93 *Fall of the Rupee*: the Indian currency had been falling for twenty years. Max Beerbohm preferred the following last sentence of this speech, relying on his memory of the first performance: 'It is somewhat too unconventional for a young girl.'

98 *He has brought his luggage with him*: Frank Dyall, who played Merriman in 1895, recalled that this line received the loudest and most sustained laugh that he had ever experienced, culminating in a round of applause. When he came off, Wilde (who was backstage) said to him: 'I am so glad you got that laugh. It shows they have followed the plot' (Hesketh Pearson, *The Life of Oscar Wilde* (1946), 257).

100 *W.*: West, one of the former London postal districts.

106 *room*: having brought his luggage, Algernon obviously intends to stay for some while.

109 S.D. *Enter Algernon*: a photograph (*Sketch*, 20 Feb. 1895) shows Allen Aynesworth wearing a conspicuously checked suit and straw boater.

125 *I am glad to hear it*: French adds 'sitting'.

133 *great disappointment*: Algernon brings up a chair and sits, rising on l. 150 and the mention of Australia, a common Victorian destination for wayward younger sons (Alexander s.d.).

161 *Quixotic*: like Cervantes's Don Quixote, a romantic idealist.

170 *Maréchal Niel?*: a species of yellow rose.

182 S.D. *Miss Prism and Dr Chasuble return*: Alexander notes that they return arm in arm.

184 *womanthrope*: Wilde coined this word for misogynist in 'The Critic as

Artist'. Chasuble gives a 'scholar's shudder', l. 186, at so ill-mixed a conjunction of Old English and Ancient Greek.

187 *neologistic*: newly invented.

188 *Primitive*: early Christian.

197 *not even to her*: French adds 'putting his hand over hers on table'.

200 S.D. *Dr Chasuble starts*: Wilde's widespread use of patterning in this play extends to gestures and phrases.

203 S.D. *Enter Jack slowly*: one of the great entrances in theatre. It is significant that Jack enters '*slowly*'. Alexander arranged a downstage movement for Prism (right) and Chasuble (left), so that their reaction to Jack was delayed, ensuring that the audience saw him first. But Beerbohm criticized Alexander, in the 1902 revival, for 'bustling on at break-neck speed' when the situation demands 'the slowest of entries'.

222 *Poor Ernest!*: Jack takes out a black-bordered handkerchief and wipes his eyes (Alexander). Michael Redgrave, Jack in the Asquith film, produced the handkerchief at 'Quite dead'.

225 *Grand Hotel*: Wilde had stayed in this luxurious hotel in the Boulevard des Capucines in 1891.

237 *manna*: the food provided miraculously for the Children of Israel in the wilderness (Exodus 16).

251 *thrift*: a euphemism for sexual continence.

267 *sprinkling*: Chasuble distinguishes baptism by sprinkling water on the forehead from baptism by total immersion, either practice being in accord with the laws and customs of the Church.

327 *Uncle Jack*: French has a s.d. for Cecily, 'pulling Jack across to Algy'.

339 *I feel very happy*: 'Algie runs L. to follow Cecily. Jack catches him by the leg with his stick and drags him back' (Alexander).

348 *dressing-case*: a dressing-case contained all the bits and pieces for the Victorian male's toilet: hair brushes, razors, pomade jars, etc. (Reginald Turner gave one to Wilde on his release from prison.)

350 *more than a week*: Algernon emphasizes his intentions by taking off his hat and putting it on the table (French).

351 *dog-cart*: a light carriage, with a compartment at the back for carrying sporting dogs.

371 *four-five train*: the five minutes past four train is clearly only one of an extremely frequent service. In the four-act version, Lady Bracknell misses eleven trains in the course of the afternoon.

405 S.D. *Algernon looks appealingly*: even Algernon does not feel confident enough to give orders to a servant and has to appeal to Cecily. By l. 433, in mid-proposal, he can rise to the challenge.

454 *On the* 14th of February: 14 February is St Valentine's Day, as well as the date of the play's first performance. French adds 'Algy embraces Cecily'.

457 *this dear old tree here*: the whole sequence is given comic emphasis by specific objects: tree, ring, bangle, and finally the letters.

509 *Bankruptcy Court*: the theme of bankruptcy loomed much larger in the four-act version.

544 S.D. *Enter Gwendolen*: Gwendolen is carrying a parasol. The Asquith screenplay specifies 'a particularly elaborate and Londonish dress'.

558 S.D. *They both sit down together*: many of Cecily and Gwendolen's movements are synchronized.

628 *Morning Post*: the society newspaper, in contrast to *The Times*, as in *An Ideal Husband*.

658 S.D. *Enter Merriman*: Merriman and the footman remain throughout the following combat.

673 *as people are in London*: Alexander and French have a s.d. at this point, with a re-entry for Merriman with 'wicker cake stand containing cut bread and butter, plate of muffins, of tea cake, puts it down behind garden seat'. French adds a servant who makes two entries, the first with a tea-tray, the second with a wicker table on which are plates and covered dishes.

691 *You have filled my tea:* with the departure of the servants, the girls rise to confront each other.

704 S.D. *Enter Jack*: Jack has by this time changed from his mourning clothes into a less formal suit.

732 *Algernon Moncrieff! Oh!:* the movements here were as patterned as the verbal exchanges, as Alexander's stage directions confirm.

771 S.D. *They retire into the house with scornful looks*: the girls' exit is emphasized by a range of gestures in different drafts and texts. In the four-act version, the scene was set indoors: 'Jack and Algernon look at each other for a short time. Then they turn away from each other. Jack, who looks very angry, walks up and down the room. Kicks footstool aside in a very irritated way. Algernon goes over to tea-table and eats some muffins after lifting up the covers of several dishes.' In the Alexander text, the girls snort as they enter the house: 'Jack hits Algie in chest with elbow imitating girls' snort.' French has coarser business: 'Algy kicks Jack, and Jack returns it spitefully'.

839 *this morning*: Jack made the arrangement at l. 279, clearly 'this afternoon', but the mistake passes unnoticed in the theatre. (In the four-act version, the Second Act was set in the morning.)

3 *Morning-room*: a more intimate place than the drawing-room, which was reserved for the most formal occasions.